The Theory of Futures Markets

B

Applied Economic Theory and Econometrics

Edited by Paul Grout, University of Bristol

Forthcoming in the series

The Theory of
Futures Markets

Edited by
Paul Weller

Copyright © Blackwell Publishers 1992

First published 1992

Blackwell Publishers
108 Cowley Road
Oxford OX4 1JF
UK

Three Cambridge Center
Cambridge, Massachusetts 02142
USA

British Library Cataloguing in Publication Data

A CIP catalogue record for this book is available from the British Library.

Library of Congress Cataloging-in-Publication Data

The Theory of Futures Markets/edited by Paul Weller.
    p.   cm. — (Applied Economic Theory and Econometrics)
Includes bibliographical references and index.
ISBN 0-631-17172-X
1. Futures market.   I. Weller, Paul.   II. Series.
HG6024.A3T46   1992
332.64′5 — dc20   91-40410   CIP

Typeset in 10 on 12 pt Times
by Colset Private Ltd., Singapore
Printed in Great Britain by Hartnolls Ltd., Bodmin, Cornwall

Contents

Contributors

Kenneth J. Arrow, Nobel Laureate and Joan Kenney Professor of Economics and Professor of Operations Research, Department of Economics, Stanford University.

Margaret M. Bray, Reader, Department of Economics, London School of Economics.

Jean-Pierre Danthine, Professor, Département d'Econométrie et d'Economie Politique, Université de Lausanne.

Sanford J. Grossman, Steinberg Trustee Professor of Finance, Wharton School, University of Pennsylvania.

David Hirshleifer, Associate Professor, The John E. Anderson Graduate School of Management, University of California, Los Angeles.

Albert S. Kyle, Associate Professor, Haas School of Business, University of California, Berkeley.

Merton H. Miller, Nobel Laureate and Robert R. McCormick, Distinguished Service Professor, Graduate School of Business, University of Chicago.

David M. G. Newbery, Director, Department of Applied Economics, Cambridge University.

Joseph E. Stiglitz, Professor, Department of Economics, Stanford University.

Robert M. Townsend, Professor, Department of Economics, University of Chicago.

Paul A. Weller, Associate Professor, Department of Finance, College of Business Administration, University of Iowa.

Makoto Yano, Associate Professor, Department of Economics, Yokohama University.

Preface

This collection of papers seeks to document, in an eclectic fashion, some of the more recent developments in the theoretical analysis of futures markets. Although on the face of it a highly specialized area, in fact the theory of futures markets involves a treatment of many issues of central importance to an understanding of asset markets in general, such as the role of the price mechanism in aggregating and disseminating private information, the effects on the allocation of risk of trade in financial assets, the possibility of strategic manipulation of market equilibrium and the determinants of market liquidity.

For this reason I hope that the contents of this volume will be of interest to a wider audience than is suggested by the title. I have deliberately included material ranging from the introductory to the advanced, and from the foundations to the frontiers of current research.

I am very grateful to all the authors who consented to have their work reprinted here. I would also like to acknowledge the role of my continuing research collaboration with Makoto Yano, evidenced by our joint contributions to the volume. Finally, I would like to thank Mark Allin at Blackwell Publishers, for his able assistance in bringing this project to fruition.

Introduction

Futures markets have increased dramatically in importance over the last decade. The volume of trade on all exchanges in the United States has expanded nearly threefold since 1980. By far the largest growth has occurred in the area of financial futures, which now account for over half the total volume on all exchanges. The daily volume of stock index futures traded rivals that of trade in the stocks themselves. Part of this increase in importance can be attributed to the fact that over the period in question there have been very significant advances in our understanding of the way in which futures markets function in general, and also of how they can be used to implement particular risk-management strategies. The papers in this volume focus upon the theoretical analysis of futures markets, and have deliberately been selected to cover a broad range of issues. In this introductory chapter we will review these issues, and preview the papers.

A futures contract involves a commitment to deliver, or to take delivery of a specified quantity of some asset or commodity at a particular future date at a price determined at the time of contracting. This description also characterizes a forward contract: the key additional element which distinguishes the two types of contract is that futures contracts are traded on organized exchanges and so acquire all the features of a liquid financial asset. It is this ability to retrade the asset which allows groups of individuals who have no intention of ever making or taking delivery of the underlying commodity to establish an important trading presence in the market.

Viewed as a security, a futures contract has two significant characteristics which contribute to the special role it performs in the economy. First, it is a derivative security: by this one means that its payoffs depend very directly upon the prices of other well-defined assets or commodities, in contrast to bonds or equities, where the link to prices is generally much more diffuse. Second, because of this direct link to prices, there will be a high correlation between the profits and losses on a given contract and the value of the endowments of those with an appreciable degree of exposure to the risk of fluctuation in the price of the underlying asset. The second characteristic is an obvious consequence of the first, and creates a use for the security as a hedging instrument, or in other words as a means of acquiring insurance against certain specific forms of risk.

The fact that futures contracts are traded on organized exchanges facilitates another important function of these markets: the dissemination of information which will affect future prices in spot markets. The extent to which the price of a futures contract can efficiently aggregate diverse private information is an issue that has been extensively investigated, but is still an area of active research.

In many futures markets, and particularly in the case of financial futures, one observes that trade in futures can often be viewed as a substitute for spot trade. These substitute trades occur as a consequence of the enhanced liquidity and reduced transactions costs associated with futures markets. The notion of liquidity in financial markets is a complex and multifaceted one, and only recently has its formal modelling been seriously attempted. But it is their liquidity which sets futures markets apart from others, such as forward and spot markets, which could in theory perform the same functions. And so a clearer theoretical grasp of this concept is arguably one of the most important requirements for advancing our understanding of why futures markets perform as they do.

We now turn to considering the way in which futures markets reallocate risk in more detail, first at the partial, and then at the general equilibrium level. The simplest model of a futures market involves trade between two groups, hedgers and speculators. Hedgers are those who have an insurance motive for engaging in trade: they may be producers, inventory holders or users of the underlying commodity, or they may hold a portfolio which contains the underlying asset. Speculators, on the other hand, trade in the contract solely in the expectation of realising a profit. Trade takes place because hedgers are prepared to pay a premium in order to avoid some of the risk they face. This is in contrast to the result of Milgrom and Stokey (1982), who show that in a purely speculative market, where there is no insurance motive for trade, if agents have common priors, then even if they subsequently acquire different information the only rational expectations equilibrium is the one in which no trade occurs.

The idea that the futures price incorporates a risk premium was first advanced by Keynes (1923), whose theory of 'normal backwardation' predicted that the price of a futures contract would have a tendency to lie below the expected spot price of a commodity. This property stemmed from his assumption that hedgers as a group would be net sellers of contracts. In order that risk-averse speculators be induced to take up the long positions necessary to equilibrate the market, positions which would expose them to additional risk, they would need to expect them to be profitable. This in turn necessitates that the delivery price on the contract, which will coincide with the spot price, must be expected to be higher than the current futures price. In such a situation the market is characterized by price bias, in that the current futures prices is a biased predictor of the spot price.

Given that an important group of hedgers in commodity markets are users, who would ordinarily be expected to hold long positions, it is not clear that the assumption that hedgers in the aggregate are short is warranted. This question is investigated in the chapter by Weller and Yano on hedging and speculation. Even in the absence of users, it is possible to show that the existence of normal backwardation will be influenced by demand conditions in the spot market for the commodity. The reason for this is that hedgers are ultimately concerned with reducing the variability of their income, not the variability of the price they receive for their output. If their output is random, hedging income risk is not the same thing as hedging price risk. This is simply illustrated by noting that if the only source of price uncertainty is variability in supply, and if spot demand is unit elastic, the hedging motive disappears completely. The picture is further complicated when one makes allowance for the presence of competitive user firms, whose objective is to offset fluctuations in profit. The impact of changing input prices on levels of profit is affected both by the conditions of market demand, and by the production technology of the firms in the market, in particular by the extent to which other inputs can be substituted for the commodity in question. However, under plausible conditions on demand elasticities, and on the elasticity of substitution between the commodity input and other factors of production, the standard 'stylized facts' of commodity futures markets can be derived – namely that producers take short positions, users take long positions, producers and users as a group are short, and normal back-wardation occurs.

The chapter by Newbery and Stiglitz develops a mean-variance model of trade in futures markets and uses it to examine the risk-reducing role of futures markets. The mean-variance model is useful in that it permits explicit solutions for individual demand functions for futures to be derived. These demand functions are linear in the futures price, and so can be straight-forwardly aggregated in order to obtain the equilibrium price as a function of attitudes to risk and other parameters. The authors are interested in comparing the effect on income variability of trade in futures with that of a centrally administered price-stabilization scheme. They show that an unbiased futures market will unambiguously provide greater insurance against income risk, essentially because of its increased flexibility. A farmer can choose in the futures market what proportion of his crop he wishes to hedge, whereas under price stabilization there is no such option. A farmer must in effect hedge the whole of his output.

Newbery and Stiglitz also consider the supply response of opening a futures market, where there is only uncertainty about the level of supply. They show in their model that average output is higher with a futures market than without. More suprisingly perhaps, they also find that producers will tend to prefer a futures market to a scheme of perfect price stabilization the more risk averse they are.

These partial-equilibrium models illustrate how a futures market can redistribute risk among economic agents, and how the futures price is influenced by circumstances in the spot market, but leave open the question of whether such markets can generate an efficient reallocation of risk at a general equilibrium level, or of whether the conclusions about the determinants of price bias carry over to a general equilibrium framework.

Since the famous work of Arrow and Debreu (Arrow, 1953, 1963–64; Debreu, 1959, ch. 7) it has been well known that trade in securities can bring about an efficient allocation of risk. But these securities are modelled as contingent claims whose payoffs are determined exogenously, and are not influenced by the equilibrium price of some other asset. They are therefore conceptually closer to equities than to derivative securities. This naturally raises the question of whether futures contracts, or indeed other derivatives, can perform the same function as Arrow securities.

The difference between the world of Arrow securities and that of futures contracts can be illustrated by means of a simple example. Consider an economy with two goods, corn and wheat, and two possible states of nature. The supply of corn differs across the two states, but the supply of wheat is unchanging. An Arrow security will pay one unit of wheat, which we select as the numeraire, in one of the states and nothing in the other. To achieve an efficient allocation of risk there must be two such securities traded, one for each state of nature. If individuals trade these securities in advance of the realization of the state of nature, and if they have rational expectations about the spot relative price of corn and wheat, they can achieve the same allocation as would have resulted from trade on a complete set of contingent commodity markets. Notice that the spot relative price of corn in terms of wheat may turn out to be the same in each state, or it may differ across states, depending upon preferences and endowments.

Now consider a situation in which a corn futures contract is the only asset traded. It is no longer irrelevant whether the spot relative price of corn varies across states. If individuals anticipate that it will be the same in each state, there will be no trade in the futures contract. The reason for this is that the equilibrium price of a futures contract in terms of wheat must be equal to the common relative price, in order to rule out infinite arbitrage profits. But then the contract will generate neither profits nor losses, and there will be no incentive to trade it. This will be a rational expectations equilibrium, but one which is not Pareto efficient, in that there will be unexploited opportunities for redistributing risk. But if the spot relative prices differ across states, a single futures contract is sufficient to achieve efficiency.

The paper by Townsend considers the circumstances under which futures markets will allocate risk efficiently, and identifies a condition guaranteeing that futures markets will perform analogously to Arrow–Debreu contingent commodity markets: the matrix of state-contingent spot prices must have rank equal to the number of states of nature. (The example discussed above considers a situation in which this condition is violated, namely when the spot relative price is the same in both states.) The familiar condition for efficiency in an Arrow–Debreu world is that there be as many linearly independent securities as states of nature. The result of Townsend provides us with a useful link between the world of Arrow securities, whose payoffs do not depend upon equilibrium spot prices, and futures contracts, whose payoffs do.

Much attention is paid in the partial-equilibrium literature to the determinants of price bias. In his paper, Hirshleifer argues that in a general equilibrium context the common determinants of hedging pressure, namely conditions of demand in the spot market, do not necessarily have the same impact upon the futures price. This results from the fact that consumers face risks which may partially or completely offset those of producers. It is only by explicitly acknowledging that transactions costs typically deter consumers from trading in futures markets that the partial equilibrium conclusions reemerge. The model that Hirshleifer uses is interesting in that he allows for sequential information arrival, which generates a motive for retrading futures contracts. The model illustrates the important proposition, first emphasized by Kreps (1982), that an opportunity to retrade securities can lead to a dramatic reduction in the number needed to complete the market. At the same time one needs to recognize that greater strain is placed upon the assumption of rational expectations. Agents need to have correct expectations about how security prices will move in response to new information over time, as well as about spot prices.

The question of what impact the presence of a futures market has on the spot market has been debated vigorously both in academic circles and in the policy arena. There have been instances where a futures market has been closed in the belief that it has been responsible for significantly increasing spot price volatility. The paper by Weller and Yano looks at this question in a general equilibrium framework. This permits proper account to be taken of the income effects associated with futures trading. In a two-agent, two-good, two-state setting, equilibria with and without a futures market are compared. What emerges is that if agents are close to income risk neutral, the opening of a futures market tends to reduce spot-price variability generated by fluctuations in supply. This is attributable to a 'pure price arbitrage' effect, where differing relative prices for state-contingent income are equalized by futures trading. However, when agents are significantly risk averse, there is an income risk sharing effect which may have the effect of increasing spot price variability. And yet the addition of a futures market leads to efficient resource allocation. The results of the paper, which apply to futures trading in foreign exchange and for broad commodity aggregates, indicate that while the effects of opening a futures market will in general be ambiguous, there is a presumption that futures markets will be spot price stabilizing. And the model is able to identify the economic factors which influence the outcome, factors such as marginal propensities to consume and elasticities of substitution in consumption.

The models discussed so far have all assumed that every trader has the same information, and so is able to form the same (rational) expectations about the relevant variables in the model. These models are therefore not able to illuminate what we observed at the outset to be one of the most important functions of a futures market: to provide a means of aggregating and transmitting private information to uninformed traders. The papers in the next section analyse various aspects of this function.

To illustrate the way in which information can be communicated through prices, consider a situation in which there are just two potential traders on the futures market. They are both risk-averse producers of a commodity with a unit elastic spot demand curve. Their individual outputs are random, as are their incomes, but aggregate income will be non-random. Suppose there are two possible levels of supply, corresponding to 'good harvest' and 'bad harvest' respectively. If both producers attach the same probabilities to the two possible outcomes, equilibrium in the futures market will be characterized by perfectly hedged positions at an unbiased futures price, i.e. where the futures price is equal to the expected spot price. The intuitive explanation for this result stems from the fact that for every feasible risky allocation there is a feasible certain allocation which has the same expected value for both producers. Any risk-averse individual will regard the risky allocation as less preferable, so it must be Pareto dominated, and cannot be a market equilibrium. And risk-averse individuals will only trade to perfectly hedged positions at an unbiased futures price.

Now suppose that one of the producers has access to a private source of information which, with some given probability, transmits one of two possible messages indicating that the producer's original prior should be revised. If the other producer's probabilities are unchanged, one of two possible equilibria will be observed, depending upon the private message received. However, because the two traders now disagree on the probabilities to be attached to the two states of nature, the equilibrium will no longer be characterized by perfect hedging at an unbiased price. But this equilibrium is not a rational expectations equilibrium, since the uninformed producer will be attaching incorrect probabilities to the two states of nature conditional on the equilibrium price. In other words, the uninformed producer will be ignoring the information contained in the futures price.

The new rational expectations equilibrium generated by the private information, if it is to be fully revealing, must have the uninformed producer associating the correct updated probabilities with the two states of nature. The crucial observation is that he can achieve this by forming expectations conditional on the futures price, which he can observe, rather than on the message itself, which by assumption he cannot.

The new rational expectations equilibrium with asymmetric information is such that the price of a futures contract can take on two possible values, associated with the two private messages to the informed trader. Conditional on the futures price, both agents associate the correct probabilities with each state of nature, and all the information contained in the private message has been revealed to the uninformed agent. This is a simple illustration of an important and very general observation in the economics of asymmetric information. Any private message, if it has economic value, will cause individuals who receive it to change their actions from what they would otherwise have been. These changed actions will generate observable consequences, from which it is possible for the uninformed to infer some, or as here, all of the private information.

Arrow examines the welfare implications of differing assumptions about the availability of information, and about expectations formation. In a simple general equilibrium model he compares the relative merits of public information but no opportunity to trade on contingent markets, and trading opportunities but no information. He shows the importance of the flexibility of the production technology in determining which arrangement is better, where flexibility measures the ability of the economy to adjust output in response to new information. If contingent commodity markets (or futures markets) are already in existence, and information is made public in advance of the opportunity to trade, then the scope for risk reallocation is reduced, and so correspondingly is welfare. Different assumptions about how expectations are formed have strikingly different implications for resource allocation. For example, if the uninformed are unaware of the fact that others have more information than they do, there may be incentives for the informed to engage in totally unproductive activity.

One of the general conclusions to emerge is that there is usually a tradeoff between the spreading of risk and efficient production. Having information released earlier allows producers to adjust their production decisions in the light of that information, but closes off opportunities to spread risk. Only if trade on futures markets were to occur before the arrival of information, but production decisions were delayed until after, would it be possible to achieve both efficient risk spreading and efficient production.

The first paper by Bray is a comprehensive survey of the role of information in futures markets. It provides an intuitive treatment of the information aggregating properties of futures prices, and analyses the robustness of the case in which the futures price fully reveals all private information. Problems of nonexistence of a rational expectations equilibrium are also discussed. She concludes with a penetrating assessment of the various models reviewed, and a list of questions for further research.

The next two papers, by Danthine and by Bray, consider the effects of asymmetric information in more detail, and at a more advanced level. Danthine is also concerned with the influence of a futures market on production decisions, and shows that in the absence of production uncertainty, the futures price plays a role identical to that of the spot price under certainty. Production decisions are not affected either by attitudes to risk or by the probability distributions which describe expectations. Even more suprisingly, perhaps, is the fact that it is of no concern whether the futures price is a biased predictor of the spot price or not. This is an indication of the prominent role that futures prices can be expected to play in guiding production decisions in those markets where it is reasonable to assume that random shocks to production are not significant.

Danthine presents an example to demonstrate the possibility in his model that the futures price will perfectly aggregate all private information, and shows also that despite the fact that in equilibrium all private information is revealed to the uninformed, nevertheless information can be of value to speculators. This stems from the fact that the model allows for a supply response on the part of producers. Roughly speaking, as more private information becomes available and is revealed in the market by the futures price, the risk premium is reduced and causes producers to plan increased supplies. This in turn increases their demand for hedging protection, and, so long as there is sufficient residual uncertainty, leads to greater expected profits for speculators, since this increased demand more than offsets the effect of the reduction in the risk premium.

The question of whether opening a futures market can be expected to have a beneficial effect on spot price volatility is also considered. This is of considerable practical importance, as we have remarked upon above. The results, however, have to be interpreted with some care, since contrary to popular perception, price volatility need not be a bad thing. Consider a situation in which producers have a choice of two technologies, one safe and one risky. The safe technology has a lower expected level of output, but output is also less variable. In the absence of a futures market, producers may well favour the safe technology. However, if there is a futures market which can provide insurance against price risk, this may encourage a shift in favour of the riskier technology. Spot prices would be more variable, but welfare could increase.

Given the early emphasis on results demonstrating that a futures price

could effectively aggregate all private information, it is important to understand the limitations of this property. This is the issue addressed in the
second paper by Bray. She shows that if there is uncertainty both about
demand and supply, one cannot expect the futures price to be fully revealing.
This observation has implications which extend much beyond the analysis of
futures markets. It enables one to circumvent the famous Grossman–Stiglitz
paradox (Grossman and Stiglitz, 1980): if price reveals all private information, and can be observed costlessly, then there will be no incentive to gather
costly private information. But then no private information will be revealed,
and there will be an incentive to gather it.

Grossman himself had argued that the addition of a suitable source of
'noise' would avoid the paradox, but as Bray observes, it would be misleading to think of her resolution of the paradox in this way. It is more
instructive to think of the situation as one in which an individual's private
information, which concerns both spot demand and his own future endowment, influences both his speculative and his hedging demand for futures
contracts. These separate effects cannot be disentangled by observing only
the futures price, which is therefore no longer a sufficient statistic for all
private information. What this means in the broader context of the theory
of asset pricing is that it is not necessary to postulate the existence of a group
of irrational 'noise' traders in order to avoid a fully revealing equilibrium.
All one requires is that there exist some (unobservable) hedging motive for
trading the asset. This approach has recently been fruitfully applied to the
question of whether informational asymmetries can become so large as to
prevent trade in an asset from occurring at all (see Bhattacharya and Spiegel,
1990). This question cannot be addressed in a model with noise traders, who
will always trade, no matter what the informational disadvantage.

Total cessation of trade in an asset represents a dramatic instance of loss
of liquidity, indicating that questions of liquidity and informational asymmetry are closely linked. But liquidity has also been a key factor in the
development of so-called 'informationless' trading strategies, exemplified
most importantly by portfolio insurance. At its simplest, this strategy is
equivalent to the purchase of a put option on a portfolio of stocks, with the
objective of placing a floor under the value of the portfolio. Since the
famous work of Black and Scholes (1973) and the extensions of Merton
(1973), it has been known that it is possible to reproduce the payoff to a put
option by transacting in bonds and in the underlying asset. But in order to
create such a 'synthetic security', adjustment of the so-called 'replicating
portfolio' has to take place frequently (strictly speaking continuously), and
would be prohibitively costly if the trades were to be executed in the spot
market for equities. However, the market for index futures offers far greater
liquidity, both in terms of simple costs of execution, and in terms of 'market
impact' costs. These latter refer to the extent to which a trade can be expected

to move prices adversely. And in the case of a well-diversified portfolio, there exists a simple arbitrage relationship between the spot price of the portfolio and the price of an index futures contract, which permits one, to a reasonable degree of approximation, to replicate spot trades in the portfolio with trades in index futures.

Grossman points out in his paper on program trading that there are problems inherent in using the futures market to produce a synthetic security. If the market is uncertain as to the proportion of traders who are using a dynamic hedging strategy involving synthetic securities, this can have the effect of significantly increasing the volatility of the underlying asset. This violates a crucial assumption underpinning the effectiveness of the dynamic hedging strategy in the first place – namely that stock prices are not themselves affected by the extent to which the strategy is adopted in the market.

These arguments have important implications for market liquidity. One of the essential ingredients of liquidity is an adequate supply of capital to undertake stabilizing trades; if it becomes more difficult to forecast the demand for such capital, the market becomes less liquid. This raises a number of important institutional and regulatory issues which Grossman discusses.

Grossman and Miller take a closer look at the determinants of market liquidity. They introduce the notion of a demand for immediacy in trade, which will vary from market to market. Futures markets constitute one end of a spectrum, where prices are volatile and the risks attendant upon delaying trade are high. In the model they consider there are market makers and outside traders, who in a futures market can be thought of as hedgers. Hedgers experience a shock to their spot market commitments, which causes them to want to hedge. It is assumed that the demand generated by this shock is exactly offset one period later by the arrival of new customers. This enables the authors to focus on the effect of a pure temporal mismatch of desired trades. They are able to solve explicitly for the relationship between the (fixed) costs of maintaining a presence in the market, and the liquidity of the market as measured by the number of market makers. They use the model to question the validity of some commonly used measures of market liquidity, and draw some thought-provoking conclusions about the part that market liquidity in both futures and cash markets played in the 1987 stock market crash.

In the early days of futures trading, markets were frequently subject to various forms of manipulation. An attempt to corner the gold market in 1869 was only foiled when President Grant ordered sales of gold from the US Treasury. More recently, the manipulation of the silver futures market by the Hunt brothers drove the price of silver, which was trading at around 6 dollars an ounce at the beginning of 1979, to a peak of over 50 dollars an ounce a year later. Such episodes have made both the exchanges themselves and the agencies which are responsible for regulating them sensitive to charges that the market may be prone to manipulation.

The final paper by Kyle considers this issue, one of great importance for the liquidity and smooth functioning of the market. How can manipulation of the market occur, and what are the factors which have a bearing on whether a manipulation is likely to be successful or not?

Kyle develops a formal model of market manipulation, in which an 'insider' is able to use private information on order flows to guide a squeeze strategy, which increases the costs of hedging and so reduces market liquidity. The insider uses hedging activity as a screen to conceal his own trades from speculators. When hedgers have large short positions, the manipulator takes up a large long position, with the intention of hanging on to it in order to drive up prices when hedgers seek to liquidate their positions. Hedgers consistently lose money in the sense that they pay a larger risk premium than they would do in the absence of manipulation. Kyle emphasizes the point that it is the feature of anonymity in the market which contributes both to liquidity and to the ability of a manipulator to successfully execute his strategy. He concludes by examining various policies which have been proposed to limit the incidence of squeezes, such as different delivery differentials, cash settlement and position limits.

The papers presented in this volume are all founded on the premise that agents are rational maximisers. No appeal has been made to the presence of 'noise traders' or other irrational elements in the market. But recent arguments have been proposed to suggest that such groups may have a significant part to play in a complete theory of asset pricing (De Long et al., 1990; Cutler et al., 1991; Danthine and Moresi, 1990). Investigating the implications of this new line of research for behaviour in futures markets represents the next important theoretical challenge which needs to be tackled.

REFERENCES

Arrow, K. J. 1953. Le role des valeurs boursières pour la répartition la meilleure des risques. *Econometrie,* Colloques Internationaux du Centre National de la Recherche Scientifique, vol. 11, Paris, 41–47.

Arrow, K. J. 1963–64. The role of securities in the optimal allocation of risk-bearing. *Review of Economic Studies,* 31, 91–96. (English translation of Arrow, 1953).

Bhattacharya, U. and Spiegel, M. 1990. Insiders, outsiders and market breakdowns. *Review of Financial Studies,* forthcoming.

Black, F. and Scholes, M. 1973. The pricing of options and corporate liabilities. *Journal of Political Economy,* 81(3), May–June, 637–54.

Cutler, D. M., Poterba, J. M. and L. H. Summers. 1991. Speculative dynamics. *Review of Economic Studies,* 58(3), 529–546.

Danthine, J.-P. and Moresi, S. 1990. Volatility, information and noise trading. Working Paper No. 10, C.E.P.R. Working Paper Series of the Network in Financial Markets, London.

Debreu, G. 1959. *Theory of Value*. New York: Wiley; New Haven: Yale University Press.

De Long, J. B., Shleifer, A., Summers, L. H. and R. J. Waldmann. 1990. The size and incidence of losses from noise trading. *Journal of Finance*, 44, 681-96.

Grossman, S. J. and Stiglitz, J. 1980. The impossiblity of informationally efficient markets. *American Economic Review*, 70, June, 393-408.

Keynes, J. M. 1923. Some aspects of commodity markets. *Manchester Guardian Commercial, Reconstruction Supplement 29*, March. (Reprinted in *The Collected Writings of John Maynard Keynes*, London: Macmillan; New York: St. Martin's Press, 1971.)

Kreps, D. 1982. Multiperiod securities and the efficient allocation of risk; a comment on the Black–Scholes option pricing model. In J. J. McCall (ed.), *The Economics of Information and Uncertainty*, Chicago: University of Chicago Press.

Merton, R. C. 1973. Theory of rational option pricing. *Bell Journal of Economics and Management Science* 4(1), Spring, 141-83.

Milgrom, P. and Stokey, N. 1982. Information, trade and common knowledge. *Journal of Economic Theory*, 26(1), February, 17-27.

Part I

Risk in Partial Equilibrium

1

An Introduction to the Theory of Hedging and Speculation in Futures Markets

Paul Weller and Makoto Yano

1 INTRODUCTION

Futures markets perform two important functions: they reallocate risk among those who choose to trade futures contracts, and they aggregate and disseminate information about the future course of prices in spot markets to any individual who elects to observe the current futures price. Our focus in this introductory chapter will be to examine the first of these two functions. A number of the other papers in this volume address various aspects of the information dissemination function.

We will start by considering a simple example in order to illustrate the issues we shall be analyzing. Suppose a wheat farmer has made a planting decision at the beginning of the growing season. He knows that his income at harvest time will depend upon the size of his crop, and on the price he receives for each bushel of wheat. At the time of planting he knows neither of these for sure. The size of the harvest will depend substantially on factors outside his control: the weather, insect infestation, and disease. The market price of wheat will be determined quite independently of any action the farmer may choose to take, since the farmer's output is only a small fraction of the total. So the situation involves a considerable degree of uncertainty as to the final outcome; uncertainty which the farmer would like to reduce if there were a means of so doing. A transaction in futures contracts provides such a means, by permitting the farmer to sell a specified quantity of his output for future delivery at a currently known price. But it is clear that although this is a way of avoiding uncertainty about the price at which he can sell his wheat, it has no direct impact upon uncertainty about the size of his harvest, although it might influence his planting decision. It is at this point that one needs to take into account the interaction between variations in price and quantity in affecting income, which is ultimately what the farmer is concerned with.

To illustrate the importance of this point, consider a situation where the outputs of all farmers are perfectly correlated, and the market demand curve is unit elastic. Then, no matter how variable the size of the harvest, demand conditions are such that incomes are perfectly stabilized. In other words, the market alone has provided perfect income insurance, and there would be no incentive for farmers to trade futures contracts, despite the fact that both output levels and prices display random fluctuation.

In general, of course, the spot market does not perform the function of stabilizing incomes perfectly, even though the negative correlation between price and output can be expected to have some stabilizing effect. This leaves a role for a futures market to perform, albeit one which will be importantly influenced by the conditions of demand in the spot market. But although the example has demonstrated the motive that a farmer would have for engaging in futures trading, we have not raised the question of who will be prepared to take the opposite side of such a transaction.

There are two distinct groups which need to be considered. The first is the group with whom the farmer would, in the absence of a futures market, be trading on the spot market; in other words, consumers and firms who use the farmer's output as a factor of production. The second is identified specifically by the nature of their trading in the futures market. We shall call them speculators.

User firms and consumers would benefit from a transaction in futures contracts in very much the same way that the farmer does, by reducing exposure to spot price variability. But, as before, we have to be careful not to assume that this necessarily represents the ultimate objective of the group.

A user firm is concerned with the profitability of its operations, which is influenced by the prices that it pays for its inputs. The usual presumption would be that the lower the price of an input, the more profit a firm is able to make. This conclusion is, however, not generally warranted when one takes into account the impact of input price changes on the price of the final output of a user. The price of the input falls as a result of an increase in supply. In a competitive environment this will lead to higher levels of output from user firms, and so will depress the price of their output. Exactly what the final effect upon profits will be depends on the characteristics of the technology of users, and also on demand conditions in the market for their output. These factors, as we shall see, have an important influence on their futures trading decisions.

The sole rationale for the existence of speculators is to trade futures contracts to their own advantage; that is to say, in order to generate positive profits from their trading activity. They are able to do this because farmers have a desire to reduce the uncertainty they face, and are willing to pay a price to accomplish this.

The example captures features which are common to a wide range of agricultural markets. The models we develop below are aimed at providing a more precise and complete exposition of the intuitive arguments sketched above.

We proceed to analyze the nature of equilibrium in a futures market, considering first a situation in which agricultural producers trade only with speculators. We examine the factors which determine whether traders take up long or short positions, what the size of these positions will be, and how the equilibrium futures price will be related to price in the spot market. User firms are then introduced, and their impact upon equilibrium in the futures market is analyzed.

1.1   A model of state-contingent income transfers

Consider first a situation in which an individual has some randomly fluctuating monetary endowment $\bar{m}$, which takes a value $\bar{m}_i$ in state i. There are two possible states, and the individual is able, before the state is realized, to trade income in one state for that in the other at some fixed 'price.' He has a von Neumann–Morgenstern utility function $u(m)$ defined on end of period income m, satisfying $u'(m) > 0$, $u''(m) \leqslant 0$. These assumptions imply that preferences display either *risk neutrality* $(u''(m) = 0)$ or *risk aversion* $(u''(m) < 0)$. The probability of state i occurring is π_i and the (Arrow–Debreu) price of income in state i is v_i. Then the optimal choice of income transfer is the solution to the problem

$$\max_{t_1, t_2} \pi_1 u(\bar{m}_1 + t_1) + \pi_2 u(\bar{m}_2 + t_2) \tag{1.1}$$

$$\text{s.t.} \quad v_1 t_1 + v_2 t_2 = 0.$$

The first-order conditions for an interior solution to this problem take the form

$$\pi_1 u'(m_1) / \pi_2 u'(m_2) = v_1 / v_2 \tag{1.2}$$

where $m_i = \bar{m}_i + t_i$. The solution to the problem can be illustrated diagrammatically as in figure 1.1. Point E represents the initial random endowment $(\bar{m}_1, \bar{m}_2)$. Point A is the equilibrium which occurs after trade, where t_1 is negative and t_2 positive. The slope of the budget constraint is $-v_1/v_2$. If we assume that the individual is risk averse $(u'' < 0)$, this is equivalent to assuming that the expected utility indifference curves are strictly convex to the origin.

The expression on the left-hand side of equation (1.2) is the marginal rate of substitution between consumption in the two states. On the 45°, or 'certainty' line, since $m_1 = m_2$, the marginal rate of substitution is indepen-

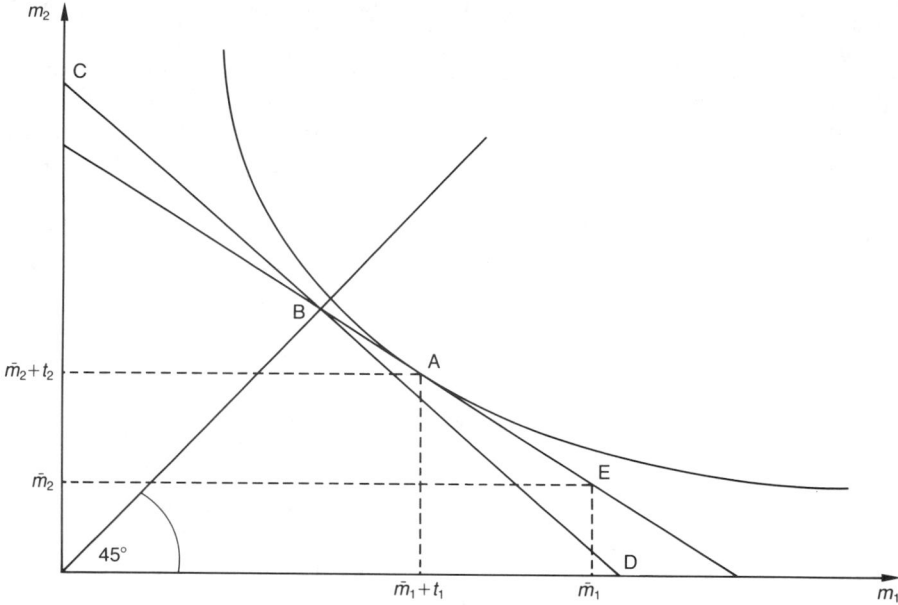

Figure 1.1   Trade in state-contingent income

dent of the individual's attitude to risk, and is equal to the ratio of the two state probabilities, π_1/π_2. On the other hand, if the individual is risk neutral, then $u'(m)$ is constant and the marginal rate of substitution is always equal to π_1/π_2. This implies (in the risk-neutral case) that expected utility indifference curves are straight line with slope $-\pi_1/\pi_2$.

From these facts a few simple observations can be made. If prices satisfy $v_1/v_2 = \pi_1/\pi_2$, then a risk-averse individual will trade so that $m_1 = m_2$. So the effects of income variability will be completely eliminated. But if we substitute this condition into the budget constraint in (1.1), we find that it implies that $\pi_1 t_1 + \pi_2 t_2 = 0$, or that the market permits *actuarially fair* transfers.

If the initial endowment is non-random, i.e. $\bar{m}_1 = \bar{m}_2$, then if $v_1/v_2 = \pi_1/\pi_2$ the individual will choose not to trade, and will set $t_i = 0$. On the other hand, if the slope of the budget constraint is not equal to the slope of an indifference curve where it intersects the 45° line, then a risk-averse individual with a non-random endowment will always trade so as to introduce some randomness into his income. Thus, in figure 1.1, if the initial endowment is at B, the individual trades to point A. Such a point will always be outside the budget set defined by the constraint $\Sigma \pi_i t_i \leqslant 0$, whose boundary is the line CBD, which has a slope of $-\pi_1/\pi_2$. So the trade to point A must satisfy the condition $\Sigma \pi_i t_i > 0$. In other words, the expected value of the transaction is positive.

There is a straightforward intuitive explanation for this. An individual who is risk averse dislikes income variability. So if he is to be induced to bear some risk, there must be some positive expected return from the transaction to compensate for the risk. Indeed, this observation enables us to deduce that if $\bar{m}_1 = \bar{m}_2$, $t_i \gtrless 0$ as $v_i/v_j \lessgtr \pi_i/\pi_j$. The budget constraint implies that $(v_i/v_j)t_i + t_j = 0$, whereas the requirement that the expected value of the transfers be positive implies that $(\pi_i/\pi_j)t_i + t_j > 0$, and the result follows. The point to be emphasized is that for a risk-averse individual whose endowment is non-random, the sign (although not the magnitude) of the transfer is independent of specific attitudes to risk.

If we return to the case illustrated in figure 1.1, we see that the trade from point E to point A can be viewed as the difference between two components, EB and BA. The trade EB would be optimal for somebody who was infinitely risk averse and possessed an initial endowment at E. Such preferences imply L-shaped indifference curves about the 45° line. Equivalently, it is the trade which minimizes income risk. The trade BA would be chosen by an individual with preferences as illustrated, and non-random endowment placing him at B.

This decomposition is of interest because we can think of the two components EB and BA as being generated by pure hedging and speculative motives, respectively. An individual who is infinitely risk averse will trade so as to minimize the variability in his income, regardless of the fact that the market might be offering very favorable terms for bearing risk. Thus the hedging, or income insurance motive, completely dominates any speculative motive for trade. The latter can be thought of as arising whenever the market offers a favorable bet, in the sense that bearing risk generates a positive expected return. So we are defining speculation as any trading activity which increases the income variability of the individual executing the trade.

We will find, when we consider the futures market in the section which follows, that the demand for futures contracts can be split up into speculative and hedging components in an exactly analogous manner.

1.2 The futures market

We consider the case of a representative agricultural producer whose output, x, fluctuates randomly. As before, we suppose that there are just two possible outcomes, which we can think of as the 'good harvest' state and the 'bad harvest' state. Total output in state i is given by x_i, $i = 1, 2$, and state 1 is the 'bad harvest' state, so that $x_1 < x_2$. There is a spot market demand curve

$x = D(p)$, which is downward sloping. The variability in supply produces a corresponding variability in the spot price, p_i, and $p_1 > p_2$.

Total revenue for the producer of the commodity, if all sales were to be made on the spot market, would be a random variable $\bar{m}_i \equiv p_i x_i$. But he has the option of trading futures contracts in advance of the realization of the state of nature. The aim of the producer, F, whose endowment is $\bar{m}_i^F$, is to maximize expected utility of end-of-period wealth $\pi_1 u^F(m_1^F) + \pi_2 u^F(m_2^F)$, where $m_i^F = \bar{m}_i^F + z^F(p_i - p^f)$, and p^f is the price of a contract promising delivery of one unit of the commodity at the end of the period. The choice variable z^F is F's demand for futures contracts and the term $z^F(p_i - p^f)$ represents the producer's gain (or loss) on a futures position of size z^F. The spot price, p_i, is also the delivery price on the futures contract. Thus a short position ($z^F < 0$) generates a profit if the spot price turns out to be lower than the futures price, and a loss if it turns out to be higher. Expectations are rational in that (a) expectations are formed with the correct state probabilities π_i, (b) the agent knows the true model of spot price determination, and this enables him to associate the correct spot prices with each state.

Let us first fix p^f exogenously. For a well-defined solution to the producer's problem we must have $p_1 > p^f > p_2$. If not, optimal choice of z^F, which can be either positive or negative, is unbounded.

The problem we have just described bears a strong similarity to that in (1.1). Indeed, if we set $v_1 = (p_1 - p^f)^{-1}$, $v_2 = (p^f - p_2)^{-1}$, $t_i = z^F(p_i - p^f)$, we find that they are equivalent. In other words, a trade in futures contracts permits transfers of state-contingent income at suitably defined implicit prices. Thus we can reinterpret figure 1.1. as an illustration of an expected utility-maximizing trade in futures contracts. Point E has coordinates $(p_1 x_1, p_2 x_2)$, and the slope of EAB is $-(p^f - p_2)/p_1 - p^f)$.

We saw earlier that if $\pi_1/\pi_2 = v_1/v_2$, all income variability is eliminated. Performing the necessary substitutions for v_1 and v_2, we find that this condition reduces to

$$p^f = \pi_1 p_1 + \pi_2 p_2 \equiv E(p) \tag{1.3}$$

The price of a futures contract is equal to the expected spot price, $E(p)$. In these circumstances the producer will choose to be *perfectly hedged* in the sense that his futures trade will have eliminated all income uncertainty. The trade will also be independent of the degree of risk aversion displayed by the producer.

The situation captured in (1.3) is termed an *unbiased* futures price, since the futures price is an unbiased predictor of the spot price. We shall have more to say about bias in futures prices when we examine market equilibrium.

To complete the model, we introduce a second group of traders in the futures market, whom we call speculators. The defining characteristic of a speculator is that he should have an income which is uncorrelated with the returns from a futures contract, and thus have no insurance or portfolio diversification motive for trading. For simplicity we assume the existence of a single representative speculator, S, who has non-random endowment $\bar{m}^S$, and who trades in order to maximize expected utility of end-of-period income $\pi_1 u^S(m_1^S) + \pi_2 u^S(m_2^S)$, where $m_i^S = \bar{m}^S + z^S(p_i - p^f)$, and, as before, the choice variable z^S represents the speculator's demand for futures contracts.

Note first that if the speculator is risk averse, $z^S \gtreqless 0$ as $p^f \lesseqgtr E(p)$. This follows from the result established above, namely that a risk-averse individual with non-random income will only trade if $\Sigma_i \pi_i t_i > 0$. But this is equivalent to $z\Sigma_i \pi_i (p_i - p^f) > 0$ or $z(E(p) - p^f) > 0$.

Thus a speculator will be long, i.e. $z^S > 0$, and he buys futures if and only if $p^f < E(p)$, or the price of a futures contract lies below the expected future spot price. He will be short if $p^f > E(p)$, and he will not trade if $p^f = E(p)$.

The factors affecting the magnitude of z^S as opposed to its sign can be understood by referring to figure 1.2. We know that $z = t_i / (p_i - p^f)$ so

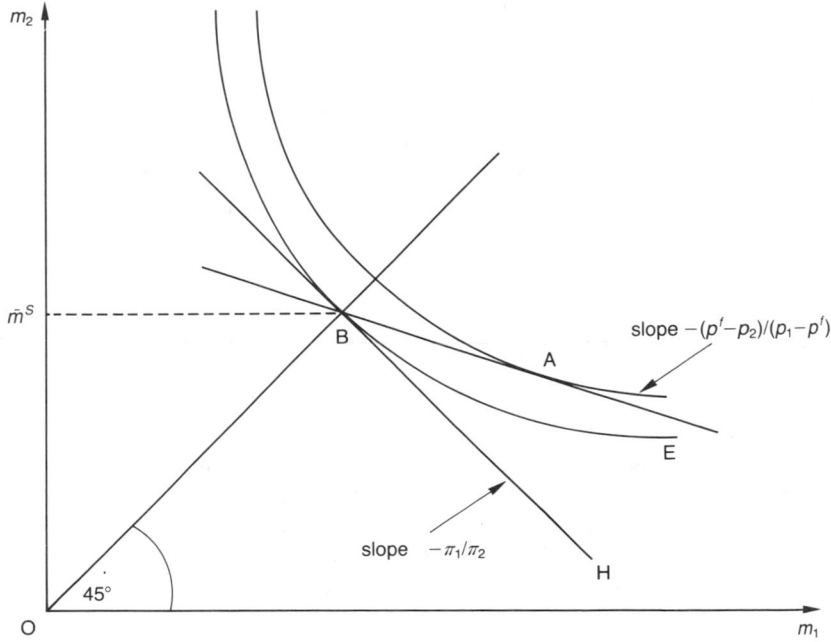

Figure 1.2 Pure speculation in futures contracts

that, for fixed prices, demand for futures contracts varies directly with the size of income transfer in equilibrium. The size of income transfer depends on (a) the curvature of the expected utility indifference curves, and (b) the slope of BAE, which is equal to $-(p^f - p_2)/(p_1 - p^f)$. The greater the curvature about the 45° line, the more risk averse the individual, and the smaller the transfer. The closer is the ratio $(p^f - p_2)/(p_1 - p^f)$ to π_1/π_2, the smaller the transfer. This is equivalent to saying that the smaller is $p^f - E(p)$ in absolute value, the smaller the transfer.

If a speculator is risk neutral, it must be the case that $p^f = E(p)$ for a solution to the expected utility maximization problem to exist, and then z^S is indeterminate. The indifference curves are straight lines with the same slope as the budget constraint implied by the condition $p^f = E(p)$, and any positive or negative value of z^S will yield the same level of utility.

1.3   Market equilibrium

We are now in a position to consider the determination of market equilibrium in the model. Spot prices are still determined by spot market equilibrium conditions, but equilibrium in the futures market requires us to treat the price of a futures contract as endogenous. The equilibrium condition takes the form

$$z^F + z^S = 0 \tag{1.4}$$

It states that the net supply of futures contracts be equal to zero.

The equilibrium is illustrated in figure 1.3 in a standard Edgeworth box diagram, where $\bar{m}^S$, the endowment of the speculator, is measured from O^S, and $\bar{m}_i^F$ is measured from O^F. The dimensions of the box represent aggregate income $\bar{m}_i \equiv \bar{m}_i^F + \bar{m}^S$ in each state, E the initial endowment point and F the equilibrium. A number of simple qualitative conclusions can be drawn.

The diagram illustrates the case where $\bar{m}_1 > \bar{m}_2$. Since we know that the slopes of the indifference curves for producer and speculator must be equal on their respective certainty lines, it is immediately evident that equilibrium can never occur above $O^S E$. Therefore, $t_1^S > 0$, which we have already shown holds if and only if $p^f < E(p)$.

But $\bar{m}_1^F > \bar{m}_2^F$ implies $p_1 x_1 > p_2 x_2$, which is true if demand for the commodity is inelastic (recall that we are assuming throughout that $x_1 < x_2$). So we have shown that inelastic spot demand will generate a downward bias in the price of a futures contract. The converse is also true. Elastic demand will be associated with an upward bias in the price of a futures contract. The intuition that lies behind this result is the following. A futures market price provides a mechanism whereby producers can transfer some of the income risk they face to speculators. In order to do this they must take losses on

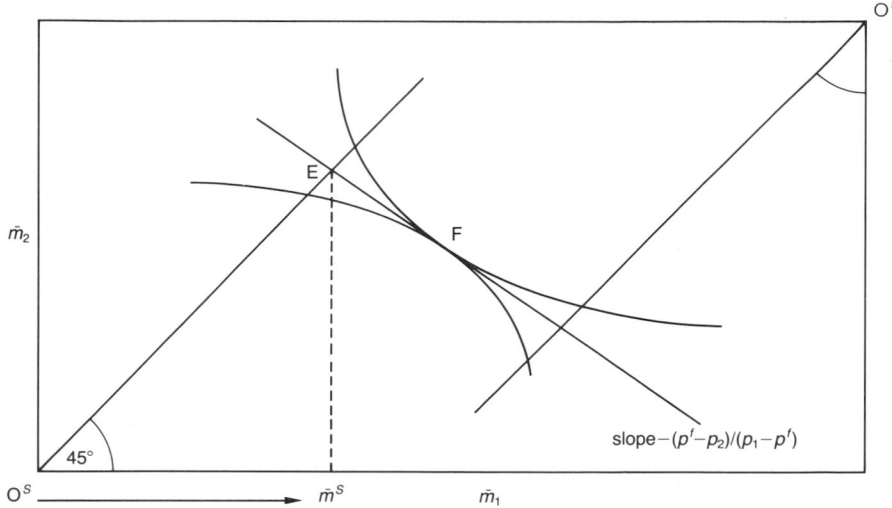

Figure 1.3   Futures market equilibrium

futures contracts in the high income state in returns for gains in the low income state. Since $t_1^F = z^F(p_1 - p^f)$ and $p^f < p_1$, if $\bar{m}_1^F > \bar{m}_2^F$ producers must be short in equilibrium $(z^F < 0)$. But then in order for the futures market to clear, speculators must be long. They will choose such a trade if the price of a contract is expected to rise sufficiently to compensate for the increase in income risk.

A simple special case arises when the spot demand curve is unit elastic. Now the representative producer faces no income risk and consequently has no motive for trading on the futures market. Thus the equilibrium is one with $p^f = E(p)$ and no trade, as is evident if we consider how the position of point F in figure 1.3 must adjust as we reduce $\bar{m}_1$. When $\bar{m}_1 = \bar{m}_2$, the two certainty lines are superimposed and equilibrium occurs at E.

This result holds despite the fact that the levels of output and spot price may be highly variable, and is a simple illustration of the fact that it is ultimately income variability rather than price variability which provides the motivation for trade in futures markets.

The above special case can be used to illustrate a more general result. Suppose we retain the assumption of unit elastic spot demand, but consider a population of heterogeneous producers whose output distributions over the two states of nature are arbitrary. The equilibrium is again characterized by an unbiased futures price, but now there is trade, and as we have established above, all producers will be perfectly hedged. This is illustrated for the case of two producers in figure 1.4. The assumption of unit elastic

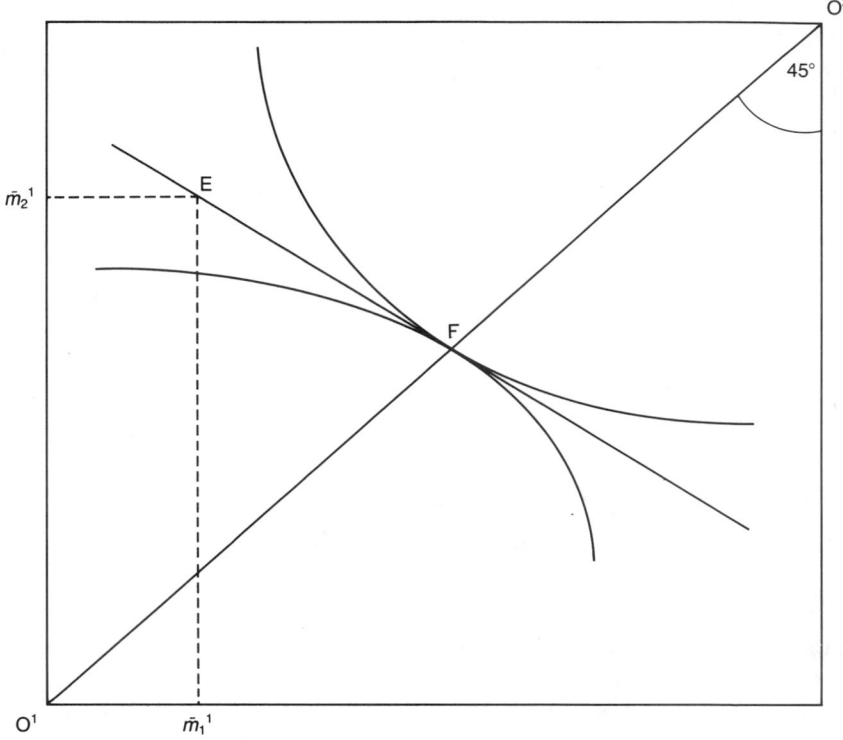

Figure 1.4 An unbiased futures market with heterogeneous risk-averse producers

spot demand implies that aggregate income does not vary across states of nature. So the box diagram is a square, and the certainty lines of the two producers, indexed 1 and 2, coincide with the diagonal. The initial endowment point at E is such that both producers have random endowments in advance of trade on the futures market. But because the endowment risk they face is perfectly negatively correlated, they trade to point F, where they are both perfectly hedged, and the futures price is unbiased. We can exclude speculators from the picture because they will choose not to trade in equilibrium. Thus we see that it is the aggregate variability of producer income which generates a role for an outside group of risk bearers, i.e. speculators.

If aggregate producer income is variable, we obtain a similar result if speculators are risk neutral. Now speculators trade, and provide an opportunity for producers to be perfectly hedged, at an unbiased futures price.

The model we have considered so far illustrates in the simplest possible way how a futures market performs its risk-sharing function, and how the trading decisions of producers and speculators are related in equilibrium. But there is an important omission from the set of individual agents who trade on the futures market. We have not allowed for the activities of manufacturers or users of the commodity in question. However, in many instances this group has a very significant presence in the futures market. In the next section we analyze a rather more complex model in which we allow for the presence of user firms.

2 HEDGING AND SPECULATION WITH USER FIRMS

We know that, in many instances, firms who use a commodity as an input to production are active traders in futures markets. And, to the extent that their profits move in the opposite direction in response to supply shocks, there should be a greater incentive for producers and users to trade futures contracts among themselves, since they ought to be prepared to provide each other with insurance at lower risk premia than would be demanded by speculators.

The purpose of the model we present in this part of the chapter is to examine the impact of user firms on equilibrium in the futures market, and to see how their presence can be expected to alter the simple patterns of hedging and speculation identified previously.

2.1 A model with user firms

The representative producer, F, and speculator, S, are characterized as before. But we introduce, in addition, a representative user firm, U, who also has a von Neumann–Morgenstern utility function defined on end-of-period profit m^U. We allow for the possibility that there are two distinct sources of demand for the agricultural producer's output: final consumption demand for the raw commodity and input demand from users.[1] $D_x(p)$ represents final consumption demand for good x, and $D_y(q)$ demand for good y, the output of the user firm. The price of good y is denoted q. The technology used to produce good y is summarized in the production function $g(w, n)$, where w is the quantity of good x used as an input, and n is an aggregate of all other factors of production. We assume that the production function displays constant returns to scale, and is strictly concave in w. The timescale over which we analyze production decisions is sufficiently short that we shall treat n as fixed, say at $\bar{n}$. But the elasticity of substitution between the two inputs to production has an important influence upon the way in which profits respond to changes in the price of commodity x. This, in turn, will affect the hedging decisions of user firms.

Before trade in the futures market, the profit of user U in state i is given by

$$\bar{m}_i^U = q_i g(w_i, \bar{n}) - p_i w_i \tag{1.5}$$

where we ignore the fixed cost component associated with $\bar{n}$. Thus the only source of uncertainty affecting profits is that associated with the fluctuation in input prices. Notice that the formulation in (1.5) allows users to select inputs contingent upon the realized state of nature. It captures the idea that the production plans of user firms are more flexible than those of producers, in that they can at least partially insulate themselves against the adverse impact of input price movements by adjusting input demand.

Thus, although we suppose that users are risk averse, they will behave as simple profit maximizers when it comes to selecting the level of the variable input w. Because, however, profit $\bar{m}^U$ is a random variable, there is an incentive to trade on the futures market.

2.2   Equilibrium in spot markets

We first examine the way in which variations in supply affect spot prices and incomes. Our model takes the following form:

$$D_x(p_i) + w_i = x_i \tag{1.6}$$

$$D_y(q_i) = g(w_i, \bar{n}) \tag{1.7}$$

$$q_i g_w(w_i, \bar{n}) = p_i \tag{1.8}$$

where g_w denotes the first partial derivative of g with respect to w.

Equation (1.6) states that the sum of the two sources of demand for the raw commodity, as final consumption and as an input for users firms, must equal total supply. Equation (1.7) states that demand for the processed or manufactured commodity should equal supply, which is equal to the output of user firms. Users are assumed to behave competitively and, as discussed above, take their decisions on the level of inputs to production after the state of nature is realized. This implies that the value marginal product of the input is set equal to its price in each state of nature, as stated in (1.8).

To analyze the comparative statics of the system (1.6)–(1.8), we denote a proportional change in a variable x by $\hat{x} = dx/x$. Suppressing subscript i for clarity, we have

$$(1 - \lambda) \varepsilon_x \hat{p} + \lambda \hat{w} = \hat{x} \tag{1.9}$$

$$-\varepsilon_y \hat{q} = \theta \hat{w} \tag{1.10}$$

$$\varepsilon_w (\hat{q} - \hat{p}) = \hat{w} \tag{1.11}$$

where $\lambda = w/x$ is the proportion of the supply of good x used in the production of good y, $\varepsilon_x = -(p/x)D_x'(p)$, $\varepsilon_y = -(q/y)D_y'(q)$ are the elasticities of consumption demand for goods x and y, $\varepsilon_w = -g_w/wg_{ww}$ is the elasticity of factor demand (where g_{ww} is the second partial derivative of g with respect to w), and $\theta = pw/qy$ is the cost-revenue ratio of users.

We find from (1.10) and (1.11) that

$$\hat{q} = \frac{\theta\,\varepsilon_w}{\varepsilon_y + \theta\,\varepsilon_w}\,\hat{p} \tag{1.12}$$

and from (1.9), (1.10) and (1.11) that

$$\hat{p} = -\frac{1}{\eta_x}\hat{x} \tag{1.13}$$

where

$$\eta_x = (1 - \lambda)\varepsilon_x + \frac{\lambda\,\varepsilon_y\,\varepsilon_w}{\varepsilon_y + \theta\,\varepsilon_w} \tag{1.14}$$

and η_x is an elasticity of (Marshallian) derived demand for x.

The effect of changes in the price of the raw commodity on that of the manufactured output is captured in (1.12). A rise in p will generate a less than proportionate rise in marginal cost, except when the production function is linear ($\varepsilon_w = \infty$). Thus the price of the manufactured output will fluctuate less than that of the raw commodity. This is reflected by the fact that $\{\theta\,\varepsilon_w/(\varepsilon_y + \theta\,\varepsilon_w)\} \leqslant 1$.

Now we define the following terms:

$$\Delta^F \equiv -\frac{1}{p}\frac{d\bar{m}^F}{dx} \tag{1.15}$$

$$\Delta^U \equiv -\frac{1}{p}\frac{d\bar{m}^U}{dx} \tag{1.16}$$

$$\Delta \equiv \Delta^F + \Delta^U \tag{1.17}$$

Observing that

$$\sigma = (1 - \theta)\varepsilon_w \tag{1.18}$$

where σ is the elasticity of substitution between w and n,[2] we find that

$$\Delta^F = \frac{1}{\eta_x}(1 - \eta_x) \tag{1.19}$$

$$\Delta^U = -\frac{1}{\eta_x}\frac{\lambda}{\varepsilon_y + \theta\,\varepsilon_w}(\varepsilon_y - \sigma) \tag{1.20}$$

The sign of Δ^F, which determines the direction of response of producers' income to changed supply, depends straightforwardly on whether the elasticity of derived demand is greater than or less than unity. The sign of Δ^U, which determines the corresponding direction of income change for users, depends upon whether the elasticity of demand for their output is greater than or less than the elasticity of substitution in production. This is explained by observing that a given increase in the supply of good x will depress its price by more if the production technology in manufacturing is relatively inflexible – that is to say, if σ is small; and the resulting increase in the output of good y will depress its price by less the more elastic is demand. A decline in an input price which is large relative to the associated decline in output price will increase profitability.

2.3   State-contingent income transfers in equilibrium

As before, we shall assume that there are only two possible states of nature. In order to simplify the exposition we suppose that $\pi_1 = \pi_2 = 1/2$. Thus $\bar{x} = (x_1 + x_2)/2$ is the mean of the output distribution of good x. If we define

$$\alpha \equiv \bar{x} - x_1 = x_2 - \bar{x} > 0 \qquad (1.21)$$

then we may use α as a measure of the variability in the supply of good x.

In order to describe equilibrium in the futures market, it is convenient to return to the analysis we developed in section 1. Define, as before, the transfer of agent j to state i, t_i^j, as

$$t_i^j \equiv m_i^j - \bar{m}_i^j = z^j (p_i - p^f) \qquad (1.22)$$

Then the first-order conditions for optimal choice of a futures position can be written

$$u_m^j (m_1^j)/u_m^j (m_2^j) = r, \qquad j = F, U, S, \qquad (1.23)$$

where $r = (p^f - p_2)/(p_1 - p^f)$.

We know that if the supply of x is non-random ($\alpha = 0$) there will be no incentive to trade on the futures market. So we analyze the effect of introducing a small amount of supply variability on the equilibrium values of t_i^j and r. Then we translate these results back into statements about spot and futures prices, and the demand for futures contracts. All the information we need is contained in (1.23), with the addition of a market clearing condition

$$\sum_j t_i^j = 0, \qquad i = 1, 2. \qquad (1.24)$$

If we totally differentiate (1.23) with respect to α, using the facts that $t_2^j = -rt_1^j$, and that in the non-random equilibrium ($\alpha = 0$ and $\bar{m}_1^j = \bar{m}_2^j$ for all j) $r = 1$ and $t_i^j = 0$, we find that

$$\frac{dt_1^j}{d\alpha} = \frac{1}{2\rho^j}\frac{dr}{d\alpha} - \frac{d\bar{m}_1^j}{d\alpha} \tag{1.25}$$

where $\rho^j = -u_{mm}^j/u_m^j$ is the coefficient of absolute risk aversion of group j. Since by assumption $\bar{m}_1^S = \bar{m}_2^S = \bar{m}^S$, implying $d\bar{m}_1^S/d\alpha = 0$, and from (1.24) $\Sigma_j dt_1^j/d\alpha = 0$, (1.25) implies

$$\frac{dt_1^F}{d\alpha} = -\frac{d\bar{m}_1^F}{d\alpha} + \gamma^F\left(\frac{d\bar{m}_1^F}{d\alpha} + \frac{d\bar{m}_1^U}{d\alpha}\right) \tag{1.26}$$

$$\frac{dt_1^U}{d\alpha} = -\frac{d\bar{m}_1^U}{d\alpha} + \gamma^U\left(\frac{d\bar{m}_1^F}{d\alpha} + \frac{d\bar{m}_1^U}{d\alpha}\right) \tag{1.27}$$

$$\frac{dt_1^S}{d\alpha} = \gamma^S\left(\frac{d\bar{m}_1^F}{d\alpha} + \frac{d\bar{m}_1^U}{d\alpha}\right) \tag{1.28}$$

where

$$\gamma^j = \left(\frac{1}{\rho^j}\right)\bigg/\left(\sum_k \frac{1}{\rho^k}\right)$$

Noting that $\Delta^S = 0$ by assumption, we summarize the relationships in (1.26)–(1.28) in the single equation

$$\frac{dt_1^j}{d\alpha} = p\Delta^j - \gamma^j p\Delta, \qquad j = F, U, S, \tag{1.29}$$

where we use the definitions of Δ and Δ^j in (1.15)–(1.17). The expression in (1.29) reveals how equilibrium income transfers depend both upon individual and aggregate patterns of income variability. We shall see in the next section that they are closely related to the demand for futures contracts.

3 SPECULATION, HEDGING, AND NORMAL BACKWARDATION

In order to analyze the interrelationships between speculation, hedging and market prices we need to calculate expressions for the futures demands of the different groups in the model. First define

$$k \equiv \bar{x}\eta_x$$

Then it is possible to show that

$$z^F \simeq k\gamma^F \Delta - k\Delta^F \tag{1.30}$$

$$z^U \simeq k\gamma^U \Delta - k\Delta^U \tag{1.31}$$

$$z^S \simeq k\gamma^S \Delta \tag{1.32}$$

For the derivation of these results see the Appendix. They hold as local approximations for small amounts of variability in the output of good x. All variables are evaluated at the equilibrium associated with non-random output $\bar{x}$.

A number of observations can be made about the expressions in (1.30)–(1.32). First, the term $k\gamma^j \Delta$ has a natural interpretation as the speculative component of futures demand, since it is the sole element in the demand of pure speculators. The less risk averse any group is, the larger is γ^j and the larger the speculative component. The term $-k\Delta^j$ is the hedging component, and is always non-zero if j's income and the output of good x (and so spot price p) are correlated. The hedging term will always reduce income variability. We can see this as follows. Suppose $\Delta^j > 0$: this implies that j's income declines as supply of the commodity x increases. So in order to reduce income variability the hedging component must transfer income from state 1 (the low supply, high spot price state) to state 2 (the high supply, low spot price state). The net transfer to state 2 attributable to the hedging component is $-k\Delta^j (p_2 - p^f)$, which is indeed positive, since we know that $p_2 < p^f$. Clearly the converse holds for $\Delta^j < 0$.

Since the ultimate objective of hedging activity is to reduce income variability, it is this feature that we shall focus upon in distinguishing between speculation and hedging. We shall say that a group is in a *net speculative position* if its income variability is increased by futures trading, and that it is in a *net hedged position* if its income variability is reduced.

It is clear that, in our model, if futures trading is to reduce the income variability of a particular group in the market it must transfer income from the high- to the low-income state for that group. This is equivalent to requiring that $dt_1^j/d\alpha$ and $d\bar{m}_1^j/d\alpha$ be of opposite sign. Introducing the definition

$$h^j = 1 - \frac{\Delta/\Delta^j}{1/\gamma^j}, \qquad j = F, U, \tag{1.33}$$

we see from (1.26) and (1.27) that

$$h^j > 0 \text{ if and only if } \frac{dt_1^j}{d\alpha} \bigg/ \frac{d\bar{m}_1^j}{d\alpha} < 0. \tag{1.34}$$

Thus for both producers and users the sign of h^j determines whether they are in net hedged or net speculative positions. It has a natural interpretation if one thinks of $1/\gamma^j$ as a measure of the extent to which group j is more or less risk averse than average, and of Δ/Δ^j as a measure of the extent to which group j faces more or less income variability than average.

It is instructive to rewrite the expressions describing the demand for futures in (1.30) and (1.31) as

$$z^F \simeq -kh^F \Delta^F \tag{1.35}$$

$$z^U \simeq -kh^U \Delta^U \tag{1.36}$$

If we compare (1.30) and (1.31) with (1.35) and (1.36), we see that if, for example, $\Delta < 0$ and $\Delta^j > 0$, it is quite possible for the speculative component to exceed the hedging component in absolute value, and for the group to be in a net hedged position. In fact, we see from the definition of h^j that if Δ and Δ^j have opposite signs, group j is always in a net hedged position. In other words, if aggregate and group (pre-trade) income variability are negatively correlated, hedging and speculative components of demand reinforce one another in terms of their impact on (post-trade) income variability.

We can now combine the analysis of the previous two sections to characterize the factors which determine whether or not a group will trade to a net hedged position or not. Using (1.17), (1.19), (1.20), and (1.33) we have the following result.

Proposition 1 *Producers are in a net hedged position* $(h^F > 0)$ *if and only if*

$$\frac{1 - \gamma^F}{\gamma^F} > -\frac{\lambda}{\varepsilon_y + \theta \varepsilon_w} \frac{\varepsilon_y - \sigma}{1 - \eta_x} \tag{1.37}$$

Users are in a net hedged position $(h^U > 0)$ *if and only if*

$$\frac{1 - \gamma^U}{\gamma^U} > -\left[\frac{\lambda}{\varepsilon_y + \theta \varepsilon_w}\right]^{-1} \left[\frac{\varepsilon_y - \sigma}{1 - \eta_x}\right]^{-1} \tag{1.38}$$

A number of observations of interest emerge from the proposition. As one would expect, the more risk averse a group is, the larger is the term $(1 - \gamma^j)/\gamma^j$ and the more likely the group is to be hedged. Since γ^j must lie between zero and one, a necessary condition for either group to be in a net speculative position is that $\varepsilon_y - \sigma$ and $1 - \eta_x$ have opposite signs. This is equivalent to saying that Δ^F and Δ^U have the same sign, or that the income variability of the two groups is positively correlated. Thus a sufficient condition for both groups to be hedged is that $\varepsilon_y - \sigma$ and $1 - \eta_x$ have the same sign, or that incomes be negatively correlated.

In the special case where there is no consumption demand for the raw commodity ($\lambda = 1$), (1.37) reduces to

$$\frac{1 - \gamma^F}{\gamma^F} > -\frac{\varepsilon_y - \sigma}{\varepsilon_y - \sigma + \varepsilon_w (1 - \varepsilon_y)} \tag{1.39}$$

and we find that a sufficient condition for producers to be in a net hedged position is that $\varepsilon_y - \sigma$ and $1 - \varepsilon_y$ have the same sign. This is true if either $\sigma < \varepsilon_y < 1$ or $1 < \varepsilon_y < \sigma$. The same condition holds also for users.

Although it is possible for either producers or users to be in a net speculative position, (1.37) and (1.38) reveal that it is not possible for *both* groups simultaneously to be in this position.[3]

The group of pure speculators, if they trade at all, must necessarily increase their income variability. They will only buy futures contracts ($z^S > 0$) if the expected return exceeds the cost, or $E(p)z^S > p^f z^S$. If we couple this observation with (1.36) we obtain the following result.

Proposition 2

$$E(p) > p^f \text{ if and only if } \Delta > 0 \tag{1.40}$$

or, normal backwardation[4] occurs if and only if aggregate income declines as the supply of good x increases.

It is worth noting that this proposition is more general than the relationship between price elasticity and bias noted in section 1. We have two distinct groups, producers and users, whose incomes are affected in different ways by demand conditions in two markets, that for the raw and for the processed or manufactured commodity. The requirement in Proposition 2 that aggregate income decline as the supply of agricultural output increases implies neither that $\varepsilon_y < 1$ nor that $\varepsilon_x < 1$.

We can see more precisely the implications of Proposition 2 for the demand elasticities in the separate markets if we use (1.19) and (1.20) to state a further proposition.

Proposition 3 *Normal backwardation occurs if and only if*

$$1 - \eta_x - \frac{\lambda}{\varepsilon_y + \theta \varepsilon_w}(\varepsilon_y - \sigma) = (1 - \lambda)(1 - \varepsilon_x) + \lambda \frac{\varepsilon_w}{\varepsilon_y + \theta \varepsilon_w}(1 - \varepsilon_y) > 0 \tag{1.41}$$

This reveals that it is necessary for one of the two demand elasticities to be less than unity for normal backwardation. Also, if $\varepsilon_x = \varepsilon_y = 1$, there will be no bias in the futures price (i.e. $p^f = E(p)$), but so long as $\sigma \neq 1$, there will still be a motive for hedging on the part of both producers and users. (We see this from (1.20), which reveals that $\Delta^U \neq 0$ if $\varepsilon_y \neq \sigma$, and from (1.31), which shows that if $\Delta = 0$ and $\Delta^U \neq 0$, then $z^U \neq 0$.) The income variability of the producers and users is perfectly negatively correlated, and they can provide each other with perfect insurance by trading futures. In this situation risk-averse speculators play no role, in that they choose voluntarily not to trade.

This point is worth emphasizing since it runs counter to the traditional view that hedging activity will necessarily produce bias in the futures price.

The term *net short hedging* is commonly used to describe the situation in which producers and users are net sellers of futures contracts, or $z^F + z^U < 0$. This characterization is somewhat misleading, implying as it does that it is always appropriate to regard both producers and users as hedgers. But there is certainly nothing inconsistent with a situation in which the two groups are net sellers of futures, and yet one group is in a net speculative position. For this reason we define the term as follows.

Definition Net short hedging is said to occur if $z^F + z^U < 0$ and $h^F > 0$, $h^U > 0$.

In other words, we observe net short hedging when both producers and users take up net hedged positions, and if the aggregate position of the two groups is short.

This enables us to state a result characterizing the stylized facts of market equilibrium.

Proposition 4 *The following statements are equivalent:*

1. In equilibrium producers are short and users are long in futures; net short hedging and normal backwardation occur.

2. $\varepsilon_y > \sigma$ and $\eta_x < 1 - \dfrac{\lambda}{\varepsilon_y + \theta \varepsilon_w} (\varepsilon_y - \sigma)$

The proof of this proposition is presented in the Appendix. Its interest stems from the fact that the circumstances described in statement 1 coincide with what are generally accepted to be the stylized facts describing equilibrium in agricultural futures markets. In addition, we are able to be precise about the sense in which producers and users are hedged. It is not simply that they are respectively short and long. Indeed, we see from (1.35) and (1.36) that whether a net hedged position is long or short depends upon the pattern of income variability summarized in the term Δ^j. Both producers and users are hedged in the sense that they have unambiguously reduced the income variability they face.

The conditions in statement 2 of Proposition 4 are plausible for a wide range of agricultural commodities traded on futures markets. If the user is a processor rather than a manufacturer, the elasticity of substitution between the commodity and other inputs can reasonably be expected to be fairly small. The condition on η_x, the elasticity of derived demand, is consistent with the fact that estimated demand elasticities for agricultural products are very commonly significantly less than one. From (1.41) it is sufficient for the condition to be satisfied that both ε_x and ε_y be less than unity.

There is a simple special case of Proposition 4 which is worth noting. If there is no demand for the raw commodity ($\lambda = 1$), then one finds that statement 1 of Proposition 4 is equivalent to the condition

$$1 > \varepsilon_y > \sigma$$

It is finally worth noting that if $\varepsilon_y = \sigma$ then users will have no hedging motive and will not trade futures. In this case it is easy to show that $\eta_x = (1 - \lambda)\varepsilon_x + \lambda\varepsilon_y$. So long as $\eta_x \neq 1$, producers will trade with speculators, and normal backwardation will occur if $(1 - \lambda)\varepsilon_x + \lambda\varepsilon_y < 1$.

APPENDIX

1   Derivation of demand functions for futures contracts

Note first that when output is non-random ($\alpha = 0$), $p_1 = p_2 = p$ and $r = 1$. Also, for $\alpha \neq 0$, $r = (p^f - p_2)/(p_1 - p^f)$. Since p_i and r are clearly differentiable in α at $\alpha = 0$, we find that the same will be true of p^f, since

$$p^f = \frac{rp_1 + p_2}{1 + r} \tag{1.42}$$

We find that $dp^f/d\alpha = 0$ at $\alpha = 0$, using the fact that $dp_1/d\alpha = -dp_2/d\alpha$. Since, for $\alpha \neq 0$,

$$z^j = \frac{t_1^j}{p_1 - p^f} \tag{1.43}$$

by L'Hôpital's rule

$$\lim_{\alpha \to 0} z^j = \frac{dt_1^j/d\alpha}{dp_1/d\alpha - dp^f/d\alpha} \tag{1.44}$$

where all derivatives are evaluated at $\alpha = 0$.

Using (1.13) and (1.29), the expressions in (1.30)–(1.32) follow immediately.

2   Proof of Proposition 4

Statement 1 in the proposition is equivalent to the following conditions:

$$z^F < 0 \qquad \text{(producers short)} \tag{1.45a}$$

$$z^U > 0 \qquad \text{(users long)} \tag{1.45b}$$

$$z^F + z^U < 0 \qquad (1.45c)$$

$$h^F > 0 \qquad \text{(net short hedging)} \qquad (1.45d)$$

$$h^U > 0 \qquad (1.45e)$$

$$p^f < E(p) \qquad \text{(normal backwardation)} \qquad (1.45f)$$

Statement 2 consists of the two inequalities

$$\varepsilon_y > \sigma \qquad (1.46)$$

$$\eta_x < 1 - \frac{\lambda}{\varepsilon_y + \theta \varepsilon_w} (\varepsilon_y - \sigma) \qquad (1.47)$$

We first show that (1.45a)–(1.45f) imply (1.46) and (1.47). Equations (1.45b) and (1.45e) imply $\Delta^U < 0$ from (1.36), which implies (1.46) by (1.20). Equation (1.45f) implies (1.47) by Proposition 3.

Next we show that (1.46) and (1.47) imply (1.45a)–(1.45f). First, (1.46) implies (1.45f) by Proposition 3. (1.45f) implies $\Delta > 0$ by Proposition 2. (1.46) implies $\Delta^U < 0$ by (1.20). But $\Delta > 0$, $\Delta^U < 0$ imply $h^U > 0$ (1.45e) by definition from (1.33). Also $\Delta^U < 0$ and $h^U > 0$ imply $z^U > 0$ (1.45b) from (1.36). But $\Delta > 0$ implies $z^S > 0$ from (1.32), which implies $z^F + z^U < 0$ (1.45c) by market clearing. Then $z^U > 0$, $z^S > 0$ imply $z^F < 0$ (1.45a) by market clearing. Finally, $\Delta > 0$, $\Delta^U < 0$ imply $\Delta^F > 0$, which with $z^F < 0$ implies $h^F > 0$ (1.45d) by (1.35).

NOTES

1 Examples of commodities for which this is true, and which are traded on futures markets, include sugar, rice, potatoes, corn, coffee, and cocoa.
2 This follows from the fact that for a linear homogeneous production function $\sigma = g_w g_n / y g_{wn}$. By Euler's theorem, $ng_n + wg_w = y$, and $wg_{ww} + ng_{wn} = 0$. Substituting for g_{wn} and using (1.8), we obtain (1.18).
3 Since $0 < \gamma^j < 1$, the necessary inequalities would imply $(1 - \gamma^F)(1 - \gamma^U) < \gamma^F \gamma^U$; thus $\gamma^F + \gamma^U > 1$, which is impossible since $\Sigma_j \gamma^j = 1$.
4 In accordance with current usage, we define normal backwardation as a situation in which $E(p) > p^f$.

2

Futures Markets and Risk Reduction

D. M. G. Newbery and J. E. Stiglitz

The response of economic agents to the presence of risk is to evolve methods of sharing and reducing this risk. The presence of risk-sharing and risk-reducing institutions may significantly modify the impact of risk-reducing policies such as commodity price stabilization. Moreover, it is typically difficult to make any general prediction about the way such impacts are modified.

The root of the problem is that the economy does not have a complete set of markets, so that the existing markets must typically serve several different functions simultaneously, and none of them quite satisfactorily. In agriculture, markets induce producers to supply commodities which are then allocated among consumers. If this were all they had to do, and if they were competitive, they would be efficient. But they also share risk between consumers and producers, and this additional role modifies the efficiency with which the market allocates commodities. If a future market is introduced, the risk-sharing role is now spread over two markets, and the operation of the spot market will be altered. The effect of price stabilization will thus depend on whether or not there is a futures market. In this chapter we are concerned with the way one particular institution, the futures market, modifies the impact of price stabilization.

In the past economists concerned with price stabilization have ignored the presence of futures markets, and, according to McKinnon (1967), this neglect is a fundamental reason why so many international commodity agreements have failed in the past. In his view futures markets dramatically modify the impact of price stabilization schemes so that it is seriously misleading to ignore their presence.

This chapter orginally appeared as chapter 13 in *The Theory of Commodity Price Stabilization: A Study in the Economics of Risk* by David M. G. Newbery and Joseph E. Stiglitz (1981), pp. 177–94. Reprinted by permission of Oxford University Press.

What we show in this chapter is that an unbiased futures market (that is, one in which the futures price is an unbiased estimator of the future cash price) provides unambiguously greater income risk insurance than perfect price stabilization. The reason is the standard revealed preference argument that an agent does better if he is free to choose the amount of price insurance as opposed to having a predetermined amount forced on him. The superior risk insurance properties of an unbiased futures market do not, however, mean that producers necessarily prefer futures markets to price stabilization, because in general price stabilization will change the average price (to the price of average output, which differs from the average price), and so generates different transfer effects and supply responses. Moreover, the result requires that futures markets be unbiased, which depends on the market structure.

We also examine the impact of price stabilization on the farmer's supply decision, and find that access to an unbiased futures market does indeed modify the impact of price stabilization on both supply and producer welfare. However, it is difficult to predict the direction in which both are modified without detailed knowledge of conditions of production and demand.

The chapter is organized as follows. We begin with a brief discussion of some of the general issues in the study of futures markets, and then address the main question of the risk-reducing role of futures markets as compared to price stabilization, assuming that average supply remains constant. In the last section we discuss the way in which the supply decision is affected by the presence of a futures market, and show how this complicates the analysis of price stabilization. Obviously our treatment of futures markets cannot be exhaustive, and the interested reader is directed to some of the excellent collections of readings available, such as Goss and Yamey (1976) or Peck (1977).

1 FUTURES MARKETS AND STORAGE

Several writers have argued that it is important to distinguish between commodities like grain which have an annual harvest and for which stocks are held continuously, and commodities like live beef cattle or fresh eggs for which there are no inventories in the normal sense. Other commodities like potatoes have discontinuous inventories since it is too costly to store them from one year to the next. The claim is that futures markets only offer significant income risk insurance to producers for discontinuously stocked commodities. To see if this claim is valid, we first note that if stocks are continuously held, then the difference between the price at different dates must be just equal to the carrying costs less convenience yield. This convenience yield measures the advantage to the stockholder of the immediate availability of the commodity compared to holding cash and buying the commodity when required. Stockholders can sell their entire stock forward on the futures market and so insure themselves against any fluctuation in the future price. Further, the futures market coordinates storage activities, for stockholders will continue to buy for storage and sell in the futures market until the futures price (reflecting expected future supplies) has been driven to the point at which no more storage is attractive. Moreover, the futures market ensures that storage is done at the lowest expected net cost.

If there were no uncertainty about future prices, and if the marginal carrying cost less marginal convenience yield on a unit of commodity held one period were c, we should expect prices at date t to satisfy

$$p_{t+1} = p_t + c_t. \tag{2.1}$$

After the harvest the price would be low, and it would steadily rise through the year to just before the next harvest, when it should reach its peak as stocks are nearly exhausted. If the net cost c is not too sensitive to stock levels, then the pattern of relative prices over the year would be fairly stable. The futures market allows stockholders to insure themselves against price uncertainties, and arbitrage will ensure that

$$_0p^f_{t+1} = {}_0p^f_t + c, \tag{2.2}$$

where $_ip^f_t$ is the futures price at date i for delivery at date t. Since the spot price at t is roughly equal[1] to the futures price for delivery at that date, $_tp^f_t$, any new information about future demand and supply which affects expectations about future prices shifts all previous prices, including the current spot price, in sympathy. This is confirmed by the empirical evidence, which also reveals that cash and futures prices are almost equally variable for continuously stocked commodities.

If it is impossible, or too expensive, to carry stocks, there is no reason for prices at successive dates to move in sympathy. In such cases the futures price is the best estimate of future cash prices, and is found to be more stable from year to year than the cash price. Table 2.1 reproduces data from Tomek and Gray (1970). Column (1) shows the variability from year to year of the futures price at the time of planting, and at the expiration of the futures contract (i.e. of the spot market after the harvest). Column (2) gives the ratio of the variances, and provides a test that the futures price is less variable than the post-harvest price from year to year. It shows that for continuously stocked crops like corn and soybeans, there is no significant difference in variability, while for the discontinuously stocked Maine potatoes the futures price is significantly more stable. Finally, column (3) gives the uncertainty surrounding the post-harvest price at the start of the season, defined as

Table 2.1 *Variability of prices 1952–68*

	Coefficient of variation (%) Annual changes (1)	F ratio[a] (2)	CV of seasonal change (%) (3)
December corn			
30 April	12.6	1.2	4.5
Last day	14.0		
November soybeans			
30 April	8.8	1.68	4.0
Last day	11.5		
November potatoes			
30 April	5.7	26.09	7.9
Last day	27.5		

[a]the 5% significance level for the difference in coefficients of variation is $F = 2.33$.
Source: Tomek and Gray (1970).

$$\text{SD} \left(\frac{p_t^f - p_t}{p_t^f} \right) ,$$

where p_t^f is the 30 April futures price and p_t is the futures price on the last day of the contract. Notice that this 'forecast error' is lower than the yearly variability of the futures price for the two continuously stocked commodities, but not for the discontinuously stocked commodity.

Tomek and Gray argue that futures markets only offer significant income risk insurance to producers for discontinuously stocked commodities, since they argue that the futures market is as risky as the spot market for continuously stocked commodities.

We shall argue that this does not necessarily follow as a consequence of the evidence in table 2.1. For example, if there were no supply risk, the futures market could eliminate all income risk for that particular year. However, income would still fluctuate from year to year, perhaps almost as much as if the farmer had not hedged in the futures market. If the farmer finances a large fraction of his crop costs by borrowing at fixed interest, then hedging within the year could still be very valuable.

There is another way to look at the distinction between the two types of commodity. Where commodities can be continuously stored, this activity itself will tend to stabilize the price (just like a buffer stock scheme). Historically, futures markets were first developed for such commodities and have as their main function the coordination of storage and the reduction of inventory price risks. For commodities which are not stocked continuously, futures markets can provide a similar kind of reduction in price variability (of the futures price) as storage did for the other crops. Thus storage and futures markets provide alternative methods of achieving the same result of reducing income variability. Futures and storage are also complementary, as futures markets coordinate the intertemporal price structure and share the risks of storage.

The main emphasis in this chapter will be on the role of futures markets in providing income insurance *within* a particular crop year, but futures markets may also stabilize prices (and, indirectly, incomes) *between* years by improving the informational efficiency of markets and reducing the importance of cobwebs and irrational expectations. Gray (1972) argues this case persuasively for potatoes, although the evidence of the onions market is mixed. Johnson (1973, in Peck, 1977, p. 329) argues that the onion market was as unstable before futures trading was suspended in 1958 as after. Powers (1970) compared price instability for beef and pork bellies for four years preceding the start of futures trading and four years afterwards and found a significant reduction in the variance of prices. There is a limit to this process though, for if too much of the instability is removed, then so are the opportunities for speculative profit and the futures market will decline. Larson (1967) attributes the decline in the once major egg futures market to increased producer concentration and reduced supply variability, which have reduced instabilities, and hence reduced the demand for futures. The butter market has apparently atrophied for similar reasons. If correct, these explanations are important for price stabilization, which would probably reduce and perhaps eliminate futures trading if prices were stabilized enough. It may then be academic to explore the extent to which the presence of a futures market modifies the impact of price stabilization. Instead the relevant comparison may be between the effect of a futures market and the effect of price stabilization with no futures market.

2   THE RISK-REDUCING ROLE OF FUTURES MARKETS

A futures market offers a farmer a guaranteed price for at least part of his crops, and hence can reduce some of the risks facing the farmer. If his output were certain, but the price were risky, he could completely eliminate income risk by selling his entire crop forward. (He may choose not to if he expects a higher price in the future; if so, then he would be *speculating* on a favourable price movement, and not *hedging* against price risk. We shall discuss his choice of forward sales in the next section, and sharpen the distinction between hedging and speculating.)

On the other hand, if there is substantial variability in his output, the variability in price may, if it is negatively correlated with output, provide income insurance and reduce the need for futures markets. For instance, if the demand function was stable and had unit price elasticity, and if all farmers faced the same risk, income would be perfectly certain and the futures market would offer no extra income insurance. Hence the extent to which the farmer will trade on the futures market and the benefit from so trading will depend on the correlation between price and output.

Consider, for example, an unbiased futures market in which the futures price p^f is equal to the expected cash price which will prevail in the market next period.

$$p^f = E\tilde{p} \equiv \bar{p}. \tag{2.3}$$

Let z be the amount of the commodity sold forward on the futures market by the representative farmer, and suppose that there is multiplicative supply risk so that his output is $\tilde{\theta}\bar{q}$. Then his income is

$$y = \tilde{p}\tilde{\theta}\bar{q} - z(\tilde{p} - p^f), \qquad E\tilde{\theta} = 1. \tag{2.4}$$

The effect of selling the crop forward on the futures market on income variability may be seen diagrammatically. There are three cases to consider. In the first case output and price are assumed to be positively correlated, so that when output is high, or θ is large, price is high. Then in the absence of futures markets, at a given level of input, the relationship between the state of nature, θ, and income is depicted in figure 2.1(a). Because the price increases with θ, income increases rapidly with θ. If the individual sells a part of his crop forward, he receives in exchange for a variable income a certain income; thus his lowest income is increased, and his highest income is reduced. If, as assumed, the futures price equalled the expected value of the spot price then mean income remains constant and so the riskiness of the individual's income would be unambiguously reduced (in the sense of Rothschild and Stiglitz (1970)). Figure 2.1(b) depicts the probability density function of his income before and after the sale of part of his crop on the futures market.

In the second case, price and output (θ) are negatively correlated, but not so negatively correlated that the price variability offsets the output variability. Hence, income variability is less than output variability. By

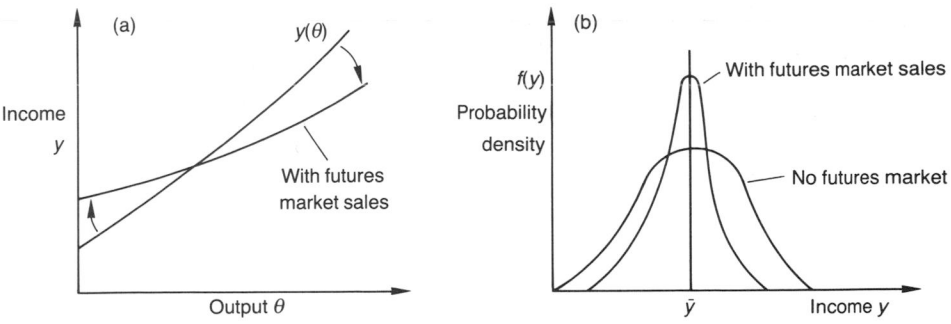

Figure 2.1 Price and output positively correlated

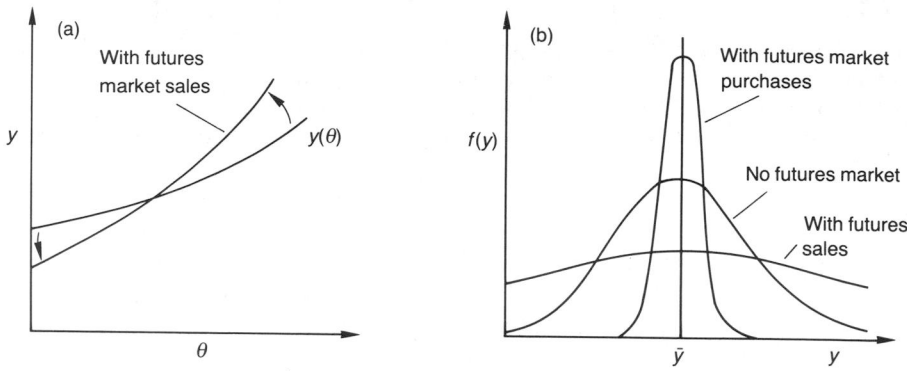

Figure 2.2   Price and output slightly negatively correlated

selling some of his crop in the futures market the individual can increase his income in states in which the price is low, i.e. in which output and income are high, at the expense, of course, of reducing it in states where income and output are low. But because of the diminishing marginal utility, since the marginal utility in the high-income states is lower than in the low-income states, he would not wish to sell his crop forward but would wish to *buy* forward. This is shown in figure 2.2.

The third case is that where prices and output are very negatively correlated, so negatively correlated that income decreases when output increases as shown in figure 2.3. This case is an important one in the subsequent analysis. Note that selling the crop on the futures market increases income when *price* is low, i.e. when output is high but income is low. Thus, in this case, he will wish to engage in an actuarially fair forward sale.

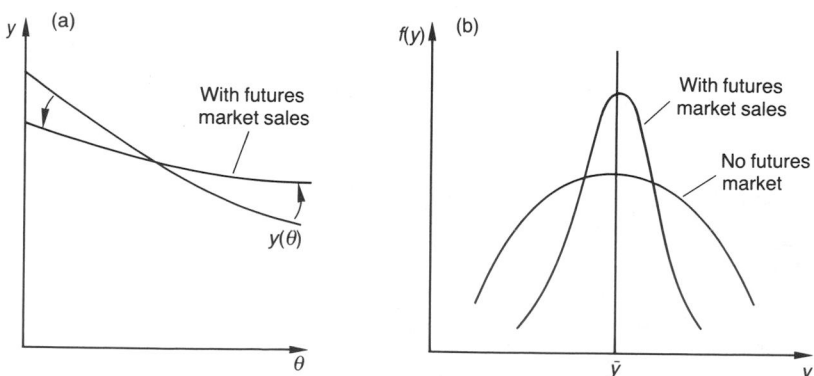

Figure 2.3   Price and output very negatively correlated

3 FUTURES MARKETS – HEDGING AND SPECULATION

Futures markets not only provide insurance against price fluctuations, but also provide opportunities for speculation. The insurance role, or hedging, typically involves taking opposite positions in the actuals and futures market. Thus a merchant who buys coffee now for storage can hedge by selling coffee futures, in which case he is 'long' in actuals and 'short' in futures. A farmer would likewise typically be a 'short hedger'. A 'long hedger' sells coffee for future delivery and buys coffee futures.

Speculation is usually contrasted as holding an uncovered position, such as selling forward without currently purchasing stocks, and instead planning to purchase in the actuals market when the time comes to make the delivery. Although much is made of this distinction, it is not very convenient for analytical purposes.

3.1 Futures markets for commodities with no storage

This will become clearer in the following model in which producers use the futures market to reduce income risk, but no one holds any stocks. The model is similar in spirit to that of McKinnon (1967) and assumes that consumers do not speculate in the futures market. If farmers and speculators have constant absolute risk aversion, and if prices and quantities are jointly normally distributed, we can employ the simple mean-variance analysis of the capital asset pricing model. Alternatively, the results can be interpreted as second-order Taylor series approximations, which are accurate for the special case of constant absolute risk aversion. Some of the implications of constant absolute risk aversion and log-normality are unreasonably strong, and must be treated with caution. In particular, as we shall show, these assumptions give rise to linear demand schedules for forward sales (or purchases), which are clearly special but very useful because they permit simple aggregation and hence explicit solutions.

We assume for the moment that farmers cannot vary their output, and examine the determination of equilibrium in the futures market and the extent to which the gains from price stabilization are modified by the presence of the futures market. In the last section we discuss the problems raised when producers can vary their supply.

If the farmer's average output is $\bar{q}$, and his forward sales are z, his income will be

$$y = \tilde{p}\tilde{\theta}\bar{q} - z(\tilde{p} - p^f), \tag{2.4}$$

where p^f is the price on the futures market. He chooses z to maximize expected utility, which, with constant absolute risk aversion, A, and joint-normality of p and $p\theta$ is equivalent to maximizing:

$$W = Ey - \tfrac{1}{2}A \operatorname{var} y \tag{2.5}$$

$$W = \bar{q}Ep\theta - z(\bar{p} - p^f) - \tfrac{1}{2}A\{\bar{q}^2 \operatorname{var}(p\theta) - 2\bar{q}z \operatorname{cov}(p, p\theta)$$
$$+ z^2 \operatorname{var} p\}. \tag{2.6}$$

If z can be positive or negative (i.e. if forward purchases are also possible)

$$z = \frac{\bar{q} \cdot \operatorname{cov}(p, p\theta)}{\operatorname{var} p} - \frac{\bar{p} - p^f}{A \operatorname{var} p}. \tag{2.7}$$

This formula can be interpreted by comparing it with the forward sales of a pure speculator who has no other sources of risky income, and who sells z' forward (or, more correctly, *buys* $-z'$ forward) to maximize

$$W' = z'(p^f - \bar{p}) - \tfrac{1}{2}A'z'^2 \operatorname{var} p.$$

$$z' = -\frac{\bar{p} - p^f}{A' \operatorname{var} p}. \tag{2.8}$$

In our very simple theory, a risk-averse speculator has no other risky income, and so can only be persuaded to take a long position (in which he *buys* futures from farmers which he will close out in the actuals market at a later date) if $p^f < \bar{p}$, that is, the futures price is a downward-biased estimate of its expiration value. The difference $\bar{p} - p^f$ is called *normal backwardation* and, in our theory, is simply a risk premium. It should be stressed that by ignoring other sources of risk and opportunities of risk-spreading our model is an over-simple description of a futures market.

The issue of market bias has attracted almost continuous attention since Keynes first advanced his theory of normal backwardation in an article in 1923, according to which the futures prices were downward-biased estimates of the final expiration values, the bias representing the risk premium for speculators. Since then considerable empirical effort has been devoted to trying to find this risk premium, with mixed success (see, for example, the selection of papers in Peck, 1977). Rather than summarize the findings here, it is enough to observe that for many markets the hypothesis of zero bias is reasonable, but for thin markets or markets which for institutional reasons are unattractive to speculators the risk premium may be positive. These issues may be explored further in the literature which shows the empirical and theoretical refinements necessary to test the hypothesis of zero bias.

We can now return to equation (2.7) and interpret the first term as the *hedging* component, and the second as the *speculative* component. The farmer can reduce or hedge his income risk by selling forward if price and income are positively correlated, but he can reduce the size of this hedge if he believes that $p^f < \bar{p}$, and to that extent he is speculating on a price risk.

If the coefficients of variation of quantity and price are σ, σ_p respectively, and if r is the correlation coefficient between price and quantity, the Appendix to this chapter demonstrates that the variances and covariances can be expressed in terms of these few parameters. In particular, equation (2.7) can be written

$$z = \bar{q}(1 + r\sigma/\sigma_p) - \frac{(\bar{p} - p^f)}{A\bar{p}^2\sigma_p^2}. \tag{2.9}$$

Thus if the only source of risk were demand risk ($\sigma = 0$), were there no bias in the futures market (so that $p^f = \bar{p}$), the farmer would sell his entire crop forward. If the only source of risk is supply variability, $r = -1$, and $\sigma/\sigma_p = \varepsilon$, the elasticity of demand, and with an unbiased futures price

$$z/\bar{q} = 1 - \varepsilon. \tag{2.10}$$

If $\varepsilon = 1$ the farmer is already perfectly hedged against income risk, and he would sell none of his crops forward.

3.2 Equilibrium in the futures market

For the futures market to be in equilibrium net sales must be zero, or, summing over farmers and speculators

$$0 = \sum z = \frac{\bar{Q}\,\text{cov}\,(p\theta,p)}{\text{var}\,p} - \frac{\bar{p} - p^f}{\text{var}\,p}\sum 1/A.$$

The bias in the market, or the normal backwardation, is

$$\bar{p} - p^f = \frac{\bar{Q}\,\text{cov}\,(p\theta,p)}{\Sigma 1/A}. \tag{2.11}$$

(The advantage of assuming constant absolute risk aversion should be apparent for the linearity of demand schedules makes it simple to aggregate and solve for the price.) It follows from equation (2.9) and the equilibrium condition that the ith agent's speculative (long) position in the forward market is

$$\frac{\bar{p} - p^f}{A^i\,\text{var}\,p} = \frac{\bar{Q}(1 + r\sigma/\sigma_p)}{A^i\Sigma 1/A}, \tag{2.12}$$

and the less risk averse the agent, the larger will be his speculative position. Agents who are risk neutral will eliminate the bias and share the speculative position between them; all other farmers will confine their activity to hedging.

Similarly, using (2.7) and the equilibrium condition, the total extent to which a farmer participates in the futures market in equilibrium can be written as

$$\frac{z}{\bar{q}^i} = \frac{\text{cov}(p, p\theta)}{\text{var}\,p}\left(1 - \frac{\bar{Q}}{\bar{q}^i A^i \Sigma 1/A}\right) = \beta(1 + r\sigma/\sigma_p), \tag{2.13}$$

where

$$\beta \equiv 1 - \frac{\bar{Q}}{\bar{q}^i A^i \Sigma 1/A}$$

is a measure of the extent to which the farmer is more risk averse than average (the terms in A) and more exposed to risk (the term $\bar{q}^i/\bar{Q}$). If all farmers are identical and there are no speculators, $\beta = 0$, while if there is one risk-neutral agent, $\beta = 1$.

The variance of a farmer's income with optimal forward sales, y^f, is, from equations (2.4) and (2.13),

$$\text{var}\,y^f = \bar{q}^2\left\{\text{var}(p\theta) - \beta(2 - \beta)\frac{\text{cov}^2(p, p\theta)}{\text{var}\,p}\right\}, \tag{2.14}$$

so provided that the farmer is a net hedger ($\beta > 0$) his income risk is unambiguously reduced.

If r is the correlation coefficient between price and output the first term is (from the Appendix to this chapter)

$$\text{var}(p\theta) = \bar{p}^2\{\sigma_p^2 + 2r\sigma\sigma_p + \sigma^2 + (1 + r^2)\sigma^2\sigma_p^2\}. \tag{2.15}$$

If the futures market is unbiased, i.e. if $\beta = 1$, his income risk is thus

$$\text{var}\,y^f = \bar{p}^2\bar{q}^2\sigma^2\{1 - r^2 + (1 + r^2)\sigma_p^2\} \tag{2.16}$$

For example, if the sole source of risk lies on the supply side so that $\sigma_p = \sigma/\varepsilon$, $r = -1$, then the ratio of income risk with a futures market to that without is, using (2.15),

$$\frac{\text{var}\,y^f}{\text{var}\,y} = \frac{\sigma^2}{\frac{1}{2}(1 - \varepsilon)^2 + \sigma^2}. \tag{2.17}$$

For plausible values of ε, σ (e.g. 0.5, 0.2) this may be quite small (25 per cent). Moreover, the futures market can completely eliminate risk which arises solely from demand fluctuations.

3.3   Comparisons with perfect price stabilization

Even if it were possible completely to stabilize the price the income risk would still be

$$\text{var } y^s = \bar{p}^2 \bar{q}^2 \sigma^2, \tag{2.18}$$

which exceeds the income risk remaining on an unbiased futures market unless the correlation between price and output is low enough, i.e. unless

$$r^2 < \frac{\sigma_p^2}{1 - \sigma_p^2} \tag{2.19}$$

(e.g. if $\sigma_p = 40\%$, $r^2 < 20\%$).

These reductions in income risk can be readily translated into measures of benefits. Thus the benefit $\frac{1}{2} R \bar{y} (\Delta \sigma_y^2)$ to a farmer of making use of an unbiased futures market compared to the case where there is only a spot market is

$$B_{FM} = \tfrac{1}{2} \bar{R} \bar{y} (\sigma_p + r\sigma)^2, \quad \bar{R} \equiv A\bar{y}. \tag{2.20}$$

($\bar{R}$ is the coefficient of relative risk aversion at mean income, $\bar{y}$, and, unlike A, is dimensionless.) This formula is accurate given our special assumptions, and is otherwise a second-order Taylor series approximation. If B_R is the *risk* benefit of perfect price stabilization (in the absence of a futures market, and ignoring the transfer benefits), then

$$B_{FM} = B_R + \tfrac{1}{2} \bar{R} \bar{y} \{ r^2 \sigma^2 - (1 + r^2) \sigma^2 \sigma_p^2 \} \tag{2.21}$$

In general, then, unbiased futures markets provide superior income risk insurance to price stabilization, because farmers are left free to choose the optimal hedge, instead of having essentially to hedge their entire crop. However, this does not imply that farmers will necessarily prefer to trade on futures markets to price stabilization, for the following reasons:

1 The futures market may be biased, especially if it is thin or unbalanced (Gray, 1960). In such cases the gain to the farmer from the futures market is

$$B_{FM} = \tfrac{1}{2} \bar{R} \bar{y} \beta (2 - \beta) (\sigma_p + r\sigma)^2, \tag{2.22}$$

which may be less than the risk benefit of price stabilization.

2 The farmer may *believe* that the futures market is biased, even if it is not, and this may discourage him from trading in it.

3 Price stabilization will typically change the price, generating an additional transfer benefit, since the price which equates average supply and demand will typically differ from the average price.

4 Both price stabilization and futures markets, by changing the farmer's risk, will in general induce a change in supply, and hence in average price (and income). The supply responses will typically differ.

5 The transactions costs of using the futures market may make trading unattractive. These costs include the usual brokerage charges, and, in

addition, the costs of having to use standard (typically large) contracts rather than the optimal amount. This last feature makes it unlikely that any but the larger farmers will be able to make use of the futures market.

Finally, it should be stressed that futures markets do not generate the arbitrage benefits (that is, the benefits of transferring goods from low-value to high-value states) which the storage associated with price stabilization can produce. Indeed, it is logical to see storage and futures markets as complementary, not competitive, activities, since futures markets both guide stockpiling decisions, and provide hedging facilities for stockholders.

This brings us to the question of the operation of the futures market for continuously stocked commodities like grain. It will be remembered from the introduction that for such commodities it appeared that the futures market offered little reduction in price variability. How can the results of this section be used to examine the force of this claim?

3.4   Futures markets for continuously stocked commodities

We implicitly assumed in the last section that the futures price stayed constant from year to year because the underlying forces of supply and demand were assumed not to change. In fact, these factors change in moderately predictable ways, and we shall suppose that at the start of the crop year, the futures price provides the best estimate of the cash price after the harvest in that particular year. The previous formulae continue to hold, but the coefficient of variation of price is now to be interpreted as the CV of differences between the futures and cash price (in an unbiased market), or, more generally, as a measure of the forecasting error:

$$(\sigma_p^e)^2 = E \left[\frac{p_t - p_t^f}{p_t^f} \right]^2. \tag{2.23}$$

It should be stressed that this is not the same as the CV of prices over time, which will typically be much larger. Similarly, the correlation coefficient between price and output is to be found by regressing the deviation in price $p_t - p_t^f$ on the deviation in output, $\theta_t - 1$. There may be large annual changes in, for example, total acreage planted, which are mainly responsible for the correlation between an individuals's output and price. It is the latter which is relevant for his hedging decision.

Once these variables have been correctly specified, equation (2.16) with σ_p^e instead of σ, gives the variance in income about the mean for that year, but not the variance of income from year to year. If the annual changes in expected price level (measured by the futures price at the start of the crop year p_t^f) are uncorrelated with the weather variable, $\tilde{\theta}$, then income in year t will be

$$\tilde{y}_t = y_t^e (1 + \tilde{u}),$$

$$y_t^e = \bar{q} E \tilde{p}_t \tilde{\theta}$$

$$= \bar{q} p_t^f (1 + r\sigma\sigma_p^e), \tag{2.24}$$

where $\tilde{u}$ is the uncertainty in income at the time of planting which can be hedged on futures markets, and variations in p_t^f are the variations which cannot be hedged. With no futures market equation (2.15) gives

$$\text{var } u = \{\sigma^2 + 2r\sigma\sigma_p^e + (\sigma_p^e)^2 + (1 + r^2)(\sigma\sigma_p^e)^2\},$$

while with optimal hedging this is replaced by the formula of equation (2.16):

$$\text{var } u^f = \sigma^2 \{1 - r^2 + (1 + r^2)(\sigma_p^e)^2\}.$$

If the coefficient of variation of the initial futures price from year to year is V_p:

$$V_p = \left\{ \sum_{t=1}^{T} (p_t^f - Ep_t^f)^2 / T \right\}^{1/2} \Big/ Ep_t^f$$

$$Ep_t^f = \sum_{t=1}^{T} p_t^f / T,$$

then the overall variability of income, measured by its coefficient of variation, can be found from equation (12.34):

$$\tilde{y}_t = \bar{q}(1 + r\sigma\sigma_p^e)\tilde{p}_t^f(1 + \tilde{u}),$$

which, if $\tilde{u}$ and p_t^f are uncorrelated, is approximately

$$CV(y) = (V_p^2 + \text{var } u)^{1/2}.$$

In table 2.1 the first term is given in column (1), the second in column (3). For the two continuously stocked commodities corn and soybeans, var u is respectively 13 and 20 per cent of V_p^2, while for the discontinuously stocked potatoes it is nearly double. Since the futures market only affects var u (directly, at least), this implies that for these commodities, futures markets may not reduce income variability by a very large factor. Futures markets are thus relatively more important in markets where stocks have not already eliminated the predictable risks.

4 THE SUPPLY RESPONSE OF INTRODUCING FUTURES MARKETS

Thus far we have assumed that supply is fixed, and the farmer merely chooses the size of his forward sales, z. Suppose that output is now a function of purchased inputs, x,

$$\tilde{y} = \tilde{p}(Q)\tilde{\theta}f(x) - wx - z(\tilde{p} - p^f) \tag{2.27}$$

The farmer will choose x so that

$$EU'\tilde{p}\tilde{\theta}f'(x) = wEU'.$$

With constant absolute risk aversion, A, equation (2.5) yields, on differentiating:

$$[E\tilde{p}\tilde{\theta} - A\{f \operatorname{var} \tilde{p}\tilde{\theta} - z \operatorname{cov}(\tilde{p}\tilde{\theta}, \tilde{p})\}]f'(x) = w. \tag{2.28}$$

If a futures market is introduced, his income risk will change, inducing a change in x, and a consequent change in $\bar{q}$. Price stabilization will induce further long-run changes. For the moment we shall be content to illustrate the effect of introducing a futures market in a simple market with a linear demand schedule and only supply risk. (The linear demand schedule ensures that price and quantity are jointly normally distributed if supply is.) The demand schedule can be written as:

$$p = \bar{p}\left(1 - \frac{1}{\varepsilon}\frac{Q - \bar{Q}}{\bar{Q}}\right), \tag{2.29}$$

where $\bar{p}$ is the mean price, $\bar{Q}$ is mean demand, and ε is the elasticity of demand at the mean price. Normalize so that $w = 1$, and suppose that

$$f(x) = \sqrt{(2\lambda x)}.$$

In this case, if $\hat{p}$ is the action certainty equivalent price, so that the farmer chooses x to maximize

$$\hat{p}f(x) - x, \tag{2.30}$$

then average supply is a linear function of $\hat{p}$:

$$\bar{q} = f(x) = \lambda\hat{p}. \tag{2.31}$$

In the absence of a futures market the certainty equivalent price is, from equation (2.28):

$$\hat{p}^0 = E\tilde{p}\tilde{\theta} - Af(x)\operatorname{var}\tilde{p}\tilde{\theta}.$$

But, from equation (2.29)

$$\tilde{p}\tilde{\theta} = \bar{p}\left\{1 - \frac{1}{\varepsilon}(\tilde{\theta} - 1)\right\}\tilde{\theta}$$

and if

$$\bar{R} \equiv \bar{p}Af(x)$$

is the coefficient of relative risk aversion at $\bar{p}$, then, using equation (2.15):

$$\hat{p}^0 \simeq \bar{p}\left\{1 - \left[\bar{R}\left(1 - \frac{1}{\varepsilon}\right)^2 + \frac{1}{\varepsilon}\right]\sigma^2\right\}. \tag{2.32}$$

In the presence of an unbiased futures market, the second term in equation (2.28) becomes (using equations (2.7) and 2.15)):

$$2A\sigma^4\bar{p}^2\bar{q}/\varepsilon^2 = 2\bar{p}\bar{R}\sigma^4/\varepsilon^2$$

so the action certainty equivalent price is, ignoring terms in σ^4:

$$\hat{p}^f = Ep\theta = \bar{p}(1 - \sigma^2/\varepsilon) \tag{2.33}$$

At the same level of inputs $\hat{p}^f > \hat{p}^0$, inducing a higher level of inputs and average output. This drives down the average price, but in equilibrium *average output is higher with a futures market than without*. The comparison of farmers' welfare is somewhat tedious, as both income risk and average income change, and it is not necessarily true that farmers are better off with a futures market. Indeed

$$U^f \gtrless U^0 \quad \text{as} \quad \varepsilon \lessgtr 1 \tag{2.34}$$

so farmers are only better off in this model if demand is inelastic.

It is also possible to calculate the effect of perfect price stabilization without a futures market for which the action certainty equivalent is:

$$\hat{p}^s = \bar{p}(1 - \bar{R}\sigma^2). \tag{2.35}$$

Average output is higher (or lower) with price stabilization than with a futures market as the coefficient of relative risk aversion $\bar{R}$ is less than (or greater than) $1/\varepsilon$. This has the interesting (and surprising) implication that the more risk averse are producers, the more they would prefer futures markets to price stabilization. (When $\bar{R} = 1/\varepsilon$, they prefer price stabilization but for $\bar{R}$ above a critical value $R_0 > 1/\varepsilon$ they prefer a futures market.)

It follows that if farmers hedge on futures markets, then it may be seriously misleading to calculate the benefits of price stabilization on the assumption that they do not, for the calculations may suggest that farmers gain from price stabilization, when in fact they would lose.

5 CONCLUSIONS

Unbiased futures markets provide superior income insurance to stabilizing the price over the period for which the futures market is open. This does not mean that futures markets are necessarily preferable to price stabilization , for in general they result in different levels of average producer income and different supply responses. If commodities are continuously stocked, then the main function of futures markets lies in coordinating and insuring stockholding activities. Such stockholding will typically be the prime source of price stabilization, with futures markets offering relatively smaller additional insurance. When commodities cannot be stocked, futures market are a relatively good form of income insurance if output and price are stongly correlated. Such commodities are unsuitable for buffer stock price stabilization schemes, and if it were desired to further stabilize price, other methods would be needed.

It might be thought that futures markets are not very important for income insurance as only large farmers are in a position to make use of them, but this would be a mistaken deduction. Merchants are unlikely to be willing to make forward contracts with small farmers unless they can hedge on futures markets, while government marketing boards in developing countries could similarly guarantee local producer prices and hedge the attendant risk on the main futures markets. Speculators are, however, rather suspicious of such activities, since they suspect that government-run marketing boards can manipulate prices and hence benefit from special inside information when trading in futures markets. The result may be a reluctance of speculators to make the market, resulting in a thin and biased futures market with lower benefits to the producers. Finally, it should be noted that futures markets only stabilize incomes over a relatively short time period, while producers may be more concerned about medium-run instabilities.

Futures markets have evolved standard contracts which specify the exact quality of the commodity, the month of delivery, the place (or places) at which delivery is to be made, and the quantity (normally quite large). Although this greatly reduces the transaction costs associated with dealing in the futures market, it is noticeable that most trading is confined to futures contracts which expire in six months or less, with markets becoming thinner for more distant contracts.

Presumably the advantages to be gained from more distant contracts diminish to the point where they no longer offset the costs of operating the markets, or alternatively, the costs of alternative institutional arrangements, such as long-term contracts or vertical integration, are lower. We shall not have much to say as to why the advantages decrease for more distant contracts, except to remark that there may not be much advantage in having futures markets covering a period longer than the period of production. For tree crops like tea, coffee, rubber, and sisal there exist alternative risk-sharing institutions, since these are frequently produced by plantations which are owned by companies whose shares are traded on stock markets, but it should be stressed that these provide markets for future profits, rather than for future prices.

The thrust of these qualifications is to suggest that futures markets are not necessarily superior to price stabilization schemes, but they are a serious alternative and, where present, may significantly alter the impact of price stabilization.

APPENDIX

Properties of joint normal distributions

If x and y are jointly normally distributed about the origin with SDs σ_1, σ_2, and correlation coefficient ρ, then write this

$$N(0, 0, \sigma_1^2, \sigma_2^2, \rho). \tag{2.36}$$

The moment generating function (m.g.f.) is

$$M(t_1, t_2) = \exp\{\tfrac{1}{2}(\sigma_1^2 t_1^2 + 2\rho\sigma_1\sigma_2 t_1 t_2 + \sigma_2^2 t_2^2)\} \tag{2.37}$$

and then

$$\mu_{rs} = Ex^r y^s = \text{coefficient of } \frac{t_1^r t_2^s}{r! s!}$$

in the expansion of the m.g.f. Therefore

$$\mu_{11} = \rho\sigma_1\sigma_2; \quad \mu_{22} = (1 + 2\rho^2)\sigma_1^2\sigma_2^2; \quad \mu_{12} = \mu_{21} = 0. \tag{2.38}$$

To evaluate $Ep\theta$, $\text{var}(p\theta)$, $\text{cov}(p, p\theta)$, write

$$p = \bar{p}(1 + x), \quad \theta = 1 + y$$

$$Ep\theta = \bar{p}E(1 + x)(1 + y) = \bar{p}(1 + \mu_{11}) = \bar{p}(1 + \rho\sigma_1\sigma_2) \tag{2.39}$$

$$\text{var}(p\theta) = \bar{p}^2 E(1 + x + y + xy - 1 - \rho\sigma_1\sigma_2)^2.$$

$$\text{var}(p\theta) = \bar{p}^2\{\sigma_1^2 + 2\rho\sigma_1\sigma_2 + \sigma_2^2 + (1 + \rho^2)\sigma_1^2\sigma_2^2\} \tag{2.40}$$

$$\text{cov}(p, p\theta) = \bar{p}^2 Ex(x + y + xy - \rho\sigma_1\sigma_2).$$

$$\text{cov}(p, p\theta) = \bar{p}^2(\sigma_1^2 + \rho\sigma_1\sigma_2). \tag{2.41}$$

Conditional probabilities

If x, y are distributed as

$$N(\mu_1, \mu_2, \sigma_1^2, \sigma_2^2, \rho), \tag{2.42}$$

then

$$y \mid x \text{ is } N\left\{\mu_2 + \rho\frac{\sigma_2}{\sigma_1}(x - \mu_1), \sigma_2^2(1 - \rho^2)\right\}, \tag{2.43}$$

so

$$Ey|x = \mu_2 + \rho \frac{\sigma_2}{\sigma_1}(x - \mu_1) \qquad (2.44)$$

If

$$x = u$$

$$y = u + v$$

and

$$(u, v) \text{ is } N(\mu_1, \mu_2, \sigma_1^2, \sigma_2^2, 0),$$

then

$$(x, y) \text{ is } N(\mu_1, \mu_1 + \mu_2, \sigma_1^2, \sigma_1^2 + \sigma_2^2, \rho), \qquad (2.45)$$

where

$$\rho = \text{corr}(u, u + v) = \frac{\sigma_1}{\sqrt{(\sigma_1^2 + \sigma_2^2)}}$$

Properties of joint log-normal distributions

If Z_1, Z_2, are jointly normally distributed:

$$N(\mu_1, \mu_2, \sigma_1^2, \sigma_2^2, r)$$

and if X_1, X_2, are log-normally distributed, with

$$X_i = \exp Z_i,$$

then

$$X_1 X_2^\beta \text{ is } \Lambda(\mu_1 + \beta \mu_2, \sigma_1^2 + 2r\beta\sigma_1\sigma_2 + \beta^2\sigma_2^2). \qquad (2.46)$$

In particular, if $X_1 = \theta$, $X_2 = (\phi/\theta)^{1/\varepsilon}$, where

$$Q = \bar{Q}\theta \qquad \theta = \Lambda(-\tfrac{1}{2}\sigma^2, \sigma^2)$$

$$Q^d = p^{-\varepsilon}\phi \quad \phi = \Lambda(-\tfrac{1}{2}\nu^2, \nu^2)$$

and

$$\text{corr}(\log\theta, \log\phi) = \rho,$$

then

$$X_2 = \Lambda\left\{\frac{1}{2\varepsilon}(\sigma^2 - \nu^2), \frac{1}{\varepsilon^2}(\sigma^2 - 2\rho\sigma\nu + \nu^2)\right\} \equiv \Lambda(\mu_2, \sigma_2^2) \qquad (2.47)$$

and

$$X_1 X_2 = \Lambda \left\{ \mu_2 - \tfrac{1}{2}\sigma^2, \left(1 - \frac{1}{\varepsilon}\right)^2 \sigma^2 + 2\left(1 - \frac{1}{\varepsilon}\right)\frac{1}{\varepsilon}\rho\sigma\nu + \frac{\nu^2}{\varepsilon^2} \right\} . \quad (2.48)$$

Equate equations (2.48) and (2.46) with $\beta = 1$ together with (2.47) to find

$$\mu_2 = -\tfrac{1}{2}\left(\varepsilon\sigma_2^2 + 2\rho\sigma\sigma_2\right).$$

NOTES

1 The price of the futures contract in its delivery month less the spot price in that
month is called the *maturity basis*. Arbitrage ensures that it is small, and the
futures seller's option to choose grades and/or delivery location typically makes
it slightly (but predictably) negative. Goss and Yamey (1976) quote the example
of cotton between 1924 and 1939 where the range was from −0.17 pence per
pound to −0.49 pence.

REFERENCES

Goss, B. A. and Yamey, B. S. (1976) *The Economics of Futures, Trading*, London,
Macmillan.
Gray, R. W. (1960) The characteristic bias on some thin futures markets. *Food
Research Institute Studies* (Nov.), reprinted in Peck (1977).
Gray, R. W. (1972) The futures market for Maine potatoes: an appraisal. *Food
Research Institute Studies*, 9, reprinted in Peck (1977).
Johnson, A. C. (1973) Effects of futures trading on price performance in the cash
onion market, 1930-1968, USDA ERS. Technical Bulletin 1470, partially
reprinted in Peck (1977).
Keynes, J. M. (1923) Some aspects of commodity markets. *Manchester Guardian
Commercial, European Reconstruction Series*, 29 March.
Larson, A. B. (1967) Price prediction on the egg futures market. *Food Research
Institute Studies*, 7(Supp.), reprinted in Peck (1977).
McKinnon, R. I. (1967) Futures markets, buffer stocks and income stability for
primary producers. *Journal of Political Economy*, 75 (Dec.), 844-61.
Peck, A. E. (ed.) (1977) *Selected Writings on Futures Markets*, vol. II, Chicago,
Chicago Board of Trade.
Powers, M. J. (1970) Does futures trading reduce price fluctuations in the cash
market? *American Economic Review*, 60, 460-4, reprinted in Goss and Yamey
(1976).
Rothschild, M. and Stiglitz, J. E. (1970) Increasing risk I: A definition. *Journal of
Economic Theory*, 2, 225-43.
Tomek, W. G. and Gray, R. W, (1970) Temporal relationships among prices on
commodity futures markets: their allocative and stabilizing roles. *American
Journal of Agricultural Economics*, 52(3) (Aug), reprinted in Peck (1977).

Part II

Risk in General Equilibrium

3

On the Optimality of Forward Markets

Robert M. Townsend

Kenneth Arrow's seminal article (1964) on the role of securities in the optimal allocation of risk bearing provided a convenient framework in which problems involving choice under uncertainty could be analyzed. By extending the commodity space to include random states of nature, classic results on the existence and optimality of a competitive equilibrium were made applicable to uncertain situations. Yet many authors have commented on the existence of the small number of markets in which claims contingent on the realization of a state are actively traded. In particular the existence of futures or forward markets in which unconditional rather than contingent claims are traded is regarded by some as a phenomenon in need of an explanation, and by others as prima facie evidence of some inefficiency.

The purpose of this paper is to show that in some cases any equilibrium allocation resulting from the operation of competitive prestate noncontingent forward markets and competitive poststate spot markets is Pareto optimal, and that any Pareto optimal allocation can be supported as a competitive equilibrium of these markets with appropriate redistribution of endowments. These propositions turn on the fact that if equilibrium spot prices satisfy certain conditions then a restriction to the trading of forward contracts will not be constraining in an equilibrium; that is, agents can achieve precisely the same allocation with forward and spot markets as they could with markets in which claims could be traded for any commodity

Reproduced by permission from *American Economic Review*, vol. 68 (1978), pp. 54–66.

An earlier version of this paper appeared in my doctoral dissertation presented at the University of Minnesota, July 1975. I am especially indebted to Neil Wallace for his advice and encouragement. I also acknowledge the assistance of Paul Anderson and helpful comments from John Chipman, John Danforth, Hayne Leland, Stephen Salant, Leonard Shapiro, and the referee, but claim full responsibility for any errors or ambiguities. Financial support from the Board of Governors of the Federal Reserve System and from the Federal Reserve Bank of Minneapolis is gratefully acknowledged. The views expressed herein are solely my own and do not necessarily represent the views of the Bank or of the Federal Reserve System.

contingent on any state.

In his article Arrow stressed that in actual markets risk bearing is not allocated by the sale of claims against specific commodities but rather by the sale of securities payable in money, and he argued that any optimal allocation could be achieved with an elementary set of such securities. These Arrow–Debreu securities, as they have become known, suffice because their returns span the space of all possible returns. That is, any security whatever can be regarded as a bundle of these elementary securities, and, as has been noted by many authors, if an arbitrary set of securities spans the space of all possible returns, then such a set of securities is essentially equivalent to the set of Arrow–Debreu securities. In particular Steinar Ekern and Robert Wilson (1974), and Roy Radner (1974) have argued that equities or shares may have the spanning property, and Steven Ross (1976) has made a similar argument for options. This paper shows that a forward contract may be viewed as a security whose return is the amount of the numeraire good (i.e., the price) for which it can be exchanged in the spot market of each state. Thus if the rank of the matrix of spot prices is equal to the number of states,[1] forward contracts also have the spanning property, and the results of this paper may be viewed as an extension of Arrow's results.[2]

This paper proceeds as follows. Section 1 presents the assumptions and technology of a pure exchange economy and describes the operation of two exchange regimes – complete prestate markets for contingent claims with no poststate spot markets and noncontingent forward markets with poststate spot markets. Section 2 formalizes the two welfare propositions given above and outlines their proofs. These results are then interpreted by way of some examples which clarify the nature of the spanning property. Section 3 presents an example which emphasizes the general equilibrium hedging property of forward contracts and provides further insight into the workings and welfare implication of forward markets when market structure is incomplete. Section 4 presents some concluding remarks. Formal proofs are shown in the Appendix.

1 DESCRIPTION OF THE MODEL AND EXCHANGE REGIMES

The model is a pure exchange economy with random endowments. There are I consumers, S mutually exclusive states of the world, and C commodities. Let π_s denote the probability that state s will occur with $0 < \pi_s < 1$. In this context endowments and consumption should be indexed by the consumer i ($i = 1, 2, \ldots, I$), state s ($s = 1, 2, \ldots, S$), and commodity c ($c = 1, 2, \ldots, C$) to which they pertain. Hence let Z_{isc} and C_{isc} denote the endowment and consumption, respectively, of consumer i in state s of commodity c, and let Z_{is} and C_{is} denote the associated C-dimensional vectors. Each consumer i maximizes expected utility:

$$\sum_{s=1}^{S} \pi_s U^i (C_{is})$$

Each is assumed to be risk averse in that function $U^i(\ )$ is strictly concave.[3]

There are various possibilities for trade in the model. In what follows, two exchange structures will be imposed exogenously and then compared. In the first exchange regime there are complete prestate markets for contingent claims. Trading in the markets for such claims takes place before random endowments are known. Also in the first regime there is no trading in spot markets subsequent to the realization of the state. In the prestate markets each consumer can issue or purchase contingent claims, where each claim entitles the holder to one unit of a specified commodity if a particular state occurs, and zero otherwise. Let X_{isc} denote the number of such unit claims on commodity c in state s held by consumer i after trading in the market for claims (with associated C-dimensional vector X_{is}). That is, $(X_{isc} - Z_{isc})$ is the demand for such claims by consumer i in the market for claims. Let r_{sc} denote the price of a unit claim on commodity c in state s in terms of some abstract unit of account. Then the budget constraint for consumer i in the markets for claims is of the form

$$\sum_{s=1}^{S} \sum_{c=1}^{C} r_{sc} (X_{isc} - Z_{isc}) = 0 \qquad (3.1)$$

After endowments are realized and some state is known to pertain, claims are honored so that $C_{is} = X_{is}$. In summary, in the first exchange regime consumer i maximizes

$$\sum_{s=1}^{S} \pi_s U^i (X_{is}) \qquad (3.2)$$

with respect to $\{X_{isc}\}$ subject to (3.1) with each $X_{is} \geq 0$.[4] An equilibrium in the first exchange regime is a set of claim prices $\{r_{sc}^*\}$ and an allocation $\{X_{isc}^*\}$, $i = 1, 2, \ldots, I$, such that $\{X_{isc}^*\}$ is maximizing for each consumer i and there is equality of the number of claims bought and sold for each state s and each commodity c, that is,

$$\sum_{i=1}^{I} (X_{isc}^* - Z_{isc}) = 0 \qquad s = 1, 2, \ldots, S; \quad c = 1, 2, \ldots, C \qquad (3.3)$$

In the first exchange regime there was a restriction that there be no trading in spot markets subsequent to the realization of a state. But that restriction cannot be constraining in a competitive equilibrium. For let P_{sc} denote the spot price of commodity c in state s (with C-dimensional vector P_s) where the Cth commodity is chosen as the numeraire. Now suppose that in state s some auctioneer calls out the vector P_s^* where

$$P_{sc}^* = r_{sc}^*/r_{sC}^* \qquad (3.4)$$

If trade is permitted, each consumer i is then confronted in the spot market of state s with the following problem: maximize $U^i(C_{is})$ with respect to C_{is} subject to the budget constraint

$$\sum_{c=1}^{C} P_{sc}^*(C_{isc} - X_{isc}^*) = 0 \qquad \text{with } C_{is} \geqslant 0$$

It may be verified that $C_{is} = X_{is}^*$ solves this problem,[5] thus the prices $\{P_{sc}^*\}$ may be viewed as the *implicit* equilibrium spot prices of the first exchange regime.

However, if each consumer i knew prior to the realization of the state that he would have the opportunity to trade in spot markets at predetermined prices $\{P_{sc}\}$ as well as in markets for contingent claims at prices $\{r_{sc}\}$, each would solve the following recursive problem. First, given income Y_{is} in state s in terms of the numeraire, commodity C, each consumer i would maximize $U^i(C_{is})$ with respect to C_{is} subject to the budget constraint $P_s \cdot C_{is} \leqslant Y_{is}$ with $C_{is} \geqslant 0$. Let $h_{is}(Y_{is}, P_s)$ denote the maximizing choice of C_{is}. Then define the indirect utility function $V^i(Y_{is}, P_s) = U^i[h_{is}(Y_{is}, P_s)]$. But Y_{is} is determined by the claims $\{X_{isc}\}$ acquired in the prestate markets for contingent claims. That is,

$$Y_{is} = \sum_{c=1}^{C} P_{sc} X_{isc} \qquad (3.5)$$

Hence in the market for contingent claims consumer i would maximize

$$\sum_{s=1}^{S} \pi_s V^i \left(\sum_{c=1}^{C} P_{sc} X_{isc}, P_s \right) \qquad (3.6)$$

with respect to $\{X_{isc}\}$ subject to the budget constraint (3.1) and income constraints $Y_{is} \geqslant 0$.[6] It should be clear that a maximizing choice $\{X_{isc}^*\}$ for this recursive problem at prices $\{P_{sc}\}$ and $\{r_{sc}\}$ cannot be unique. For if $\{X_{isc}^*\}$ were a maximizing choice, so also would be all bundles $\{X_{isc}^{**}\}$ such that

$$\sum_{c=1}^{C} P_{sc} X_{isc}^{**} = \sum_{c=1}^{C} P_{sc} X_{isc}^*$$

for each state s. Roughly speaking, given the opportunity to trade in spot markets at spot prices $\{P_{sc}\}$, consumer i cares only about the income he will have in the various states.

The indeterminacy of the recursive problem just described suggests that some further restrictions can be placed on trades without altering the ability of the consumer to acquire (ultimately) the maximizing consumption bundles. Indeed one such restriction was placed on the consumer in the first exchange regime – that there be no trading in spot markets.[7] This ·paper examines restrictions associated with forward contracts. For each consumer i and each commodity c these restrictions are of the form $(X_{isc} - Z_{isc}) = (X_{itc} - Z_{itc})$ for all states s and t. Thus, for example, if consumer i purchases a specified number of claims on commodity c contingent on state s, then he must also purchase the same number of claims on commodity c contingent on all other states. In effect only unconditional claims can be purchased or issued in such forward markets.

Thus in the second exchange regime of this paper each consumer can trade unconditional forward contracts in prestate markets and can also trade in poststate spot markets. The decision problem which confronts a consumer in such a regime is now formalized. Let Q_{ic} denote the number of unconditional claims on commodity c purchased forward by consumer i in forward markets. (Thus if Q_{ic} is negative, commodity c is sold forward.) Let f_c denote the forward price of an unconditional unit claim on commodity c in terms of some abstract unit of account. Then the budget constraint for consumer i in forward markets is

$$\sum_{c=1}^{C} f_c Q_{ic} = 0 \tag{3.7}$$

Having acquired forward contracts $\{Q_{ic}\}$, consumer i enters spot market s with income

$$Y_{is} = \sum_{c=1}^{C} P_{sc} Z_{isc} + \sum_{c=1}^{C} P_{sc} Q_{ic} \tag{3.8}$$

Thus, with trading permitted in spot markets, consumer i maximizes

$$\sum_{s=1}^{S} \pi_s V^i \left(\sum_{c=1}^{C} P_{sc} (Z_{isc} + Q_{ic}), P_s \right) \tag{3.9}$$

with respect to $\{Q_{ic}\}$ subject to the budget constraint (3.7).

An equilibrium of the second exchange regime is a set of forward prices $\{f_c^*\}$, a set of spot prices $\{P_{sc}^*\}$, a forward position $\{Q_{ic}^*\}$, $i = 1, 2, \ldots, I$, and a consumption allocation $\{X_{isc}^*\}$ $i = 1, 2, \ldots, I$, such that $\{Q_{ic}^*\}$ and $\{X_{isc}^*\}$ are maximizing for each consumer i in forward markets and spot markets, respectively. That is $\{Q_{ic}^*\}$ maximizes (3.9) subject to (3.7) under $\{f_c^*\}$ $\{P_{sc}^*\}$ with

$$X_{is}^* = h_{is} \left(\sum_{c=1}^{C} P_{sc}^* (Z_{isc} + Q_{ic}^*), P_s^* \right)$$

Forward markets clear for each commodity c,

$$\sum_{i=1}^{I} Q_{ic}^* = 0 \qquad c = 1, 2, \ldots, C \tag{3.10}$$

and spot markets clear for each commodity c in each state s,

$$\sum_{i=1}^{I} [X_{isc}^* - (Z_{isc} + Q_{ic}^*)] = 0 \qquad s = 1, 2, \ldots, S \quad c = 1, 2, \ldots, C$$

$$\tag{3.11}$$

2   ON THE EQUIVALENCE OF THE TWO EXCHANGE REGIMES

In this section it will be argued that, subject to some restrictions on the matrix of (implicit) spot prices, any Pareto optimal allocation can be supported as a competitive equilibrium of the second exchange regime with suitable redistribution of endowments and that competitive equilibria of the second regime are Pareto optimal. More formally we have the following results.

Proposition 1   Suppose that a Pareto optimal allocation $\{X_{isc}^*\}$, $i = 1, 2, \ldots, I$, can be supported as a competitive equilibrium of the first exchange regime with endowments $\{Z_{isc}\}$, $i = 1, 2, \ldots, I$, and claim prices $\{r_{sc}^*\}$ such that the $S \times C$ matrix $p'' = [P_{sc}^*]$ (where $P_{sc}^* = r_{sc}^*/r_{sC}^*$) is of rank S. Then $\{X_{isc}^*\}$, $i = 1, 2, \ldots, I$, can be supported with the same endowments as a competitive equilibrium of the second exchange regime with forward markets in S commodities.

Proposition 2   Suppose there exists a competitive equilibrium of the second exchange regime with forward markets in S commodities with spot prices $\{P_{sc}^*\}$ and consumption allocation $\{X_{isc}^*\}$ $i = 1, 2, \ldots, I$ such that the corresponding $S \times S$ matrix $P = [P_{sc}^*]$ is of rank S. Then the consumption allocation $\{X_{isc}^*\} i = 1, 2, \ldots, I$ is Pareto optimal.

The formal proofs of these propositions are contained in Appendix A, but are now outlined with some motivating remarks. As for the first proposition it is clear from the classical theorems of welfare economics that any Pareto-optimal allocation can be supported as a competitive equilibrium of the first exchange regime with suitable redistribution of endowments in the various states. Having specified this same distribution of endowments, the second exchange regime is imposed. Then it is argued that each consumer is endowed implicitly with forward contracts; each consumer can issue forward contracts up to his ability to honor such claims with his income in the various states. Also, each consumer must have sufficient income in the various states to purchase the optimal allocation assigned to him. This determines the forward contracts he must acquire in the forward markets. It is then shown that at appropriately selected spot and forward prices the resulting excess demands are consistent with the budget constraint of each consumer and that the acquired forward contracts are indeed maximizing. Finally it is shown that all markets clear.

Proposition 1 also has an important corollary:

Corollary *If there exists a competitive equilibrium of the first exchange regime such that the matrix P″ is of rank S, then there exists a competitive equilibrium of the second exchange regime with a consumption allocation which is Pareto optimal.*

This follows from the fact that the equilibrium allocation of the first regime is Pareto optimal and by hypothesis can be supported in a competitive equilibrium without any redistribution of endowments.

The idea underlying the proof of the second proposition is that an equilibrium consumption allocation of the second regime can be supported as an equilibrium allocation of the first regime and hence is Pareto optimal.

It remains to examine the hypothesis that the matrix of spot prices have rank equal to the number of states. Essentially this hypothesis ensures that the returns of forward contracts span the space of all possible returns. In order to clarify the role of this spanning property, two examples are now described, one with the spanning property and one without.

For the first example there are three commodities and three states and the 3×3 matrix of spot prices is assumed to be of rank three. Suppose that a nonnegative vector of incomes $\{Y_{is}; s = 1, 2, 3\}$ is to be attained by a forward position $\{Q_{ic}; c = 1, 2, 3\}$. Then equations (3.7) and (3.8) are of the form

$$\sum_{c=1}^{3} f_c Q_{ic} = 0 \tag{3.12}$$

$$Y_{is} = \sum_{c=1}^{3} P_{sc} Z_{isc} + \sum_{c=1}^{3} P_{sc} Q_{ic} \qquad s = 1, 2, 3 \tag{3.13}$$

Setting $f_3 = 1$, solving for Q_{i3} in (3.12), and substituting into (3.13) yields

$$Y_{is} = \hat{Y}_{is} + \sum_{c=1}^{2} (P_{sc} - f_c) Q_{ic} \qquad s = 1, 2, 3 \tag{3.14}$$

$$Y_{is} = \sum_{c=1}^{3} P_{sc} Z_{isc} \qquad s = 1, 2, 3 \qquad\qquad (3.15)$$

Equation (3.14) is a parametric representation of a plane in three space through the endowed state distribution income point $\{\hat{Y}_{is}\}$. With suitable specification of the spot and forward prices, each consumer i can exchange income in any one state for income in any other without altering income in the third as illustrated in figure 3.1. Thus in effect in the second regime each consumer i maximizes

$$\sum_{s=1}^{3} \pi_s V^i (Y_{is}, P_s)$$

with respect to $\{Y_{is}\}$ as determined by the choice of $\{Q_{ic}\}$ subject to constraints (3.14). Moreover, as each consumer i is confronted with a budget plane with the same gradient (determined by the prices $\{f_c\}$ and $\{P_{sc}\}$ each will have the same rate of substitution of income (the numeraire good) across states in an equilibrium, and the equilibrium allocation will be optimal.

For the second example there are three states but only two goods so that the matrix of spot prices cannot be of rank three. Then setting $f_2 = 1$, the analogue of (3.13) is of the form

$$Y_{is} = \hat{Y}_{is} + Q_{i1} (P_{s1} - f_1) \qquad s = 1, 2, 3 \qquad\qquad (3.16)$$

Equation (3.16) is a parametric representation of a line in three space. If for example $P_{11} < f_1 = P_{21} < P_{31}$ it is impossible to alter income in the second

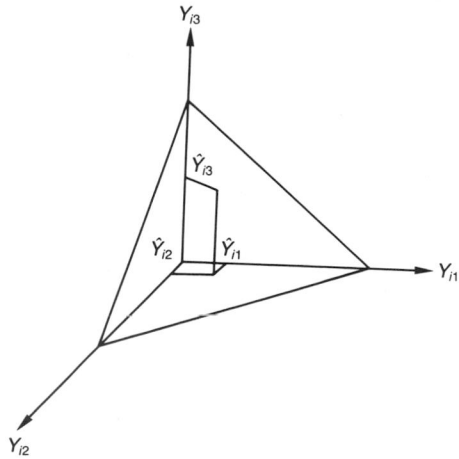

Figure 3.1

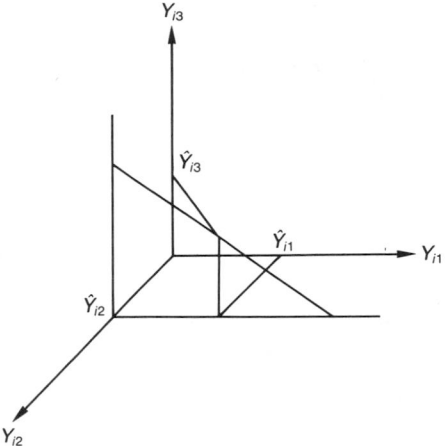

Figure 3.2

state. This is illustrated in figure 3.2. If for example $P_{11} < f_1 < P_{21} < P_{31}$, it is impossible to alter income in one state without altering income in the other two. Though in an equilibrium of the second regime each consumer is confronted with a budget line of the same slope (determined by the prices $\{f_c\}$ and $\{P_{sc}\}$), in general each will not have the same rate of substitution of income across states. This example thus illustrates the potential for inefficiency when states outnumber commodities.

An attempt is now made to relate Proposition 1 to the results of Arrow. His principal conclusion is that an optimal allocation of risk bearing can be achieved in a distribution economy (with money) by competitive markets in elementary securities. He emphasizes that a security is a claim payable in money in contrast to claims against specific commodities. But of course in the context of an exchange economy money can be no more than a numeraire. Thus, for example, if the Cth good is selected as the numeraire of each spot market, an elementary security yielding one monetary unit in state s and zero otherwise can be nothing other than a claim on commodity C in state s. It is shown in Appendix B of this paper that in an exchange economy any optimal allocation can be achieved with a set of S securities with linearly independent returns, where these returns are in terms of the amount of the numeraire good which a bearer can purchase in the spot market of each state. This then is the generalized analogue of Arrow's theorem for an exchange economy. Arrow–Debreu securities (claims on the numeraire good only) can be viewed as a particularly simple set of such securities. And subject to a rank condition on a matrix of spot prices P, forward contracts also constitute a spanning set. A forward purchase on commodity c, for example, has state-dependent return represented by the cth column of the matrix P. The condition that P be of rank S is equivalent to the condition that the column vectors of returns of the S forward 'securities' be linearly independent.

3   FORWARD TRADING AS GENERAL EQUILIBRIUM HEDGING

This section is intended to give some further insight into the workings of forward markets in a general equilibrium setting. A simple example is presented which illustrates that with active spot markets, forward contracts serve as a hedge against exogenously random endowments *and* endogenously random spot prices. This general equilibrium hedging model of forward markets may be contrasted with the classic partial equilibrium approach of John M. Keynes (1950) and John Hicks (1946) which emphasizes a distinction between hedgers and speculators. In particular, in the model of this paper maximizing behavior on the part of risk-averse agents does not necessarily involve the elimination of risk by purchasing the consumption bundle forward. The example also allows some inferences concerning the existence and optimality of a competitive equilibrium of the second exchange regime when market structure is incomplete.

For the example there are two representative consumers, S states of the world ($S \geqslant 2$), and two commodities. The first consumer is endowed with the first commodity only, and the second consumer is endowed with the second commodity only. That is, $Z_{isc} = 0$ if $i \neq c$. Without loss of generality it is supposed that Z_{1s1} is strictly increasing in s. It is also assumed that Z_{2s2} is equal to some constant Z_2 for all states.

Preferences are identical for both consumers. Each has a utility function of the form ($U(,) = g[W(,)]$) where $W(,)$ displays constant elasticity of substitution and $g( )$ is a monotone increasing function. Hence $W(,)$ is of the form

$$W(C_{is1}, C_{is2}) = [(\alpha)C_{is1}^{-\rho} + (1-\alpha)C_{is2}^{-\rho}]^{-1/\rho} \qquad \text{if } \sigma \neq 1$$

$$W(C_{is1}, C_{is2}) = C_{is1}^{\alpha} C_{is2}^{1-\alpha} \qquad \text{if } \sigma = 1$$

where σ, the elasticity of substitution, equals $1/(1+\rho)$ and $0 < \alpha < 1$. It is further assumed that $g(W) = W^{\mu}$, where $0 < \mu < 1$, or $g(W) = \ln W$.

Let the second commodity be chosen as the numeraire in the forward markets. Then each consumer i maximizes

$$\sum_{s=1}^{S} \pi_s V \left(\sum_{c=1}^{2} Z_{isc} P_{sc} + Q_{i1}(P_{s1} - f_1), P_s \right) \tag{3.17}$$

with respect to Q_{i1}, yielding necessary and sufficient first-order conditions

$$\sum_{s=1}^{S} \pi_s (P_{s1} - f_1) V_1 \left\{ \sum_{c=1}^{2} Z_{isc} P_{sc} + \psi^i(f_1) [P_{s1} - f_1], P_s \right\} = 0 \quad (3.18)$$

where $\psi^i(f_1)$ denotes the maximizing choice of Q_{i1} as a function of f_1. It can be shown that $\psi_1^i(f_1) < 0$.[8]

It also can be shown that for this example equilibrium spot prices are independent of the existence and direction of forward trading as

$$P_{s1} = \left(\frac{\alpha}{1-\alpha}\right) \left(\frac{Z_2}{Z_{1s1}}\right)^{1/\sigma} \quad (3.19)$$

Consequently P_{s1} is strictly decreasing in S. It also follows that

$$P_{s1} Z_{1s1} = \left(\frac{\alpha}{1-\alpha}\right) Z_2^{1/\sigma} Z_{1s1}^{(\sigma-1)/\sigma} \quad (3.20)$$

Equation (3.20), which displays the value of the exogenous endowment of the first consumer as a function of s and σ, will be useful in what follows.

There remains the task of establishing the existence and direction of equilibrium forward trading. We have the following proposition.

Proposition 3 *Under the assumptions of the example there exists a competitive equilibrium of the second regime. Moreover,*

(i) *if $\sigma > 1$, then $Q_{11} > 0$*
(ii) *if $0 < \sigma < 1$, then $Q_{11} < 0$*
(iii) *if $\sigma = 1$, then $Q_{11} = 0$*

The idea underlying the proof of the proposition is illustrated in figure 3.3. The object is to find forward prices f'' and f' at which the first and second consumer, respectively, would not wish to trade, and to show these prices differ in an appropriate way. The equilibrium price f^* can then be found and the properties of the proposition verified. A formal proof of the proposition is contained in Appendix C.

The results of the proposition are not as counterintuitive as they may first seem. Consider the case $\sigma > 1$. From (3.20), $P_{s1} Z_{1s1}$ is strictly increasing in s. Hence the first consumer is relatively more anxious to engage in a venture which is strictly decreasing in s than is the second consumer. Forward purchase of the first commodity with per unit return $(P_{s1} - f_1)$ represents such a venture. Thus each consumer purchases forward the single commodity with which he is endowed. Maximizing behavior in this general equilibrium hedging model need not entail purchasing the consumption bundle forward.

What can be said of the optimality of a competitive equilibrium allocation of the second exchange regime when market structure may be incomplete (as

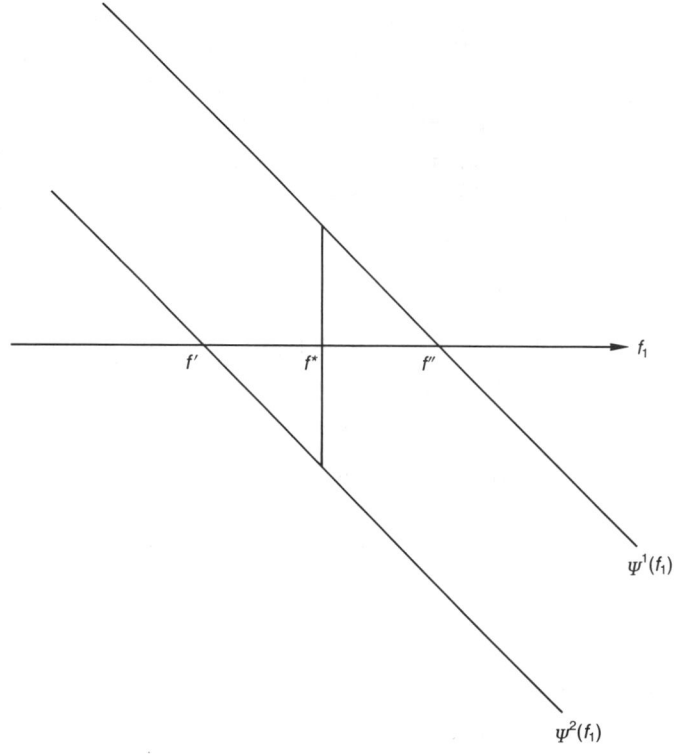

Figure 3.3

in the example of this section with $S > 2$)? If tastes are identical and homothetic (as in the example), it is possible to make some welfare comparisons. For if tastes are identical and homothetic, spot market prices are independent of the existence and direction of prestate forward trading. If there are forward markets and if a consumer chooses not to participate in such markets, then his consumption possibility set is precisely what it would have been had there been no forward markets at all. Hence the possibility of forward trading can only make him better off. This yields the next result.

Proposition 4 *If tastes are identical and homothetic, then a competitive equilibrium allocation of the second exchange regime is Pareto noninferior and possibly Pareto superior to the competitive equilibrium allocation with all markets for claims prohibited.*

4 CONCLUDING REMARKS

Jacques Drèze (1972) has stressed the need for research into the functions and shortcomings of existing institutions and for the application of standard welfare economics based on Pareto optimality to limited exchange opportunities for risk bearing. The objective of this paper was to examine the workings and welfare implications of forward markets and to place those markets in the context of complete markets for contingent claims. It was found that with at least as many commodities as states, prestate forward markets with poststate spot markets may support Pareto optimal allocations. Thus the existence of forward markets in some commodities rather than markets for contingent claims should not be taken as prima facie evidence of some inefficiency.[9]

APPENDIX

A Proof of Proposition 1

As P'' is of rank S, $C - S$ columns may be deleted from P'' while leaving a square matrix P of rank S. Then without loss of generality commodities with prices in P are numbered one through S. Let $\hat{Y}_{is} = \Sigma_{c=1}^{C} P_{sc}^{*} Z_{isc}$ with associated $S \times 1$ vector $\hat{Y}_{i}$. Then each consumer i is endowed implicitly with forward contracts $\{E_{ic}; c = 1, 2, \ldots, S\}$ with associated $S \times 1$ vector E_{i} such that

$$\sum_{c=1}^{S} P_{sc}^{*} E_{ic} = \hat{Y}_{is} \qquad s = 1, 2, \ldots, S \tag{3.21}$$

or in matrix notation $PE_{i} = \hat{Y}_{i}$. Let $Y_{is}^{*} = \Sigma_{c=1}^{C} P_{sc}^{*} X_{isc}^{*}$ with associated $S \times 1$ vector Y_{i}^{*}. Then if the optimal allocation $\{X_{isc}^{*}\}$, $i = 1, 2, \ldots, I$, is to be achieved consumer i must enter spot markets holding forward contracts $\{F_{ic}; c = 1, 2, \ldots, S\}$ with associated $S \times 1$ vector F_{i} such that

$$\sum_{c=1}^{S} P_{sc}^{*} F_{ic} = Y_{is}^{*} \qquad s = 1, 2, \ldots, S \tag{3.22}$$

or in matrix notation $PF_{i} = Y_{i}^{*}$.

Choose spot prices $P_{sc} = P_{sc}^{*}$ and choose forward prices $f_{c} = f_{c}^{*}$, $c = 1, 2, \ldots, S$, where $f_{c}^{*} = \Sigma_{s=1}^{S} r_{sc}^{*}$. Define an $S \times S$ diagonal matrix D with diagonal elements r_{sC}^{*} and zeros elsewhere.

First it is shown that individual budget constraints are satisfied. From (3.21) and (3.22), $DPQ_{i}^{*} = D(Y_{i}^{*} - \hat{Y}_{i})$, where $Q_{i}^{*} = F_{i} - E_{i}$, with typical row s,

$$\sum_{c=1}^{S} r_{sc}^{*} Q_{ic}^{*} = \sum_{c=1}^{C} r_{sc}^{*} (X_{isc}^{*} - Z_{isc}) \tag{3.23}$$

Summing over the rows (3.23) yields

$$\sum_{c=1}^{S} f_{c}^{*} Q_{ic}^{*} = \sum_{s=1}^{S} \sum_{c=1}^{C} r_{sc}^{*} (X_{isc}^{*} - Z_{isc}) \tag{3.24}$$

By hypothesis the right side of (3.24) equals zero, and hence so does the left side.

Now suppose that Q_i^* were not a maximizing forward position for some consumer i given prices $\{f_c^*\}$, $\{P_{sc}^*\}$. That is, suppose there existed some choice Q_i^{**} of forward contracts and associated consumption $\{X_{isc}^{**}\}$ in spot markets such that

$$\sum_{s=1}^{S} \pi_s U^i (X_{is}^{**}) > \sum_{s=1}^{S} \pi_s U^i (X_{is}^{*}) \tag{3.25}$$

Since these choices are feasible, the budget constraint in forward markets is satisfied, i.e., $\Sigma_{c=1}^{S} f_c^* Q_{ic}^{**} = 0$, and there is sufficient income to purchase $\{X_{isc}^{**}\}$ in spot markets. i.e., $PQ_i^{**} = Y_i^{**} - \hat{Y}_i$ where Y_i^{**} is the $S \times 1$ vector associated with $Y_{is}^{**} = \Sigma_{c=1}^{C} P_{sc} X_{is}^{**}$. With virtually the same manipulations that yielded (3.24), one obtains

$$\sum_{c=1}^{S} f_c^* Q_{ic}^{**} = \sum_{s=1}^{S} \sum_{c=1}^{C} r_{sc}^{*} (X_{isc}^{**} - Z_{isc}) \tag{3.26}$$

But

$$\sum_{c=1}^{S} f_c^* Q_{ic}^{**} = 0 \tag{3.27}$$

and therefore

$$\sum_{s=1}^{S} \sum_{c=1}^{C} r_{sc}^{*} (X_{isc}^{**} - Z_{isc}) = 0 \tag{3.28}$$

so that $\{X_{isc}^{**}\}$ was feasible under the budget constraint of the first regime. This is the desired contradiction.

It remains to show that forward markets clear. From (3.21) and (3.22),

$$\sum_{i=1}^{I} Q_i^* = P^{-1} \sum_{i=1}^{I} (Y_i^* - \hat{Y}_i) \tag{3.29}$$

But

$$\sum_{i=1}^{I} (Y_{is}^* - \hat{Y}_{is}) = \sum_{c=1}^{C} P_{sc}^* \sum_{i=1}^{I} (X_{isc}^* - Z_{isc}) \tag{3.30}$$

From (3.3) the right side equals zero. Substitution into (3.39) yields the desired result.

Finally, each spot market s is in equilibrium at the prices $\{P^*_{sc}\}$. For at these prices consumers achieve the same distribution of incomes across states as in the equilibrium of the first regime. That is, each consumer is on the same budget hyperplane in each state. As spot markets were implicitly in equilibrium at these same prices (see section 1) they will continue to be so (see (3.35) below).

Proof of Proposition 2

The idea underlying the proof is that the consumption allocation of the second regime can be obtained as an equilibrium allocation of the first regime. Without loss of generality, assume the first S commodities are traded forward in the second regime. Let $\{f^*_c\}$ and $\{Q^*_{ic}\}$ $c = 1, 2, \ldots, S$; $i = 1, 2, \ldots, I$, denote the equilibrium forward prices and forward positions, respectively, of the second regime. Then let the claim prices $\{r^*_{sc}\}$ be chosen such that

$$f^*_c = \sum_{s=1}^{S} r^*_{sc} \qquad c = 1, 2, \ldots, S \tag{3.31}$$

$$r^*_{sc} = P^*_{sc} r^*_{sC} \qquad s = 1, 2, \ldots, S; \quad c = 1, 2, \ldots, C \tag{3.32}$$

(Note that by substituting (3.32) into (3.31) one obtains the system

$$f^*_c = \sum_{s=1}^{S} P^*_{sc} r^*_{sC} \qquad c = 1, 2, \ldots, S \tag{3.33}$$

With P of full rank, there exists a unique solution for r^*_{sC}, $s = 1, 2, \ldots, S$, in (3.33) so (3.31) and (3.32) are well defined.)

As $\{X^*_{isc}\}$ is the final allocation, it must be, as in the proof of Proposition 1, that (3.24) holds. But by hypothesis the left side of (3.24) equals zero. Hence $\{X^*_{isc}\}$ satisfies the budget constraint (3.1) under $\{r^*_{sc}\}$.

Now suppose $\{X^*_{isc}\}$ were not maximizing under the first regime. Suppose there exist some $\{X^{**}_{isc}\}$ such that (3.28) and (3.25) hold. But then define $\{Q^{**}_{ic}\}$ such that there is sufficient income to purchase $\{X^{**}_{isc}\}$. That is, (3.26) applies. From (3.28), the right side of (3.26) equals zero. Hence $\Sigma^{S}_{c=1} f^*_c Q^{**}_{ic} = 0$. This contradicts $\{Q^*_{ic}\}$ as maximizing.

Finally note that the markets for claims are in equilibrium. For let $\{\hat{X}_{isc}\}$ denote the forward position of consumer i in the second regime after trading in forward markets but before trading in spot markets. Then

$$X^*_{isc} = (Z_{isc} + Q^*_{ic}) + (X^*_{isc} - \hat{X}_{isc}) \qquad s = 1, 2, \ldots, S; \quad c = 1, 2, \ldots, C \tag{3.34}$$

Summing (3.34) over i yields

$$\sum_{i=1}^{I} (X_{isc}^* - Z_{isc}) = \sum_{i=1}^{I} Q_{ic}^* + \sum_{i=1}^{I} (X_{isc}^* - \hat{X}_{isc}) \qquad s = 1, 2, \ldots, S;$$
$$c = 1, 2, \ldots, C$$
(3.35)

As forward and spot markets clear in the second regime, the right side of (3.35) equals zero.

B   Generalization of Arrow's theorem

In what follows a security is defined to be a linear combination of unit claims on the SC contingent commodities. That is, a security of type τ entitles the holder to β_{sc}^{τ} units of commodity c in state s, $c = 1, 2, \ldots, C, s = 1, 2, \ldots,$ S. Let $R_{s\tau}$ denote the return (in terms of commodity C) of security τ in state s so that given spot prices $\{P_{sc}\}$, $R_{s\tau} = \Sigma_{c=1}^{C} P_{sc} \beta_{sc}^{\tau}$.

Proposition B1   *Suppose that a Pareto optimal allocation* $\{X_{isc}^*\}$, $i = 1, 2, \ldots, I$, *can be supported as a competitive equilibrium with complete markets for contingent claims and with no trade in spot markets with endowments* $\{Z_{isc}\}$ $i = 1, 2, \ldots, I$, *and claim prices* $\{r_{sc}^*\}$. *Suppose also that there exist S securities where security of type τ has return $R_{s\tau}^*$ in state s as determined by the spot prices $P_{sc}^* = r_{sc}^*/r_{sC}^*$ such that the $S \times S$ matrix of security returns $R = [R_{s\tau}^*]$ is of rank S. Then $\{X_{isc}^*\}$, $i = 1, 2, \ldots, I$, can be supported with the same endowments as a competitive equilibrium with prestate markets for the S securities and poststate spot markets.*

PROOF   Let $P_{sc} = P_{sc}^*$. Let $\hat{Y}_{is} = \Sigma_{c=1}^{C} P_{sc}^* Z_{isc}$ with associated $S \times 1$ vector $\hat{Y}_i$. Then each consumer i is endowed implicitly with $\tilde{E}_{i\tau}$ units of security of type τ with associated $S \times 1$ vector $\tilde{E}_i$ defined by

$$R\tilde{E}_i = \hat{Y}_i \tag{3.36}$$

Let $Y_{is}^* = \Sigma_{c=1}^{C} P_{sc}^* X_{isc}^*$ with associated $S \times 1$ vector Y_i^*. Then if the allocation $\{X_{isc}^*\}$ is to be attained, consumer i must enter spot markets with securities $\tilde{F}_{i\tau}$ with associated $S \times 1$ vector $\tilde{F}_i$ defined by

$$R\tilde{F}_i = Y_i^* \tag{3.37}$$

Subtracting (3.37) from (3.36), premultiplying by the $S \times S$ diagonal matrix D with elements r_{sC}^*, and summing over rows yields

$$\sum_{\tau=1}^{S} \tilde{f}_{\tau}^* (\tilde{F}_{i\tau} - \tilde{E}_{i\tau}) = \sum_{s=1}^{S} \sum_{c=1}^{C} r_{sc}^* (X_{isc}^* - Z_{isc}) \tag{3.38}$$

where $\tilde{f}_{\tau}^* = \Sigma_{s=1}^{S} r_{sC}^* R_{s\tau}^*$ is taken as the price of security τ. By hypothesis the right side of (3.38) equals zero so the $\tilde{Q}_i^* = \tilde{F}_i - \tilde{E}_i$ security trades are consistent with the budget constraint of consumer i in the prestate security markets.

Moreover, $\{\tilde{Q}_i^*\}$ is maximizing for consumer i. The argument is virtually identical to the one given in Proposition 1 with E_i, F_i, Q_i^*, f_c^*, and P replaced by $\tilde{E}_i$, $\tilde{F}_i$, $\tilde{Q}_i^*$, f_τ^*, and R, respectively.

Also, security markets clear. The excess demand for security τ is

$$\sum_{i=1}^{I} (\tilde{F}_{i\tau} - \tilde{E}_{i\tau}) \tag{3.39}$$

From (3.36), $\tilde{E}_i = R^{-1}\hat{Y}_i$, using the fact that R is of full rank. That is,

$$\tilde{E}_{i\tau} = \sum_{s=1}^{S} \alpha_{\tau s} \hat{Y}_{is} \tag{3.40}$$

where the $\{\alpha_{\tau s}\}$ are expressions involving the terms of R. These may be regarded as constants. Similarly one obtains

$$\tilde{F}_{i\tau} = \sum_{s=1}^{S} \alpha_{\tau s} Y_{is}^* \tag{3.41}$$

Then substituting (3.40) and (3.41) into (3.39) and recalling the definitions of Y_{is}^* and $\hat{Y}_{is}$ one obtains

$$\sum_{s=1}^{S} \alpha_{\tau s} \sum_{c=1}^{C} P_{sc}^* \sum_{i=1}^{I} (X_{isc}^* - Z_{isc}) \tag{3.42}$$

which equals zero by the market-clearing conditions of the first regime.

Finally it may be argued as in Proposition 1 that spot markets clear.

Proposition B2 *Suppose that there exists a competitive equilibrium with prestate markets in S securities and with poststate spot markets with spot prices $\{P_{sc}^*\}$ and a consumption allocation $\{X_{isc}^*\}$ $i = 1, 2, \ldots, I$ such that the matrix of security returns $R = [R_{s\tau}^*]$ is of rank S. Then the consumption allocation $\{X_{isc}^*\}$, $i = 1, 2, \ldots, I$, is Pareto optimal.*

PROOF Let $\{\tilde{f}_\tau^*\}$ and $\{\tilde{Q}_{i\tau}^*\}$, $i = 1, 2, \ldots, I$, denote the equilibrium security prices and security trades, respectively. Then choose claim prices $\{r_{sc}^*\}$ to satisfy

$$\tilde{f}_\tau^* = \sum_{s=1}^{S} r_{sC}^* R_{s\tau}^* \qquad \tau = 1, 2, \ldots, S \tag{3.43}$$

$$r_{sc}^* = P_{sc}^* r_{sC}^* \tag{3.44}$$

(As R is of full rank, these equations are well defined.) Then as in Proposition 2, it can be shown that $\{X_{isc}^*\}$ is a maximizing choice of each consumer

i in claims markets of the first regime. Finally let $\{\tilde{X}_{isc}\}$ denote the implicit forward position of consumer i after trading in security markets. Then

$$X^*_{isc} = Z_{isc} + \sum_{\tau=1}^{S} \beta^\tau_{sc}\tilde{Q}^*_{i\tau} + (X^*_{isc} - \hat{X}_{isc}) \tag{3.45}$$

$$s = 1, 2, \ldots, S; \quad c = 1, 2, \ldots, C$$

Summing over i in (3.45) yields

$$\sum_{i=1}^{I}(X^*_{isc} - Z_{isc}) = \sum_{\tau=1}^{S} \beta^\tau_{sc}\sum_{i=1}^{I}\tilde{Q}^*_{i\tau} + \sum_{i=1}^{I}(X^*_{isc} - \hat{X}_{isc}) \tag{3.46}$$

$$s = 1, 2, \ldots, S; \quad c = 1, 2, \ldots, C$$

As security markets and spot markets clear, the right side of (3.46) equals zero.

Two special cases of the propositions should be noted. First if there exist S commodities such that the corresponding $S \times S$ matrix P of spot prices is of full rank, setting $R = P$, Propositions 1 and 2 follow. Also with S elementary Arrow–Debreu securities (where a security of type s yields one unit of commodity C in state s and zero otherwise) $R = I$, the identity matrix, and the propositions apply.

C Proof of Proposition 3

Under the assumptions of the example the indirect utility function is of one of the following two forms:

$$V(Y_{is}, P_s) = \varphi(P_s)^\mu (Y_{is})^\mu \tag{3.47}$$

$$V(Y_{is}, P_s) = \ln Y_{is} + \ln \varphi(P_s) \tag{3.48}$$

where $\varphi(P_s)$ is an expression in terms of α, σ, and P_s. Define

$$G^i(Q_{i1}, f_1) = \sum_{s=1}^{S} \pi_s(P_{s1} - f_1) V_1\left(\sum_{c=1}^{2} P_{sc}Z_{isc} + Q_{i1}(P_{s1} - f_1), P_s\right) \tag{3.49}$$

Let f'' be defined by the equation $G^1(0, f'') = 0$ so that

$$\sum_{s=1}^{S} \pi_s(P_{s1} - f'')\mu(P_{s1}Z_{1s1})^{\mu-1}\varphi(P_s)^\mu = 0 \tag{3.50}$$

$$\sum_{s=1}^{S} [\pi_s(P_{s1} - f'')]/[P_{s1}Z_{1s1}] = 0 \tag{3.51}$$

for forms (3.47) and (3.48) of $V(\cdot, \cdot)$, respectively. Let f' be defined by the equation $G^2(0, f') = 0$ so that

$$\sum_{s=1}^{S} \pi_s (P_{s1} - f')\mu(Z_2)^{\mu-1}\varphi(P_s)^\mu = 0 \tag{3.52}$$

$$\sum_{s=1}^{S} [\pi_s (P_{s1} - f')]/[Z_2] = 0 \tag{3.53}$$

for forms (3.47) and (3.48) of $V(\cdot,\cdot)$, respectively. Now consider the following cases:

Case 1: $\sigma > 1$

With $\sigma > 1$ it follows from (3.20) that $P_{s1}Z_{1s1}$ is strictly increasing in s. Therefore, both forms (3.47) and (3.48), $f'' > f'$. Let $\psi(f_1) = \Sigma_{i=1}^{2}\psi^i(f_1)$. Then $\psi(f_1)$ is continuous. As $d\psi^i(f_1)/df_1 < 0$, $i = 1, 2, \psi(f'') < 0$ and $\psi(f') > 0$; see figure 3.3. Therefore, there exists some f^*, $f' < f^* < f''$, with $\psi(f^*) = 0$. Hence f^* is the unique equilibrium forward price with $\psi^1(f^*) > 0$.

Case 2: $0 < \sigma < 1$

With $0 < \sigma < 1$, $P_{s1}Z_{1s1}$ is strictly decreasing in s. Consequently $f'' < f'$ and there exists some f^*, $f'' < f^* < f'$, with $\psi^1(f^*) < 0$.

Case 3: $\sigma = 1$

With $\sigma = 1$, $P_{s1}Z_{1s1}$ is constant in s, so that $f^* = f' = f''$ and $\psi^i(f^*) = 0$.

NOTES

1 This is not possible if there are more states than commodities.

2 The extension, however, is not quite as immediate as it may first appear to be. Both Arrow's model and his result have been given a variety of interpretations. Arrow modeled a distribution economy in which money as an actual commodity plays a role. In contrast, in the exchange economy of this paper there is no money per se. Thus Arrow's proof may not be applied directly. Though the principal results of this paper are known by some, there does appear to be a need for a clarifying exposition. (The analogue of Arrow's theorem for an exchange economy is presented in Appendix B.)

3 It is also assumed that $U^i(\ )$ is continuously differentiable with $U_C^i(0) = \infty$.

4 $\{X_{isc}\}$ denotes the SC-dimensional vector with elements X_{is}, $s = 1,2,\ldots, S$; $c = 1, 2, , C$. This shorthand notation is used below for this and other variables if no ambiguity results.

5 For suppose $C_{is} = X_{is}^{**}$ solves this problem with $U^i(X_{is}^{**}) > U^i(X_{is}^*)$ and $\Sigma_{c=1}^{C}(X_{isc}^{**} - X_{isc}^*)P_{sc}^* = 0$. Then from (3.4) one obtains $\Sigma_{c=1}^{C}(X_{isc}^{**} - X_{isc}^*)r_{sc}^* = 0$. This in conjunction with (3.1) establishes that $\{X_{isc}^{**}\}$ was obtainable in the first regime but not chosen, the desired contradiction.

6 Here and below, these income constraints rule out bankruptcy; each consumer is

assumed to honor all contracts into which he has entered, and with these constraints each has sufficient income to do so. However, it is *not* required that delivery be made in spot markets of commodities sold in the markets for claims. It is supposed that each consumer accepts delivery of all commodity bundles which when valued at spot prices yield incomes equivalent to the yield of the claim in question. It can also be established that under previous assumptions $V^i(\cdot, P_s)$ is strictly concave and continuously differentiable with $V_1^i(0, P_s) = \infty$. Hence in a maximizing position $Y_{is} > 0$ and the income constraints need not be made explicit.

7   It can be established rigorously that such a restriction is not constraining.

8   The objective function is strictly concave and continuously differentiable in Q_{il}. Moreover, the income constraints $Y_{is} \geqslant 0$ restrict the choice of Q_{il} to a compact set. Hence there exists a unique maximizing choice of Q_{il}. Also with $V_1^i(0, P_s) = \infty$, this choice must be an interior solution and the implicit-function theorem applies. With decreasing absolute risk aversion, the derivative of $\psi^i(\ )$ can be signed.

9   The ultimate intent of a paper of this sort is to explain why futures contracts with subsequent spot markets is a prominent institutional configuration. If agents were indifferent between complete markets for contingent claims and futures contracts with subsequent spot markets, and if there were a cost associated with the former contracts which is not associated with the latter, then one structure would emerge endogenously. A cost which might be associated with contingent but not with futures contracts could be the cost of state verification. It is in this sense that the requirement that P'' be of rank S is somewhat disappointing. If P'' is of rank S, then no two rows of P'' can be identical. Agents will be fully informed by the spot market prices of which state has occurred. State verification is costless and is no obstacle to the making of contingent contracts. Futures contracts with subsequent spot markets may allow agents to do just as well, but there is nothing in the model to lead them to choose one structure over the other.

REFERENCES

K. J. Arrow, The role of securities in the optimal allocation of risk bearing, *Rev. Econ. Stud.*, Apr. 1964, 31, 91–6.

J. Drèze, Econometrics and decision theory, *Econometrica*, Jan. 1972, 40, 1–17.

S. Ekern and R. Wilson, On the theory of the firm in an economy with incomplete markets, *Bell J. Econ.*, Spring 1974, 5, 171–80.

John R. Hicks, *Value and Capital*, Oxford 1946, 135–9.

John M. Keynes, *A Treatise on Money*, London 1950, 142–7.

R. Radner, A note on unanimity of stockholders' preferences among alternative production plans: a reformulation of the Ekern–Wilson model, *Bell J. Econ.*, Spring 1974, 5, 181–4.

S. A. Ross, Options and efficiency, *Quart. J. Econ.*, Feb. 1976, 90, 75–89.

4

Hedging Pressure and Futures Price Movements in a General Equilibrium Model

David Hirshleifer

Two issues central to the analysis of futures markets are the determination of optimal hedging/speculative positions for the various classes of traders (e.g., producers and outsiders) and the existence of price bias, that is, deviations of the futures price from the expected value of the later spot price. A major branch of the futures pricing literature attributes bias to hedging pressure by producers.[1]

In the original normal backwardation theory of Keynes and Hicks, producers take short positions in the futures market to hedge their initial long positions in the commodity. Their supply of futures contracts, or hedging pressure, tends to drive down the futures price relative to the expected value of the later spot price, to generate a downward bias (normal backwardation) in the futures price. Speculators who enter on the long side of futures contracts bear a risk, and being risk averse are therefore compensated by a positive expected profit on their positions. More recent work[2] in which producers face quantity risk as well as price risk has shown that they might take long instead of short futures positions – in which case their hedging pressure would instead promote an upward price bias ('contango'). Specifically, producers will want to hedge their overall income risk by going long if quantity is relatively variable compared to price (elastic demand) and going short in the opposite case. So upward or downward bias in the futures price depends on whether the aggregate hedging position by producers is long or short.[3]

Reproduced from *Econometrica*, vol. 58 (1990), pp. 411–28.

This paper is adapted from a chapter of my dissertation at the University of Chicago. I thank my dissertation committee: D. Carlton, G. Becker, D. Diamond, C. Kahn, and L. Telser. Especially helpful comments were provided by M. Brennan, B. Trueman, and two anonymous referees of this journal. I also thank G. Constantinides, E. Fama, V. France, M. Grinblatt, S. Grossman, D. Lucas, A. Subrahmanyam, S. Titman, and S. Yeh. I am happy to acknowledge financial support from the Earhart Foundation and the Center for the Research of Security Prices at the University of Chicago.

The hedging pressure literature usually assumes, first, that only a single risky security is traded, and second, that the only sources of risk in the economy are random supply/demand shocks for the futures-traded commodity. In contrast, the branch of the futures literature based on the capital asset pricing model (CAPM) allows for many risky tradable endowments. However, by assuming that equity claims to producers' future revenues are tradable,[4] the traditional CAPM rules out the incentive for producers to hedge using futures; they instead trade to well-diversified portfolios along the efficient frontier.[5]

Both the hedging pressure and traditional CAPM models are 'partial equilibrium,' in the sense that they do not model the consumption choice between the futures-traded and other commodities. Instead, decisionmakers maximize expected utility derived from generalized wealth, which is equivalent to assuming only a single consumption good. The primary purpose of the current paper is to reexamine the effect of hedging on the futures risk premium within a general equilibrium (multi-good) setting.[6] The paper differs from the standard hedging pressure and CAPM literatures in that (a) demand for the futures-traded commodity is determined as an optimizing consumption choice among different goods, and (b) in selecting futures positions, individuals take into account that the relative prices of the goods they consume are changing. Allowing for more than a single consumption good makes it possible to examine how the consumption preferences such as complementarity affect equilibrium risk premia.

To investigate how hedging by producers influences risk premia, the case of zero complementarity (additive separability) is examined with both costless and costly futures trading. When trading is costless, the main pricing prediction of the hedging pressure theory is refuted. As consumer preferences vary, the spot market demand elasticity changes, causing aggregate hedging to change from short to long. Nevertheless, the futures price remains unbiased,[7] so hedgers are able to reduce their risk without paying a premium to speculators. Furthermore, under more general preferences there is still no presumption that producer hedging will promote futures price bias.

The source of the disagreement between the different classes of models is a neglected element in the partial-equilibrium account, the risks borne by consumers of the commodity. Here, since consumers' risks prove to be inverse to those of producers, the hedging pressures of the two groups are in opposite directions. Therefore, the two groups reduce their own type of risk by mutually hedging on the futures market, with neither receiving a premium from the other.

However, the partial-equilibrium models are certainly realistic in limiting the participation of consumers in the futures market. Owing to fixed setup costs (such as finding a broker or learning about the market), few commodity consumers trade futures[8] to hedge relative price changes, despite the consumption-hedging incentives described by Breeden (1984). Randomness in the price of a single commodity such as corn is relatively inconsequential to a consumer of many commodities, but imposes a substantial risk on a specialized producer. Setup costs will therefore differentially tend to deter small consumers rather than producers of the commodity from participating in the futures market.

I show here that nonparticipation by consumers restores the effect of hedging pressure on price bias. Consider the 'traditional' case in which producers hedge short (price risk outweighs quantity risk). Since the consumers who remove themselves from the futures market would have hedged long, nonparticipation creates an imbalance between the hedging pressure of producers and of the remaining consumers. Balance is restored by a downward price bias, which discourages short hedging while encouraging the remaining consumers to enlarge their long positions. The analysis therefore shows that hedging-induced futures price bias derives fundamentally from barriers to futures trading that impact differently upon consumers rather than producers.[9]

The paper is structured as follows. The economic setting is described in section 1. Section 2 analyzes futures price bias and dynamic hedging strategies in markets without transaction costs. Section 3 shows how fixed setup costs of trading in the futures market affect the price bias. Section 4 concludes the paper.

1 THE ECONOMIC SETTING

Each individual is endowed with a stochastically variable quantity of a risky commodity Z and a known quantity of the numeraire commodity N ('all other goods').[10] In the assumed regime of futures markets (FM), traders can exchange only riskless claims to Z and N. Thus, the purchase of a unit of Z entitles the buyer to receive that unit in each and every state of the world. The model is therefore in real rather than nominal terms (see Grauer and Litzenberger, 1979). The market regime excludes the possibility of trading claims that are state-contingent, e.g., insurance contracts or equity shares. Spot and futures markets are assumed to be competitive, and individuals are assumed to have homogeneous beliefs.

Traders maximize expected utility by choosing consumption levels of goods N (the numeraire) and Z (the risky good). All individuals have identical preferences over the two goods summarized by the utility function $U(n, z)$. All consumption takes place at date 1.[11] We assume that there are S possible states of the world at date 1. Information is publicly revealed through a sequence of m information events with binary outcomes, which are jointly conclusive[12] (i.e., together they determine the state of the world, so that $S = 2^m$).

The information event j is a random variable θ^j where possible outcomes are denoted a^j and b^j. The history of information events through j is $(\theta^1, \theta^2, \ldots \theta^j)$ and will be denoted by s^j. The entire ordered sequence of information events 1 through m, starting at date 0 and ending at consumption date 1, determines the final state s^m (or more briefly, s). The initial probabilities are π_s^0 for the different states, and after later events $\theta^1, \ldots, \theta^j$, the probability of state s conditional on history s^j is denoted π_s^j.

The sequence of market trading is as follows. Each participant begins with an endowment gamble $E = (\bar{n}; \bar{z}_1, \ldots, \bar{z}_S)$, where $\bar{n}$ is his initial (nonrandom) endowment of N available for consumption at date 1, and $\bar{z}_s, s = 1, \ldots, S$ is his state-conditional endowed quantity of Z. A grower typically would be endowed with some state-distributed pattern of Z (his prospective output of corn, say), while a consumer would be endowed only with N ($\bar{z}_s \equiv 0$). Before the first information event, each individual trades on the futures market to a speculative gamble $T^0 = (n^0; z_1^0, \ldots, z_S^0)$. The futures transaction involves a purchases of ξ^0 units of corn at price P^0 (in units of N). (Thus, for a buyer z_s^0 exceeds $\bar{z}_s$ by ξ^0 for each and every s.) After the first information event θ^1, an individual revises his beliefs to π_s^1 and retrades (by buying or selling ξ^1 contracts at price P^1) to a new trading position T^1. This process of information arrival and retrading continues until θ^m arrives and resolves the final state of the world. Individuals then trade at the ultimate (spot) price P^m to their final consumption positions $(n^m; z_s^m)$. (We have listed only z_s^m after the semicolon, the quantity of Z in the single state actually realized.)

The individual's trading problem may then be written as

$$\max_{\{(\xi^k(s^k)\}} E[U(\tilde{n}^m, \tilde{z}^m)] \qquad \text{subject to} \qquad (4.1)$$

$$n^0 = \bar{n} - P^0\xi^0, \qquad n^k = n^{k-1} - P^k\xi^k,$$

$$z_s^0 = \bar{z}_s + \xi^0, \qquad z_s^k = z_s^{k-1} + \xi^k \qquad (k = 1, \ldots, m; s = 1, \ldots, S).$$

The trading strategies ξ^k are functions of s^k, the history through k. The selection of the ξ^k's, by the trading constraints, pins down z_s^k and n^k as functions of s^k also, a dependence which is left implicit. Prices P^k are also functions of history. $\tilde{z}^m$ is a random variable that takes on value z_s^m in state s. $\tilde{n}^m$ is also in general random, since it arises from a trading strategy which depends on stochastic information arrivals.

1.1   Effective completeness of the futures markets regime

Throughout the paper, we will make the mild assumption that the arrival of different information events leads to different prices (otherwise, perturb the endowments to shift prices slightly). This implies the following lemma (all proofs are in the Appendices).

Lemma 1   The regime of futures markets is effectively complete.

To see why, let us define wealth contingent on state s, W_s^m, for an agent after all information has been revealed (when θ_m arrives) but prior to the final round of trading. Let contingent wealth be the value of his total holdings n^{m-1} and z_s^{m-1} of N and Z in state s, denominated in units of N,

$$W_s^m \equiv n^{m-1} + P^m z_s^{m-1} \tag{4.2}$$

The meaning of a shift in a trader's 'wealth' occurring at rounds prior to m is developed formally in Appendix 1. In general, if there are enough securities to adjust the level of 'wealth' achieved owing to different outcomes at each information event, then the market is effectively complete. The futures contract suffices here because of the binomial information structure.[13] At each event a futures position shifts wealth across outcomes, so ex ante we can calculate effective prices for transferring wealth from one final state to another. The information structure therefore allows us to exploit the tractable properties of complete market allocations, without eliminating the need for traders to use futures contracts.[14] The binary information structure is the discrete time analog to a diffusion framework with a single state variable, in which two securities complete the market.

2   HEDGING AND BIAS WITH ZERO TRANSACTION COSTS

We will first examine the pricing of futures contracts in section 2.1, and then in section 2.2 derive conclusions about optimal hedging and its relationship to pricing.

2.1   Futures price bias

In a futures market regime with zero transaction costs, preference complementarity is an important determinant of the direction of futures price bias. Let E^j be the expectation conditional on history s^j.

Proposition 1   Under a regime of futures markets, if preferences are: (a) additively separable, then prices follow a martingale, that is, $P^j = E^j[P^k]$ for all $k > j$; (b) homothetic, then with positive (negative) complementarity $U_{nz} \gtreqless 0$, the futures price is a downward (upward) biased predictor of the later spot price $P^j \lesseqgtr E^j[P^m]$.

In the general theory of asset pricing, an asset's (excess) expected return rises with the covariance of its return with each investor's marginal utility of wealth. A 'risk premium' is a reward that an asset must offer to compensate for the shortcoming of paying off more in states where wealth adds little to utility. In part (a) of Proposition 1, the covariance of the futures payoff with marginal utility is zero, because of certainty in the aggregate quantity of N. Writing the additively separable preferences as $U(n, z) = u(n) + v(z)$, then with common beliefs individuals trade to a Pareto optimal allocation in which each consumes a nonstochastic amount of N.[15] It follows that the marginal utility of possessing one more unit of wealth at time m, which by a standard envelope condition is equal to the marginal utility of consuming one more unit of N, is constant across states.

In part (b), the reason for downward bias when there is positive complementarity is easily seen when it is noted that, with homothetic preferences, the consumptions of N are nonstochastic.[16] Therefore the marginal utility of wealth is highest when consumption of Z is high, which occurs when the spot price is low. So the futures contract pays off the least (in units of N) when marginal utility is high; this adverse risk characteristic leads to a positive premium for holding the futures contract, i.e., a downward bias.[17]

For the remainder of the paper, we assume additively separable preferences, so that part (a) of Proposition 1, which predicts martingale pricing, is the relevant case. Unbiasedness is not a general prediction about risk premia; it arises from three stylized features of the current model: separability, effectively complete markets, and nonrandom endowment of the numeraire.[18] The martingale case will be useful for two reasons. First, it provides a clear counterexample to the proposition in partial equilibrium models that with risk-averse individuals, the futures price bias is upward or downward according to the sign of producer hedging. Second, it will serve as a baseline from which to highlight the effect of transaction costs on the premium examined in section 3.

The counterexample shows that martingale pricing is consistent with either long or short hedging. In particular, section 2.2 shows that, consistent with partial equilibrium models, here hedging by producers tends to be long or short according to the elasticity of demand. This will illustrate how the attempt of hedgers to transfer risk to risk-averse speculators need not produce any bias in the futures price.

2.2 Optimal hedging

The basic intuition is captured by the case of a typical producer in a market with a single conclusive information arrival. Suppose that there are two types of agents, a representative producer/consumer, whose output of Z is positively proportional to the aggregate output of Z, and a pure consumer, whose output of Z is identically zero for all states. If spot demand for Z is unitary elastic, then price and output move in inverse proportion,[19] so if the grower does not trade, the numeraire value of his endowment is equal in the two states. Similarly, the value of a pure consumer's endowments is the same across states; if utility as a function of wealth were state independent, there would be no risk to transfer, and we would expect a zero hedge.[20]

With inelastic demand, a typical grower finds that the value of his Z endowment is higher in the low output state, labeled b, than the high output state a, because low output $\bar{z}_b$ is more than offset by a disproportionately high spot price. So he is motivated to offer futures on sufficiently favorable terms to induce consumers to bear part of his (predominantly price) risk. The sale of a 1:1 bundle of claims to Z in either state reduces the value of the grower's Z holdings more in state b than in state a, whereas the numeraire payment he receives is of the same value in either state. So selling futures short raises state-a wealth and reduces state-b wealth, which stabilizes the grower's endowed wealth gamble. With elastic demand, revenue is instead higher in state b, so the grower is motivated to go long in futures.

To formalize this argument with many trading rounds, we will assume the property of revenue ordering.

Definition *Revenue ordering* is said to obtain if at each information event θ^j, the expected spot price $E^j[P^m]$ rises when the expected expenditure on Z, $E^j[P^m z^m]$ rises (falls) for inelastic (elastic) demand.

Proposition 2 *Under the assumptions of representative producers and consumers, revenue ordering, and additively separable preferences, producers take long/short futures positions and consumers take short/long positions in all trading rounds if demand is elastic/inelastic.*

Although one would normally expect revenue ordering to obtain, it could conceivably fail because of the nonlinear relationship between spot price, output, and sales revenue. As shown in Appendix 2, a specific case in which revenue ordering obtains is the additive logarithmic (LOG) family of utility functions

$$U(n, z) = \alpha \log(n) + \log(z - \beta), \tag{4.3}$$

where α and β are constants, $\alpha > 0$. Both elastic and inelastic spot demand for Z is possible under LOG preferences, depending on the sign of β. Alternatively, revenue ordering will obtain under the assumption of a good-bad information structure as defined in section 3.

The inelastic demand case of Proposition 2 is similar to Keynes' and Hicks' scenario, in that futures sales by producers to outsiders are a means of transferring price risks. However, since prices follow a martingale, there is no "normal backwardation" in the futures price. With elastic demand, contrary to normal backwardation theory, growers will hedge themselves by *buying* corn futures from consumers.

The direction of hedging in Proposition 2 matches the predictions of partial equilibrium models of producer hedging. And yet Proposition 1 showed that the prediction for bias of partial equilibrium analysis fails. In the example, futures price bias is unrelated to either demand elasticity or to the direction of aggregate hedging. Complementarity of preferences does not resolve the disagreement. As part 2 of Proposition 1 showed, positive complementarity promotes downward bias regardless of elasticity of demand, while hedging will still tend to be long or short according to demand elasticity.

This demonstrates a significant inconsistency between the general versus partial equilibrium approaches. The full resolution of this dissonant chord will be deferred until the discussion of bias in section 3 below. There we will see how setup costs of trading can reinstate the bias/hedging/elasticity relation. To identify more clearly the source of the discrepancy, recall that when demand is inelastic, producers desire to hedge short. The partial equilibrium argument is that outsiders require a downward bias to compensate for the risk of their long futures position; similarly, an upward bias results from elastic demand. This neglects the state dependence in the indirect utility of wealth function of the traders.

Suppose, instead that besides trading corn futures, outsiders also eat corn. Then the marginal utility of (N-denominated) wealth function depends not only on the trader's wealth, but on the price of corn. Traders optimally arrange their consumptions of N to be level across states. Even though their wealth is not equated across states, they trade to where their *marginal utility of wealth* ($= u'(n)$) is. Therefore they are not on the margin willing to pay a premium for a security to shift contingent wealths across states.

A deeper understanding in terms of hedging pressure is provided by considering the consumption levels consumers would achieve if they were able to trade only in the final spot market, not in the prior futures markets. Consumers begin with a nonstochastic endowment of N, so without futures trading, their wealths are independent of state. Since the final spot price at which they can purchase Z is random, they do bear consumption risk. With inelastic demand, a consumer spends more on corn when the price is high than when it is low, so a high price reduces his consumption of N. This implies high marginal utility of the numeraire. Thus, a long position is a good hedge for a consumer, because the futures contract pays off more when his marginal utility of wealth is higher. Similarly, with elastic demand short positions are good hedges for consumers.

It follows that consumers and producers are *mutually* hedging by taking the opposite sides of the futures transaction. Unlike the pure speculators of partial equilibrium models, consumers are not reluctant acceptors of futures positions. The hedging pressure of producers is met by a comparable hedging pressure of consumers. With additive preferences, these hedging incentives happen to offset precisely, so that neither group pays a premium.

3 THE MODEL WITH POSITIVE TRANSACTION COSTS

Because people diversify their consumption across commodities, but specialize in production, they are many more consumers than producers in any commodity market. When demand is inelastic, as is typical for agricultural commodities, and with costless trading, growers are predicted here to sell futures to consumers. The disproportion in numbers of the two groups implies that in the equilibrium of section 2 the long futures position of a typical consumer is small compared with the short position of a typical producer.

Few consumers actually trade futures, in contrast with the predictions of section 2, as well as those of conventional models of asset pricing. Evidently, some fixed costs limit the participation of outsiders who do not have a stake in production.[21] A fixed setup cost drives consumers, who would be small traders, rather than growers differentially from the futures market. This does not mean we apply the original model as if consumers did not exist, for though the actors are late, they arrive in time for the last scene, the spot market. The missing demand in the prior-to-final trading rounds biases the futures market price as compared to the model with costless exchange (as is formalized below).

The constriction of consumer demand for futures contracts (in the inelastic case) or supply of futures (elastic case) introduces downward and upward biases respectively in the futures price as a predictor of the spot price. Instead of a martingale, the benchmark case, there is systematic backwardation or contango according to demand elasticity. The larger the trading costs, the more consumers will be frozen out of the prior rounds, and so the larger the bias. For the inelastic case, this is reminiscent of Hicks' (1939) view that there is a congenital weakness on the demand side in futures markets, leading to 'normal backwardation.'

With many information arrivals and a fixed cost that is incurred before each futures trade, the number of futures participants after the first round of trading depends on the content of the initial information message, and so is itself a stochastic variable. We simplify here by assuming that there is only a one-shot setup cost t (in numeraire units). An individual incurs a deadweight cost t only at his first trade, so that he may trade at any later round without additional cost. (The one-shot assumption is reasonable if the cost of participation consists mainly of learning how to trade in futures, understanding the basic supply/demand characteristics of the market, or of searching for a good broker.)

The proposition that follows assumes that consumers rather than producers are driven by the fixed cost from the futures market. When there are many consumers relative to producers, the positions of consumers under zero transaction costs will be very small compared to producers. A sufficiently small transaction cost will therefore deter only consumers.[22]

Two technical assumptions are needed. First is that the spot price for Z, P^m is a decreasing function of aggregate output. This could conceivably fail if there were a peculiar pattern of wealth effects. (Such a possibility could be ruled out by the stronger assumption of preferences which lead to aggregation, such as the LOG family or homothetic preferences.) The second assumption is that the arrival of information is unambiguously good or bad news, in the following sense.

Definition   A *good-bad information structure* is one in which $j = 1, \ldots, m$, the distribution of aggregate output of Z conditioned on history s^{j-1} and event a^j first order stochastically dominates the distribution given b^j.

Proposition 3   *Under the assumptions of a good-bad information structure, a fixed setup cost of participation in the futures market, and that the spot price declines with aggregate output, if demand is inelastic/elastic, the futures price is a downward/upward biased predictor of the futures price at any later time, and of the later spot price.*

The intuition for this result is easy to see in the case of a single information event (which automatically has a good-bad information structure). Consider inelastic demand. Producers hedge short, but since transaction costs deter some of their trading partners, they are not as short as they would be if trading were costless. So their wealth is higher in the high price state and lower in the low price state in comparison with a costless trading regime.

This means that the marginal utility of wealth, instead of being equated across states, is low when the futures payoff is high,[23] leading to a positive risk premium. Thus the partial equilibrium result which failed in general equilibrium without transaction costs – to wit, that inelastic demand leads to downward bias and elastic demand to upward bias – is reinstated in a general equilibrium with transaction costs.[24]

This is despite the fact that qualitatively, the conclusions about hedging drawn in section 2 are not greatly affected by the addition of transactions costs. Identical producers will still hedge long or short according to demand elasticity, although the amount by which they do so is reduced by an adverse risk premium effect. Consumers, of course, are affected since some will refrain from trading instead of taking small positions on the futures market.

A subtlety brought out by the model about multiple information arrivals is that if the information structure is ambiguous, the price bias might fail to correspond in the expected way with the direction of hedging. Instead of assuming good-bad stochastic dominance, suppose only that the *expected* output were higher in a^j than b^j. Then even though the spot price decreases across final states with aggregate Z, it is possible for the expected spot price (and also, it turns out, the time j futures price) to be *higher* in a^j than in b^j. While atypical, this type of case may occur if the event is relatively uninformative about the *level* of Z, but materially affects variance or higher-order moments.

4 CONCLUSION

Examining futures pricing in a multi-good setting reveals some effects that are not present in partial equilibrium models. Proposition 1 showed that positive complementarity in preferences between consumption goods promotes downward futures price bias, and negative complementarity promotes upward bias. More importantly, contrary to the prediction of single-good partial-equilibrium theory, hedging pressure does not cause futures price bias in a model with costless trading. The paper has provided an example where the optimal futures hedging positions of identical growers are determined by demand price elasticity (Proposition 2). With additively separable preferences, futures prices are unbiased predictors of later spot prices regardless of demand elasticity (Proposition 1), even though hedging is long or short for elastic and inelastic demand respectively. With nonadditive preferences as well, there is no tendency for the bias to match the direction of producer hedging.

The divergence of these results from those of standard hedging pressure theory is due to allowing for hedging incentives of consumers, which are opposite to the hedging incentives of producers. However, the standard partial-equilibrium models are certainly realistic in (implicitly) assuming nonparticipation by consumers. This feature can be incorporated in a general equilibrium framework by adding a fixed setup cost of trading. Fixed costs of trading futures differentially drive the smaller traders (consumers) rather than the larger traders (producers) from the futures market. Allowing for trading costs reinstates the prediction of downward bias (backwardation) under inelastic demand, when producers hedge short; correspondingly, the model predicts upward bias (contango) for elastic demand, when producer hedging is long (Proposition 3). This effect, being systematic, is in contrast with the implications of imperfect-arbitrage models in which trading costs merely add a band of inaccuracy around the perfect market baseline prediction.

This effect also contrasts with pricing relations derived from models with costless trading, which frequently can be obtained by assuming identical individuals, so that securities are priced to deter trading. Here, the predictions for bias arise from differential exclusion of some potential traders from the futures market, nonparticipation being a function of the endowments of the trader. The model therefore reflects in an essential way a feature of commodity futures markets which traditional theorists have considered important for pricing and the success of contracts: that the market brings about an interaction between distinct classes of traders, producers ('hedgers') and outsiders ('speculators').

In other contexts also, risks that are concentrated among a few traders should be more influential for pricing than dispersed risks. We would expect, for example, that the pricing of bonds and interest rate futures contracts would reflect more the hedging incentives of owners or managers of financial institutions than those of small homeowners.

The central theme of this paper may be summarized as follows. Partial-equilibrium models of commodity futures pricing are logically incomplete, since they neglect the consumption choice amongst different goods whose prices vary. However, they are realistic in an important respect – implicitly allowing for transaction costs. To combine logical completeness with realism, predictions should be derived from general equilibrium models that explicitly include the costs that limit market participation. This will sometimes, though not necessarily always, justify the predictions of partial-equilibrium models.

APPENDIX 1   FUTURES PRICES WITH COSTLESS TRADING

Proof of Lemma 1

A backwards recursion method is used. Contingent wealth W_s^m as defined by (4.2) may be viewed as a consumption good for which investors will have an induced (state-dependent) utility function $V(W^m; P^m)$. To show that at any time a dynamic trading strategy can be used to span the states of nature, consider first a shift in trading strategy of $\Delta\xi^{m-1}$ at $m - 1$. This increases wealth by $\Delta W_s^m = \Delta\xi^{m-1}(P^{m(a)} - P^{m-1})$ or $\Delta\xi^{m-1}(P^{m(b)} - P^{m-1})$ after outcomes a^m and b^m respectively. Hence

$$0 = \Delta W_a^m [P^{m(b)} - P^{m-1}] - \Delta W_b^m [P^{m(a)} - P^{m-1}], \qquad (4.4)$$

where a and b abbreviate the states that follow a^m and b^m, so the market at date $m - 1$ is effectively complete so long as $P^{m(b)}$, $P^{m(a)} \neq P^{m-1}$. If $P^{m(b)} \neq P^{m(a)}$, then the former condition must hold, since otherwise a riskless arbitrage opportunity would be available.

Next, as inductive hypothesis assume spanning at an arbitrary time j. Let S^j refer to the set of states which remain possible outcomes subsequent to history s^j. Spanning implies that there exist implicit state prices for terminal wealth $P_{W_s}^{j(a)}$ and $P_{W_s}^{j(b)}$ after outcomes a^j and b^j respectively such that

$$\sum_{s \in S^{j(a)}} P_{W_s}^{j(a)} \Delta W_s^{j(a)} = 0, \quad \sum_{s \in S^{j(b)}} P_{W_s}^{j(b)} \Delta W_s^{j(b)} = 0, \tag{4.5}$$

where ΔW_s^j is defined as the change in terminal state-s wealth selected at date j. Let $\Delta^{j(a)}$ and $\Delta^{j(b)}$ be the shifts in dynamic trading strategy that generate the wealth shifts $\Delta W_s^{j(a)}$, $s \in S^{j(a)}$ and $\Delta W_s^{j(b)}$, $s \in S^{j(b)}$. At $j - 1$, consider a shift in position of $\Delta \xi^{j-1}$ at $j - 1$, followed by an offsetting shift of opposite sign at j to close this position, and in addition the shifts $\Delta^{j(a)}$ and $\Delta^{j(b)}$. Then in addition to producing $\Delta W_s^{j(a)}$ and $\Delta W_s^{j(b)}$ for the remaining possible states, $P^{j(a)} - P^{j-1}\xi^{j-1}$ extra units of wealth are provided in all states subsequent to a^j, and $P^{j(b)} - P^{j-1}\xi^{j-1}$ extra units of wealth in all states subsequent to b^j. Hence, the total wealth shift brought about in state s is

$$\Delta W_s^{j-1} = \Delta W_s^j + (P^j - P^{j-1}) \Delta \xi^{j-1}. \tag{4.6}$$

So solving (4.6) for $\Delta W_s^{j(a)}$ and $\Delta W_s^{j(b)}$ and substituting into (4.5) gives

$$0 = \sum_{s \in S^j} P_{W_s}^j [\Delta W_s^{j-1} - (P^j - P^{j-1}) \Delta \xi^{j-1}]. \tag{4.7}$$

Solving for and then eliminating $\Delta \xi^{j-1}$ in (4.7) as applicable after a^j and b^j, and defining $K_a \equiv \Sigma_{s \in S^{j(a)}} P_{W_s}^{j(a)}$ and $K_b \equiv \Sigma_{s \in S^{j(b)}} P_{W_s}^{j(b)}$, then so long as $P^j \neq P^{j-1}$, we obtain

$$0 = -K_b (P^{j(b)} - P^{j-1}) \sum_{s \in S^{j(a)}} P_{W_s}^{j(a)} \Delta W_s^{j-1} +$$

$$K_a (P^{j(a)} - P^{j-1}) \sum_{s \in S^{j(b)}} P_{W_s}^{j(b)} \Delta W_s^{j-1}. \tag{4.8}$$

This is a linear budget constraint on wealth shifts chosen at $j - 1$, so since $P^{j(a)} \neq P^{j(b)}$, the states are spanned by dynamic trading strategies initiated at $j - 1$. Therefore, by induction, the market is effectively complete at all dates.

Semi-contingent markets

It is convenient for later proofs to introduce an artificial trading regime, *semi-contingent markets* (SCM), to describe the equilibrium in the assumed FM regime. The efficient allocation achieved under FM could be characterized by examining the trading problem of a one-shot complete market for contingent claims on the two goods. However, with additive separability or with homotheticity, since endowments and consumption of N are nonrandom, contingent trading in N is a degree of freedom for which traders have no use. It is therefore convenient to price contingent claims to Z in terms of *uncontingent* claims to numeraire N. In SCM, which is also effectively complete, there is a single round of trading, and contingent claims to Z are tradable. However, when a trader buys or sells units of N, the same quantity must be delivered in each state of the world.

We consider the decision of a trader on a semi-contingent market opened by surprise immediately following event θ^j, so let $\bar{n}^j$ and $\bar{z}^j_s$ refer to the trader's position in N and Z at time j. Let n^j be the final level of consumption of N selected, z^j_s be consumption of Z in state s, and let ϕ^j_s be the price of a claim to state-s Z.

The trader's problem under SCM is then

$$\max_{n^j, \{z^j_s\}, s \in S^j} E[u(n^j, \tilde{z}^j)] \qquad \text{subject to} \tag{4.9}$$

$$\bar{n}^j + \sum_s \phi^j_s \bar{z}^j_s = n^j + \sum_s \phi^j_s z^j_s,$$

where $\tilde{z}^j$ takes on value z^j_s in state s. This yields the optimality conditions

$$\frac{U_z(n^j, z^j_s)}{E^j[U_n(n^j, \tilde{z}^j)]} = \frac{\phi^j_s}{\pi^j_s}, \qquad s \in S^j. \tag{4.10}$$

Proof of Proposition 1

Suppose that a SCM were opened at time j, and consumption positions selected. Next, suppose that agents were given a new opportunity to trade on a spot market opened at the final date m. With either separable or homothetic preferences, each individual's consumption of N is constant across states, so that the initial SCM is effectively complete. Thus, no retrading in the new spot market would take place. Applying (4.10) at time m and at time j, dividing, and noting that $\phi^{m(s)}_s = P^{m(s)}$ shows that the market will clear if no-one trades at time m ($n^m = n^j_s = z^m_s$), and if the spot price is

$$P^{m(s)} = \left(\frac{E^j\left[U_n\left(n^j, \tilde{z}^j\right)\right]}{U_n\left(n^j, z_s^j\right)} \right) \frac{\phi_s^j}{\pi_s^j} \equiv \frac{\phi_s^j}{w_s^j}, \qquad \sum_{s \in S^j} w_s^j = 1. \tag{4.11}$$

Since both FM and SCM are effectively complete, the price in the FM regime of a futures contract must be the sum of the prices of the elements of the state claim bundle it provides:

$$P^j = \sum_{s \in S^j} \phi_s^j. \tag{4.12}$$

(a)   With additive separability, since n^j is constant, U_n is nonstochastic. Hence, substituting for ϕ_s^j in (4.12) from (4.11).

$$P^j = \sum_{s \in S^j} \pi_s^j P^{m(s)} = E^j\left[\tilde{P}^m\right]. \tag{4.13}$$

It follows by the rule of iterated expectations that

$$P^j = E^j\left[E^k\left[\tilde{P}^m\right]\right] = E^j\left[\tilde{P}^k\right], \qquad k > j.$$

(b)   Let a similar ordering between two variables x and y be denoted by $x \sim y$, i.e., as one goes up so does the other. With positive complementarity, we have the similar ordering across states $U_n\left(n^j, z_s^j\right) \sim z_s^j \sim -P^{m(s)}$. (To see that $z_s^j \sim -P^{m(s)}$, note that with homotheticity we can view the final consumption choice as being made by a representative individual endowed with the same N, but with more Z in state s' than state s. If P^m were unchanged, then he would consume more of both N and Z in state s', if P^m were to rise, then the opportunity set for net purchase (sale) of N would be strictly improved (worsened), so by revealed preference he would also purchase more N in state s', inconsistent with market clearing.) Hence

$$P^j = \sum_{s \in S^j} w_s^j P^{m(s)} < \sum_{s \in S^j} \pi_s^j P^{m(s)} = E^j\left[\tilde{P}^m\right], \tag{4.14}$$

where the inequality follows because probability weight is shifted toward lower prices under the martingale measure w_s^j compared with the true probabilities π_s^j in the first-order stochastic dominance sense. The argument with negative complementarity is similar.

APPENDIX 2   OPTIMAL HEDGING AND LOG PREFERENCES

Definition   Let *wealth* at time j, W^j be the numeraire value of the agent's position as taken after information event θ^{j-1} evaluated in terms of the prices of contingent Z which would obtain if an *SCM* market for final consumption claims were opened at time j. So

$$W^j = n^{j-1} = \sum_{s \in S^j} \phi^j_s z^{j-1}_s. \tag{4.15}$$

Lemma 2 *With additively separable preferences, in a FM regime contingent wealths follow a martingale.*

PROOF First, it may be noted that by (4.11) that SCM prices follow a martingale, because at any time j, letting $k = m$,

$$\phi^j_s = \pi^j_s \phi^m_s = E^j[\tilde{\phi}^m], \tag{4.16}$$

where $\tilde{\phi}^m$ takes on value ϕ^m_s in state s, and zero otherwise. It follows that at any time j, expected wealth is

$$E^j[W^{j+1}] = E^j[n^j] + \sum_{s \in S^j} (E^j[\tilde{\phi}^{j+1}_s]) z^j_s$$

$$= n^j + \sum_{s \in S^j} \phi^j_s z^j_s, \tag{4.17}$$

where $\tilde{\phi}^{j+1}_s$ is a random variable taking on the value of the SCM price for state-s Z that applies at time $j + 1$ when event θ^{j+1} occurs. But by the FM trading constraints (4.1),

$$E^j[W^{j+1}] = n^{j-1} - P^j \xi^{j-1} + \sum_{s \in S^j} \phi^j_s(z^{j-1}_s + \xi^{j-1})$$

$$= W^j + \xi^{j-1} \left(-P^j + \sum_{s \in S^j} \phi^j_s \right).$$

The last term is zero, by (4.12), so wealth follows a martingale.

Proof of Proposition 2

1 *Similar ordering of consumption bundles*: Consumptions of N are identical across states. By effective completeness, consumption of Z is the same as it would be in a SCM regime. By the SCM optimality condition (4.10), since $v'(z_s)$ is a strictly monotonic function of z_s and the right hand side is the same for all individuals, consumption of Z is similarly ordered (as one goes up, so does the other).

2 *Ordering of contingent wealths and spot prices over states*: To achieve similar ordering of consumption in an FM regime, contingent wealth in the final trading rounds must, for all individuals, be ordered similarly across states. If demand is inelastic/elastic, then a trader's expenditure on Z, $P^m z^m$ is similarly/inversely ordered with P^m. Recalling that by effective com-

pleteness consumption n is constant across states, it follows that to pay for this the wealth for each trader must be similarly/inversely ordered with spot price as demand is inelastic/elastic.

3 *Ordering of wealths and futures prices*: Let us now verify how time j wealths are ordered with respect to the futures price. Suppose that for event θ^j, that $W_a^j > W_b^j$. Then since consumption of N is the same in all states, it follows by Lemma 2 that $E_a^j[P^m z^m] > E_b^j[P^m z^m]$. By revenue ordering expected revenue is higher/lower when expected price is higher for inelastic/elastic demand, so

$$E_a^j[P^m] \gtreqless E_b^j[P^m] \qquad \text{as demand is inelastic/elastic.}$$

Since the futures price at time j is equal to the expected value of the spot price,

$$P_a^j \gtreqless P_b^j, \qquad \text{as demand is inelastic/elastic.}^{25}$$

4 *Long and short positions*: At time j, consumers' wealths satisfy

$$W^j = P^j H^{j-1} + n^{j-1}, \tag{4.19}$$

where $H^{j-1} \equiv \Sigma_{k=0}^{j-1} \xi^k$ is the total futures position at time $j - 1$. So by (4.18) to make wealth similarly/inversely ordered with the futures price when demand is inelastic/elastic, a long/short total futures position must be taken by consumers. By market clearing, it follows that short/long positions are taken by producers.

Revenue ordering and elasticity properties of LOG utility

We first show that for an individual with LOG preferences, expenditure on Z in the spot market, $P^m z^m$ is linearly related across states to the spot price P^m. In the final trading round, suppressing m superscripts, the budget constraint is

$$W = Pz + n. \tag{4.20}$$

This gives the optimality condition

$$\frac{U_n}{U_z} = \frac{1}{P}. \tag{4.21}$$

For LOG preferences (4.3), by (4.20) and (4.21) and solving for expenditure on Z,

$$Pz = \frac{n}{\alpha} + \beta P. \tag{4.22}$$

where n is optimally independent of state. Revenue ordering follows immediately by taking the expected value of (4.22), since n is nonstochastic. To demonstrate that demand is elastic/inelastic as β is $< / > 0$, solve (4.22) for z and differentiate with respect to price.

APPENDIX 3   TRANSACTION COSTS AND RISK PREMIA

Proof of Proposition 3

We will prove that futures price P^j is a downward/upward biased predictor of $P^{j+1}, j = 0, \ldots, m - 1$ from which the proposition immediately follows.

1   *Similar ordering of futures traders' marginal utilities*: The opportunity to trade futures in the rounds preceding the final spot market may be viewed as being equivalent to opening a complete market at time zero in terminal wealths W^m. Traders have an indirect utility function $V(W^m; P^m)$ for terminal wealth which is state dependent through P^m. So the effective completeness of the FM regime implies a Pareto optimal allocation of contingent wealths *among those trading futures*. (This is only efficient relative to the constraint that wealths cannot be shifted between futures traders and nontraders.) In such a constrained Pareto optimal allocation, all traders select similarly ordered marginal utilities of wealth across states, i.e., for all traders i and k, $V_W^i \sim V_W^k$. For if marginal utilities crossed i.e., $V_W(W_i^{m(s)}; P^{m(s)}) < V_W(W_i^{ms'}; P^{m(s')})$ for trader i, yet $V_W(W_k^{m(s)}; P^{m(s)}) > V_W(W_k^{m(s')}; P^{m(s')})$ for trader k, then they could jointly raise their expected utilities by agreeing that i gives ε units of state-s wealth to k in return for $\varepsilon(\pi^s/\pi^{s'})$, of state-$s'$ wealth, ε small.

2   *Ordering of marginal utilities with the spot price*: Consider now the final spot market after θ^m arrives. By a standard envelope condition for a single-round consumption decision, $\partial V(W; P)/\partial W = u'(n)$ (m superscripts suppressed). So traders' marginal utilities are inversely ordered across states with final consumption of N. Since $V_W(W; P)$ is similarly ordered for all traders across states, traders order similarly their consumptions of N as well, $n^i \sim n^k$.

By the definition of spot demand elasticity, for given wealth the expenditure on Z increases (decreases) with the spot price of Z if demand is inelastic (elastic). The wealth of a consumer who does not trade futures equals his endowed quantity of N, which is the same across states. Let an r superscript indicate a consumer who refrains from trading. Since his expenditure on Z increases (decreases) with the spot price for inelastic (elastic) demand, $Pz^r \sim P$ $(-P)$, his consumption of N, $W - P^r z^r$, decreases (increases) with P, so $-n^r$ $(n^r) \sim P$.

Since traders similarly order their consumption of N, which in the aggregate (net of costs t) is nonrandom, by adding up of social totals the consumption of N by traders increases (decreases) with P, i.e., n' ($-n'$) $\sim P$. It follows by the envelope condition that for inelastic/elastic demand, marginal utility of traders $-V'_W(W; P)$ ($V'_W(W; P)$) $\sim P$.

3 *Bias*: We will now show that the futures price must be biased appropriately, since no change in an optimal trading strategy can increase expected utility. Starting after event θ^j, let the possible prices at time $j + 1$ be $P^{(j+1)a}$ and $P^{(j+1)b}$. Consider an increase in the futures position ξ^j by ε, which is closed at $j + 1$ by a sale of ε units of futures. Any profits or losses from this perturbation in the trading strategy shows up as a (negative) increase in wealth W^m of $(P^{(j+1)a} - P^j)\varepsilon$ in each state which can arise subsequent to a^{j+1}, and an increase of $(P^{(j+1)b} - P^j)\varepsilon$ in each state arising subsequent to b^{j+1}.

The impact of the trading perturbation on expected utility is

$$\frac{\mathrm{d}E^j[V(W^m; P^m)]}{\mathrm{d}\xi^j} = \Pr(a^{j+1}|s^j)E^{(j+1)a}\left[\frac{\mathrm{d}W^m}{\mathrm{d}\xi^j}V_W\right]$$

$$+ \Pr(b^{j+1}|s^j)E^{(j+1)b}\left[\frac{\mathrm{d}W^m}{\mathrm{d}\xi^j}V_W\right] \qquad (4.23)$$

where

$$\frac{\mathrm{d}W^m}{\mathrm{d}\xi^j} = \begin{cases} P^{(j+1)a} - P^j < 0 \text{ if } a^{j+1} \text{ occurs,} \\ P^{(j+1)b} - P^j < 0 \text{ if } b^{j+1} \text{ occurs.} \end{cases} \qquad (4.24)$$

The inequalities above must hold, because labeling a^{j+1} so that $P^{(j+1)a} < P^{(j+1)b}$, if either failed it would be possible through either a long or short perturbation to increase wealth in all states subsequent to *both* outcome a^{j+1} or b^{j+1}. With a good-bad information structure, the distribution of Z given a^{j+1} first order dominates the distribution given b^{j+1}. The spot price is decreasing with aggregate Z, and is monotonic across states with the marginal utilities of traders. It follows that the distribution of traders' marginal utilities given event a^{j+1} is greater (lower) than that given event b^{j+1} for inelastic (elastic) demand, so $E^{(j+1)a}[V_W] \geq E^{(j+1)b}[V_W]$ for inelastic (elastic) demand.

Consider the case of inelastic demand. By (4.23), setting to zero the gain from perturbing the optimal trade,

$$0 = (E^{(j+1)a}[V_W])[\Pr(a^{j+1}|s^j)P^{(j+1)a} + \Pr(b^{j+1}|s^j)P^{(j+1)b}$$

$$- P^j] - (E^{(j+1)a}[V_W] - E^{(j+1)b}[V_W])\Pr(b^{j+1}|s^j)[P^{(j+1)b} - P^j]. \qquad (4.25)$$

Since the subtracted term is positive, the first term is also positive, so $P^j < E^j[P^{j+1}]$. The argument for elastic demand is similar.

NOTES

1 Some traditional sources include Keynes (1923), Hicks (1939), Stein (1961), Stoll (1979).
2 Rolfo (1980), Newbery and Stiglitz (1981), Newbery (1983), Anderson and Danthine (1983), D. Hirshleifer (1988a, b).
3 A recent study by Chang (1985) lends support to this thesis, in that futures prices for grains on average rise when hedgers are short, and fall when hedgers are long.
4 That is, the CAPM in effect assumes that all producers costlessly issue equity shares in their businesses.
5 The models of Stoll (1979) and D. Hirshleifer (1988a) combined producer hedging with a stock market. In such a setting, the futures price bias has additive components, the first due to the futures contract's 'beta' (covariance of its return with the return on the stock market portfolio of all tradable endowments), and a second due to hedging by producers of their revenue risks from sales of the commodity. Breeden's (1980, 1984) general equilibrium consumption-based CAPM also allows for nontraded endowments, and therefore implicitly for producer hedging.
6 A general equilibrium literature has examined a different set of issues. J. Hirshleifer (1977), Grauer and Litzenberger (1979), Richard and Sundaresan (1981), and Breeden (1980, 1984) examine futures pricing in multi-good settings, but not the role of producer hedging in futures pricing. Stiglitz (1983) and Britto (1984) provide a number of useful results concerning hedging by producers; the current paper differs from these in that all rather than a subset of traders are concerned with two consumption goods, and in its focus on nontrading by some investors.
7 The conditions discussed below leading to unbiased futures pricing are not new. However, it does not seem to have been recognized that this general equilibrium prediction conflicts with the hedging pressure prediction of recent partial-equilibrium models with risk-averse speculators.
8 Stock mutual funds do not trade in commodity futures, so investors who wish to include commodities in their portfolios must resort to specialized futures funds. Pension funds face regulatory constraints on trading commodity futures. Alternatively, shifting risk from growers to consumers by off-exchange forward contracting would clearly be very costly, if it operates through the intermediation of millers, bakers, and retailers at different stages in the production process.
9 This explains Gray's (1960) finding that bias tends to be more pronounced in thin (low participation) futures markets.
10 We may interpret Z as corn, say, and N as noncorn consumption. The purpose of assuming a fixed endowment of N is to focus on hedging pressure. The Mayers (1972) CAPM with nonmarketable assets showed that a security's risk premium is influenced not only by its covariation with nonmarketable endowments (reflecting hedging incentives), but also by covariation with marketable assets ('beta'). Stock market risk would enter the current model, if in addition to the imperfectly marketable risky endowment of Z, equity shares were traded on stochastic endowments of N.

11 Introducing consumption at date zero would not substantively alter any of the results provided here. On the other hand, multi-date consumption and resettlement would introduce considerations not addressed here.

12 The binomial information process is used for tractability, as discussed further below. Cox, Ross, and Rubinstein (1979) used a binomial state process to provide insight about hedging behavior in options. Unlike their model, this paper does not assume an exogenous process for prices.

13 It is well known that multiple trading rounds can reduce the number of long-lived securities needed to effectively complete a market. See e.g., Kreps (1982); see Duffie and Huang (1985) for a continuous time analysis. Here, absent transaction costs, an efficient allocation is achieved using only the futures contract for the exchange of N for Z.

14 Unlike options pricing models, here there are no redundant securities. With more than two possible information outcomes at each event, more securities would be required to complete the market. This would introduce portfolio considerations which will not be our focus here.

15 Proof: For any given allocation, replace each individual's consumption of N with its expected value. This is feasible, and by additive separability of preferences, the concavity of $u(n)$, and Jensen's inequality, the new allocation yields a higher level of expected utility.

16 Under homotheticity, the ratio of N to Z consumption in each state is the same for all individuals, and so is in proportion to the social totals; with constant aggregate supply of N, this implies that each individual's consumption of N is nonstochastic.

17 Homotheticity in part (b) of Proposition 1 rules out wealth-induced differences in preferences, to ensure that higher aggregate output of Z leads to higher (lower) marginal utility of N. A stronger version of part (b) states that the futures price is a downward (upward) biased predictor of all later futures prices, not just the final spot price; this requires the additional assumption of a good-bad information structure, as defined in section 3.

18 Similar martingale results with nonrandom quantity of the numeraire were provided by J. Hirshleifer (1977) in a two-state model, and Richard and Sundaresan (1981) in a continuous time setting. Salant (1976) stressed the sensitivity of this result to the assumption of additive separability.

19 Throughout the paper, we refer to general equilibrium demand elasticity, that is, the percentage rate of change in gross demand for Z as its spot price varies in response to shifts in the Z endowment.

20 Of course, here marginal utility is a function not only of wealth, but also of the random spot price. However, because marginal utilities of endowed wealth are affected by price in a similar way across states for both groups, futures positions with unitary elastic demand will still be null.

21 More generally, there are scale economies in trading on the individual level. Declining unit costs of trading are reflected in minimum contract sizes, brokerage commissions (to the extent that these are higher for smaller trades), and most importantly, the time and cognitive costs of learning to trade intelligently. Of course, costs may be reduced to some extent by trading through financial intermediaries (futures mutual funds). The fixed cost then would be the minimal

cost per customer of transacting with the intermediary.

22 For a larger setup cost, some producers may be driven from the futures market as well. But so long as a disproportionate number of demanders versus suppliers of futures are excluded, the tendency toward bias will remain.

23 The trading cost makes the market bindingly incomplete, so that the efficient outcome of nonrandom consumption of N is not achieved.

24 The more general theme suggested here, that nonparticipation by consumers causes the direction of bias to be related to the hedging positions of producers, could lead to different predictions in other settings. For example, the inclusion of a second production stage would introduce another set of hedgers, processors of the commodity. Under inelastic demand, processors' positions would be complementary with those of growers (see D. Hirshleifer; 1988b). With limited participation by growers as well as consumers, this could lead to an upward rather than downward bias.

25 So long as demand elasticity is not unitary, then since by assumption prices differ, $P_a^j \neq P_b^j$, wealths must be unequal.

REFERENCES

Anderson, Ronald W., and Jean-Pierre Danthine (1983) Hedger diversity in futures markets. *Economic Journal* 93, 370–89.

Breeden, Douglas (1980) Consumption risk in futures markets. *Journal of Finance* 35, 503–20.

――― (1984) Futures markets and commodity options: hedging and optimality in incomplete markets. *Journal of Economic Theory* 32, 275–300.

Britto, R. (1984) The simultaneous determination of spot and futures prices in a simple model with production risk. *Quarterly Journal of Economics* 99, 351–65.

Chang, Eric (1985) Returns to speculators and the theory of normal backwardation. *Journal of Finance* 40, 193–208.

Cox, John, Stephen Ross and Mark Rubinstein (1979) Options pricing: a simplified approach. *Journal of Financial Economics* 7, 229–63.

Duffie, Darrell and Chi-Fu Huang (1985) Implementing Arrow-Debreu equilibria by continuous trading of few long-lived securities. *Econometrica* 54, 1161–84.

Grauer, Frederick L. A. and Robert H. Litzenberger (1979) The pricing of commodity futures contracts nominal bond and other risky assets under commodity price uncertainty. *Journal of Finance* 34, 69–83.

Gray, Robert W. (1960) The characteristic bias in some thin futures markets. *Food Research Institute Studies* 2, 296–312.

Hicks, John R. (1939) *Value and Capital*. Cambridge: Oxford University Press, pp. 135–40.

Hirshleifer, David (1988a) Residual risk, trading costs, and commodity futures risk premia. *Review of Financial Studies* 1, 173–93.

――― (1988b) Risk, futures pricing, and the organization of production in commodity markets. *Journal of Political Economy* 96, 1206–20.

Hirshleifer, Jack (1977) The theory of speculation under alternative regimes of markets. *Journal of Finance* 32, 975–99.

Keynes, John Maynard (1923) Some aspects of commodity markets. *Manchester Guardian Commercial*. European Reconstruction Series, Section 13, 784–6.

Kreps, David (1982) Multiperiod securities and the efficient allocation of risk: a comment on the Black-Scholes option pricing model, in *The Economics of Information and Uncertainty*, ed. J. J. McCall. Chicago: University of Chicago Press.

Mayers, David (1972) Non-marketable assets and capital market equilibrium under uncertainty, in *Studies in the Theory of Capital Markets* ed. M. Jensen. New York: Praeger.

Newbery, David M. G. (1983) Futures trading, risk reduction and price stabilization, ch. 9 in *Futures Markets* ed. M. Streit. London: Basil Blackwell.

Newbery, David M. G. and Joseph E. Stiglitz (1981) *The Theory of Commodity Price Stabiization: A Study in the Economics of Risk*. Oxford: Clarendon Press.

Richard, Scott, and Suresh Sundaresan (1981) A continuous time equilibrium model of forward prices and futures prices in a multigood economy. *Journal of Financial Economics* 9, 347–71.

Rolfo, Jacques (1980) Optimal hedging under price and quantity uncertainty: the case of a cocoa producer. *Journal of Political Economy* 88, 100–16.

Salant, Stephen W. (1976) Hirshleifer on speculation. *Quarterly Journal of Economics* 90, 667–76.

Stein, Jerome (1961) The simultaneous determination of spot and futures prices. *American Economic Review* 51, 1012–25.

Stiglitz, Joseph E. (1983) Futures markets and risk: a general equilibrium approach, in *Futures Markets* ed. M. Streit. London: Basil Blackwell.

Stoll, Hans (1979) Commodity futures and spot price determination and hedging in capital market equilibrium. *Journal of Financial and Quantitative Analysis* 14, 873–94.

5

Forward Exchange, Futures Trading, and Spot Price Variability: A General Equilibrium Approach

Paul Weller and Makoto Yano

1 INTRODUCTION

The central issue addressed in this paper has long been a subject for debate, both practical and academic. It concerns the effect of forward and futures trading on the stability of spot prices in the markets for both foreign exchange and for commodities. In the real world, this issue is of obvious importance; some active futures markets have been closed on the grounds of their alleged destabilizing effects on prices.[1] Thus it is no surprise that this topic has been the subject of extensive empirical research.[2] Recently, moreover, a number of theoretical studies on this topic have appeared (see Peck, 1976; Turnovsky, 1979, 1983; Sarris, 1980; Kawai, 1983a, 1983b, 1984; Turnovsky and Campbell, 1985). The existing studies without exception adopt a partial equilibrium approach. As a general consequence of this, therefore, these studies ignore completely any income effects generated by the creation of forward and futures markets.

The present paper, in contrast, takes a general equilibrium approach in order to analyze the question in the context of markets where income effects can be expected to play a significant role. We shall argue in section 3 that forward and futures transactions in foreign exchange and in agricultural output may be thought of as dealing in futures contracts for broad commodity aggregates; income effects which appear in the spot markets for such aggregates affect futures transactions significantly. In order to analyze such

Reproduced from *Econometrica*, vol. 55 (1987), pp. 1433–50.

We are grateful to D. Easley, R. Guesnerie, M. Miller, J. Pomery, T.N. Srinivasan, S. Turnovsky, and two referees of this journal for helpful suggestions and correspondence.

We would also like to thank the Economics Department at Cornell where Makoto Yano was a faculty member and Paul Weller was a visiting faculty member when the work reported here was initiated.

general equilibrium effects, we develop a rational expectations model with futures and spot markets. The effect of opening a forward or futures market is isolated by comparing equilibria in our futures-spot market model when the futures market is open and when it is closed. The difference in spot price variability between the two equilibria is characterized by such familiar parameters as marginal propensities to consume, elasticities of compensated demand, and degrees of risk aversion.

Our study involves the comparison of equilibria in two different market systems and is thus conceptually distinct from standard comparative static analysis. Such a comparison is intractable in a complex model. In order to overcome this difficulty, we introduce output risk into the simple two-agent, two-good trade model and consider only the case where the variance of output is small. This enables us to derive a linear approximation to the change in spot price variability which results from the opening of a futures market.

In this context we identify an important channel not, so far as we know, previously even commented upon in the literature, through which forward and futures markets affect spot price variability.[3] Individuals who trade in forward and futures contracts bear capital gains and losses in the spot market when the contracts are settled. These gains and losses result in income transfers which influence demands and so spot prices. This suggests the existence of an important parallel between our analysis and that of international transfers (see Samuelson, 1952; Jones, 1975, for example).

The structure of this study follows. Section 2 sets out the model in a general setting. Section 3 discusses the interpretation of the model. Section 4 outlines the technique of analysis we use. Section 5 derives expressions for spot price variability in economies with and without forward and futures trading. Section 6 makes the comparison of spot price variability in these two economies. Section 7 discusses the variability in real income and its relationship to that in spot prices. Section 8 makes concluding remarks.

2   MODEL

Our model is an extension of the standard two-good, two-agent exchange model. It is described in a general setting here in order to emphasize that our analysis applies to various types of futures and forward transactions. The next section discusses possible interpretations of the model in the contexts of forward foreign exchange and commodity futures trading. The goods are referred to as A and B, the agents as α and β. The output of good A depends upon random factors. There are two states of nature; and state $i(= 1, 2)$ is realized with probability ϕ_i. The endowment of agent α consists of the entire output of good A, whose distribution is $(X_{A1}^\alpha, X_{A2}^\alpha)$. The entire output of good B is independent of states and constitutes the endowment of agent β. Its distribution is (X_B^β, X_B^β). The preferences of agent $j (= \alpha, \beta)$ are represented by von Neumann-Morgenstern utility functions $\Sigma_i \phi_i u^j (D_{Ai}^j, D_{Bi}^j)$, where (D_{Ai}^j, D_{Bi}^j) is the vector of agent j's consumption of goods A and B in state i. The function u^j is defined on the nonnegative orthant of the two-dimensional real space, R_+^2. We make the following assumption.

Assumption 1 $X_{Ai}^\alpha > 0, i = 1, 2,$ and $X_B^\beta > 0$. The utility function of agent $j (= \alpha, \beta), u^j \colon R_+^2 \to R$ is continuous, strictly quasi-concave, and concave on R_+^2, and continuously twice differentiable on the interior of R_+^2. Moreover, the partial derivatives of u^j are always positive.

Let p be the relative price of good A in terms of good B. We define the indirect utility function

$$v^j(p, Y) = \max \{u^j(D_A, D_B) : pD_A + D_B = Y\} \tag{5.1}$$

for $j = \alpha, \beta$. For later purposes we also define agent j's (vector) demand function $(D_A^j (p, Y), D_B^j (1/p, Y/p))$ as that which solves the maximization problem in equation (5.1).[4] Assumption 1 implies that for $Y > 0$ and $p > 0$ the indirect utility function and the demand function are continuously twice and once, respectively, differentiable.

We consider a single-period model. The futures market for good A opens at the beginning of the period, before the state of nature is realized. Exchange on spot markets occurs at the end of the period, after the state is realized. A futures contract stipulates that one unit of good A is to be delivered when the spot market opens. We shall examine a rational expectations equilibrium. Thus, each agent is assumed to know the correct distribution of the spot relative price when futures trading takes place. Let (p_1, p_2) be the distribution of the spot relative price of good A in terms of good B. We denote by (I_1^j, I_2^j) the distribution of agent j's income from production in the spot market. That is,

$$I_i^\alpha = p_i X_{Ai}^\alpha \quad \text{and} \quad I_i^\beta = X_B^\beta. \tag{5.2}$$

Let q be the price of a futures contract in terms of the numeraire, or good B, and F^j be agent j's demand for futures contracts. Then, $(p_i - q) F^j$ and $I_i^j + (p_i - q) F^j$ are the capital gain and the income, respectively, that agent j expects in the spot market in state i. In the futures market agent j chooses F^j so as to maximize his expected utility. Thus, we have the following condition.

Condition 1 $F = F^j, j = \alpha, \beta$, solves

$$\max_{F} \sum_{i} \phi_i v^j (p_i, I_i^j + (p_i - q)F) .$$ (5.3)

The market clearing condition in the futures market is as follows.

Condition 2 $F^\alpha + F^\beta = 0$.

After the state of nature is realized, the spot markets for goods A and B open. In the spot market in state i agent j chooses his demand vector (D_{Ai}^j, D_{Bi}^j) so as to maximize his utility, given his income $I_i^j + (p_i - q)F^j$. Thus, we have the following condition.

Condition 3 $(D_A, D_B) = (D_{Ai}^j, D_{Bi}^j), j = \alpha, \beta$ and $i = 1, 2$, solves

$$\max_{(D_A, D_B)} u^j (D_A, D_B) \text{ subject to}$$ (5.4)

$$p_i D_A + D_B = I_i^j + (p_i - q) F^j.$$

The necessary market clearing conditions in spot markets are as follows.

Condition 4 $D_{Bi}^\alpha + D_{Bi}^\beta = X_B^\beta, i = 1, 2$.

Conditions 1–4 describe a general equilibrium rational expectations model of futures and spot markets. We introduce the following definition.

Definition 1   The vector of a futures price and a spot price distribution, (q, p_1, p_2), is a rational expectations equilibrium in the *futures-spot market system* associated with the output distribution of good A, $(X_{A1}^\alpha, X_{A2}^\alpha)$, if there is a vector $(F^j, D_{Ai}^j, D_{Bi}^j; j = \alpha, \beta, i = 1, 2)$ which satisfies Conditions 1–4, given (q, p_1, p_2).

Setting F^j identically equal to zero in Condition 3 we may consider the spot market equilibrium in the absence of a futures market.

Definition 2   A spot price distribution (p_1, p_2) is an equilibrium in the *pure-spot market system* associated with the output distribution of good A, $(X_{A1}^\alpha, X_{A2}^\alpha)$, if there is a vector $(D_{Ai}^j, D_{Bi}^j; j = \alpha, \beta, i = 1, 2)$ which simultaneously satisfies Conditions 3, 4, and $F^j = 0, j = \alpha, \beta$, given (p_1, p_2).

We are interested in analyzing the long-run effect of opening a futures market. To this end, it is assumed that the economy is initially in equilibrium in the pure-spot market system with good A output distribution $(X_{A1}^\alpha,$

X_{A2}^{α}). Denote the spot price distribution in this equilibrium by (p_1^0, p_2^0). Suppose that the futures market for good A opens. We assume that the economy adjusts over time to a rational expectations equilibrium in the futures-spot market system. We denote the spot price distribution in this rational expectations equilibrium by (p_1^f, p_2^f). The effect of opening a futures market on spot price variability is captured by comparing these two spot price distributions, (p_1^0, p_2^0) and (p_1^f, p_2^f). A major part of the present study is devoted to this comparison.

In the existing literature on the analysis of the effect of opening a futures market, rational expectations equilibria are considered in a partial equilibrium framework. Turnovsky (1983) and Kawai (1983a, 1983b, 1984) explicitly introduce agents' optimization behaviour which is not treated in earlier studies, and which gives rise to log-linear demand and supply functions. This enables them to use techniques similar to those in macro rational expectations models.

In those studies, however, the general equilibrium effect of opening a futures market is ignored. As we shall discuss in the next section, there are a number of important issues which are treated more suitably in a general equilibrium framework. To consider such effects, we introduce several simplifying assumptions which are different from those in the partial equilibrium analysis of Turnovsky and Kawai. We conclude this section with some remarks on the nature of these assumptions.

First, we work with only two states of nature; thus, we cannot without loss of generality consider randomness in the endowment of more than one good. In other words, any additional source of randomness must be perfectly correlated with the original source. If one is prepared to accept this restriction, results similar to those presented below hold even if both agents are assumed to possess risky endowments, which may consist of both goods. Second, we deliberately choose not to incorporate in the model supply responses of producers. This is to focus upon what we consider to be the most fundamental differences between general and partial equilibrium effects. Third, we concentrate on randomness in production as the source of a motive for trading in futures markets. We do not consider the case of uncertainty on the demand side, but our approach could be adapted to analyze this by introducing state-contingent utility functions. Fourth, since our aim is to provide a description of the long-run effect of opening a futures market and to neglect short-run transitional phenomena, the one-period framework is appropriate. The two-agent, two-good model is sufficiently familiar to require no special remarks.

3   INTERPRETATION OF THE MODEL

3.1   Forward and futures markets for foreign exchange

If we think of each agent in the model as a country, the pure spot economy is an exchange model of international trade where each country produces a different spectrum of goods. Each spectrum may be identified with a broad commodity aggregate which can be treated as a single good. The relative price, p, is a real exchange rate. In order to reduce the income instability resulting from exogenous supply shocks, a country may trade claims to future delivery of its output. So long as domestic price levels are assumed to be constant, this is precisely equivalent to trading forward or futures contracts in foreign exchange.[5]

This interpretation of the model raises issue which are most appropriately treated in a general equilibrium framework; income effects cannpt be ignored since the commodities consumed are broad aggregates. It also suggests a number of interesting extensions, all of which add considerably to the complexity of the model. We may want to allow both countries to have random outputs which are less than perfectly correlated or to produce the same goods in different proportions. If so, it becomes necessary to work with more than two states of nature. We may also wish to distinguish between the real exchange rate and the terms of trade, which are the same under the above interpretation of our model. An interesting way to make such a distinction is to introduce a nontradable goods sector. Since a real exchange rate is the relative price of the aggregated goods and services of a country, it differs from the terms of trade in the presence of nontraded goods.

3.2   Futures markets for agricultural commodities

Goods A and B in our model may be thought of as the outputs of the agricultural and nonagricultural sectors, respectively. The production structure of our model incorporates a stylized representation of the fact that agricultural output in the aggregate tends to be subject to greater random fluctuation than nonagricultural output. Since the output of the agricultural sector is in general an aggregate of a number of commodities, our general equilibrium analysis is appropriate in comparing an economy which has a well-developed set of futures markets for agricultural commodities with one which lacks such markets.

4   FUTURES-SPOT MARKET SYSTEM AND ARROW SECURITIES

We show that the futures-spot market system above is complete in the sense of Arrow and Debreu. The intuition behind this result is that the three prices, q, p_1, and p_2, in the model determine three relative prices in a world of four state-contingent commodities. Thus, there is an equivalence between this system and that with Arrow securities. This equivalence is utilized in the later sections.

A state i Arrow security is a security which pays out one unit of the numeraire in state i and nothing in the other state. Thus, in the ex-ante security market agent j may supply I_i^j units of state i Arrow securities. His demand for state i Arrow securities is denoted by Y_i^j, and r is the relative price of a state 1 Arrow security in terms of state 2 Arrow securities. Following Arrow (1963), we may introduce the following definition.

Definition 3   The vector of a security price and a spot price distribution, (r, p_1, p_2), is a rational expectations equilibrium in the *Arrow-securities-spot market system* if there is a vector $(Y_i^j, D_{Ai}^j, D_{Bi}^j; j = \alpha, \beta, i = 1, 2)$ which satisfies the following conditions together with Condition 4.

Condition 1' $(Y_1, Y_2) = (Y_1^j, Y_2^j), j = \alpha, \beta$, solves

$$\max_{(Y_1, Y_2)} \sum_i \phi_i v^j(p_i, Y_i) \quad \text{subject to} \tag{5.5}$$

$$rY_1 + Y_2 = rI_1^j + I_2^j.$$

Condition 2' $Y_1^\alpha + Y_1^\beta = I_1^\alpha + I_1^\beta$.

Condition 3' $(D_A, D_B) = (D_{Ai}^j, D_{Bi}^j), j = \alpha, \beta, i = 1, 2$, solves

$$\max_{(D_A, D_B)} u^j(D_A, D_B) \quad \text{subject to} \tag{5.6}$$

$$p_i D_A + D_B = Y_i^j.$$

By Assumption 1, an equilibrium exists both in the Arrow-securities-spot market system and in the pure spot market system. The relationship of these two market systems is characterized by the following lemma.

Lemma 1   Suppose $p_1 \neq p_2$. Let

$$r(q - p_1) = p_2 - q. \tag{5.7}$$

Then, the price vector (q, p_1, p_2) *is an equilibrium in the futures-spot market system if and only if the price vector* (r, p_1, p_2) *is an equilibrium in the Arrow-securities-spot market system.*

PROOF   The equivalence of Conditions 1–3 and Conditions $1'$–$3'$ may be shown by setting

$$Y_i^j = I_i^j + (p_i - q) F^j, \qquad j = \alpha, \beta \qquad \text{and} \qquad i = 1, 2, \tag{5.8}$$

if $p_i \neq q$ for $i = 1, 2$. If (q, p_1, p_2) is an equilibrium in the futures-spot market system, $p_1 \neq p_2$ implies this condition since q has to lie strictly between p_1 and p_2. Conversely, if (r, p_1, p_2) is an equilibrium in the Arrow-securities-spot market system, $p_1 \neq p_2$ implies $q \neq p_i$ for $i = 1, 2$ since (5.7) implies $p_2 - q = r(p_2 - p_1)/(r + 1)$ and $q - p_1 = (p_2 - p_1)/(r + 1)$.

For the sake of simplicity, we assume $\phi_1 = \phi_2$ and $X_{A1}^\alpha \geqslant X_{A2}^\alpha$. (As is seen below, we do not lose generality with these assumptions.) Let $\bar{X}_A^\alpha = E(X_{Ai}^\alpha)$, the expected value of the output of good A. Then, $R = X_{A1}^\alpha - \bar{X}_A^\alpha = \bar{X}_A^\alpha - X_{A2}^\alpha$ may be regarded as a measure of output fluctuation. We denote by $(p_1^0(R), p_2^0(R))$ and $(r(R), p_1(R), p_2(R))$ equilibrium price vectors in the pure-spot and Arrow-securities-spot market systems, respectively. By Lemma 1, if $p_1(R) \neq p_2(R)$, the spot price distribution $(p_1(R), p_2(R))$ is associated with an equivalent equilibrium in the futures-spot market system. Thus, we may examine the effect of opening a futures market on spot price variability by comparing spot price distributions $(p_1^0(R), p_2^0(R))$ and $(p_1(R), p_2(R))$. In general, it is an intractable problem to carry out a comparison of equilibria in systems with different numbers of markets. Thus, we use linear approximations to these distributions around the risk-free output distribution of good A, or around $R = 0$. To this end, we note that if good A output has a uniform distribution $(\bar{X}_A^\alpha, \bar{X}_A^\alpha)$, the pure-spot market system has an equilibrium where the spot relative price and spot allocation are independent of states. We make the following assumption.

Assumption 2   The pure-spot market system with a uniform output distribution $(\bar{X}_A^\alpha, \bar{X}_A^\alpha)$ *has a unique equilibrium where each agent consumes a positive amount of each good in each state.*

It is standard in the literature dealing with comparative statics to assume uniqueness of equilibrium. We denote by $\bar{p}$ and $(\bar{D}_A^j, \bar{D}_B^j; j = \alpha, \beta)$ the spot relative price and spot allocation, respectively, of the unique equilibrium in Assumption 2. Thus, $\bar{D}_A^j > 0$ and $\bar{D}_B^j > 0$. Let $\bar{Y}^j = \bar{p}\bar{D}_A^j + \bar{D}_B^j$.

Lemma 2   *The Arrow-securities-spot market system with output distribution* $(\bar{X}_A^\alpha, \bar{X}_A^\alpha)$ *has a unique rational expectations equilibrium* $(r, p_1, p_2) = (1, \bar{p}, \bar{p})$ *with associated allocation vector* $(Y_i^j, D_{Ai}^j, D_{Bi}^j; j = \alpha, \beta, i = 1, 2) = (\bar{Y}^j, \bar{D}_A^j, \bar{D}_B^j; j = \alpha, \beta, i = 1, 2)$.

PROOF   It is obvious that the price and allocation vectors in the lemma are an equilibrium in the Arrow-securities-spot system. ($r = 1$ follows from the assumption $\phi_1 = \phi_2$.) The Arrow-securities-spot system with $(\bar{X}_A^\alpha, \bar{X}_A^\alpha)$ is equivalent to a complete market general equilibrium system without 'intrinsic' uncertainty. Thus, as shown by Malinvaud (1972) and Cass and Shell (1983), the spot price and spot allocation in equilibrium must be state-independent. Thus, by Assumption 2 we have uniqueness.

5   SPOT PRICE VARIABILITY

First, we prove a lemma.

Lemma 3   *If* (r, p_1, p_2) *is an equilibrium in the Arrow-securities-spot market system with good A output distribution* $(\bar{X}_A^\alpha + R, \bar{X}_A^\alpha - R)$, *there are* T_1^α *and* T_2^α *such that* $(r, p_1, p_2, T_1^\alpha, T_2^\beta)$ *solves the simultaneous equation system,*

$$\frac{v_Y^\alpha(p_1, p_1(\bar{X}_A^\alpha + R) + T_1^\alpha)}{v_Y^\alpha(p_2, p_2(\bar{X}_A^\alpha - R) - rT_1^\alpha)} = r, \tag{5.9}$$

$$\frac{v_Y^\beta(p_2, X_M^\beta + T_2^\beta)}{v_Y^\beta(p_1, X_M^\beta - T_2^\beta/r)} = \frac{1}{r}, \tag{5.10}$$

$$rT_1^\alpha = T_2^\beta, \tag{5.11}$$

$$D_B^\alpha\left(\frac{1}{p_1}, \frac{p_1(\bar{X}_A^\alpha + R) + T_1^\alpha}{p_1}\right) - T_1^\alpha = p_1 D_A^\beta(p_1, X_B^\beta - T_1^\alpha), \tag{5.12}$$

$$D_B^\alpha\left(\frac{1}{p_2}, \frac{p_2(\bar{X}_A^\alpha - R) - T_2^\beta}{p_2}\right) + T_2^\beta = p_2 D_A^\beta(p_2, X_B^\beta + T_2^\beta), \tag{5.13}$$

where $v_Y^j = \partial v^j(p, Y)/\partial Y$.

Moreover, let (p_1^0, p_2^0) be an equilibrium in the pure-spot market system with $(\bar{X}_A^\alpha + R, \bar{X}_A^\alpha - R)$. Then, (p_1^0, p_2^0) satisfies

$$D_B^\alpha \left(\frac{1}{p_1^0}, \bar{X}_A^\alpha + R \right) = p_1^0 D_A^\beta \left(p_1^0, X_B^\beta \right),$$ (5.14)

$$D_B^\alpha \left(\frac{1}{p_2^0}, \bar{X}_A^\alpha - R \right) = p_2^0 D_A^\beta \left(p_2^0, X_B^\beta \right).$$ (5.15)

PROOF   By the budget constraint of Condition 1′, if we set $T_1^\alpha = Y_1^\alpha - I_1^\alpha$ and $T_2^\beta = Y_2^\beta - I_2^\beta$, we have $Y_2^\alpha = I_2^\alpha - rT_1^\alpha = p_2(\bar{X}_A^\alpha - R) - rT_1^\alpha$ and $Y_1^\beta = I_1^\beta - T_2^\beta/r = X_M^\beta - T_2^\beta/r$, using (5.2) and the definition of $\bar{X}_A^\alpha$. Therefore, given Assumption 2 Conditions 1′–3′ imply equations (5.9)–(5.13). The second statement is obvious.

Index $\rho^j(p, Y) = -v_{YY}^j(p, Y)/v_Y^j(p, Y)$ is agent j's coefficient of absolute income-risk aversion, where $v_{YY}^j = \partial v_Y^j/\partial Y$. Agent j is income-risk averse if $\rho^j > 0$. Indices

$$m_A^j(p, Y) = p \, \partial D_A^j(p, Y)/\partial Y \quad \text{and}$$

$$m_B^j(p, Y) = (1/p)\partial D_B^j(1/p, Y/p)/\partial(Y/p)\,|_{\mathrm{d}p=0} = 1 - m_A^j(p, Y)$$

are agent j's marginal propensities to consume goods A and B. Indices

$$\varepsilon_B^\alpha(p, Y) = -\frac{\dfrac{1}{p}}{D_B^\alpha\left(\dfrac{1}{p}, \dfrac{Y}{p}\right)} \left.\frac{\partial D_B^\alpha\left(\dfrac{1}{p}, \dfrac{Y}{p}\right)}{\partial\left(\dfrac{1}{p}\right)}\right|_{\mathrm{d}\left(Y/p\right)=0} ;$$

and

$$\varepsilon_A^\beta(p, Y) = -\frac{p}{D_A^\beta(p, Y)} \frac{\partial D_A^\beta(p, Y)}{\partial p}$$

are the elasticities of agents α and β's demands for goods B and A. Moreover, indices $s_B^\alpha(p, Y) = \varepsilon_B^\alpha(p, Y) - m_B^\alpha(p, Y)$ and $s_A^\beta(p, Y) = \varepsilon_A^\beta(p, Y) - m_A^\beta(p, Y)$ are the elasticities of agents α's and β's compensated demands for goods B and A.[6] Thus, we have $s_B^\alpha > 0$ and $s_A^\beta > 0$. We make the following assumptions.

Assumption 3   *At least one agent is income-risk averse.*

Assumption 4   *The agent (α) who produces the risky output (A) has a nonunitary marginal propensity to consume his output.*

Assumption 5   *If the agent (β) who produces the nonrisky output (B) is* *income-risk neutral, he has a nonzero marginal propensity to consume his output.*

Assumptions 3, 4, and 5, respectively, imply $\rho^\alpha + \rho^\beta > 0$, $m_A^\alpha \neq 1$, and that $m_B^\beta \neq 0$ if $\rho^\beta = 0$. We now state our first main result. Let $y \cong x$ mean that x is a linear approximation to y. We have the following theorem.

Theorem 1   Let $\phi_1 = \phi_2$ and $R = X_{A1}^\alpha - E(X_{Ai}^\alpha) = E(X_{Ai}^\alpha) - X_{A2}^\alpha$. Then, there exists $\varepsilon > 0$ such that if $|R| < \varepsilon$, the pure-spot and futures-spot market systems with good A output distribution $(X_{A1}^\alpha, X_{A2}^\alpha)$ have uniquely determined equilibria where the distributions of the spot relative price of good A, $(p_1^0(R), p_2^0(R))$ and $(p_1^f(R), p_2^f(R))$, respectively, are differentiable functions of R. Moreover, we have

$$\frac{p_2^0(R) - p_1^0(R)}{2E(p_i^0(R))} \cong \frac{m_B^\alpha}{(\Delta \bar{M}/\bar{p})} R \,, \tag{5.16}$$

$$\Delta = s_B^\alpha + s_A^\beta - m_A^\alpha + m_A^\beta > 0 \,, \tag{5.17}$$

$$\frac{p_2^f(R) - p_1^f(R))}{2E(p_i^f(R))} \cong \frac{\rho^\beta m_B^\alpha + \rho^\alpha m_B^\beta}{(\delta/\bar{p})} R \,, \tag{5.18}$$

$$\delta = (\rho^\alpha + \rho^\beta)(s_B^\alpha + s_A^\beta)\bar{M} + (m_A^\alpha - m_A^\beta)^2 > 0 \,, \tag{5.19}$$

where agent j's coefficient of absolute income-risk aversion, $\rho^j \geqslant 0$, his marginal propensities to consume goods A and B, m_A^j and m_B^j, the elasticities of agents α's and β's compensated demands for good B and A, $s_B^\alpha > 0$ and $s_A^\beta > 0$, the spot relative price of good A, $\bar{p}$, and the value of trade in terms of good B, $\bar{M} > 0$, are all evaluated at the equilibrium of the pure-spot market system with good A output distribution $(E(X_{Ai}^\alpha), E(X_{Ai}^\alpha))$.

PROOF   Let $v_{Yp}^j = \partial v_Y^j/\partial p$. Then, we have

$$v_{Yp}^j(p, Y) = - v_{YY}^j(p, Y)D_A^j(p, Y) - v_Y^j(p, Y)\frac{m_A^j(p, Y)}{p}.^7 \tag{5.20}$$

We want to apply the implicit function theorem to system (5.9)–(5.13) around vector $b \equiv (r, p_1, p_2, T_1^\alpha, T_2^\beta, R) = (1, \bar{p}, \bar{p}, 0, 0, 0)$ which, by Lemmas 2 and 3, solves that system. Let $\hat{x} = dx/x$. By (5.20), the total differentiation of (5.9)–(5.11) at b implies

$$2\rho^\alpha d T_1^\alpha = - \hat{r} + (m_A^\alpha - \rho^\alpha \bar{p}(\bar{D}_A^\alpha - \bar{X}_A^\alpha))(\hat{p}_2 - \hat{p}_1) - 2\rho^\alpha \bar{p}dR \,, \tag{5.21}$$

$$2\rho^\beta d T_2^\beta = \hat{r} - (m_A^\beta - \rho^\beta \bar{p}\bar{D}_A^\beta)(\hat{p}_2 - \hat{p}_1) \,, \tag{5.22}$$

$$d T_1^\alpha = d T_2^\beta \,. \tag{5.23}$$

Note that in the expressions above as well as below, parameters ρ^j, m_B^j, $m_A^j, \varepsilon_A^j, \varepsilon_B^j, s_A^j$, and s_B^j are all evaluated at $(p, Y) = (\bar{p}, \bar{Y}^j)$. By (5.21)–(5.23), we have

$$\mathrm{d}\,T_1^\alpha = \mathrm{d}\,T_2^\beta = \frac{1}{2(\rho^\alpha + \rho^\beta)}\,(m_A^\alpha - \rho^\alpha \bar{p}\,(\bar{D}_A^\alpha - \bar{X}_A^\alpha)$$

$$- m_A^\beta + \rho^\beta \bar{p} \bar{D}_A^\beta)\,(\hat{p}_2 - \hat{p}_1) - \frac{\rho^\alpha}{\rho^\alpha + \rho^\beta}\bar{p}\mathrm{d}R\,. \tag{5.24}$$

By (5.23) the total differentiation of (5.12) and (5.13) at b implies

$$\hat{p}_2 = -\hat{p}_1, \tag{5.25}$$

$$\hat{p}_2 - \hat{p}_1 = -\frac{m_A^\alpha - m_A^\beta}{\bar{D}_B^\alpha \Delta}\,(\mathrm{d}\,T_1^\alpha + \mathrm{d}\,T_2^\beta) + \frac{m_B^\alpha}{\bar{D}_B^\alpha \Delta/\bar{p}}\,2\mathrm{d}R, \tag{5.26}$$

where (5.26) follows since $m_B^j(p, Y) = (1/p)\,\partial D_B^j(1/p, Y/p)/\partial\,(Y/p)$ $|_{\mathrm{d}p\,=\,0}$, and where $\Delta = \varepsilon_B^\alpha + \varepsilon_A^\beta - 1$. Then, Assumption 2 implies $\Delta > 0$, which implies (5.17).[8] Since $\bar{p}\bar{D}_A^\alpha = \bar{p}(\bar{X}_A^\alpha - \bar{D}_A^\alpha) = \bar{D}_B^\alpha$ by Condition 4 and by β's spot budget constraint, expressions (5.24), (5.26), and (5.17) imply

$$\hat{p}_2 - \hat{p}_1 = 2(\rho^\beta m_B^\alpha + \rho^\alpha m_B^\beta)\,\frac{\bar{p}}{\delta}\mathrm{d}R\,, \tag{5.27}$$

where $\bar{D}_B^\alpha = \bar{M}$ gives δ as in (5.19). Since our assumptions imply $\delta > 0$, we may apply the implicit function theorem to (5.9)–(5.13). Thus, we have $\varepsilon > 0$ such that if $|R| < \varepsilon$, there is a unique differentiable function $(r(R),$ $p_1^f(R), p_2^f(R), T_1^\alpha(R), T_2^\beta(R))$ which satisfies (5.9)–(5.13).

Let $q(R)$ be defined by setting $(r, p_1, p_2) = (r(R), p_1^f(R), p_2^f(R))$ in (5.7). Since, by (5.25) and (5.27), $p_1^f(R) \neq p_2^f(R)$ for any small R, Lemma 1 implies that $(q(R), p_1^f(R), p_2^f(R), T_1^\alpha(R), T_2^\beta(R))$ is an equilibrium in the futures-spot system with $(\bar{X}_A^\alpha + R, \bar{X}_A^\alpha - R)$. To show the uniqueness of equilibrium, by Lemma 1 it suffices to show that the futures-spot system with small $R \neq 0$ has no equilibrium where $p_1^f = p_2^f$. If such an equilibrium exists, for some $R \neq 0$ there is no trade on the futures market; the pure-spot market system must have an equilibrium where $p_1^0 = p_2^0$. This is ruled out by Assumption 4, since by setting $\mathrm{d}T_1^\alpha = \mathrm{d}T_2^\beta$ in (5.26) we have

$$\hat{p}_2^0 - \hat{p}_1^0 = \frac{m_B^\alpha}{\bar{D}_B^\alpha \Delta/\bar{p}}\,2\mathrm{d}R\,. \tag{5.28}$$

Moreover, by the implicit function theorem we have function $(p_1^0(R), p_2^0(R))$ in the statement of the theorem. Since, given $p_1(0) = p_2(0) = \bar{p}$, we have

$$\frac{p_2(R) - p_1(R)}{2E(p_i(R))} \left(\frac{d}{dR} \frac{p_2(R) - p_1(R)}{2E(p_i(R))} \right) R = \frac{\hat{p}_2 - \hat{p}_1}{2dR} R,$$

(5.27) and (5.28) imply (5.16) and (5.18) together with $\bar{M} = \bar{D}_B^\alpha$.

Expressions (5.16) and (5.18) capture the degree of risk in the spot price distribution in the pure-spot and futures-spot market systems, respectively. In particular, the absolute values of the left-hand sides of expressions (5.10) and (5.18) represent the spot price variabilities, where we adopt the following definition.

Definition 4 $V = E(|x_i - E(x_i)|)/E(x_i)$ is the *variability* of a distribution (x_1, x_2).

We draw a few conclusions from expressions (5.16) and (5.18). First, *in the state where the supply of the good (A) with random output is larger, its spot relative price is lower both before and after opening a futures market, given that the good (B) with nonrandom output is normal for both agents.* Thus the presence of futures trading cannot under the normality assumption lead to perverse relative price effects, or what one might refer to as 'over-stabilization.' In the futures-spot market system the spot price variability depends upon both agents' marginal propensities to consume a good unlike in the pure-spot market system. This is explained by the fact that income risks are shared by means of income transfers which directly influence the demands of both agents.

Remark 1 As seen in the proof of Lemma 3, $Y_1^\alpha = p_1(\bar{X}_A^\alpha + R) + T_1^\alpha$ and $Y_2^\beta = X_M^\beta + T_2^\beta$. Therefore, comparing the spot budget constraints in Conditions 3 and 3', we have $T_1^\alpha = (p_1 - q)F^\alpha$ and $T_2^\beta = (p_2 - q)F^\beta$. This implies that T_1^α and T_2^β are the capital gains of agents α and β in states 1 and 2, respectively, which the purchases of futures contracts, F^α and F^β, generate. Therefore, we may regard a futures transaction as an *ex ante* exchange of state-contingent spot incomes, since capital gains T_1^α and T_2^β may be interpreted as the excess demands of agents α and β for states 1 and 2 spot incomes, respectively.

Remark 2 The spot price distribution in the pure-spot market system depends upon good A output distributions $(\bar{X}_A^\alpha + R, \bar{X}_A^\alpha - R)$. Term $(m_B^\alpha/(\bar{D}_B^\alpha \Delta/\bar{p}))(2dR)$ in equation (5.26) captures the *direct effect* of output risk on spot price risk. The coefficient $m_B^\alpha/(\bar{D}_B^\alpha \Delta/\bar{p})$, which is well known in deterministic trade theory (see Caves and Jones, 1981, 4.S. 14), shows the change in the relative price of good A in the pure-spot market system when good A output increases by one unit. In the futures-spot market system, capital gains and losses influence the spot price distribution. This is illustrated by the first term on the right-hand side of equation (5.26), $-((m_A^\alpha - m_A^\beta)/\bar{D}_B^\alpha \Delta)$ $(dT_1^\alpha + dT_2^\beta)$, which we refer to as the *indirect effect* of output risk in the futures-spot market system. These capital gains and losses are nothing more than *ex post* income transfers between the two agents. The coefficient capturing the indirect effect, $-((m_A^\alpha - m_A^\beta)/\bar{D}_B^\alpha \Delta)$, which is also well known in trade theory (see Caves and Jones, 1981, 4.S. 21), shows the effect of an income transfer from agent β to agent α on the relative price of good A. Note that the second term on the right-hand side of equation (5.26) is the same as the term in equation (5.28) showing the direct effect in the pure-spot market system. Thus, in the futures-spot market system output risk has both direct and indirect effects on spot price risk. The effect of opening a futures market is captured by the indirect effect, $-((m_A^\alpha - m_A^\beta)/\bar{D}_B^\alpha \Delta)$ $(dT_1^\alpha + dT_2^\beta)$.

Remark 3 An important technical trick we develop in this study is to carry out the analysis of the futures-spot market system in the Arrow-securities-spot market system. Since, given the uniform output distribution ($\bar{X}_A^\alpha$, $\bar{X}_A^\alpha$), the spot price $\bar{p}$ is state independent and must be equal to the price of a futures contract, demand and supply in the futures market are indeterminate. This prevents us from applying the implicit function theorem directly to the equilibrium conditions in the futures-spot market system. Our method avoids this difficulty.

Remark 4 The assumption of $\phi_1 = \phi_2$ is made purely for the sake of simplifying our notation. Equations (5.9)–(5.13) indicate that we have a result similar to Theorem 1 even without this assumption.

6 DECOMPOSITION OF THE EFFECT OF OPENING A FUTURES MARKET

For the sake of simplicity, we focus upon the normal case where the supply of the good with random output and its spot relative price are negatively correlated. To this end, let us make the following assumption.

Assumption 6 The good (B) with nonrandom output is a normal good for both agents.

We prove the following theorem.

Theorem 2 Denote by V^0 and V^f the variability of equilibrium spot price *distributions in the pure-spot and futures-spot market systems with good A output distribution $(X^\alpha_{A1}, X^\alpha_{A2})$, respectively. Then, we have*

$$V^0 - V^f \cong (\sigma_P + \sigma_I)R, \tag{5.29}$$

$$\sigma_P = \frac{m^\alpha_B (m^\alpha_A - m^\beta_A)^2}{(\Delta\delta\bar{M}/\bar{p})} \geqslant 0, \tag{5.30}$$

$$\sigma_I = \frac{(m^\alpha_A - m^\beta_A)(\rho^\beta m^\alpha_B + \rho^\alpha m^\beta_B - \rho^\alpha(s^\alpha_B + s^\beta_A))}{(\Delta\delta/\bar{p})}, \tag{5.31}$$

where all the parameters are those in Theorem 1.

PROOF   By Assumption 6 and Definition 3, $V^k = (p^k_2(R) - p^k_1(R))/2E(p^k_i(R)), k = 0, f$. Thus, expressions (5.27) and (5.28) imply the theorem.

$V^0 - V^f$ captures the extent to which spot price variability is altered by opening a futures market. We decompose $V^0 - V^f$ into two parts, $\sigma_P R$ and $\sigma_I R$. We call σ_P the *coefficient of pure price arbitrage* and σ_I the *coefficient of income-risk-sharing*. The reason for adopting this terminology can be explained as follows.

Consider the situation in which both agents are close to income risk neutral, so that ρ^α and ρ^β are nearly zero. In this case from (5.30) and (5.31) σ_I becomes negligible relative to σ_P, and the change in spot price variability $V^0 - V^f$ is approximated by $\sigma_P R$. When agents are income risk neutral, no benefit is gained from the sharing of risk. But in the absence of a futures market, differing implicit relative prices for state contingent income are established for the two agents. A futures market provides the possibility of arbitrage between the previously unconnected 'markets,' and leads to an equalization of implicit relative prices. This effect is summarized by the coefficient σ_P. In accord with intuition, this arbitrage effect always works in the direction of increasing the stability of spot prices, since $\sigma_P \geqslant 0$. Indeed, equation (5.18) together with the expression for V^k in the proof of Theorem 2 indicates that as ρ^α and ρ^β approach zero, so does V^f. In other words, if both agents are almost income risk neutral, opening a futures market eliminates spot price risk almost completely.[9]

The coefficient of income-risk sharing, σ_I, shows the effect on spot price variability that is attributable to the function of a futures market as an income-risk-sharing device. That is, σ_I captures the entire effect of opening a futures market if futures trading is explained completely by the income-risk sharing motive, or if there is an infinitely income-risk averse agent. As an agent becomes more income-risk averse, the income-risk sharing motive outweighs any response to relative prices in determining a trade pattern in the futures market. Thus, the coefficient of pure price arbitrage becomes negligible. Mathematically, this fact is shown by

$$\lim_{\rho^\alpha \to \infty} \sigma_I = \frac{(m_A^\alpha - m_A^\beta)(m_B^\beta - s_B^\alpha - s_A^\beta)}{(\Delta(s_B^\alpha + s_A^\beta)\bar{M}/\bar{p})},$$ (5.32)

$$\lim_{\rho^\beta \to \infty} \sigma_I = \frac{(m_A^\alpha - m_A^\beta)m_B^\alpha}{(\Delta(s_B^\alpha + s_A^\beta)\bar{M}/\bar{p})},$$ (5.33)

$$\lim_{\rho^\alpha \to \infty} \sigma_P = \lim_{\rho^\beta \to \infty} \sigma_P = 0.$$ (5.34)

Note that the sign of the coefficient of income-risk sharing σ_I is ambiguous. The implication of this coefficient is explained in detail in section 7.

The total effect of a futures market is characterized by the sum of the two coefficients, $\sigma_P + \sigma_I$. Therefore, the direction of the effect of opening a futures market on spot price variability is ambiguous. However, since σ_P is always positive, there is a presumption in favor of the situation where a futures market is spot price stabilizing.

This presumption is stronger the less risk-averse agents are.

7 REAL INCOME VARIABILITY AND SPOT PRICE VARIABILITY

Clearly, the real income of an agent in the spot market varies over states of nature. The consideration of real income variability helps us to understand the impact of the coefficient of income-risk-sharing, σ_I, on spot price variability. Note that we measure 'real income' in units of *ex post* or 'spot' utility. Then we have the following theorem.

Theorem 3 Assume the conditions and notation in Theorem 1. Then, if $|R| < \varepsilon$, the equilibrium distributions of agent j's ex post utility in the pure-spot and futures-spot market systems with good A output distribution $(X_{A1}^\alpha, X_{A2}^\alpha)$ are expressed by the differentiable functions of R, $(u_1^{j0}(R), u_2^{j0}(R))$ and $(u_1^{jf}(R), u_2^{jf}(R))$, respectively, for $j = \alpha, \beta$. Moreover, we have

$$\frac{u_1^{\alpha 0}(R) - u_2^{\alpha 0}(R)}{2E(u_i^{\alpha 0}(R))} \cong \frac{\bar{v}_Y^\alpha}{\bar{v}^\alpha} \frac{s_B^\alpha + s_A^\beta - m_B^\beta}{(\Delta/\bar{p})} R,$$ (5.35)

$$\frac{u_1^{\beta 0}(R) - u_2^{\beta 0}(R)}{2E(u_i^{\beta 0}(R))} \cong \frac{\bar{v}_Y^\beta}{\bar{v}^\beta} \frac{m_B^\alpha}{(\Delta/\bar{p})} R,$$ (5.36)

$$\frac{u_1^{\alpha f}(R) - u_2^{\alpha f}(R)}{2E(u_i^{\alpha f}(R))} \cong \frac{\bar{v}_Y}{\bar{v}^\alpha} \frac{\rho^\beta \bar{M}(s_B^\alpha + s_A^\beta) + m_B^\beta(m_A^\alpha - m_A^\beta)}{(\delta/\bar{p})} R,$$ (5.37)

$$\frac{u_1^{\beta f}(R) - u_2^{\beta f}(R)}{2E(u_i^{\beta f}(R))} \cong \frac{\bar{v}_Y^\beta}{\bar{v}^\beta} \frac{\rho^\alpha \bar{M}(s_B^\alpha + s_A^\beta) - m_B^\alpha(m_A^\alpha - m_A^\beta)}{(\delta/\bar{p})} R, \qquad (5.38)$$

where $\bar{v}^j = v^j(\bar{p}, \bar{Y}^j)$ and $\bar{v}_Y^j = v_Y^j(\bar{p}, \bar{Y}^j)$.

PROOF   By Theorem 1 and its proof, we have functions $r(R)$, $T_1^\alpha(R)$, and $T_2^\beta(R)$ which satisfy equations (5.9)–(5.13) for R, $|R| < \varepsilon$, together with $p_1^f(R)$ and $p_2^f(R)$. Thus we have

$$(u_1^{\alpha f}(R), u_2^{\alpha f}(R)) = (v^{\alpha f}(p_1^f(R), p_1^f(R)(\bar{X}_A^\alpha + R) + T_1^\alpha(R)),$$
$$v^{\alpha f}(p_2^f(R), p_2^f(R)(\bar{X}_A^\alpha - R) - rT_1^\alpha(R))$$

which is differentiable. Let $u_1^\alpha = v^\alpha(p_1, p_1(\bar{X}_A^\alpha + R) + T_1^\alpha)$ and $u_2^\alpha = v^\alpha(p_2, p_2(\bar{X}_A^\alpha - R) - rT_1^\alpha)$. Totally differentiating these at $r = 1$, $T_1^\alpha = 0$, $p_1 = p_2 = \bar{p}$, and $R = 0$, we have

$$\hat{u}_1^\alpha - \hat{u}_2^\alpha = \frac{\bar{v}_Y^\alpha}{\bar{v}}(2\bar{p}\mathrm{d}R + 2\mathrm{d}T_1^\alpha + \bar{p}(\bar{D}_A^\alpha - \bar{X}_A^\alpha)(\hat{p}_2 - \hat{p}_1)). \qquad (5.39)$$

Since, as in the discussion at the end of the proof of Theorem 1, we have

$$\frac{u_1^{\alpha f}(R) - u_2^{\alpha f}(R)}{E(u_i^{\alpha f}(R))} \cong \left(\frac{1}{\bar{v}^\alpha}\frac{\mathrm{d}}{\mathrm{d}R}(u_1^\alpha - u_2^\alpha)\right) R,$$

by equations (5.24), (5.27), and (5.39) we have expression (5.37), using $\bar{p}(\bar{X}_A^\alpha - \bar{D}_A^\alpha) = \bar{D}_B^\alpha = \bar{p}\bar{D}_B^\alpha = \bar{M}$. In a similar way, we have expression (5.38). We define $(u_1^{\alpha 0}(R), u_2^{\alpha 0}(R)) = (v^\alpha(p_1^0(R), p_1^0(R)(\bar{X}_A^\alpha + R)),$ $v^\alpha(p_2^0(R), p_2^0(R)(\bar{X}_A^\alpha - R))$, which is differentiable. Let $u_1^\alpha = v^\alpha(p_1, p_1(\bar{X}_A^\alpha + R))$ and $u_2^\alpha = v^\alpha(p_2, p_2(\bar{X}_A^\alpha - R))$. Totally differentiating these at $p_1 = p_2 = \bar{p}$ and $R = 0$, we have

$$\hat{u}_1^\alpha - \hat{u}_2^\alpha = \frac{\bar{v}_Y^\alpha}{\bar{v}^\alpha}(2\bar{p}\mathrm{d}R + \bar{p}(\bar{D}_A^\alpha - \bar{X}_A^\alpha)(\hat{p}_2 - \hat{p}_1)). \qquad (5.40)$$

Thus, using equations (5.28) and (5.17), and $p(\bar{X}_A^\alpha - \bar{D}_A^\alpha) = \bar{D}_B^\alpha = \bar{p}\bar{D}_A^\beta = \bar{M}$, we have expression (5.35). In a similar way we obtain expression (5.39).

Expressions (5.35) and (5.36) are well known in trade theory (see Caves and Jones, 1981, 4.S. 15). They capture the conditions under which an agent's 'real income,' $(u_1^{j0}, u_2^{j0}), j = \alpha, \beta$, is positively correlated with the output of good A, $(\bar{X}_A^\alpha + R, \bar{X}_A^\alpha - R)$, in the pure-spot market system. Given $m_B^\alpha > 0$, for agent β real income is always positively correlated with the random output by the terms-of-trade effect. For agent α a negative correlation can occur, if $s_B^\alpha + s_A^\beta - m_B^\beta < 0$. (Such a phenomenon is known as immiserizing growth in the trade literature.) Expressions (5.37) and (5.38) indicate that opening a futures market changes the conditions guaranteeing a positive correlation between real income and output distributions. Let us suppose that one of the two agents is infinitely income-risk averse, but the other is not. Since by definition $\delta \to \infty$, expressions (5.37) and (5.38) imply

$$\lim_{\rho^\alpha \to \infty} \frac{u_1^{\alpha f}(R) - u_2^{\alpha f}(R)}{2E(u_i^{\alpha f}(R))} \cong 0, \tag{5.41}$$

$$\lim_{\rho^\beta \to \infty} \frac{u_1^{\beta f}(R) - u_2^{\beta f}(R)}{2E(u_i^{\beta f}(R))} \cong 0, \tag{5.42}$$

These results indicate that an infinitely income-risk averse agent trades in the futures market so as to eliminate all 'real income', risk. We are now able to relate this effect of a futures market on 'real income' variability to that on spot price variability. Suppose that agent α is infinitely income-risk averse ($\rho^\alpha = \infty$), but that agent β is not. If $s_B^\alpha + s_A^\beta - m_B^\beta > 0$, expression (5.35) implies that agent α has a higher 'real income' in state 1 than in state 2 before the futures market opens. When it opens, agent α therefore trades in futures contracts to take a capital gain in state 2 and a capital loss in state 1 in order to absorb the risk in real income completely. Thus, in the spot market an income transfer is made from agent α to agent β in state 1 and from β to α in state 2. Suppose $m_A^\alpha - m_A^\beta < 0$. Then, the transfers create an excess demand for good A in state 1 and an excess supply of good A in state 2, at the spot price distribution $(p_1^0(R), p_2^0(R))$. The excess demand raises the relative price of good A in state 1, and the excess supply lowers it in state 2. This implies that the futures market is spot-price stabilizing, since p_1^0 $(R) < p_2^0(R)$ by expression (5.16) and Assumption 6. Therefore, $\rho^\alpha = \infty$, $s_B^\alpha + s_A^\beta - m_B^\beta > 0$ and $m_A^\alpha - m_A^\beta < 0$ imply stabilization of the spot-price distribution $(p_1^0(R), p_2^0(R))$ in the presence of a futures market. It is this relationship that is captured by equations (5.32) and (5.34). In a similar way, we may explain equations (5.33) and (5.34). The fact that, in equation (5.33), the sign of $\lim_{\rho^\beta \to \infty} \sigma_I$ does not depend upon $s_B^\alpha + s_A^\beta$ unlike that of $\lim_{\rho^\alpha \to \infty} \sigma_I$ is due to the fact that the fluctuation of β's real income is entirely attributable to the terms-of-trade effect, which is captured by expressions (5.16) and (5.36).

8 CONCLUSIONS

We have characterized the effect of forward and futures trading on spot price variability and on spot real income variability in markets for foreign exchange and for agricultural commodities. The importance of a general equilibrium approach in analyzing such markets has been explained. Analysis of the effect of opening a market is intractable in a complex model. Thus, we have focused upon a two-by-two-by-two setting where the production risk in the economy is small. In order to compare equilibria in economies with and without a futures market, we have linearly approximated them around the equilibria in the economies where there is no production risk. In contrast, the partial-equilibrium approach allows Turnovsky (1983), Kawai (1983a, 1983b, 1984), and Turnovsky and Campbell (1985) to consider an arbitrary size of risk.

Our major conclusions follow. If agents are close to income-risk neutral, the opening of a futures market tends to reduce spot-price variability generated by production risk (pure price arbitrage effects). It is interesting to observe that Turnovsky (1983) and Kawai (1983a, 1983b, 1984) obtain similar results in a partial-equilibrium setting which is entirely different from the setting of the present study. If agents are risk averse, the effect of futures trading on spot-price variability is explained by this pure price arbitrage effect and an income risk sharing effect. It is shown that the income risk sharing effect is closely related to the effect of futures trading on real income variability. The direction of the income risk sharing effect is ambiguous. Therefore, there is a presumption that forward and futures trading are spot-price stabilizing. This presumption is stronger if the income-risk aversion of agents is weaker. A forward or futures market affects spot price variability only if agents have different tastes (or, more specifically, different marginal propensities to consume goods).

We have deliberately chosen not to incorporate in the model the supply responses of producers to the opening of a futures market in order to simplify our analysis and to capture the most basic difference between general and partial equilibrium effects. Turnovsky (1983), Kawai (1983a, 1983b, 1984), and Turnovsky and Campbell (1985) consider both supply and demand responses to the opening of a futures market in their partial equilibrium framework. In general, the general equilibrium approach and the partial equilibrium approach have different limitations and provide different insights. In this sense we regard our study as complementary to their work.

NOTES

1   An example is the closing of the futures market for onions in the US in 1958 (v. Goss and Yamey (1976), p. 59, footnote 99).
2   See Turnovsky (1983) for a list of such studies in the context of commodity markets.
3   There are two important channels through which forward and futures trading

affect spot price distributions. This study focuses on the one discussed above. The other is that producers and storage operators behave differently in the presence of a futures market. The implications of this observation have been extensively discussed in the literature. See, for example, Danthine (1978), Anderson and Danthine (1983), Newbery and Stiglitz (1981), Britto (1984), among others.

4   We specify the demand for the numeraire good B in this way for convenience of exposition. The treatment of both goods is symmetric in that their demand functions depend upon the relative price of the good and income measured in terms of the other good.

5   We make no distinction between forward and futures contracts, in common with much of the literature. Simple arbitrage considerations ensure that prices in forward and futures markets will be closely related, and the reasons for operating in one market rather than the other raise institutional issues which are not of relevance here.

6   These relationships follow straightforwardly from the relevant Slutsky equations.

7   This result is obtained by differentiating the identity $v_p^j(p, Y) \equiv - v_Y^j(p, Y) D_A^j(p, Y)$ with respect to Y.

8   As noted above, $p_1 = \bar{p}$, $T_1^\alpha = 0$, and $R = 0$ satisfies equation (5.12). That is, $D_B(1/\bar{p}, \bar{X}_A^\alpha) = \bar{p}D_A^\beta(\bar{p}, X_B^\beta)$. Note, by the definition of demand function D_A^α, we have $(1/\bar{p})D_B^\alpha(1/\bar{p}, \bar{X}_A^\alpha) = \bar{X}_A^\alpha - D_A^\alpha(\bar{p}, \bar{X}_A^\alpha)$. Thus, if we define the excess demand function $ED_A(p) = D_A^\beta(p, X_B^\beta) + D_A^\alpha(p, \bar{X}_A^\alpha) - \bar{X}_A^\alpha = D_A^\beta(p, X_B^\beta) - D_B^\alpha(1/p, \bar{X}_A^\alpha)/p$, it must follow that $ED_A(\bar{p}) = 0$. Therefore if $dX_A^\alpha = dX_B^\beta = 0$ we have

$$\frac{dED_A}{\bar{D}_A^\beta} = \frac{\bar{p}}{\bar{D}_A^\beta} \frac{\partial D_A^\beta(\bar{p}, X_B^\beta)}{\partial p} \hat{p} + \frac{1/\bar{p}}{\bar{D}_B^\alpha} \frac{\partial}{\partial(1/p)} D_B^\alpha\left(\frac{1}{\bar{p}}, \bar{X}_A^\alpha\right) \hat{p} + \hat{p} = - \Delta\hat{p}.$$

We know that if $\bar{p}$ is the unique equilibrium, $\bar{p}ED_A(p) + ED_B(p) > 0$ for all p satisfying $p \neq \bar{p}$. (See Arrow and Hahn (1971), Theorem 17, chapter 9.) By Walras' law $ED_B(p) = -pED_A(p)$. Therefore $(p - \bar{p}) ED_A(p) < 0$. Expanding this expression in a Taylor series about $\bar{p}$ to second order, we find that $\partial ED_A(\bar{p})/\partial p < 0$, which implies that $\Delta > 0$.

9   If $\rho^\alpha = \rho^\beta = 0$, $p_2^f(R) - p_1^f(R) \cong 0$ by expression (5.18). In this case, from Lemma 2, it is not guaranteed that $(p_1^f(R), p_2^f(R))$ is an equilibrium spot price distribution in the futures-spot market system, although it is one in the Arrow-securities-spot market system if $m_A^\alpha \neq m_A^\beta$ (i.e. if $\delta > 0$).

REFERENCES

Anderson, R. W. and J.-P. Danthine (1983) Hedger diversity in futures markets. *Economic Journal* 93, 370–89.

Arrow, K. J. (1963) The role of securities in the optimal allocation of risk bearing. *Review of Economic Studies* 31, 91–6.

Arrow, K. J. and F. H. Hahn (1971) *General Competitive Analysis*. Edinburgh: Oliver and Boyd.

Britto, R. (1984) The simultaneous determination of spot and futures prices in a simple model with production risk. *Quarterly Journal of Economics* 99, 351-65.

Cass, D. and K. Shell (1983) Do sunspots matter?, *Journal of Political Economy* 91, 193-227.

Caves, R. and R. Jones (1981) *World Trade and Payments*, 2nd edn. Boston: Little, Brown.

Danthine, J.-P. (1978) Information, futures markets and stabilizing speculation. *Journal of Economic Theory* 17, 79-98.

Goss, B. A. and B. S. Yamey (1976) *The Economics of Futures Trading*. New York: John Wiley.

Jones, R. W. (1975) Presumption and the transfer problem. *Journal of International Economics* 5, 263-74.

Kawai, M. (1983a) Spot and futures prices of nonstorable commodities under rational expectations. *Quarterly Journal of Economics* 98, 235-54.

———— (1983b) Price volatility of storable commodities under rational expectations in spot and futures markets. *International Economic Review* 24, 435-58.

———— (1984) The effect of forward exchange on spot-rate volatility under risk and rational expectations. *Journal of International Economics* 16, 155-72.

Malinvaud, E. (1972) The allocation of individual risks in large markets. *Journal of Economic Theory* 4, 312-28.

Newbery, D. M. G. and J. E. Stiglitz (1981) *The Theory of Commodity Price Stabilization*. Oxford: Oxford University Press.

Peck, A. E. (1976) Futures markets, supply response and price stability. *Quarterly Journal of Economics* 90, 407-23.

Samuelson, P. A. (1952) The transfer problem and transport costs. *Economic Journal* 62, 278-304.

Sarris, A. (1980) Commodity price stabilization with private storage and futures markets. Working Paper no. 112, Division of Agricultural Sciences, University of California, Berkeley.

Turnovsky, S. J. (1979) Futures markets, private storage and price stabilization. *Journal of Public Economics* 12, 301-27.

———— (1983) The determination of spot and futures prices with storable commodities. *Econometrica* 51, 1363-88.

Turnovsky, S. J. and R. B. Campbell (1985) The stabilizing and welfare properties of futures markets: a simulation approach. *International Economic Review* 26, 277-303.

Part III

Information

6

Risk Allocation and Information: Some Recent Theoretical Developments

K. J. Arrow

I propose to set forth here some new developments in the theory of risk allocation in a market economy. In contrast to earlier work, these revolve about the effects of information on the viability and efficiency of risk-bearing markets. Specific questions raised are the allocative effects of additional publicly available information and of possibly differing private information.

Markets are means for the mutually beneficial exchange of goods and for inducing the transformation of goods from one form to another. We will take it as axiomatic that individuals are risk-averse, so that the bearing of risks is a cost and the shifting of risks to others a good. The existence of insurance, common stocks, and many other devices testifies to the validity of the assumption of risk aversion, though it must be admitted that gambling and perhaps some speculative activity might be regarded as evidence for risk preference in some contexts.

As part, then, of the general use of the market for exchanging goods, we expect to find markets in which risks are traded. The risks are shifted to those more able to bear them until at the margin the cost to the risk bearer is equal to the benefit to the risk shifter. More specifically, there are, in addition to the usual commodities, a set of *contingent commodities*: a unit contingent commodity is an agreement to deliver one unit of a specific good or (more generally in practice) to pay one unit of money if and only if a specified event has occurred. An insurance policy is a good example.

If an event is certain to occur, then a commodity contract contingent on its occurrence is identical with the corresponding unconditional contract, and creation of the contingent commodity market has no economic significance. If an event is certain not to occur, then a commodity contingent on

Reproduced from *The Geneva Papers on Risk and Insurance*, no. 8 (1978). Originally presented as the First Annual Lecture of the Geneva Association, November 1977.

that event must have price zero, and again existence of the contingent market has no economic significance. However, if there is uncertainty about the event, then in general a market for contracts contingent upon that event will be viable; there will be a price at which supply and demand will balance with some buyers and some sellers.

In fact if markets are created for every commodity for every contingency, then the general competitive equilibrium leads to an efficient allocation of risk bearing (Arrow, 1953; Debreu, 1953, 1959, ch. 7).

The existence of competitive equilibrium with universal contingent contracts follows by suitable reinterpretation of the usual existence results. Even if the markets only exist for some contingencies, existence of equilibrium can still be demonstrated (Radner, 1968). However, as is usual when markets are absent, the market allocation of risk bearing is no longer efficient; there exist conceivable reallocations which would make everyone better off.

It is a matter of some controversy how to represent the concept of uncertainty. The most usual doctrine represents uncertainty by probabilities, and I shall follow that convention here. It certainly is the only theory that has shown itself to be useful in deriving any results. Within this framework, however, is a point which has created controversy for generations: is probability objective or subjective? That is, given an event, is there one probability to which all reasonable people must subscribe, or can individuals differ? The currently most accepted doctrine is the subjective probability theory: probabilities express individual beliefs just as utilities express individual tastes. Individual behavior is determined by maximizing expected utility, where the expectation is computed according to the individual's own probabilities.

Under the subjective probability theory, there are two motives for trading in contingent commodities. One is the desire to avoid risks fundamental to insurance; this depends on the existence of uncertainty and would hold even if everyone agreed on the probabilities. The other motive derives from differences of opinion; if I judge an event more probable than you do, then, other things being equal, there will be a price at which I am willing to sell a contract contingent on that event and you are willing to buy it. Betting on horse races is a pure example. For a more serious example, it is clear that many of the participants on the commodity futures or stock markets are basing their actions on anticipations of the future; since some sell and some buy, these anticipations must differ. From this viewpoint, the efficiency of the competitive market in contingent claims remains valid, in the sense that there is no alternative feasible allocation which will yield every individual a higher expected utility based on his or her own probabilities.

Both the subjective and the objective probability theories, however, recognize that there may be differences of opinion based on different observations. As part of the complete structure of probability beliefs about the world, every individual has conditional probabilities. The probability that an event A occurs will in general be changed by the knowledge that another event B has occurred. Thus, the probability that it will snow on January 1, 1990 in Cambridge, Massachusetts, will be some number which will be approximately the proportion of the times it has snowed on January 1 over the years for which observations have been made. But on December 31, 1989, a more relevant probability will be that given by the weather map on that date – roughly, the proportion of times that a similar weather map has been followed by snow the next day.

Therefore, two individuals with the same probability beliefs may nevertheless have different probabilities for the same event when entering the market, because they have observed different other events. The existence of information derived from observations can have profound effects on the working of the risk-sharing markets. Indeed, the problem of differential information has long been known in the insurance literature under such headings as 'moral hazard' and 'adverse selection.'

In this chapter I want to survey some aspects of the effects of information on the markets for contingent goods, by means of a toy example studied under different informational assumptions. The theory is still under development and was influenced by many scholars; I give specific references in appropriate places.

First, some definitions. By 'information,' I mean any observation which effectively changes probabilities according to the principles of conditional probability. The prior probabilities are defined for all events, an event being described by statements about both the variables that are relevant to individual welfare and those that define the range of possible observations. Given an observation, there is a conditional or posterior distribution of possible values of the welfare-relevant variables.

Consider first the case of a single individual. Suppose information is offered to him or her at no cost. Should the individual accept it? Clearly the answer is yes. He or she cannot be worse off because the information can always be disregarded. In more technical language, the individual, in the absence of information, will have to make a decision. That is, he or she will have to choose among a set of alternative actions. Since the consequences of each action are uncertain, the choice will be made so as to maximize expected utility. Now suppose the individual is told that information will be made available; that is, an observation which specifies which of a number of possible alternative events occurred will be made and transmitted to him. The decision can be made after the observation has been received and therefore maximizes expected utility computed according to the probabilities conditional on the observation. The decision made will now depend on the actual event observed. To put it slightly differently, the individual can, before receiving the information, choose a *decision function*, which specifies the decision made for each possible observation. The decision made in the absence of information is a special kind of decision function, one which specifies the same decision for any possible observation. Therefore, the optimal decision function must be at least as good, in the expected-utility sense, as a constant decision, simply from the definition of the word 'optimal.' In general, the best decision function will be better, in the expected-utility sense, than the best decision which disregards the observation.

This analysis neglects the cost of acquiring and using the information. The most important and most stubborn of these costs are the limits on individual information-processing capacity. These costs are extremely important in actual economic life, but I wish to neglect them for the present discussion. The point to be stressed here is rather the difference between the individual and the social values of information, even apart from costs. As will be seen, when risks are allocated by the market, information may be harmful rather than beneficial.

Let us review briefly the theory of allocation under contingent contracts by means of the simplest possible example. Suppose the world can be in only two possible states, although it is not known to any party which is the truth. Further, suppose there are only two individuals. More precisely, to preserve the competitive flavor, we should assume two types of individuals, with indefinitely many in each type and with identity of tastes and endowments among all individuals within a type. The effect is the same as if there were two individuals, each of whom, however, behaved like a perfect competitor in taking prices as parameters. Call the members of our tiny economy Walras and Böhm-Bawerk. Suppose further that their subjective probabilities for the two events are the same. (I shall maintain throughout the hypothesis that the subjective probabilities of the events held *prior* to any observations are the same to all individuals. Any differences in probability judgments when entering a market are attributed to different observations.) In fact, to make the examples even simpler, it will be assumed that the probability of each event is 1/2 for each individual. Suppose that, of the two states, state 1 is relatively more favorable to Walras than to Böhm-Bawerk. The Walras sells contracts payable if state 1 occurs and buys contracts payable if state 2 occurs.

Let me state a whimsical, more specific example which will be used throughout the chapter as a theme for variations. Suppose there are two commodities, 'wheat' and 'barley,' which are perfect substitutes in consumption but produced under different conditions. If v is the total amount of wheat and barley consumed by an individual, then the individual's von Neumann–Morgenstern utility is assumed to be log v. Walras has initially a stock of 1 unit of wheat, Böhm-Bawerk a stock of 1 unit of barley; there is no production. There are two weather states, with probability 1/2 each: in

Table 6.1   Output as a function of state of the world

	State of the world	
Individual	W	B
Walras	1	0
Böhm-Bawerk	0	1

state W, all the barley is destroyed and none of the wheat; in B, all the wheat is destroyed and none of the barley. The effective initial holdings of the consumers' good, 'wheat plus barley,' are given in table 6.1

There are two contracts on the market: delivery of the consumers' good if W and delivery of the good if B. Because of the total symmetry of the assumptions, the two contracts have equal unit prices. In equilibrium, Walras sells 1/2 unit of wheat if W and buys 1/2 unit of barley if B. Böhm-Bawerk does the opposite. The expected utilities of Walras and Böhm-Bawerk are the same, both being $(1/2) \log (1/2) + (1/2) \log (1/2) = \log (1/2)$. For ease of understanding, it is preferable to state the *certainty-equivalent income* instead of expected utility, that is, that income which, if obtained with certainty, would have a utility equal to the given expected utility. If y^* is the certainty-equivalent income, then

$$\log y^* = E(\log y),$$

or

$$y^* = \text{antilog } E(\log y),$$

where y is the variable consumption.

To cover the general case, let p_W and $p_B = 1 - p_W$ be the probabilities of states W and B, respectively, from the viewpoint of any particular individual. Let y_W and y_B be the individual's consumption under the respective states. Then, his or her certainty-equivalent income is

$$y^* = y_W^{p_W} y_B^{p_B}.$$

In the present case, $p_W = p_B = 1/2$, *so that*

$$y^* = (y_W y_B)^{1/2}. \tag{6.1}$$

It is seen that with perfect contingent markets but no information,

$$y_W^* = y_B^* = 1/2. \tag{6.2}$$

A major theme of this chapter is the surprising fact that an increase in information may *lower* the efficiency of the market, as first noted by Hirshleifer (1971). The simplest illustration already occurs if information is introduced into the above example. Suppose the information is *public*, by which is meant that both parties know it. Because there are only two possible states of the world, information consists of knowing which state will prevail. Clearly, if W is known, Böhm-Bawerk will have no purchasing power; therefore no transactions will take place (this is in fact the competitive equilibrium allocation, with all prices for the contingent commodities as possible equilibria). Then Walras will consume 1 unit, for utility 0, Böhm-Bawerk 0 units, for utility $-\infty$, if W occurs. If B occurs, the allocation is reversed. Ex ante, states W and B occur with probability 1/2 each; hence, for each individual the expected utility is $-\infty$, and therefore,

$$y_W^* = y_B^* = 0. \tag{6.3}$$

Thus, the existence of public information effectively prevents the sharing of risk bearing and destroys the corresponding utility gain.

In the preceding example, public information effectively reduced the market to autarchy. The information eliminated the possibility of trading risks without doing any offsetting good. The reason for this is that the information has no social use in a pure exchange economy. If production is introduced, however, it is reasonable to suppose that information enhances productive capability. If inputs are made before outputs, then, under uncertainty, outputs are a random function of inputs. Information reduces the uncertainty of output for any given input, and therefore should improve the allocation of resources for production.

Let me now introduce a simple example, which generalizes the previous one and at the same time demonstrates the possibility that information increases productivity. Instead of being endowed with wheat or barley, let each member of the market be endowed with land which can be sown to either wheat or barley according to the decision of the owner. We retain the assumption about the unknown state of the world; in W weather, only wheat grows; in B weather, only barley. Walras is better off than Böhm-Bawerk in W weather in the sense that if they both plant their entire land (one unit for each) in wheat, then Walras' output is greater than Böhm-Bawerk's; the opposite holds in B weather. The production hypothesis is summarized in table 6.2. The parameter a satisfies the condition, $0 \leq a < 1$. The utility functions and prior probabilities of the two states are as before. If $a = 0$, this production model is equivalent to the pure exchange model; Walras' land can only be used for wheat, so that his output is the same as his endowment in the pure exchange model for each state, and the same is true of Böhm-Bawerk.

Each individual can sow part of his land to wheat and part to barley; the amounts produced under each state are proportional to the amounts sown. Thus, if Walras plant 2/3 of his land in wheat and 1/3 in barley, his output is 2/3 if W, $a/3$ if B.

Table 6.2 Output as a function of production decision and state of the world

Individual	State of the world	
	W	B
Walras	1 if sown to wheat	a if sown to barley
	0 if sown to barley	0 if sown to wheat
Böhm-Bawerk	a if sown to wheat	1 if sown to barley
	0 if sown to barley	0 if sown to wheat

If $a = 1$, then Walras and Böhm-Bawerk have identical production possibilities. No trade will occur in either the presence or the absence of information. But public information is certainly productive; if it is known that state W obtains, both will plaint to wheat, if B both to barley.

Retain the assumption that information is public. We can compare attained welfare levels with or without information and with or without the existence of contingent markets. There are four possible cases.

Case 1: No information, no contingent markets

Since each has to be autarchic, each plants so as to maximize the expected utility of consumption. Let Walras, for example, plant w in wheat and $b = 1 - w$ in barley. His output is w if W, ab if B. His expected utility is $(1/2) \log w + (1/2) \log (ab) = (1/2) \log w + (1/2) \log b + (1/2) \log a$. The optimal policy is clearly independent of a; it is $w = b = 1/2$. The situation for Böhm-Bawerk is symmetric. Straightforward calculation shows that

$$y_W^* = y_B^* = a^{1/2}/2.$$

Case 2: Contingent markets without information

There are now markets for wheat-claims conditional on W and for barley-claims contingent on B. Because of the symmetry of the assumptions, it is obvious that the prices of the two kinds of claims are the same.

Each individual can be thought of as made up of a firm and a consumer. The consumer's income is the profit of the firm. The firm can be thought of as supplying two joint products, wheat-claims if W and barley-claims if B. As in the usual theory of firms and households under certainty, the firm should maximize its profits independently of the tastes of the owning household. In this case, profits equal the total value of contingent claims sold. We assume honesty in sale, in that the number of claims sold for a given state does not exceed the amount the firm could supply in that state.

Since the prices of the two kinds of claims are equal, it is clear that Walras should sow his entire land to wheat and sell 1 unit of wheat claims; any land transferred to barley would yield a lesser value sold in the ratio $a : 1$. Similarly, Böhm-Bawerk sows his land to barley and sells one unit of barley claims. Under expected-utility maximization, each individual will spend half his income on claims of each kind; hence, each will receive $1/2$ unit of wheat if W and $1/2$ unit of barley if B, so that his income is $1/2$ with certainty.

Since $a < 1, 1/2 > a^{1/2}/2$; hence, introducing contingent markets without information increases the welfare of both.

Case 3:   Information without contingent markets

In the absence of contingent markets, there is no trade either before or after realization of the state of the weather. Clearly, both individuals plant wheat if W and barley if B. Walras realizes and consumes 1 if W and a if B, while Böhm-Bawerk has the same up to a permutation of the states. Therefore, each has a certainly-equivalent income of $(1 \cdot a)^{1/2}$. Each is obviously better off than in case 1. Introduction of public information increases welfare if there are no contingent markets, because it permits adaptation of production.

Is the outcome of case 3 better than that of case 2? Is it better to introduce public information or contingent markets, if only one is possible? Comparison of the certainty-equivalent incomes shows that case 3 yields better outcomes if and only if $a^{1/2} > 1/2$, or $a > 1/4$. The coefficient a measures what may be termed the *flexibility* of the economy, its ability to increase production in response to information.

Public information is better than the introduction of contingent markets if the economy is sufficiently flexible and not otherwise.

Case 4:   Information and contingent markets

It has already been pointed out that public information prevents the execution of mutually advantageous contingent contracts. But it should be noted that, technically speaking, the contingent markets are not 'destroyed.' Rather, the prices are such that each individual finds it most advantageous neither to buy nor to sell. Specifically, if state W obtains, barley claims have zero price. Then both individuals plant only wheat. Neither can plan to buy wheat claims, since they cannot sell barley claims. On the other hand, since both know that W obtains, neither will want to sell wheat claims, since all they could do with the proceeds would be to buy barley claims, which have no use. Hence supply and demand balance on both markets. However, from the welfare point of view, the situation is identical with that of public information and no markets.

The results of this section are set forth in table 6.3. Certainty-equivalent income for (No, No) is less than any of the other three. Certainty-equivalent

Table 6.3   Certainty-equivalent incomes for different combinations of public information and contingent markets

Public information	Contingent markets	Certainty-equivalent income
No	No	$a^{1/2}/2$
No	Yes	$1/2$
Yes	No	$a^{1/2}$
Yes	Yes	$a^{1/2}$

income for (Yes, No) is greater than that for (No, Yes) if and only if $a > 1/4$.

Now suppose that information is not public; specifically, assume that one member of our toy economy has information that the other does not have. For definiteness, we suppose that Walras knows the state of the weather while Böhm-Bawerk does not. Call this the hypothesis of *differential* information.

The concept of differential information is becoming increasingly recognized as central to many features of economic organization. The problems of adverse selection and moral hazard in insurance are special cases, as will be discussed subsequently; their implications for the general theory of risk bearing were suggested in Arrow (1965) and have been greatly developed in recent years. Akerlof (1970) showed how markets might disappear altogether when the parties have different information and know it.

When there is differential information, the prices obtaining on markets may be a means of transmitting information. The existence and efficiency properties of equilibria under these circumstances have been studied by Green (1973), Kihlstrom and Mirman (1975), Grossman (1976), Grossman and Stiglitz (1976), and Shubik (1977), among many others. These concepts will be illustrated in our very simple model.

Case 5:   Differential information without contingent markets

Walras plants entirely to wheat if W, to barley if B. His output is 1 if W, a if B; hence, his certainty-equivalent income is $a^{1/2}$, just as in the case of public information and no contingent markets. Böhm-Bawerk is in the same situation as if there were no public information and no contingent markets; hence, his certainty-equivalent income is $a^{1/2}/2$.

If there are contingent markets, then all depends on what Böhm-Bawerk can infer about what Walras knows. First, we must note that in any case, the equilibrium on the contingent markets cannot be the same as if there were no information. In the last case, prices for the two kinds of contingent contracts (wheat if W, barely if B) must be equal. But suppose the state is in fact W; Walras will buy no barley claims and will therefore sell no wheat claims. At the original prices, Böhm-Bawerk's demands and supplies are unchanged.

Hence, there is now excess supply of barley claims and excess demand for wheat claims, so the original prices can no longer be in equilibrium.

How does Böhm-Bawerk respond to the discovery that the previous equilibrium no longer holds? There are (at least) two possibilities. One is in the spirit of competitive theory – he simply takes market prices as parameters and responds to them by profit maximization and utility maximization. We may call this the *parametric price* assumption. Alternatively, he may be aware that Walras knows the true state; since the market prices reflect Walras' behavior, Böhm-Bawerk can infer the true state and act accordingly. The equilibrium price for each state must be such that if it is read as a signal for the truth of that state, the resulting behavior will sustain it as an equilibrium. This is the assumption of *rational expectations*.

Before taking up the two cases, some terminology and general remarks are in order. In either case, there will be in general a different set of prices if W occurs than if B occurs; this was also true in the (trivial) case of public information and contingent markets (case 4). Take barley-claims to be numéraire in each state of nature. Then the price system in each state reduces to the price of wheat-claims in terms of barley-claims (possibly infinite if barley-claims are free goods). Let p^W and p^B be the prices of wheat-claims in terms of barley-claims in the states W and B, respectively; the pair (p^W, p^B) will be referred to as the *equilibrium price system*.

It is important to note that the supply conditions are independent of information once the prices are given; this is a fundamental property of contingent markets. Each of our agents can be thought of as combining a firm and a consumer. The firm sells claims contingent on the state of the weather. Its aim is to maximize its profits in the transactions; given the contingent prices, it cannot do better by using information. To validate any planned sales of contingent claims, the firms must actually plant the corresponding amounts. Note that demands indeed respond to information; hence, the system as a whole is influenced by information, and supplies may indeed respond to information, but only through the prices of contingent contracts.

In our simple linear technologies, there will be for each firm one wheat-claim price, p, at which it is indifferent between producing barley and wheat (and therefore between selling barley-claims and wheat-claims). For all smaller wheat-claim prices it produces only barley, for all larger ones only wheat. Walras would realize p if he produced only wheat, a if he produced only barley. Therefore, he produces barley if $p < a$, wheat if $p > a$, and is indifferent between them when $p = a$. In the last case, he is also indifferent among all alternatives which allocate a fraction r of his land to wheat and $1 - r$ to barley and therefore produces r of wheat and $a(1 - r)$ of barley for any $r, 0 \leq r \leq 1$. It also follows that Walras' income as a function of the wheat-claim price is

$$Y_w(p) = \max(p, a). \tag{6.4}$$

Similarly, Böhm-Bawerk produces only barley if $p < a^{-1}$, only wheat if $p > a^{-1}$. If $p = a^{-1}$, he is equally willing to produce ar of wheat and $1 - r$ of barley for any $r, 0 \leq r \leq 1$. His income is

$$Y_B(p) = \max(ap, 1) \tag{6.5}$$

With these remarks, we can study the equilibrium price systems and associated quantity allocations under the alternative assumptions of parametric prices and rational expectations.

Case 6:   Differential information with contingent markets and parametric prices

The determination of the equilibrium price system is elementary but slightly tedious; it will be found in the appendix at the end of the chapter. The results are

$$p^W = a^{-1}, \quad p^B = a \quad \text{if } a \geq 1/2, \tag{6.6}$$
$$= 1/2 \quad \text{if } a < 1/2.$$

The production and consumption allocations are interesting. Since $p^W = a^{-1} > a$, Walras will produce only wheat-claims if W prevails. His supply will be 1. Also, from (6.4), his income is p^W; since he only buys wheat-claims (knowing that W prevails), he buys 1 unit of wheat-claims, and therefore exactly consumes his own supply. Böhm-Bawerk, not knowing which state prevails, buys both kinds of claims. To meet his demand for wheat-claims, he must therefore produce some of his own, as well as some barley-claims. At $p^W = a^{-1}$, he will in fact be willing to produce both. Precisely, he plants one-half his land in wheat, one-half in barley, and therefore consumes $a/2$ if W prevails.

Suppose B is true, so that the price is p^B. The case $a < 1/2$, where the technology is relatively inflexible, is most interesting. Since $p^B = 1/2 > a$, Walras will find it profitable to plant only wheat and therefore sell only wheat-claims, even though he knows that B is true! Since $p^B = 1/2 < a^{-1}$, Böhm-Bawerk plants only barley and sells barley-claims. Therefore, one unit of barley is produced if B holds. However, Walras' income is $1/2$, which he spends entirely on barley-claims. Walras and Böhm-Bawerk therefore consume $1/2$ each. The production, though not the consumption, reflects a striking misallocation.

If $a \geq 1/2$, then still $p^B < a^{-1}$, so that Böhm-Bawerk plants only barley. However, Walras will plant some of his land in each, $(2a)^{-1}$ in wheat and $1 - (2a)^{-1}$ in barley. His product, if B prevails, is $a - (1/2)$ of barley, while Böhm-Bawerk's output of barley is 1, for a total output of $a + (1/2)$.

Walras' income is a, spent entirely on barley-claims, so that he receives a units of barley, while Böhm-Bawerk's consumption is the remainder, $1/2$.

If we work through the certainty-equivalent incomes, we find

$$y_W^* = 2^{-1/2} \text{ if } a < 1/2,$$
$$= a^{1/2} \text{ if } a \geq 1/2; \tag{6.7}$$
$$y_B^* = a^{1/2}/2 \, [a^{1/2}/2] \quad \text{in any case.}$$

Comparison with the results in table 6.3 shows that Walras is at least as well off under differential information as in any previous case. Böhm-Bawerk, on the otherr hand, has the same welfare level as in the absence of both contingent markets and information and is worse off than in the presence of either.

Case 7: Differential information with contingent markets and rational expectations

It is obvious that if both wind up knowing the true state, the situation is the same as with public information and contingent markets (case 4). Barley-claims are free goods in state W, wheat-claims in state B; the contingent markets are ineffective, and the real outcome is the same as with public information and no markets (case 3).

It may be a useful exercise to restate this conclusion more formally. It is asserted that the equilibrium price system is $p^W = \infty, p^B = 0$. Clearly, with these prices, both individuals plant only wheat if W, only barley if B. Further, if W holds, both know it, Walras by assumption and Böhm-Bawerk by inference from observing p^W, and therefore both demand only wheat-claims; the same holds, *mutatis mutandis*, if state B holds.

In the spirit of general equilibrium theory, one may ask if the equilibrium price system is unique. In this case, it is not, and the formal argument is instructive. Suppose there is another equilibrium price system, p^W, p^B. First suppose that $p^W \neq p^B$. Then Böhm-Bawerk can infer from the market price which state holds. If W is true, both demand only wheat-claims. Hence, both must supply only wheat-claims. But this policy will be profit-maximizing for both whenever $p^W \geq a^{-1}$. Similarly, equilibrium will hold if B is true whenever $p^B \leq a$. Hence, any pair satisfying these conditions is an equilibrium price system.

Is it possible that $p^W = p^B$ in some equilibrium price system? If it did, then Böhm-Bawerk would *not* be able to infer which state prevailed. His demands for the two kinds of claims would therefore be the same as if he took prices parametrically. Since the rational expectations and parametric price models differ only with respect to Böhm-Bawerk's demand, it follows

Table 6.4 Payoffs under alternative assumptions

Assumption on markets	Productivity parameter (a)	Individual	
		Walras	Böhm-Bawerk
None	$0 \leqq a < 1$	$a^{1/2}$	$a^{1/2}/2$
Parametric prices	$1/2 \leqq a < 1$	$a^{1/2}$	$a^{1/2}/2$
Parametric prices	$0 \leqq a < 1/2$	$2^{-1/2}$	$a^{1/2}/2$
Rational expectations	$0 \leqq a < 1$	$a^{1/2}$	$a^{1/2}$

Walras knows the state of the world, Böhm-Bawerk does not.

that, if $p^W = p^B$, the pair of prices would be a rational expectations price equilibrium system if and only if it is a parametric price equilibrium system. But, from (6.6), there is not in this example any parametric price equilibrium system with $p^W = p^B$.

In this example, there is no rational expectations equilibrium with $p^W = p^B$. But it is certainly possible to have such equilibria in other contexts. Therefore, rational expectations equilibria do not necessarily convey information held by one individual to the uninformed. As table 6.4 shows, the informed party, Walras, is as well off with differential information as with public information and better off if the uninformed party takes prices parametrically and if the technology is not very flexible. The uninformed party, on the contrary, is as badly off as if there were neither information nor contingent markets unless he uses the observed prices to form rational expectations; in that case, the situation is essentially the same as with public information.

These examples all show compromise between spreading the risk bearing and efficiency of production. Can both kinds of efficiency be achieved?

First, what is the optimal allocation in an ideal system? Clearly, if W obtains, both parties should plant to wheat; the total production would be $1 + a$. Similarly, if B obtains, a total output of $1 + a$ is also obtainable. If, in each state, the total output is divided equally between the two, then each consumes $(1 + a)/2$ with certainty. Since $(1 + a)/2 > a^{1/2}$ and also $(1 + a)/2 > 1/2$ whenever $0 < a < 1$, this is better than any allocation achieved through the market structures analyzed so far. The allocation is Pareto-optimal; it is the only one which is also symmetric between the participants.

Could this allocation be achieved through a market mechanism? It can, if the contingent markets operate *before* information is available while production takes place after. In this case. Walras knows that he could produce one unit if W, a units if B, and will sell claims accordingly. The market prices for the two kinds of claims are equal, say to one. Then Walras' and Böhm-Bawerk's incomes are each $1 + a$; they each purchase $(1 + a)/2$

of each kind of claim, thereby realizing the optimal allocation.

Whether this principle has significant application can only be determined in individual cases. It depends on the possibility of ensuring that contingent markets are in existence before information can be known.

To conclude, I give some real-world cases in which problems of market organization are illustrated by the new theoretical developments. Examples of differential information abound. In the field of insurance, both adverse selection and moral hazard arise from differential information. In the case of adverse selection, the insured has a greater knowledge of the risks than the insurer. His or her demand behavior will change accordingly. In equilibrium, the insurer is correct on the average but cannot distinguish among insured with varying risks. Those with higher risks find their insurance underpriced relative to the true risks and will thus buy more insurance than is efficient. Therefore, the average risk per dollar of insurance is higher; the premium must rise and might conceivably rise to the point of eliminating low-risk individuals from the market. If the insurance company can observe the total amount of insurance purchased by an individual, it might infer his risk status and use that information in setting rates. The differential information is that which enables the individual insured to know his or her particular risks.

In the case of moral hazard, the individual can make decisions which cannot be monitored successfully by the insurance company. Thus, in the case of health insurance, the ill person demands medical services based on his perception of his illness. But if the cost of medical services is partly or wholly covered by the insurance, he or she will demand more than if the full cost were not covered. The insurer is not, however, able to distinguish among medical needs.

It is for reasons such as these that other kinds of cost controls are widely proposed and beginning to be enforced; at least in the United States. The market is no longer regarded as thoroughly efficient, and nonmarket controls are invoked.

Differential information is manifested in another form in connection with quality of product. The quality of medical services is a particularly acute form of this problem. Here, the seller in general knows much more than the buyer; the latter is not in a strong position to insist on quality standards. It is unlikely that a market mechanism of any kind will be very useful. Society has been adapting to this example of market by regulation and by ethical codes, such as those governing the practices of medicine and law.

For a final example among a vast number of possibilities, I mention the allocation of resources to the production of information itself. The main form is research and development of new products. There are conflicting tendencies to overinvestment and underinvestment. In the case where public information renders contingent markets useless, there can be overinvestment by social standards. Since differential information is advantageous (at least in the parametric price case), each individual may be willing to expend resources to find the information; but if both succeed, they may have made both worse off. On the other hand, information is hard to make into a private good; if discovered, it is likely to leak in some form, and therefore the investor will not get the full reward.

My main stress in this chapter is not on the particular applications, most of which remain to be worked out, but to exemplify as simply as possible some new tendencies in economic thinking about risk bearing.

APPENDIX

As promised earlier, I work out here in detail the equilibrium price system and quantity allocations for case 6, where there are contingent markets, differential information, and parametric prices.

First, note that Böhm-Bawerk, who receives no information directly and makes no inferences from observed prices, is uncertain about the state of the weather. He therefore demands some claims of each kind. Hence, in equilibrium, there must be a willingness to supply claims of both kinds. From the discussion of supply in the text, we see that at any equilibrium, we must have

$$a \leqq p \leqq a^{-1}. \tag{6.8}$$

With this range of prices, the incomes of the two individuals are

$$Y_W(p) = p, \qquad Y_B(p) = 1. \tag{6.9}$$

Let d stand for demand for wheat-claims, with subscripts representing the agents. Böhm-Bawerk's demand is independent of state. For any market price, p, his demands come from maximizing

$$(1/2)\log w + (1/2)\log b$$

subject to $pw + b = 1$, where w and b are the demands for wheat-claims and barley-claims respectively. Then,

$$d_B(p) = w = (2p)^{-1}. \tag{6.10}$$

Walras' demand for wheat-claims depends on the state, to be indicated by a superscript. If W holds, Walras spends his entire income on wheat-claims; if B holds, he spends none of his income on wheat-claims;

$$d_W^W(p) = 1, \qquad d_W^B(p) = 0. \tag{6.11}$$

If d^W and d^B represent total demands in states W and B, respectively,

$$d^W(p) = 1 + (2p)^{-1}, \qquad d^B(p) = (2p)^{-1}. \tag{6.12}$$

Walras will supply 1 unit of wheat-claims if $p > a$; he will supply any amount from 0 to 1 indifferently if $p = a$. Similarly, Böhm-Bawerk will supply no wheat-claims if $p < a^{-1}$ and will be indiffernt at any amount from 0 to a if $p = a^{-1}$. Hence, total supply is indifferent over the interval $\langle 0, 1 \rangle$ if $p = a$, equals 1 if $a < p < a^{-1}$, and is indifferently anything in the interval $\langle 1, 1 + a \rangle$ if $p = a^{-1}$.

If $d(p)$ is the demand function, then p is an equilibrium in any of the three following circumstances: $(1) p = a, 0 \leqq d(a) \leqq 1$; $(2) a < p < a^{-1}, d(p) = 1$; $(3) p = a^{-1}, 1 \leqq d(a^{-1}) \leqq 1 + a$. (Note that clearing the wheat-claims market automatically clears the barley-claims market).

Suppose state W holds. Since $d^W(p) > 1$, the only possible equilibrium is at $p = a^{-1}$. Since $1 < d^W(a^{-1}) = 1 + (a/2) < 1 + a$, it is in fact true that $p^W = a^{-1}$. Total output is $1 + (a/2)$, of which 1 is supplied by Walras. From (A-4), Walras' demand for wheat-claims is also 1, which is realized.

In state W, then, Böhm-Bawerk commits himself to producing $a/2$ of wheat if W; this can be done by sowing one-half his land in wheat and half in barley. He buys $a/2$ wheat claims and $1/2$ barley-claims; the former is realized.

In state B, matters are a little more complex. Is it possible that $p^B = a$? From (6.12) and the equilibrium conditions, $p^B = a$ if and only if $(2a)^{-1} \leqq 1$, or $a \geq 1/2$. In that case, Böhm-Bawerk produces only barley. However, he demands $(2a)^{-1}$ of wheat-claims, which is supplied by Walras. This means that Walras must plant $(2a)^{-1}$ of his land in wheat, even though he knows that no wheat will grow; he plants the remainder in barley, with a realized output of $a[1 - (2a)^{-1}] = a - (1/2)$. Walras' demand for barley-claims which is realized, is a (his total income). Böhm-Bawerk's demand for barley-claims is $1/2$.

It is impossible that $p^B = a^{-1}$; for $d^B(a^{-1}) = a/2$, from (A-5), and $a/2 < 1$. However, it is possible that $a < p < a^{-1}$; this occurs only when $d^B(p) = 1$, that is, $p = 1/2$, and it is an equilibrium when $a < 1/2 < a^{-1}$. Since the second inequality must hold, we have that

$$p^B = 1/2 \quad \text{when} \quad a < 1/2.$$

Here, Walras has an income $1/2$ and a demand $1/2$ for barley-claims. Because $p^B > a$, he plants only wheat, although he knows that no wheat will grow, a remarkable inefficiency. Böhm-Bawerk grows only barley; since Walras receives $1/2$, Böhm-Bawerk will also receive $1/2$.

REFERENCES

Akerlof, G. A. (1970) The market for 'lemons'; quality uncertainty and the market mechanism. *Quarterly Journal of Economics* 84:488–500.

Arrow, K. J. (1953) Le rôle des valeurs boursières pour la répartition la meilleure des risques. *Econométrie*, Colloques Internationaux du Centre National de la Recherche Scientifique, vol. 11, Paris, 41–7. English translation, 1963–64.

Arrow, K. J. (1963–64) The role of securities in the optimal allocation of risk-bearing. *Review of Economic Studies* 31:91–6. English translation of Arrow (1953).

Arrow, K. J. (1965) *Aspects of the Theory of Risk-Bearing*. Helsinki: Yrjö Jahnssonin säätio. Lecture 3, reprinted in Arrow (1970, ch. 5).

Arrow, K. J. (1970) *Essays in the Theory of Risk-Bearing*. Amsterdam: North-Holland.

Debreu, G. (1953) Une économie de l'incertain. Paris: Electricité de France, mimeographed.

Debreu, G. (1959) *Theory of Value*. New York: Wiley; New Haven; Yale University Press.

Green, J. (1973) Information, efficiency, and equilibrium. Harvard Institute of Economic Research, Discussion Paper no. 284.

Grossman, S. (1976) On the efficiency of competitive stock markets where traders have diverse information. *Journal of Finance* 31:573–85.

Grossman, S., and Stiglitz, J. (1976) Information and competitive price systems. *American Economic Review* 66:246–52.

Hirshleifer, J. (1971) The private and social value of information and the reward to inventive activity. *American Economic Review* 61:561–74.

Kihlstrom, R. E., and Mirman, L. J. (1975) Information and market equilibrium. *Bell Journal of Economics and Management Science* 6:357–76.

Radner, R. (1968) Competitive equilibrium under uncertainty. *Econometrica* 36:31–58.

Shubik, M. (1977) Competitive equilibrium, contingent commodities, and information. *Journal of Finance* 32:189–93.

7

Rational Expectations, Information, and Asset Markets: An Introduction

Margaret M. Bray

1 INTRODUCTION

Financial markets are a subject of perpetual fascination to economists and
others. There are very large sums of money to be gained and lost on them.
They are obviously crucially important not only to the people and institutions who invest directly, but also to the many others who invest indirectly
through holding unit trusts (mutual funds), pension or life assurance
policies. Moreover the financial markets do not operate in isolation; they
affect and are affected by the rest of the economy.

One important economic function of such markets is the spreading and
sharing of risk. An entrepreneur can reduce the risks which he carries by
selling shares in his firm. Investors may be willing to carry some of the risk
because they are less risk averse than the entrepreneur. They may also be
willing to invest even if they are more risk averse because the market allows
them to hold a diversified portfolio which reduces risk. Investing £10,000 in
ten different firms whose profits are imperfectly correlated is very much less
risky than investing £10,000 in one of the firms. The view that such markets
perform a socially important function in spreading risk reasonably well is
widely held, (see Arrow, 1964; and Diamond, 1967; for theoretical models).
But there are distinguished dissidents; in Chapter 12 of the *General Theory*,
Keynes argues forcefully that the markets increasingly provide a casino for
speculators, rather than a guide for investors, and may be socially useless or
even positively dangerous.

Recent theoretical work on asset markets, based on the rational expectations hypothesis, has argued that they may have an additional informational
role. Traders have information which affects their evaluation of the value of

I am grateful to Craig Alexander, Jeremy Edwards, Anna Lemessany, Peter Sinclair, and
Martin Weale for comments on an earlier version of this paper.

assets, the demand for the assets, and thus prices. Other traders may attempt to infer the information from prices. The major achievement of recent work has been to develop a coherent description of this phenomenon and use it to ask how well the markets transmit and aggregate the information.

Much of this literature is highly technical, and inaccessible without a considerable mathematical apparatus. Yet the basic issues can be understood with much less background, as this paper seeks to demonstrate. It is written as an introduction to recent work on information in asset markets, assuming intermediate microeconomics, enough calculus to differentiate a quadratic, a little manipulation of linear equations, and enough probability theory to know about means, variances, and conditional distributions. I use expected utility theory, but anyone who does not know the theory, and is willing to take on trust my assertion that it is a sensible way to model choice under uncertainty, should be able to follow the argument.

Much of the paper is concerned with elaborating a simple model. The model introduced in section 2 is the standard deterministic partial equilibrium model of supply and demand in a spot market, modified by the assumption that production decisions must be made before the market operates on the basis of price expectations. I use this model to introduce a perfect foresight equilibrium; the deterministic version of a rational expectations equilibrium. In section 3 I introduce a futures market, operating at the date when production decisions are made. A futures contract is a financial asset, whose gross return is the spot price. I argue that arbitrage implies that in this deterministic model, if expectations are held with certainty, the futures price must be equal to the present discounted value of the expected spot price. Section 4 introduces briefly the expected utility theory of choice under uncertainty. Section 5 applies this theory to a stochastic version of the model on the assumption that dealers are risk neutral, using an arbitrage argument to establish that the futures price is equal to the present discounted value of the expected spot price. Section 6 shows how the simple arbitrage argument breaks down when risk-neutral dealers have diverse information, introducing the informational role of asset prices. The formal definition of a rational expectations equilibrium in an asset market with asymmetric information is introduced in section 7. Section 8 introduces risk aversion, simplifying matters mathematically by working with exponential utility functions, and normal random variables. The joint equilibrium of the spot and futures market when dealers are risk averse is calculated, on the assumption that no-one has any private information about the spot price when trading on the futures market. Information is introduced in section 9, firstly on the assumption that all dealers have the same information, secondly on the assumption that there are informed and uninformed traders, but the informed traders all have the same information, and thirdly on the assumption that dealers have diverse information. In this model the futures market is remarkably informationally efficient; it aggregates information perfectly. Section 10 is concerned with the implications and robustness of the informational efficiency result in this and related models. In the models which I use calculating the rational expectations equilibrium is relatively straightforward, but in section 11 I introduce a version of the spot and futures market model which has no rational expectations equilibrium. I discuss the nature and significance of the problems associated with the existence of rational expectations equilibrium, and the literature on the subject. Section 12 attempts an evaluation of the models, discussing the assumptions, concentrating largely on the rational expectations assumption, and referring briefly to the empirical and experimental evidence. Section 13 discusses some open questions prompted by these models.

The results which I establish have no claims to originality; the first model which I develop has its origins in the cobweb model (Kaldor, 1934), and in Muth's paper on rational expectations (1961). The futures market model is based on Danthine (1978), and related to Grossman (1976, 1977) and Bray (1981). The non-existence example in section 11 is new in detail, but is similar to that of Kreps (1977). I give references to other, related literature, where appropriate. A more technical introduction to this and many other topics can be found in Radner's (1982) survey of 'equilibrium under uncertainty' and in the symposium issue (April 1982) of the *Journal of Economic Theory* on 'Rational expectations in microeconomic models', in particular the introduction by Jordan and Radner. Stiglitz (1982) discusses a range of issues concerned with information and capital markets.

2   SUPPLY AND DEMAND WITH A PRODUCTION LAG: PERFECT FORESIGHT EQUILIBRIUM

In the standard model of supply and demand, production and consumption decisions are taken simultaneously, based on the price. If production takes time, production decisions have to be based on the expected price. For example, a farmer plants a crop in January which will be harvested and sold in June. To begin with assume that there is no uncertainty, an assumption which will be relaxed in section 4. Demand $D(p_s)$ is a deterministic function of p_s, the spot price of wheat in June. Supply $S[p_s^e]$ is a deterministic function of p_s^e, the farmers' point expectation belief in January about what the spot price will be in June. For now, assume that all farmers are subjectively certain about what the price will be, and all have the same beliefs. If the market in June clears, supply equals demand. $D[p_s] = S[p_s^e]$. The expected price determines production which in turn determines the actual price. In fact the price p_s, is a function of the expected price.

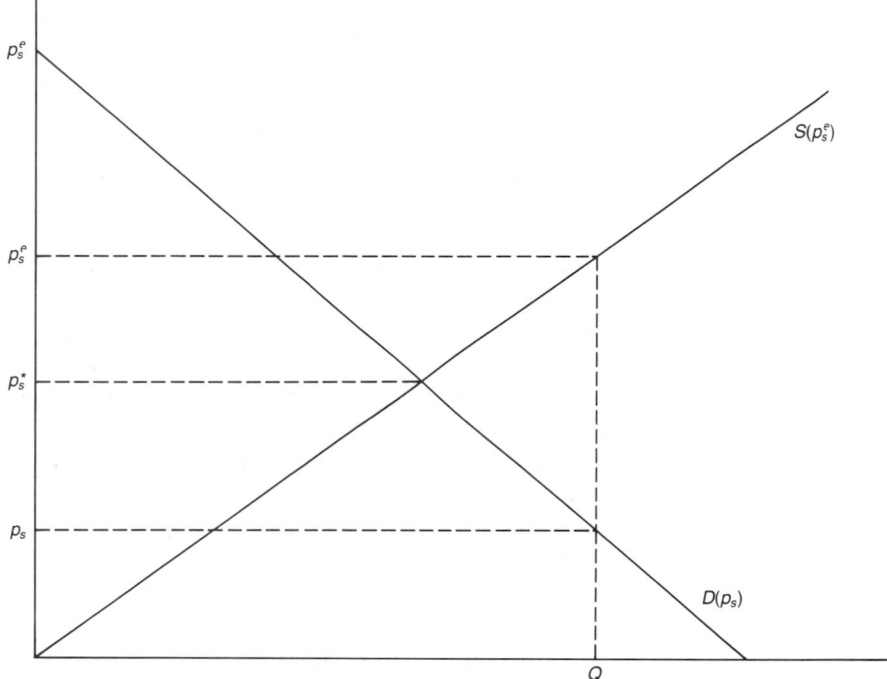

Figure 7.1

In figure 7.1, when the price is p_s^e, $Q = S[p_s^e]$ is produced. When Q is put on the spot market in June the price is p_s. If $p_s \neq p_s^e$ the farmers, despite their subjective certainty, are wrong. Beliefs are wrong unless $p_s^e = p_s^*$, the price at which the supply and demand curves intersect so $S[p_s^*] = D[p_s^*]$. This could well be described as a self-fulfilling belief. However, the standard terminology is a perfect foresight equilibrium or more recently (following Muth, 1961) a rational expectations equilibrium.

A rational expectations equilibrium can be defined as a situation in which people do not make systematic mistakes in forecasting. In this case where beliefs are point expectations held with certainty, rational expectations equilibrium requires that beliefs be correct, i.e. that people have perfect foresight. The rational expectations assumption is now used very widely, but remains controversial. The assumption avoids many of the difficult dynamic problems apparently associated with expectation formation, making it possible to proceed with other questions. For the time being I will simply assume rational expectations without further discussion, returning to the matter in section 12.

3   FINANCING PRODUCTION: FUTURES MARKETS AND ARBITRAGE

The revenue from selling the crop arrives some time after most of the production costs are incurred. This leaves a farmer with the problem of finding funds to cover the investment in planting the crop. He may have sufficient wealth to finance this from his own resources. If not he will have to borrow.

Assume that everyone knows that the price in June will be p_s. There are perfect capital markets, that is the farmer can borrow or lend as much as he wishes at the same interest rate. £1 borrowed in January must be repaid with $£(1 + r)$ in June. Suppose that a farmer has wealth W_0 in January, and incurs the costs of producing output y, which have a present discounted value in January of $C(y)$. He invests the remainder of his wealth $W_0 - C(y)$ at interest rate r until June. His wealth in June is the sum of his revenue from output $p_s y$ and the return on his other investment

$$W = p_s y + (W_0 - C(y))(1 + r) = p_s y - C(y)(1 + r) + W_0(1 + r)$$

The value of profits from production in June is $p_s y - C(y)(1 + r)$. Note that $W_0 - C(y)$ may be negative, in which case the farmer is borrowing to cover some of his costs. The farmer maximizes his June wealth by maximizing profits. If C is a convex function of y and $p_s > C'(0)(1 + r)$, this is done by setting $p_s = C'(y)(1 + r)$. The value of y is independent of his initial wealth, which simply determines how much, if anything he has to borrow.

The farmer may also finance his production by selling on the futures market. A futures market is an institution on which money is exchanged for promises to deliver goods in the future. For example, a farmer may sell wheat in January for delivery in June. As before, suppose the farmer has wealth W_0 in January, produces, y, incurring costs $C(y)$, and sells z on the futures market at price p_f. This leaves him $W_0 - C(y) + p_f z$ to invest at interest r. In June he sells the remainder of his output $y - z$ on the spot market. His wealth in June is

$$W = p_s(y - z) + (W_0 - C(y) + p_f z)(1 + r)$$

$$= p_s y - C(y)(1 + r) + (p_f(1 + r) - p_s)z + W_0(1 + r). \quad (7.1)$$

The farmer maximizes his wealth, as before by choosing output y so $p_s = C'(y)(1 + r)$. If $p_f > p_s/(1 + r)$, so that the futures price exceeds the present discounted value of the spot price, he can make arbitrarily large profits by selling on the futures market. He will increase z indefinitely, and will wish to set $z > y$, selling more on the futures market than he produces, meeting the shortfall $z - y$ by buying on the spot market. However, he is unlikely to find a willing buyer at this price. There are two possible classes of buyers, consumers and speculators. Consumers (e.g. food manufacturers and wholesalers) may choose to buy futures in January rather than waiting to buy on the spot market in June, thus hedging against uncertainty about the June spot price. For the sake of simplicity I will assume that consumers do not participate in the futures market; if they did it would complicate the models without substantially affecting the conclusions. Speculators buy futures contracts, which they sell on the spot market, never actually taking delivery of the goods, in the hope of making a profit on the difference between the futures price and the present value of the spot price. Suppose a speculator with wealth W_0 in January buys x futures contracts in January, sells x on the spot market in June, and invests the rest of his wealth in the safe asset paying interest r. His wealth will be

$$W = p_s x + (W_0 - p_f x)(1 + r)$$
$$= (p_s - p_f(1 + r))x + W_0(1 + r). \tag{7.2}$$

If $p_f > p_s/(1 + r)$ both speculators and farmers will wish to sell futures. With no willing buyers the market cannot clear. If $p_f < p_s/(1 + r)$ both speculators and farmers will want to buy futures. Thus the only price at which the futures market can clear is when $p_f = p_s/(1 + r)$. This is an example of an arbitrage argument – these arguments are based on the premise that in equilibrium it cannot be possible for anyone to make arbitrarily large certain profits. If the market is perfectly arbitraged, $p_s = p_f(1 + r)$. The wealth in June of farmers and speculators does not depend on the size of their future trades. In this deterministic model with perfect foresight, a futures contract is a safe asset paying interest r. There is no reason for anyone to use the futures market in preference to borrowing or lending at rate r elsewhere. If the futures market ceased to exist no-one would be any better or worse off.

In fact under certainty there seems little reason for the futures market to exist. Any understanding of futures markets, and other asset markets such as the stock market, depends upon introducing uncertainty.

4 CHOICE UNDER UNCERTAINTY

The farmer faces risks in both the quantity and price of output. A futures market allows the farmer to shift the price risks to speculators. If his output y is certain he can completely eliminate the risk by setting $z = y$, selling his entire output on the futures market. But why will the speculator be willing to assume the risk, and at what price? The currently available answers to this, and many other questions about economics under uncertainty, are derived from a widely accepted model of choice under uncertainty: the theory of expected utility. An introduction to the theory can be found in, among other places, Deaton and Muellbauer (1980), in a survey by Schoemaker (1982) or, in a valuable collection of readings, Diamond and Rothschild (1978).

Assume that an investor has decided to invest a certain amount W_0 for a period. He has a number of different assets to choose between, and a definite set of beliefs about the joint probability distribution of the returns on the different assets. He cares only about the probability distribution of his wealth $\tilde{W}$ at the end of the period, which depends upon the way he allocates his initial wealth W_0 between the different assets. The theory of expected utility shows that if his preferences over the probability distribution of $\tilde{W}$ satisfy some plausible assumptions he will choose a portfolio which maximizes the mathematical expectation $EU(\tilde{W})$ of a function $U(\tilde{W})$ given his beliefs about the probabilities. For a discrete probability distribution $EU(\tilde{W}) = \Sigma_i U(W_i)p_i$, where W_i is wealth in state i and p_i the probability of state i. For a continuous probability distribution

$$EU(\tilde{W}) = \int_{-\infty}^{\infty} U(W)f(W)\,\mathrm{d}W$$

where f is the probability density function. In both cases the probability distribution depends upon the investor's beliefs, and his choice of portfolio.

The theory has two essential elements, the utility function and the probability distribution, which determines the mathematical expectation. The functional form of the utility function U describes attitudes to risk. U is increasing provided investors prefer more to less wealth. If $U(\tilde{W}) = \tilde{W}$ the investor is risk neutral, caring only about expected wealth, and not at all about its riskiness. If $U(\tilde{W})$ is strictly concave the investor is risk averse, strictly preferring investments yielding the expectation of $\tilde{W}$ for sure, to random $\tilde{W}$. Risk aversion in investment choices for an individual seems highly plausible, and is often assumed.

The assumption that uncertainty can be described in terms of probability distributions is widely made today, but historically has not commanded universal acceptance. Keynes was a notable dissenter. There is very little controversy about applying the mathematical theory of probability to assess the probabilities associated with a series of similar events, where after a time there is enough data to construct probabilities from frequency distributions (for example weather or life expectancy data), situations described by Knight (1921) as risk. The argument is rather whether meaningful probabilities can be assigned to unique events, where there is no objective frequency data to rely on, situations described by Knight as uncertainty. The subjectivist or Bayesian viewpoint on probability is that Knight's distinction is invalid. It is always possible to elicit probabilities by forcing people to make bets (see Raiffa, 1968). There is, however, no guarantee in subjectivist theory that different people will form the same probability distributions, unless there is frequency data to base them on, which brings us back to Knight's risk. For some purposes it is enough to assume that people act as if they had subjective beliefs expressible as probability distributions. However, many models postulate that people have the same correct beliefs about probability distributions (rational expectations). These models do not seem to be applicable to situations which Knight would describe as uncertain.

I am now in a position to use the theory of expected utility to extend the theory of asset pricing under certainty to uncertainty. Initially I will assume risk neutrality, and then proceed to consider risk aversion.

5   RISK NEUTRALITY: ARBITRAGE AGAIN

Returning to the futures market example, suppose that once farmers have chosen their level of inputs their output y is certain. The June spot price is uncertain because spot demand is uncertain. A risk neutral farmer will choose his output y and futures sales z to maximize the expected value of his wealth; from (7.1) this is

$$E\tilde{W} = E\tilde{p}_s y - C(y)(1 + r) + (p_f(1 + r) - E\tilde{p}_s)z + W_0(1 + r).$$

(Throughout this paper a tilde ~ above a variable indicates that it is random.) A speculator will choose his futures purchases x to maximize the expected value of his wealth; from (7.2) this is

$$E\tilde{W} = (E\tilde{p}_s - p_f(1 + r))x + W_0(1 + r).$$

Decisions depend upon the mathematical expectation $E\tilde{p}_s$ of $\tilde{p}_s$, its average value. The risk-neutral dealers do not care about any other characteristics of the probability distribution. $E\tilde{p}_s$ is not a point expectation held with certainty; the dealers are aware that there is uncertainty and would expect to observe that usually $E\tilde{p}_s \neq \tilde{p}_s$.

Precisely the same arbitrage argument as before implies that unless $p_f = E\tilde{p}_s/(1 + r)$ there are unlimited positive expected profits to be made and the market cannot clear. The argument is less compelling than under certainty. Although a speculator may wish to exploit opportunities for making positive expected profits he may not be able to do so. Suppose that $E\tilde{p}_s > p_f(1 + r)$, so buying futures contracts generates a positive expected return. A risk-neutral speculator will choose to spend his entire wealth on futures contracts, and will also wish to borrow without limit to exploit further the opportunity for profit. There is a chance that the spot price will be so low that he cannot repay his debts; lending to the speculator becomes risky. Speculators may face either a higher interest rate than r, or limits on credit, limiting their ability to arbitrage the market.

6   DIVERSE INFORMATION

The simple arbitrage argument also breaks down if different dealers (farmers and speculators) have different beliefs about the expected spot price. This is not incompatible with the dealers having rational expectations, if they have access to different information. Suppose for example that $\tilde{p}_s = \tilde{I} + \tilde{e}$ where $\tilde{I}$ and $\tilde{e}$ are independent random variables, $E\tilde{e} = 0$, and so $E\tilde{p}_s = E\tilde{I}$. There are two types of dealers. The informed dealers observe $\tilde{I}$ before the futures market opens; their expectation of $\tilde{p}_s$ is conditional upon $\tilde{I}$, $E[\tilde{p}_s | \tilde{I}] = \tilde{I}$. The uninformed dealers observe nothing; their expectation of $\tilde{p}_s$ is $E\tilde{p}_s = E\tilde{I}$. If both types of dealers are risk neutral, face no borrowing constraints, and stick to their beliefs, the informed will want to buy or sell an unlimited amount unless $p_f = E[\tilde{p}_s | \tilde{I}]/(1 + r) = \tilde{I}/(1 + r)$, and the uninformed dealers will want to buy or sell an unlimited amount unless $\tilde{p}_f = E\tilde{p}_s/(1 + r)$. Unless by coincidence $E[\tilde{p}_s | \tilde{I}] = E\tilde{p}_s$ (i.e. if $\tilde{I} = E\tilde{I}$), the market apparently cannot clear.

It is, however, most unlikely that the uninformed dealers will stick to their beliefs. Knowing that there are informed dealers in the market whose trading affects the futures price, they will try to make inferences from the futures price about the spot price. They are using the price of a financial asset, a futures contract, to make judgements about its quality. Judging quality from price is not confined to financial markets. Consumers may also do so, assuming that cheap goods are also cheap and nasty. One of the major successes of recent economic theory has been the development of models which take this into account.

In these models prices have two roles: their conventional role in determining budget sets for consumers and profit opportunities for firms, and an additional role in transmitting information. Hayek (1945), in a discussion of decentralization and planning, argues that the conventional role of prices must also be understood as an informational one. In standard Walrasian competitive equilibrium models, once households and firms know current prices they have no use for any further information about the plans, characteristics and opportunities of others in the economy; they need make no attempt to infer this information from prices. As Grossman (1981) argues, recent models of asymmetric information move beyond this: some agents want some information held by others, in this case information about the spot price in the future. They try to infer as much information as they can from current prices. In some cases the price system may be entirely efficient at transmitting information, prices are so informative that there is no additional information currently known to anyone in the economy which would be helpful. In other cases prices may be less informationally efficient, conveying some information, but still leaving a frustrated desire to see the current contents of someone else's mind, or computer file. In either case agents are trying to look beyond prices to solve an inference problem, which is unnecessary in standard Walrasian models. The central question addressed by the models which I am about to discuss is how informationally efficient are prices? These models make use of the idea of a rational expectations equilibrium. I will now show how this equilibrium is defined, and explain how it yields an equilibrium price for this example.

7 RATIONAL EXPECTATIONS EQUILIBRIUM AND RISK NEUTRALITY

The definition of a rational expectations equilibrium for the spot and futures markets has four parts. A very similar definition can be formulated for any asset market model. The first part describes how dealers form their beliefs.

Part 1 Each dealer (farmer or speculator) observes some private information $\tilde{I}_i$ and the futures price $\tilde{p}_f$. Given this information he has beliefs about the spot price $\tilde{p}_s$ which can be expressed as a conditional probability distribution.

For example, dealer i might believe that given the futures price $\tilde{p}_f$ and private information, $\tilde{I}_i$, the conditional distribution of $\tilde{p}_s$ was normal with mean $E[\tilde{p}_s | \tilde{p}_f, \tilde{I}_i] = \frac{1}{2}\tilde{p}_f + \frac{1}{4}\tilde{I}_i$ and variance $\frac{1}{8}$. At this stage I have not required that the beliefs be correct, only that they exist.

The second part of the definition states that given their beliefs dealers choose their portfolio in accordance with expected utility theory.

Part 2 Each dealer chooses the holding of futures contracts, and for farmers, output, which maximizes his expected utility given his beliefs about the spot price, conditional upon his private information and the futures price.

Parts 1 and 2 of the definition give the supply and demand for futures. Note that supply and demand are affected by both the numerical value of the futures price and information, and by beliefs. If a risk-neutral dealer believes that $E[\tilde{p}_s | \tilde{p}_f, \tilde{I}_i] = \frac{1}{2}\tilde{p}_f + \frac{1}{4}\tilde{I}_i$, he will buy or sell an unlimited amount depending on whether $\tilde{p}_f - [\frac{1}{2}\tilde{p}_f + \frac{1}{4}\tilde{I}_i]/(1+r)$ is positive or negative.

To emphasize this point I will write $d_i[\tilde{p}_f, \tilde{I}_i; B_i]$ for dealer i's demand for futures, where B_i is shorthand for beliefs.

The next part of the definition is as follows.

Part 3 The spot and futures prices are at levels where both markets clear.

In different years the information will be different, so if the markets are to clear prices must be a function of the information. Demand and the market clearing prices also depend upon beliefs, so I will write

$$\tilde{p}_f = f[\tilde{I}_1, \tilde{I}_2, \ldots, \tilde{I}_n; B_1, B_2, \ldots, B_n]$$

$$\tilde{p}_s = g[\tilde{I}_1, \tilde{I}_2, \ldots, \tilde{I}_n; B_1, B_2, \ldots, B_n].$$

An omniscient economist could calculate the function f. Knowing the joint distribution of $[\tilde{I}_1, \tilde{I}_2, \ldots, \tilde{I}_n]$ the economist could then calculate the joint distribution of $[\tilde{p}_f, \tilde{p}_s, \tilde{I}_1, \tilde{I}_2, \ldots, \tilde{I}_n]$, and so the conditional distribution of $\tilde{p}_s$ given $\tilde{p}_f$ and $\tilde{I}_i$ for each i. This would tell the economist what the correct beliefs for each dealer would be; call them $\hat{B}_i$. As the joint distributions depend upon the original beliefs, $[B_1, B_2, \ldots, B_n]$, the correct beliefs $[\hat{B}_1, \hat{B}_2, \ldots, \hat{B}_n]$ also depend upon the original beliefs. A more formal way of saying the same thing is that $[\hat{B}_1, \hat{B}_2, \ldots, \hat{B}_n]$ is a function of $[B_1, B_2, \ldots, B_n]$.

The last part of the definition is as follows.

Part 4 Each agent has rational expectations. Agents have correct beliefs about the joint probability distribution of the futures price, spot price and private information, so

$$B_i = \hat{B}_i \qquad i = 1, 2, \ldots, n.$$

Note that this states that beliefs about the entire conditional probability distribution are correct. Much of the macroeconomic literature works with models where only the conditional mean is relevant, but the rational expectations hypothesis is not confined to such models.

This definition may appear unnecessarily long winded. Stating that the beliefs are correct in Part 1 would make for greater brevity, but stating the definition in this way gives more insight. It is helpful in calculating the rational expectations equilibrium in simple models, where making a guess about the functional form of beliefs, calculating supply and demand, and then checking to see if there is indeed a set of beliefs which generates rational expectations often works. This approach is also very helpful in understanding issues associated with the existence and stability of rational expectations equilibrium.

I have stated the definition in terms of a spot and futures market, but very similar definitions can be formulated for any set of financial asset markets. I have not been specific about the information. $\tilde{I}_i$. All that is required is that it be a random variable, but it may be continuous or discrete, a scalar or a vector. It may always take the same value, $\tilde{I}_i = 0$, in which case it is effectively no information.

I will now calculate the rational expectations equilibrium for the futures market example with risk-neutral dealers. Here the informed agents observe $\tilde{I}$ and the uninformed agents observe nothing. Recall that $\tilde{p}_s = \tilde{I} + \tilde{e}$, $\tilde{I}$ and $\tilde{e}$ are independent and $E\tilde{e} = 0$. In accordance with Part 1 of the definition, suppose that the informed dealers believe that $E[\tilde{p}_s | \tilde{I}, \tilde{p}_f] = \tilde{I}$, and the uninformed dealers believe that $E[\tilde{p}_s | \tilde{p}_f] = \lambda \tilde{p}_f$ where λ is a constant. Utility maximization (Part 2 of the definition) for risk-neutral dealers implies that the informed dealers will want to buy or sell an unlimited amount unless $E[\tilde{p}_s | \tilde{I}, \tilde{p}_f] = \tilde{p}_f(1 + r)$, and the uninformed dealers will want to buy or sell an unlimited amount unless $E[\tilde{p}_s | \tilde{p}_f] = \tilde{p}_f(1 + r)$. Thus market clearing (Part 3 of the definition) implies that

$$E[\tilde{p}_s | \tilde{I}, \tilde{p}_f] = \tilde{I} = \tilde{p}_f(1 + r)$$

and

$$E[\tilde{p}_s | \tilde{p}_f] = \lambda \tilde{p}_f = \tilde{p}_f(1 + r).$$

This is impossible unless $\lambda = 1 + r$ and $\tilde{p}_f = \tilde{I}/(1 + r)$. It remains to check that Part 4 of the definition holds. If $\tilde{p}_f = \tilde{I}/(1 + r)$, knowing $\tilde{p}_f$ tells the informed dealers nothing about $\tilde{I}$ and $\tilde{p}_s$ that they did not know already from observing $\tilde{I}$ directly. As $\tilde{p}_s = \tilde{I} + \tilde{e}$, the correct conditional expectation for the informed dealers is $E[\tilde{p}_s | \tilde{I}] = E[\tilde{p}_s | \tilde{I}, \tilde{p}_f] = \tilde{I}$. The uninformed dealers observe $\tilde{p}_f = \tilde{I}/(1 + r)$, so can infer $\tilde{I}$ from $\tilde{p}_f$; knowing that $E[\tilde{p}_s | \tilde{I}] = \tilde{I}$, their correct conditional expectation is $E[\tilde{p}_s | \tilde{I}] = E[\tilde{p}_s | \tilde{p}_f] = \tilde{I} = (1 + r)\tilde{p}_f$, which is the form assumed with $\lambda = 1 + r$. This is a rational expectations equilibrium.

This is a very striking result, indicating that the market is completely efficient as a transmitter of information from the informed to the uninformed. Much of the recent theoretical work on asset markets has been concerned with investigating the circumstances under which a rational expectations equilibrium exists, and is informationally efficient.

This example has a number of peculiar features. The assumption of risk neutrality is special, and I have argued that even with risk neutrality the market may not be perfectly arbitraged. In equilibrium neither farmers nor speculators have any reason to trade futures. The expected profits from trade are always zero. It seems possible that the futures market will die away. But without a futures market the informational differences will persist, so there will be a motive for trade. These peculiarities stem from the risk-neutrality assumption.

8   RATIONAL EXPECTATIONS EQUILIBRIUM UNDER RISK AVERSION

I will now introduce risk aversion into the model. This can generate considerable mathematical complexities, which I will minimize by assuming that both farmers and speculators have utility functions of the form

$$U_i(\tilde{W}) = -\exp(-k_i\tilde{W})$$

where k_i is a positive constant. Remember that 'exp' is an abbreviation for 'exponential' and not for 'expectation'.

This utility function is widely used and has some attractive properties. Its first derivative is positive $(U' > 0)$ implying that utility is increasing in wealth. The second derivative is negative $(U'' < 0)$, implying risk aversion. The constant $k_i = -U''/U'$ is the coefficient of absolute risk aversion: higher values of k_i imply greater risk aversion. Above all there is the very useful result that if $\tilde{W}$ is normal with mean $E\tilde{W}$ and variance var $\tilde{W}$,

$$E\{-\exp(-k\tilde{W})\} = -\exp(-k[E\tilde{W} - \tfrac{1}{2}k\,\mathrm{var}\,\tilde{W}]).\qquad(7.3)$$

This result implies that the expected utility maximising portfolio is one that maximises $E\tilde{W} - \tfrac{1}{2}k$ var $\tilde{W}$. As I will demonstrate this makes for a very tractable model of asset demand, which is linear in expected asset return and prices. The major unattractive feature of the utility function, which I will also demonstrate is that asset demand is independent of wealth.[1]

I will now use (7.3) to analyse the behaviour of the spot and futures market model under risk aversion. The first step in defining and calculating the rational expectations equilibrium is a description of the information and beliefs. The first case I will look at is where dealers have no private information. Each farmer and speculator has the same belief that

$$\tilde{p}_s \sim N(\mu, \sigma^2).\qquad(7.4)$$

Later I will look at a version of the model where each agent has the same piece of information, and then at versions with diverse private information. Once the mathematics has been done for the first case the others follow very simply.

Equation (7.4) gives the beliefs described in Part 1 of the definitions of a rational expectations equilibrium. I will use this to derive the utility maximizing speculators' demand for futures, and the farmers' demand for futures and spot supply (Part 2 of the definition). I will then make an assumption about spot demand which enables me to write down market clearing conditions for the spot and futures markets (Part 3 of the definition). These conditions will generate a 'correct distribution' for the spot price which will depend upon the parameters of the model, including μ and σ^2. I will show that there are values of μ and σ^2 which generate correct beliefs (Part 4 of the definition), thus deriving the rational expectations equilibrium.

There are n dealers, m farmers and $n - m$ speculators. Farmers are indexed by $i = 1, 2, \ldots, m$, and speculators by $i = m + 1, \ldots, n$.

8.1 Speculators

Speculator i has a utility function $-\exp[-k_i \tilde{W}_i]$. If he buys x_i futures at price p_f, sells them on the spot market at price $\tilde{p}_s$, gets interest r on a safe asset, and has initial wealth W_{i0}, his final wealth $\tilde{W}_i$ is from (7.2) a random variable

$$\tilde{W}_i = (\tilde{p}_s - p_f(1 + r))x_i + W_{i0}(1 + r).$$

As speculators believe that $\tilde{p}_s \sim N(\mu, \sigma^2)$, they believe that $\tilde{W}_i$ is normal, and

$$E\tilde{W}_i = (\mu - p_f(1 + r))x_i + W_{i0}(1 + r)$$

$$\text{var } \tilde{W}_i = \sigma^2 x_i^2.$$

From (7.3) the speculator will choose x_i to maximize

$$E\tilde{W}_i - \tfrac{1}{2}k_i \text{var } \tilde{W}_i = (\mu - p_f(1 + r))x_i + W_{i0}(1 + r) - \tfrac{1}{2}k_i\sigma^2 x_i^2.$$

Thus

$$x_i = \frac{1}{k_i\sigma^2}(\mu - p_f(1 + r)) \qquad (i = 1, \ldots, n). \qquad (7.5)$$

The speculator buys futures if $\mu > p_f(1 + r)$, there is a positive expected profit to be made on holding futures, and sells futures if $\mu < p_f(1 + r)$, there is an expected loss to be made on holding futures. His trades are inversely proportional to σ^2, the variance of the spot price, and to k_i, which measures risk aversion. Note that x_i does not depend on initial wealth W_{i0}, owing to the special utility function for which the coefficient of absolute risk aversion $k_i = -U''/U'$ does not depend on wealth.

8.2 Farmers

The speculators choose to take on risk by entering the futures market. If the farmers' output in certain they can entirely avoid risk by hedging: selling their entire output on the futures market. If they sell more or less than this they are assuming risk which they could avoid, in pursuit of profits, effectively acting as speculators. If y_i is farmer i's output, and z_i his future sales, $x_i = y_i - z_i$ can be thought of as speculative purchases of futures. The farmer's wealth is from (7.1) a random variable

$$\tilde{W}_i = (p_f y_i - C(y_i))(1 + r) + (\tilde{p}_s - p_f(1 + r))x_i + W_{i0}(1 + r).$$

The first term is profits from production if all output is sold on the futures market. The second term is profits from speculation. The third term is the future value of initial wealth. As he believes that $\tilde{p}_s \sim N(\mu, \sigma^2)$ he believes that $\tilde{W}_i$ is normal, with mean and variance

$$E\tilde{W}_i = (p_f y_i - C(y_i))(1 + r) + (\mu - p_f(1 + r))x_i + W_{i0}(1 + r)$$

$$\text{var } \tilde{W}_i = \sigma^2 x_i^2.$$

If the farmer has a utility function $-\exp(-k_i \tilde{W}_i)$ from (7.3) he chooses (x_i, y_i) to maximize

$$E\tilde{W}_i - \tfrac{1}{2} k_i \text{var } \tilde{W}_i = (p_f y_i - C(y_i))(1 + r) + (\mu - p_f(1 + r))x_i +$$
$$W_{i0}(1 + r) - \tfrac{1}{2}\sigma_i^2 x_i^2.$$

I will assume that the farmer's costs are

$$C(y_i) = \tfrac{1}{2} cy_i^2$$

where c is a positive constant. Thus the farmer will maximize

$$(p_f y_i - \tfrac{1}{2} cy_i^2)(1 + r) + (\mu - p_f(1 + r))x_i + W_{i0}(1 + r) - \tfrac{1}{2}\sigma_i^2 x_i^2.$$

The first-order condition for y_i implies that $p_f = cy_i$. The futures price determines the level of output, which is set so that the futures price is equal to the marginal cost of production. This result is valid for arbitrary utility functions. In this case it implies that

$$y_i = c^{-1}p_f \qquad (i = 1, \ldots, m). \tag{7.6}$$

The first-order condition for x_i implies that

$$x_i = \frac{1}{k_i\sigma^2}(\mu - p_f(1 + r)) \qquad (i = 1, \ldots, m). \tag{7.7}$$

The farmer's speculative demand for futures is precisely the same as if he were a pure speculator. This result is not valid if output is uncertain, but is convenient. (See Bray, 1981.)

8.3   The futures market

The futures market clearing condition is

$$\sum_{i=1}^{n} x_i = \sum_{i=1}^{m} y_i.$$ (7.8)

The sum of speculative demand for futures from farmers and speculators is equal to farmers' output, sold forward to hedge against uncertainty. Using the expressions for x_i, and y_i, (7.5)–(7.7),

$$\sum_{i=1}^{n} \frac{1}{k_i \sigma^2} (\mu - p_f(1 + r)) = \sum_{i=1}^{m} c^{-1} p_f = mc^{-1} p_f.$$ (7.9)

Thus the futures price depends upon the distribution of the spot price μ and σ^2. However, the spot price depends upon the physical quantity produced, $\sum_{i=1}^{m} y_i$, which in turn depends upon the futures price. The equilibria of the spot and futures markets have to be considered simultaneously.

8.4   The spot market

Assumption   Spot demand is

$$D(\tilde{p}_s) = \tilde{a} - b\tilde{p}_s$$

where $\tilde{a}$ is a normal random variable with mean $E\tilde{a}$ and variance var $\tilde{a}$, and b a positive constant.

Thus spot demand is subject to random variation as $\tilde{a}$ varies. Spot supply comes from two sources. Farmers sell any output which they have not already sold on the futures market, so farmer i sells spot $x_i = y_i - z_i$. Speculator i sells spot everything which he bought on the futures market from farmers, x_i. Total spot sales $\sum_{i=1}^{n} x_i$ are thus equal to farmers' total output $\sum_{i=1}^{m} y_i$. (This is implied by the futures market clearing condition (7.8)). As (7.6) implies that $\sum_{i=1}^{m} y_i = mc^{-1} p_f$ the spot market clears when

$$\tilde{a} - b\tilde{p}_s = mc^{-1} p_f.$$ (7.10)

8.5   Rational expectations equilibrium

Eliminating p_f from the market clearing conditions (7.9) and (7.10) implies that

$$\tilde{p}_s = b^{-1} \tilde{a} - b^{-1} mc^{-1} \phi^{-1} \mu$$ (7.11)

where

$$\phi = 1 + r + mc^{-1} \sigma^2 \left[\sum_{i=1}^{n} k_i^{-1} \right]^{-1}.$$ (7.12)

As $\tilde{a}$ is normal and all the other terms on the right-hand side of (7.11) are constants, $\tilde{p}_s$ is normal. The dealers' beliefs about the form of the distribution of $\tilde{p}_s$ are correct. From (7.4) they believe that $\tilde{p}_s \sim N(\mu, \sigma^2)$. Equation (7.11) implies that

$$E\tilde{p}_s = b^{-1}E\tilde{a} - b^{-1}mc^{-1}\phi^{-1}\mu \qquad (7.13)$$

and

$$\text{var } \tilde{p}_s = b^{-2}\text{var } \tilde{a}. \qquad (7.14)$$

Beliefs about the mean and variance are correct if $E\tilde{p}_s = \mu$ and var $\tilde{p}_s = \sigma^2$. In this case (7.13) and (7.14) imply that the beliefs are correct if and only if

$$\sigma^2 = b^{-2}\text{var } \tilde{a} \qquad (7.15)$$

$$E\tilde{p}_s = \theta^{-1}\phi E\tilde{a} \qquad (7.16)$$

where substituting for σ^2 in (7.12),

$$\phi = 1 + r + mc^{-1}b^{-2}\text{var } \tilde{a} \left[\sum_{i=1}^{n} k_i^{-1} \right]^{-1} \qquad (7.17)$$

and

$$\theta = b\phi + mc^{-1}. \qquad (7.18)$$

Thus from (7.11), (7.16) and (7.18) as $\mu = E\tilde{p}_s$

$$\tilde{p}_s = \theta^{-1}\phi E\tilde{a} + b^{-1}(\tilde{a} - E\tilde{a}) \qquad (7.19)$$

and from (7.10) and (7.19)

$$p_f = \theta^{-1}E\tilde{a}. \qquad (7.20)$$

If the futures price is given by (7.20) and dealers' beliefs about the expected spot price by (7.15)–(7.18), the futures market clears. The futures price determines output. Output determines the distribution of the spot price. At this futures price, and this expected spot price, dealers' beliefs about the distribution of the spot price are correct. This is a rational expectations equilibrium.

Introducing risk aversion changes the model in several respects. If all dealers are risk neutral, arbitrage implies that $(1 + r)p_f = E\tilde{p}_s$: the expected return on risky futures is the same as the return on the safe asset. Dealers are indifferent about how many futures they hold, and have no positive reason to trade on the futures market. In this model with risk aversion (7.16) and (7.20) imply that $\phi p_f = E\tilde{p}_s$, and from (7.17) $\phi > 1 + r$. The risk premium $\phi - (1 + r)$ is an increasing function of the variance of the spot price b^{-2} var $\tilde{a}$, and each dealer's risk aversion parameter k_i.

Speculators are willing to take on some of the farmer's risk in order to earn a positive expected return. This model in fact overemphasizes the riskiness of speculative portfolios, because it considers only a single risky asset. In practice speculators can diminish, but not eliminate, risk by holding a portfolio of several risky assets whose returns are imperfectly correlated.

Both speculators and farmers wish to hold definite amounts of futures, and the market will trade actively. As $\mu = E\tilde{p}_s > p_f(1 + r)$, (7.5) and (7.7) imply that demand from speculators, and the speculative element of farmers' demand, will be strictly positive in equilibrium. Farmers as a whole must be net sellers of futures, to meet the demand from speculators. But an unusually risk-tolerant farmer might be a net purchaser.

9 RATIONAL EXPECTATIONS EQUILIBRIUM AND INFORMATION

In the model which I have just analysed the spot price is stochastic and differs from year to year, but the futures price is a constant, a function of the parameters of the model, including the mean and variance of $\tilde{a}$, the stochastic intercept in the spot demand function, which is by assumption the source of all the uncertainty.

I am now going to modify the model by assuming that dealers have information about $\tilde{a}$ in January when the futures market operates. I will look at three different information structures of increasing complexity, asking in each case how well the futures price reflects the information.

Example 1 *Symmetric information* Assume that

$$\tilde{a} = \tilde{I} + \tilde{e} \tag{7.21}$$

$\tilde{I}$ and $\tilde{e}$ are independent scalar normal random variables, $E\tilde{I} = E\tilde{a}$, and $E\tilde{e} = 0$. As the sum of normal variables is normal $\tilde{a}$ is still normal, var $\tilde{a} =$ var $\tilde{I} +$ var $\tilde{e}$. Assume also that all dealers, farmers and speculators observe $\tilde{I}$ each January. Conditional upon the information $\tilde{I}$ each dealer believes correctly that $\tilde{a}$ is a normal random variable whose mean $E(\tilde{a}|\tilde{I}) = \tilde{I}$ is random, whereas var $(\tilde{a}|\tilde{I}) =$ var $\tilde{e}$ is not random. The model is unchanged, apart from the fact that beliefs about the mean of $\tilde{a}$ change from year to year. The rational expectations equilibrium can be calculated as before. Parelleling (7.14) and (7.16)–(7.20),

$$\text{var}\,[\tilde{p}_s|\tilde{I}] = b^{-2}\,\text{var}\,[\tilde{a}|\tilde{I}] = b^{-2}\,\text{var}\,\tilde{e} \tag{7.22}$$

$$E\,[\tilde{p}_s|\tilde{I}] = \theta^{*-1}\phi^*E\,(\tilde{a}|\tilde{I}) = \theta^{*-1}\phi^*\tilde{I} \tag{7.23}$$

where

$$\phi^* = 1 + r + mc^{-1}b^{-2}\operatorname{var}\left[\tilde{a}|\tilde{I}\right]\left[\sum_{i=1}^{n}k_i^{-1}\right]^{-1} \tag{7.24}$$

$$\theta^* = b\phi^* + mc^{-1} \tag{7.25}$$

$$\tilde{p}_s = \theta^{*-1}\phi^*E\left(\tilde{a}|\tilde{I}\right) + b^{-1}[\tilde{a} - E\left(\tilde{a}|\tilde{I}\right)] = \theta^{*-1}\phi^*\tilde{I} + b^{-1}\tilde{e} \tag{7.26}$$

and

$$\tilde{p}_f = \theta^{*-1}E\left(\tilde{a}|\tilde{I}\right) = \theta^{*-1}\tilde{I}. \tag{7.27}$$

These equations differ from (7.14) and (7.16)–(7.20) in two ways. Firstly, the terms relating to the unconditional distribution of $\tilde{a}$, $E\tilde{a}$ and var $\tilde{a}$ in the previous equations have been replaced by the corresponding terms for the distribution conditional upon the information $E(\tilde{a}|\tilde{I})$ and var $(\tilde{a}|\tilde{I})$. Secondly, the futures price $\tilde{p}_f$ is now a random variable rather than a constant.

The expressions θ^* and ϕ^* are not random because var $(\tilde{a}|\tilde{I})$ is not random. Thus provided the numerical values of θ^* and ϕ^* are known it is possible to infer $\tilde{I}$, and $E[\tilde{p}_s|\tilde{I}]$ from $\tilde{p}_f$.

$$E[\tilde{p}_s|\tilde{I}] = \theta^{*-1}\phi^*\tilde{I} = \phi^*\tilde{p}_f$$

and so the conditional distribution of $\tilde{p}_s$ given $\tilde{p}_f$ is normal,

$$E[\tilde{p}_s|\tilde{p}_f] = E[\tilde{p}_s|\tilde{I}] = \phi^*\tilde{p}_f \tag{7.28}$$

and

$$\operatorname{var}\left[\tilde{p}_s|\tilde{p}_f\right] = \operatorname{var}\left[\tilde{p}_s|\tilde{I}\right] = b^{-2}\operatorname{var}\left(\tilde{a}|\tilde{I}\right) = b^{-2}\operatorname{var}\tilde{e}. \tag{7.29}$$

Anyone knowing the numerical value of ϕ^* would form the same conditional expectation of the spot price $\tilde{p}_s$ from the futures price $\tilde{p}_f$, as if he knew the information $\tilde{I}$. This observation is perhaps not very interesting in the context of this example, in which, by assumption all the dealers know $\tilde{I}$, but it is helpful in analysing the next two examples.

Example 2   As in the previous example

$$\tilde{a} = \tilde{I} + \tilde{e}$$

$\tilde{I}$ and $\tilde{e}$ are independent, and normal. $E\tilde{a} = E\tilde{I}$, and $E\tilde{e} = 0$. However, now only some of the dealers observe $\tilde{I}$. The others have no private information. In the rational expectations equilibrium the uninformed dealers will infer what information they can about the spot price from the futures price. If the futures price is completely efficient as an information transmitter the uninformed traders will trade as if they had the information.

This observation suggested to Radner (1979) and Grossman (1978) that models with asymmetric information could be analysed by considering the corresponding model in which the information is pooled and made available to all dealers (called a full communications equilibrium by Radner, an artificial economy by Grossman). If the futures price is a perfect transmitter of information in the rational expectations equilibrium of the original model, dealers' beliefs about the distribution of the spot price given the futures price in the original model will be the same as if they had the information available to them in the full communications equilibrium. Thus supply, demand and prices will be the same in the full communications equilibrium as in the rational expectations equilibrium of the original model.

Observing this point Radner and Grossman argued that the first step in analysing this type of model should be to examine the full communications equilibrium. This is much easier than looking at the rational expectations equilibrium with asymmetric information directly, because if dealers know all the information which could possibly be reflected in prices already they have no motive for using prices as information, so prices do not affect beliefs in the full communications equilibrium. Having characterized prices in the full communications equilibrium, ask what dealers' correct beliefs would be conditional on the full communications equilibrium prices. In particular, ask whether the beliefs are the same as they would be if dealers know all the information. If they are, it has been established that a rational expectations equilibrium exists in which beliefs, prices, supply and demand are the same as in the full communications equilibrium.

Consider the four-part definition of a rational expectations equilibrium in an asset market with asymmetric information. The first part refers to beliefs, the second to utility maximization given beliefs, the third to market clearing, and the fourth to correct beliefs. If the full communications equilibrium prices allow dealers to form precisely the same beliefs as if they had all the information, utility maximization leads to the same trades as in the full communications equilibrium. As the trades are the same the market clears at the same prices. The beliefs generating the trades are correct. This is a rational expectations equilibrium. This argument breaks down if beliefs given the full communications equilibrium prices are not the same as beliefs given all the information. In this case if a rational expectations equilibrium exists prices transmit some, but not all information.

In this example the full communications equilibrium is one in which all dealers observe $\bar{I}$. This is precisely example 1 where I have already argued that conditioning on the futures price alone leads dealers to the same beliefs as if they knew the information $\tilde{I}$. Thus the full communications equilibrium prices of example 1 are also rational expectations equilibrium prices for example 2. In this rational expectations equilibrium the futures price transmits all the information from the informed to the uninformed dealers.

Example 3 *Diverse information*   I now generalize the information structure considerably. Suppose that each dealer observes a random information variable $\tilde{I}_i$. This may be a scalar or a vector. It may be constant, in which case it is effectively no information. The only restriction is that $(\tilde{a}, \tilde{I}_1, \tilde{I}_2, \ldots, \tilde{I}_n)$ has a joint normal distribution. It seems an impossible task to ask a single price to aggregate all this diverse information, so that in the rational expectations equilibrium, dealers can trade as if they had all the information. Yet this is in fact so, owing to the following properties of normal random variables.

Lemma   *Conditional distributions of normal random variables*   *If $[\tilde{a}, \tilde{I}_1, \tilde{I}_2, \ldots, \tilde{I}_n]$ has a joint normal distribution,*

$$\tilde{I} = E[\tilde{a}|\tilde{I}_1, \tilde{I}_2, \ldots, \tilde{I}_n]$$

and

$$\tilde{e} = \tilde{a} - \tilde{I}$$

then $\tilde{I}$ and $\tilde{e}$ are independent normal random variables, $E\tilde{a} = E\tilde{I}$, $E\tilde{e} = 0$, var $\tilde{a} =$ var $\tilde{I} +$ var $\tilde{e}$. The conditional distribution of $\tilde{a}$ given $\tilde{I}$ is the same as the conditional distribution of $\tilde{a}$ given $\tilde{I}_1, \tilde{I}_2, \ldots, \tilde{I}_n$. Both conditional distributions are normal, with mean

$$E(\tilde{a}|\tilde{I}) = E[\tilde{a}|\tilde{I}_1, \tilde{I}_2, \ldots, \tilde{I}_n] = \tilde{I}$$

and variance

$$\text{var}(\tilde{a}|\tilde{I}) = \text{var}[\tilde{a}|\tilde{I}_1, \tilde{I}_2, \ldots, \tilde{I}_n] = \text{var } \tilde{a} - \text{var } \tilde{I} = \text{var } \tilde{e}.$$

Proof   See appendix

This result shows that for the purposes of forming beliefs about $\tilde{a}$, knowing $\tilde{I} = E[\tilde{a}|\tilde{I}_1, \tilde{I}_2, \ldots, \tilde{I}_n]$ gives the same information as knowing $\tilde{I}_1, \tilde{I}_2, \ldots, \tilde{I}_n$. The conditional mean $\tilde{I}$, a single number, aggregates perfectly all the diverse information. (It is a sufficient statistic for the information.)

This result can be used to compare two full communications equilibria, for the spot and futures market model. In the first equilibrium dealers observe the vector of random variables $\tilde{I}_1, \tilde{I}_2, \ldots, \tilde{I}_n$. In the second they observe $\tilde{I} = E[\tilde{a}|\tilde{I}_1, \tilde{I}_2, \ldots, \tilde{I}_n]$. In both equilibria the conditional distribution of $\tilde{a}$ is normal, with the same mean and variance. Thus the equilibrium prices are the same. The equilibrium in which all dealers observe $\tilde{I}$ is the equilibrium of the first model studied in this section. The prices in both equilibria are given by (7.22)–(7.27). In these equilibria, from (7.27)

$$\tilde{p}_f = \theta^{*-1}\tilde{I} = \theta^{*-1}E[\tilde{a}|\tilde{I}_1, \tilde{I}_2, \ldots, \tilde{I}_n] \tag{7.30}$$

and from (7.22) and (7.23)

$$\text{var}[\tilde{p}_s|\tilde{p}_f] = \text{var}[\tilde{p}_s|\tilde{I}] = \text{var}[\tilde{p}_s|\tilde{I}_1, \tilde{I}_2, \ldots, \tilde{I}_n] = b^{-2}\text{var}\,\tilde{e} \tag{7.31}$$

$$E[\tilde{p}_s|\tilde{p}_f] = E[\tilde{p}_s|\tilde{I}] = E[\tilde{p}_s|\tilde{I}_1, \tilde{I}_2, \ldots, \tilde{I}_n] = \theta^{*-1}\phi^*\tilde{I} = \phi^*\tilde{p}_f \tag{7.32}$$

and

$$\tilde{p}_f = \theta^{*-1}\tilde{I} = \theta^{*-1}E[\tilde{a}|\tilde{I}_1, \tilde{I}_2, \ldots, \tilde{I}_n]. \tag{7.33}$$

Conditioning only on the futures price, dealers form the same beliefs about the spot price as they would if they know either $\tilde{I} = E[\tilde{a}|\tilde{I}_1, \tilde{I}_2, \ldots, \tilde{I}_n]$, or the entire information vector $\tilde{I}_1, \tilde{I}_2, \ldots, \tilde{I}_n$. By the same argument as before these must also be rational expectations equilibrium prices for the model in which dealer i observes information $\tilde{I}_i$.

This is a much stronger result than before. It argues that a market price can not only transmit a single piece of information from one set of dealers to another, but also aggregate a large and diverse set of information perfectly.

10   THE ROBUSTNESS OF THE INFORMATIONAL EFFICIENCY RESULT

In the previous section I showed that in a simple futures market model the market price can aggregate diverse information so efficiently that each dealer's beliefs about the return on holding an asset (the spot price) given only its price are the same as if he had access to all the information to the market. He finds his own private information completely redundant.

This surprising result is not limited to futures markets. From a speculator's point of view a futures contract is one of many financial assets; others include shares and bonds issued by firms, and government securities. The original version of this model (Grossman, 1976) considered a stock market. The stock lasts for one period, and pays a random gross return $\tilde{R}$. An investor with wealth W_{i0} who buys x_i units of the stock at price p and invests $W_{i0} - px_i$ in a safe asset paying interest r, has final wealth

$$\tilde{W}_i = (\tilde{R} - p(1 + r))x_i + W_{i0}(1 + r).$$

The gross return $\tilde{R}$ plays a role precisely analogous to the spot price in the futures market. If R is normally distributed and the investor has an exponential utility function $-\exp [-k_i \tilde{W}_i]$ the argument used to derive the speculators' demand for futures yields the investors' demand for the stock

$$x_i = \frac{1}{k_i \operatorname{var} \tilde{R}} (E\tilde{R} - p(1 + r)) . \tag{7.34}$$

If there are n investors and a fixed supply of the stock S, market clearing requires that

$$\sum_{i=1}^{n} \frac{1}{k_i \operatorname{var} \tilde{R}} (E\tilde{R} - p(1 + r)) = S . \tag{7.35}$$

The stock and futures market models are mathematically very similar, apart from the fact that the supply of the asset in the stock market is taken as exogenous.

Now suppose the investors have diverse information, $\tilde{I}_1, \tilde{I}_2, \ldots, \tilde{I}_n$, and $[\tilde{R}, \tilde{I}_1, \tilde{I}_2, \ldots, \tilde{I}_n]$ is joint normal. Experience with the futures market model suggests looking at the full communications equilibria, in which market clearing implies that

$$\sum_{i=1}^{n} \frac{1}{k_i \sigma^2} [E[\tilde{R}|\tilde{I}_1, \tilde{I}_2, \ldots, \tilde{I}_n] - (1 + r)\tilde{p}] = S$$

where $\sigma^2 = \operatorname{var} [\tilde{R}|\tilde{I}_1, \tilde{I}_2, \ldots, \tilde{I}_n]$, so

$$E[\tilde{R}|\tilde{I}_1, \tilde{I}_2, \ldots, \tilde{I}_n] = \sigma^2 \left[\sum_{i=1}^{n} k_i^{-1} \right]^{-1} S + (1 + r)\tilde{p} . \tag{7.36}$$

Anyone knowing the numerical value of $\sigma^2 [\sum_{i=1}^{n} k_i^{-1}]^{-1} S$ and $(1 + r)$ could infer $E[\tilde{R}|\tilde{I}_1, \tilde{I}_2, \ldots, \tilde{I}_n]$ from the price $\tilde{p}$, and would form the same beliefs about $\tilde{R}$ as if he knew $\tilde{I}_1, \tilde{I}_2, \ldots, \tilde{I}_n$. By a now familiar argument this implies that the full communications equilibrium is also a rational expectations equilibrium; the rational expectations equilibrium price aggregates the information perfectly.

Grossman wrote the paper embodying this result before he had the idea of using an artificial economy, or full communications equilibrium, to analyse the model. He had to use more complex arguments and was not able to prove such a general result. The paper was important firstly because it was the first satisfactory asset market model embracing risk aversion and asymmetric information, and secondly because Grossman pointed out a most important paradox. In Grossman's model, just as in the spot and futures market model, knowing the asset price renders dealers' private information redundant. If this information is costly no dealer has any incentive to gather the information, particularly if he knows that another dealer is using the same information. Yet if no-one gathers the information it cannot be reflected in the price, which generates incentives to gather the information.

Grossman and Stiglitz (1980) resolve this paradox by modifying the model slightly. Suppose now that the asset supply is a normal random variable $\tilde{S}$. The relationship between the full communications equilibrium price $\tilde{p}$, $E[\tilde{R}|\tilde{I}_1, \tilde{I}_2, \ldots, \tilde{I}_n]$ and $\tilde{S}$ is given by (7.36), modified only by replacing the constant S by random $\tilde{S}$:

$$E[\tilde{R}|\tilde{I}_1, \tilde{I}_2, \ldots, \tilde{I}_n] = \sigma^2 \left[\sum_{i=1}^{n} k_i^{-1} \right]^{-1} \tilde{S} + (1 + r)\tilde{p}. \tag{7.37}$$

Even if the numerical values of $\sigma^2 [\Sigma_{i=1}^{n} k_i^{-1}]^{-1}$ and $(1 + r)$ are known it is impossible to infer $E[\tilde{R}|\tilde{I}_1, \tilde{I}_2, \ldots, \tilde{I}_n]$ from $\tilde{p}$ because $\tilde{S}$ is different each time the market operates. Conditioning on $\tilde{p}$ does not yield the same information as conditioning on $\tilde{I}_1, \tilde{I}_2, \ldots, \tilde{I}_n$. The full communications equilibrium is not a rational expectations equilibrium. (This is also true in the spot and futures market model, if farmers' output is uncertain, and dealers have information about both spot demand and output (Bray, 1981).)

Grossman and Stiglitz calculate the rational expectations equilibrium for a version of the stock market model in which there are two groups of dealers. The informed dealers all observe the same information, on which they base their expectations. The uninformed dealers form their expectations on the basis of the price. The informativeness of the price increases as the proportion of informed dealers increases. In the absence of information costs the informed dealers have higher expected utility than the uninformed, because they are less uncertain of the asset return (its conditional variance is lower for the informed than the uninformed). If information is costly, informed dealers may be better or worse off. If the proportion of informed dealers is large and the price conveys much of the information to the uninformed dealers, they are likely to be worse off. If the proportion of informed dealers is small and the price conveys little information to the uninformed, they are likely to be better off. Grossman and Stiglitz show that for each level of information costs there is an equilibrium proportion of informed dealers, so that the benefits of the information just balance the costs, and dealers are indifferent between being informed and uninformed. They derive a variety of interesting comparative static results from this model.

11   EXISTENCE OF RATIONAL EXPECTATIONS EQUILIBRIUM

Expectations play a crucial role in all the models which I have presented, as in many others. Whenever I have needed to close models by specifying expectations I have followed standard practice in postulating rational expectations. In each case I have been able to show that a rational expectations equilibrium exists by solving explicitly for the equilibrium. This is not always possible. Indeed in some examples, such as the one which follows, it can be shown that there is no set of prices and beliefs which satisfy Parts 3 and 4 of the definition. There is no rational expectations equilibrium.

The example is similar in form to that of Kreps (1977). It is a somewhat modified version of the spot and futures market model. For mathematical simplicity assume that there is one farmer and one speculator. Each maximizes the expectation of a utility function $-\exp(-\tilde{W})$. The speculator believes the spot price $\tilde{p}_s \sim N(\mu, \sigma^2)$. The interest rate $r = 0$. Arguing as before, the speculator's excess demand for futures is

$$x_s = \frac{1}{\sigma^2}(\mu - p_f). \tag{7.38}$$

The farmer has a cost function for output $C(y) = sy + \frac{1}{2}y^2$. He also believes that $\tilde{p}_s \sim N(\mu, \sigma^2)$. Utility maximization for the farmer implies that he sets output so $C'(y) = p_f$ or

$$y = p_f - s. \tag{7.39}$$

He hedges by selling y on the futures market, and in addition speculates by buying futures

$$x_f = \frac{1}{\sigma^2}(\mu - p_f). \tag{7.40}$$

Futures market clearing implies that $x_s + x_f = y$, or from (7.38)–(7.40),

$$\frac{2}{\sigma^2}(\mu - p_f) = p_f - s. \tag{7.41}$$

Spot demand is

$$D(p_s) = \tilde{a} - \tilde{p}_s$$

where $\tilde{a}$ is a normal random variable, and var $\tilde{a} = 1$. Spot market clearing implies that $D(\tilde{p}_s) = y$, that is

$$\tilde{a} - \tilde{p}_s = p_f - s. \tag{7.42}$$

Equation (7.42) implies that

$$E\tilde{p}_s = E\tilde{a} - p_f + s \tag{7.43}$$

and

$$\text{var } \tilde{p}_s = \text{var } \tilde{a} = 1. \tag{7.44}$$

If the farmer and speculator are to form rational expectations $\mu = E\tilde{p}_s = E\tilde{a} - p_f + s$, and $\sigma^2 = \text{var}\,\tilde{p}_s = 1$. The futures market clearing condition (7.41) becomes

$$2(E\tilde{a} - p_f + s - p_f) = p_f - s$$

so

$$p_f = \tfrac{1}{5}\left(2E\tilde{a} + 3s\right). \tag{7.45}$$

Spot market clearing and rational expectations imply (7.43), which with (7.45) implies that

$$E\tilde{p}_s = \tfrac{1}{5}\left(3E\tilde{a} + 2s\right). \tag{7.46}$$

So far I have had no difficulty in calculating the rational expectations equilibrium, but introducing asymmetric information can cause complications. Suppose that there are only two sorts of weather, good and bad. The farmer observes the weather; the speculator does not. If the weather is good $E\tilde{a} = \tfrac{5}{4}$ and $s = \tfrac{1}{6}$. If it is bad $E\tilde{a} = 1$ and $s = \tfrac{1}{3}$.

There are only two possibilities: either the futures price is different in different weather or it is not. If the futures price is different the speculator can infer the weather from the price. Trades and prices will be the same as if both farmer and speculator knew the weather. In this case in good weather $E\tilde{a} = \tfrac{5}{4}$, $s = \tfrac{1}{6}$, from (7.45) $p_f = \tfrac{3}{5}$ and from (7.46) $E\tilde{p}_s = \tfrac{49}{60}$. In bad weather $E\tilde{a} = 1$, $s = \tfrac{1}{3}$, from (7.45) $p_f = \tfrac{3}{5}$, and from (7.46) $E\tilde{p}_s = \tfrac{44}{60}$. Thus the futures price is the same in both weathers, contradicting the supposition that it was different.

The alternative supposition is that the futures price is the same whatever the weather, in which case the speculator's demand will be the same. If the farmer has rational expectations his excess demand for futures will be using (7.39), (7.40) and (7.43), and recalling that $\sigma^2 = 1$ and $\mu = E\tilde{p}_s$,

$$x_f - y = (E\tilde{p}_s - p_f) - (p_f - s) = E\tilde{p}_s + s - 2p_f$$

$$= E\tilde{a} + 2s - 3p_f.$$

In good weather $E\tilde{a} + 2s = \tfrac{19}{12}$, in bad weather $E\tilde{a} + 2s = \tfrac{5}{3}$. If p_f is independent of the weather the speculator's demand for futures is independent of the weather, but the farmer's is not. The futures market cannot clear at the same price in both weathers. This exhausts the possibilities. In this example the assumptions of market clearing and rational expectations are logically inconsistent. There is no rational expectations equilibrium.

In defining a rational expectations equilibrium for an asset market model in section 3 I argued that the market clearing condition induces a mapping from the beliefs people hold to the correct beliefs. This is an almost universal feature of models with expectations. It crops up, for example, in equation (7.13), which gives the correct expected spot price $E\tilde{p}_s$ as a function of the subjectively held expectation μ. A rational expectations equilibrium is a fixed point of this mapping. Fixed-point theorems give conditions under which mappings have fixed points; notably continuity. The non-existence problems for rational expectations models with asymmetric information stem from discontinuities in the mapping, where a small change in prices can induce a large change in the information which can be inferred from them. In the example, if prices are identical in both weathers, the speculator cannot infer the weather, but if they are very slightly different he can.

Checking that an equilibrium exists is an essential preliminary to using a model; assuming that an equilibrium exists and arguing from there, can yield no valid conclusions if in fact no equilibrium exists. Knowing the circumstances under which a model has an equilibrium puts logical limits on the range of applicability.

Existence problems are attacked from two directions, existence theorems and non-existence examples. Existence theorems establish that under certain conditions, typically conditions on preferences, technology, and the structure of transactions and information, an equilibrium exists. For some special models equilibrium can be shown to exist by calculating the equilibrium, but in general the problem is attacked indirectly, often using fixed-point theorems which establish that a set of equations has a solution, but not what the solution is. Non-existence examples show that in certain cases no equilibrium exists. These examples are helpful because they show certain conjectured general existence results cannot be valid; a claim that all models of a certain type have an equilibrium is wrong if a single such model has no equilibrium, just as a single black swan is enough to invalidate the claim that all swans are white.

The non-existence example which I demonstrated earlier is not robust; a small change in the parameters of the model would allow an equilibrium to exist, non-existence is a freak eventuality. Radner (1979) studies a much more general asset market model which shares two features with this example. In both models there are only a finite number of different possible information signals. In the example there are two, good weather or bad weather. In Radner's model there may be a large but finite number of different signals received by a finite number of individuals. The vector of joint signals can only take a finite number of different values. In Radner's model, as in my example, there may be no rational expectations equilibrium. Radner shows rigorously that equilibrium exists generically. Generic existence is defined precisely in the paper; the idea which it captures is that whilst equilibrium may fail to exist in some special cases, almost any perturbation of the model will restore existence. Radner's proof proceeds by considering the full communications equilibrium, in which dealers pool all their information signals before trading. The price vector in the full communications equilibrium $\tilde{p}$ is a function of the joint signal $\tilde{s}$, $\tilde{p} = p(\tilde{s})$. If the price vector is different whenever any element in the signal is different, the price reveals the signal, and the full communications equilibrium is a rational expectations equilibrium, in which prices fully reveal the information.

The crucial question is whether the map from the signals into prices is invertible. There are a finite number, m, of signals, whereas prices can be any vector in R^{n+}, so there are an infinity (indeed a continuum) of different possible prices. Radner's result confirms the intuition that if the utility functions generating demand are reasonably well behaved, the map from signals to prices fails to be invertible only in special circumstances, in which case a small perturbation of the model restores invertibility.

The assumption that there are a finite number of different possible signals plays a crucial role in this invertibility argument. If there are a continuum of different possible signals the argument may break down. Jordan and Radner (1982) devise an example with an informed dealer and an uninformed dealer and one relative price. The informed dealer observes a signal $\tilde{s}$ in $[0, 1]$. Given the price, the informed dealer's demand changes with the signal; if there are two different signals $s_1 \neq s_2$, with $p(s_1) = p(s_2)$ the informed dealer's demand is different for the two signals, but the uninformed dealer who observes only the price has the same demand. The market cannot clear at the same price for both s_1 and s_2. On the other hand, if the function is invertible the uninformed dealer can infer s from p, the prices are the same as in the full communications equilibrium. But Jordan and Radner show that the full communications equilibrium price function has the form shown in figure 7.2, and is not invertible. This is a robust example, changing the parameters of the model changes the price function a little, but does not make it invertible.

The importance of invertibility for the existence of rational expectations equilibria in which prices reveal all the information suggests that the relative dimensions of the signal space and the price space may be important. This is confirmed by Allen (1982), who shows that if the dimension of the signal space is less than the dimension of the price space a fully revealing rational expectations equilibrium exists generically. Jordan (1983) shows that if the dimension of the price space is lower than the dimension of the signal space rational expectations equilibrium exists, generically, but is not fully revealing.

The literature on fully revealing equilibria is concerned with equilibria in which dealers can infer the entire information signal from the prices. This is sufficient to enable them to form the same expectations as if they saw the signal. But it is not necessary; dealers want to know about a vector or asset returns $\tilde{R}$. If $\tilde{R}$ and the information $\tilde{I}$ are joint normal, knowing $E(\tilde{R}|\tilde{I})$ tells them as much as knowing $\tilde{I}$. The vector $E(\tilde{R}|\tilde{I})$ has the same dimension as

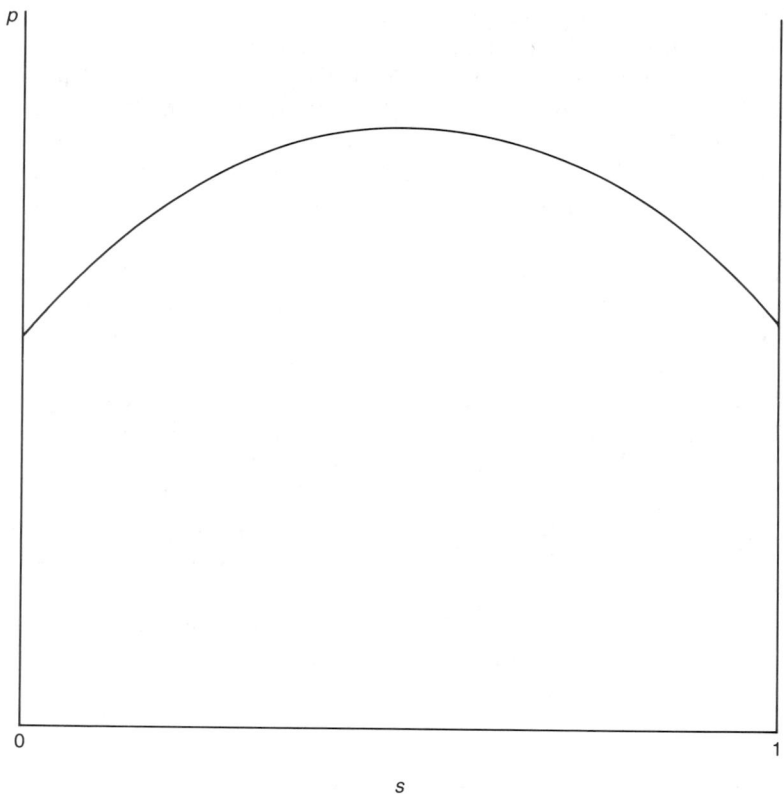

Figure 7.2

$\tilde{R}$, the number of risky assets. This may be much lower than the dimension of $\tilde{I}$. Grossman (1978) uses this result to analyse a stock market model in which returns are normal, and dealers care only about the mean and variance of return. By applying the capital asset pricing model Grossman shows that provided the market portfolio is not a Giffen good, dealers can infer $E(\tilde{R}|\tilde{I})$ from the information, and so a rational expectations equilibrium exists in which dealers trade as if they had all the information. Grossman also exploits the properties of normal random variables in his paper on futures markets (1977), showing how they can act to transmit information.

The existence of rational expectations equilibrium in asset markets is an attractive and challenging problem for mathematical economists. A more sophisticated discussion and further references are in Radner (1982), which surveys the literature on equilibrium under uncertainty, and in Jordan and Radner (1982), which introduces a symposium issue of the *Journal of*

Economic Theory, on rational expectations in microeconomic models, which includes a number of related papers. More recent work on the matter includes Jordan (1982a, 1982b), Allen (1983), and Anderson and Sonnenschein (1985).

12 EVALUATING THE MODELS

A model is a simplified, stylized description of certain aspects of the economy. It omits many details in order to concentrate on certain features and their interrelationships. One of the major objectives of modelling is often to show that the description is logically consistent by demonstrating that an equilibrium exists, an issue which I have discussed at some length. If a model is to be used as a basis for saying something about real economies logical consistency is essential; even grossly unrealistic models may be useful in establishing logical limits to rhetoric. But is is obviously desirable that a model be a correct, as well as a consistent, description.

Unfortunately there is no clear and universally applicable criterion for the correctness of models. Any model omits details, abstracts and simplifies. Reality is too complicated to be thought about in totality. Assumptions in economic models are most unlikely to be completely adequate descriptions of behaviour. The question to ask is whether they are plausible enough to generate implications which say something about the aspects of reality with which the model is concerned. This is inevitably a matter of judgement, and must often depend upon the use to which a model is being put.

The three major assumptions made in the financial market models which I described are that markets clear, that agents are price-takers and that they have rational expectations. These assumptions are very widely made; they are also central to the 'new-classical' macroeconomics (Begg 1982a). Market clearing and price-taking seem in general quite plausible for financial markets, where prices move readily, there is little evidence of sustained excess supply and demand, and there are a large number of traders.

The rational expectations hypothesis can be stated loosely, that people do not make systematic mistakes in forecasting; more precisely, people's subjective beliefs about probability distributions correspond to the objective probability distributions. Employing the rational expectations hypothesis imposes two logical requirements, that objective probability distributions exist, and that a rational expectations equilibrium exists. In constructing a model an economist creates the objective probability distributions, but these models can only be applied to situations where the distributions could in principle at least be derived from data. This requires that the structure and parameters of the economy are in some way constant through time. Rational expectations models describe long-run stationary equilibria.

One important criticism of the rational expectations hypothesis is that it assumes that agents know too much. Consider the spot and futures market model with asymmetric information. In rational expectations equilibrium the uninformed dealers believe correctly that the conditional distribution of the spot price given the futures price is normal, has conditional mean given by (7.28), $E[\tilde{p}_s | \tilde{p}_f] = \phi^* \tilde{p}_f$, and a constant conditional variance. All they need to know is the fact of normality and the numerical value of ϕ^* and var $[\tilde{p}_s | \tilde{p}_f]$. The uninformed dealers do not have to know the structure of the model, just two parameters of the reduced form. Further, by observing the markets operating in rational expectations equilibrium for a number of years the numbers ϕ^* and var $[\tilde{p}_s | \tilde{p}_f]$ could be estimated by standard statistical techniques. Apparently it is quite easy to learn how to form rational expectations.

In financial markets there are very large amounts of money at stake; and there is every incentive to apply the considerable abilities and resources of professional investors to make the best possible forecasts. However, the argument that it is easy or even possible to learn how to form rational expectations by applying standard statistical techniques is misleading. Economists are interested in expectations because they believe that expectations affect what happens. This belief is reflected in the models; if agents in these models do not have rational expectations the model behaves differently from the rational expectations equilibrium. In section 7 I defined a rational expectations equilibrium as a fixed point of the mapping from subjectively held beliefs into 'correct beliefs' induced by the market clearing condition. Outside rational expectations equilibrium subjective beliefs differ from both correct beliefs and the rational expectations equilibrium beliefs. For example, in the spot and futures market model in rational expectations equilibrium dealers believe that $E[\tilde{p}_s | \tilde{p}_f] = \phi^* \tilde{p}_f$. If dealers believe that $E[\tilde{p}_s | \tilde{p}_f] = \phi \tilde{p}_f$ where $\phi \neq \phi^*$, the correct conditional expectation will be of the form $E[\tilde{p}_s | \tilde{p}_f] = \hat{\phi} \tilde{p}_f$ where $\hat{\phi} \neq \phi$, the expectation is incorrect, and $\hat{\phi} \neq \phi^*$, the correct expectation is not the same as in the rational expectations equilibrium. Changing to the 'correct' expectation formation rule $E[\tilde{p}_s | \tilde{p}_f] = \hat{\phi} \tilde{p}_f$, changes the behaviour of the model, and this rule becomes incorrect. The obvious question to ask is whether repeated changes of the expectation formation rule ultimately lead to a rational expectations equilibrium. Is it possible to describe a plausible learning process which ultimately yields rational expectations? The answer depends upon how 'plausible' is understood. One possibility is to insist that agents learn using correctly specified Bayesian models. David Kreps and I argue elsewhere (Bray and Kreps, 1986) that it is in fact not plausible, because it in effect assumes a more elaborate and informationally demanding form of rational expectations equilibrium. However, if agents do learn in this way and if the model has suitable continuity properties, expectations eventually become rational in the conventional sense.

Another possible way to model learning is to assume that agents estimate the model as if it were in rational expectations equilibrium, for example in the spot and futures market model they regress $\tilde{p}_s$ on $\tilde{p}_f$ using ordinary least squares, and use the estimated regression coefficients in forecasting $\tilde{p}_s$ from $\tilde{p}_f$. In Bray (1982) I studied this procedure for the model of example 2 where there are uninformed dealers, and informed dealers, all of whom have the same information. I found that provided the uninformed dealers did not form too large a proportion of the market, the model would eventually converge to its rational expectations equilibrium. Bray (1983)[2] and Bray and Savin (1986) study similar econometric learning processes for a simple macroeconomic model and a version of the cobweb model. In both these models if the parameters of the supply and demand functions have the usual signs, agents eventually learn how to form rational expectations. In all these examples agents are estimating misspecified economic models, so convergence to rational expectations equilibrium is not based on standard theorems on the asymptotic properties of estimators, is somewhat surprising, and hard to prove. Convergence to rational expectations equilibrium may be slow, and takes place only if the parameters of the model lie in a certain range. Although many of the examples which have been studied converge in economically plausible circumstances there is no general theory which establishes that convergence will always take place.

Expectations are important for economics; they crop up unavoidably in considering a vast range of issues. The enormous virtue of the rational expectations hypothesis is that it gives a simple, general and plausible way of handling expectations. It makes it possible to formulate and answer questions, for example, on the efficiency of markets as transmitters as information, which would otherwise be utterly intractable. All recent progress on the economics of information is built on the rational expectations hypothesis.

Consider for a moment the alternative hypotheses. One possibility is that agents use a simple forecasting rule which generates systematic mistakes. In any application it is necessary to specify the rule, for example adaptive expectations. If there is good evidence that people do forecast in this way this is attractive, but it seems implausible that in the long run in a stable environment they will fail to notice their mistakes and modify the rule. Another alternative is to try to model the dynamics of the learning process. At present this seems to make for models which are too complicated and mathematically difficult to use for addressing most questions. Rational expectations equilibrium is a way of avoiding many difficult dynamic issues; if an issue is intractable in the current state of knowledge, circumventing it is probably the most fruitful research strategy.

Another alternative is to rely on survey data for expectations. Where possible this may be valuable in empirical work, if not very helpful for theorists.

A further alternative is to follow Keynes and argue that expectations cannot be described as probability distributions, they are volatile, and not susceptible to formal description. This makes it impossible to incorporate expectations explicitly into formal models, except by treating them as exogenous. Begg (1982b) argues that this is Keynes' strategy in the *General Theory* and is followed in traditional textbook treatments of Keynesian theory. In some cases I think this is an entirely defensible, indeed attractive strategy for modelling short-term events. The danger is that if expectations are unobservable, inexplicable, exogenous and volatile it leaves the model with no predictive and very little explanatory power as anything can be attributed to a shift in expectations. The rational expectations hypothesis also postulates unobservable expectations, but otherwise in total opposition to Keynes treats expectations as explicable, exogenous, and stable (unless the underlying model changes, in which case expectations change appropriately). In medium to long-term models the extreme rational expectations hypothesis is more attractive than the extreme exogenous expectations hypothesis. There is currently no generally acceptable intermediate hypothesis. Note that although Keynes himself would probably shudder if he knew, there is no reason why rational expectations should not be incorporated into 'Keynesian' models, which would have quite different properties from the 'new-classical' rational expectations models. (See Begg 1982b).

The rational expectations hypothesis seems at present much the most satisfactory generally applicable hypothesis on expectations formation. But it must be remembered that rational expectations models describe long-run equilibria, on the assumption that the dynamics induced by learning eventually converge to rational expectations equilibrium. We have no good reason to believe that this assumption is always, or even often, valid.

I have discussed the assumptions of the financial market models at some length. The other criteria for the correctness of the models as descriptions is to look at implications of the models, and compare them with data. There are two sources of data, experimental data from laboratory situations, and empirical data from real markets. Ultimately the objective is to understand real markets, but laboratory data generated by setting up a market with groups of students enables the experimenter to control and design the experiment, eliminating the host of extraneous factors which affect real market data.

Plott and Sunder (1982) set up a series of asset markets with informed and uninformed traders. The return on the asset depended on which of two or three states of the world occurs. The informed traders all had the same piece of information, in most cases telling them which state of the world had occurred. Plott and Sunder calculated two prices for each market, firstly the rational expectations equilibrium price in which the uninformed dealers inferred as much as possible from the price, secondly the prior information price in which the uninformed dealers traded only on the basis of their prior information. Although the rational expectations model was not a perfect fit, prices did show a tendency to move towards their rational expectations equilibrium level. Plott and Sunder interpret the data as supporting the rational expectations rather than the prior information model.

Real market data has been used to test the efficient markets hypothesis, that using information in addition to the current price of an asset does not make for better predictions, and the market price efficiently aggregates all the information. Three different forms of the hypothesis have been considered: the weak form, considering the information in past prices; the semi-strong form, considering more general publicly available information; and the strong form, considering private information. The empirical literature is vast; Brealey (1983) provides a very readable introduction, and numerous references. Broadly the literature supports the weak and semi-strong forms of the efficient markets hypothesis, but private information does seem to give some advantage. The efforts of numerous academic investigators have failed to uncover a rule for forecasting market prices in order to manage a portfolio which does significantly better than holding a fixed, well-diversified portfolio. These results are consistent with the theoretical models which I have been describing and can be taken as support for the application of the rational expectations hypothesis to financial markets.

13   FURTHER QUESTIONS

These models answer some questions, but provoke others. Many of the models consider asset markets in isolation, taking the return generated by the asset as exogenous. (The spot and futures market model is an exception.) But financial markets are part of a larger system. One of their major functions is to enable enterprises to spread, and share risk, with consequences for output, investment and employment. It now appears that the markets may also have a role as transmitters of information. The ramifications of this role are not understood, but may be investigated using techniques similar to those which I have described.

Another set of open questions concern the mechanism of price formation. In these models price is a function of information, for example in the spot and futures market model where dealers have diverse information the futures price $\tilde{p}_f = \theta^{*-1} E[\tilde{a} | \tilde{I}_1, \tilde{I}_2, \ldots, \tilde{I}_n]$, (7.30), where θ^* is a parameter, and $\tilde{I}_i$ agent i's information, a normal random variable. As the information varies from year to year the price varies. If the dealers have diverse information no individual dealer can check that the price is at the correct level given all the information. If a dealer thinks that the futures price is high or low given his private information, he can only conclude that other dealers have different information which leads them to expect a high or low spot price. Any numerical value of $\tilde{p}_f$ can clear the market; it is far from clear what pushes $\tilde{p}_f$ to its correct value. (This point is originally due to Beja, 1976).

Universal price-taking is of course a convenient fiction. People set prices, unilaterally, by auction procedures, or by haggling. If there is a very limited range of prices at which goods can be sold, price-taking is a good approximation. It may be necessary to consider the detailed mechanics of price making, the activities of brokers, jobbers, and market makers, to understand some aspects of the determination of prices in asset markets. In discussing their experimental results Plott and Sunder suggest that some of the information is transmitted by the oral auction process which they use, including unaccepted bids and offers. If this is so it provides an additional reason for looking at the institutional details of market structure.

The models which I have presented have a very stark, simple, time structure: things happen at only two dates. In practice many financial markets operate repeatedly, the same asset is traded at a large number of dates, indeed trade may best be modelled as a continuous time process. There is a literature on continuous-time models of financial markets (e.g. Black and Scholes, 1973; Merton, 1973), but this literature takes no account of informational asymmetries. Continuous-time models with asymmetric information are attractive means of investigating the rate at which markets disseminate information, although they may pose formidable technical difficulties. There is certainly a case for looking at a richer temporal structure than has been considered up to now.

APPENDIX

Proof of lemma.   Conditional distributions of normal random variables

Anderson (1958) shows that

$$\tilde{I} = E[\tilde{a}|\tilde{I}_1, \tilde{I}_2, \ldots, \tilde{I}_n] = E\tilde{a} + \sum{}_{ay} \sum{}_{yy}^{-1} (\tilde{y} - E\tilde{y}) \qquad (7.47)$$

where $\tilde{y}$ is notation for the vector $[\tilde{I}_1, \tilde{I}_2, \ldots, \tilde{I}_n]$, $\Sigma_{ay} = \text{cov}(\tilde{a}, \tilde{y})$, $\Sigma_{yy} = \text{var}(\tilde{y})$. Equation (7.47) implies that $\tilde{I}$ is a linear function of $[\tilde{I}_1, \tilde{I}_2, \ldots, \tilde{I}_n]$. As linear functions of normal random variables are normal, $\tilde{I}$ and $\tilde{e} = \tilde{a} - \tilde{I}$ are normal

$$\text{cov}(\tilde{e}, \tilde{y}) = \text{cov}[\tilde{a} - E\tilde{a} - \sum{}_{ay} \sum{}_{yy}^{-1} (\tilde{y} - E\tilde{y}), \tilde{y}]$$

$$= \sum_{ay} - \sum_{ay} \sum_{yy}^{-1} \sum_{yy} = 0.$$

Thus $\tilde{e}$ and $\tilde{y}$ are uncorrelated, and as they are normal independent. Since $\tilde{I}$ is a linear function of $\tilde{y}$, $\tilde{I}$ and $\tilde{e}$ are uncorrelated, that is

$$\text{cov}(\tilde{I}, \tilde{e}) = \text{cov}(\tilde{I}, \tilde{a} - \tilde{I}) = 0 \tag{7.48}$$

and so $\tilde{I}$ and $\tilde{e}$ are independent.

From (7.47),

$$E\tilde{a} = E\tilde{I} \tag{7.49}$$

and so $E\tilde{e} = E\tilde{a} - E\tilde{I} = 0$. As $\tilde{I}$ and $\tilde{e}$ are independent,

$$\text{var}\,\tilde{a} = \text{var}(\tilde{I} + \tilde{e}) = \text{var}\,\tilde{I} + \text{var}\,\tilde{e}.$$

As $\tilde{I}$ is a function of $\tilde{I}_1, \ldots, \tilde{I}_n$ and $\tilde{e}$ is independent of $\tilde{I}_1, \tilde{I}_2, \ldots, \tilde{I}_n$ the conditional distribution of $\tilde{a} = \tilde{I} + \tilde{e}$ given $\tilde{I}_1, \tilde{I}_2, \ldots, \tilde{I}_n$ is normal (as $\tilde{e}$ is normal), with mean

$$E[\tilde{a}|\tilde{I}_1, \tilde{I}_2, \ldots, \tilde{I}_n] = E[\tilde{I}|\tilde{I}_1, \tilde{I}_2, \ldots, \tilde{I}_n] + E[\tilde{e}|\tilde{I}_1, \tilde{I}_2, \ldots, \tilde{I}_n]$$

$$= \tilde{I} + E\tilde{e} = \tilde{I} = E(\tilde{a}|\tilde{I})$$

and

$$\text{var}[\tilde{a}|\tilde{I}_1, \tilde{I}_2, \ldots, \tilde{I}_n] = \text{var}[\tilde{e}|\tilde{I}_1, \tilde{I}_2, \ldots, \tilde{I}_n] = \text{var}\,\tilde{e} = \text{var}(\tilde{a}|\tilde{I}).$$

It can be shown that the conditional expectation of $\tilde{a}$ given $\tilde{I}_1, \tilde{I}_2, \ldots, \tilde{I}_n$ is the unique linear function of $\tilde{I}$ or $\tilde{I}_1, \tilde{I}_2, \ldots, \tilde{I}_n$ satisfying 7.48 and 7.49. These equations characterize the conditional expectation of one normal random variable given another. (See Bray (1981) for an application of this fact.)

NOTES

1 $E(\exp(-k\tilde{W})$ is the moment generating function of the random variable $\tilde{W}$, an object which mathematicians find interesting. The result is proved in most texts on probability, e.g. Meyer (1970).

2 Bray (1983) is much the shortest and simplest of these papers on learning, and the best introduction to the issues as I see them. Bray and Savin (1984) contains computer simulations which shed light on the rates of convergence and divergence, and discusses the relationship between this work, and time-varying parameter models in econometrics. Related literature is surveyed briefly in Blume, Bray and Easley (1982). Bray and Savin (1984) contains more recent references.

REFERENCES

Allen, B. (1982) Strict rational expectations equilibria with diffuseness. *Journal of Economic Theory* 27, 20–46.

Allen, B. (1983) Expectations equilibria with dispersed information: existence with approximate rationality in a model with a continuum of agents and finitely many states of the world. *Review of Economic Studies* 50, 267–85.

Anderson, T. W. (1958) *An Introduction to Multivariate Statistical Analysis*. Wiley, New York.

Anderson, R. M. and Sonnenschein, H. (1985) Rational expectations equilibrium with econometric models. *Review of Economic Studies* 52(3), 359–69.

Arrow, K. (1964) The role of securities in the optimal allocation of risk-bearing. *Review of Economic Studies* 31, 91–6.

Begg, D. K. H. (1982a) *The Rational Expectations Revolution in Macroeconomics*. Philip Allan, Oxford.

Begg, D. K. H. (1982b) Rational expectations, wage rigidity and involuntary unemployment: a particular theory. *Oxford Economic Papers* 34, 23–47.

Beja, A. (1976) The limited information efficiency of market processes, Research Program in Finance Working Paper No. 43, University of California, Berkeley.

Black, F. and Scholes, M. (1973) The pricing of options and corporate liabilities. *Journal of Political Economy* 81, 637–59.

Blume, L., Bray, M. M. and Easley, D. (1982) Introduction to the stability of rational expectations equilibrium. *Journal of Economic Theory* 26, 313–17.

Bray, M. M. (1981) Futures trading, rational expectations, and the efficient markets hypothesis. *Econometrica* 49, 575–96.

Bray, M. M. (1982) Learning, estimation, and the stability of rational expectations. *Journal of Economic Theory* 26, 318–39.

Bray, M. M. (1983) Convergence to rational expectations equilibrium. In *Individual Forecasting and Aggregate Outcomes* ed. R. Frydman and E. S. Phelps, Cambridge: Cambridge University Press.

Bray, M. M. and Kreps, D. M. (1986) Rational learning and rational expectations. In *Essays in Honor of K. J. Arrow*, eds W. Heller, D. Starrett and R. Starr, Cambridge University Press.

Bray, M. M. and Savin, N. E. (1986) Rational expectations equilibria, learning and model specification, Econometrica 54, 1129–60.

Brealey, R. (1983) *An Introduction to Risk and Return*. 2nd edn Blackwell, Oxford.

Danthine, J. P. (1978) Information, futures prices and stabilising speculation. *Journal of Economic Theory* 17, 79–98.

Deaton, A. and Muellbauer, J. (1980) *Economics and Consumer Behaviour*. Cambridge University Press, Cambridge.

Diamond, P. A. (1967) The role of a stock market in a general equilibrium model with technological uncertainty. *American Economic Review* 57, 759–73.

Diamond, P. A. and Rothschild, M. (1978) *Uncertainty in Economics*. Academic Press, New York.

Grossman, S. J. (1976) On the efficiency of competitive stock markets where traders have diverse information. *Journal of Finance* 31, 573–85.

Grossman, S. J. (1977) The existence of futures markets, noisy rational expectations and informational externalities. *Review of Economic Studies* 44, 431–49.

Grossman, S. J. (1978) Further results on the informational efficiency of competitive stock markets. *Journal of Economic Theory* 18, 81–101.

Grossman, S. J. (1981) An introduction to the theory of rational expectations under aysmmetric information. *Review of Economic Studies* 48, 541–60.

Grossman, S. J. and Stiglitz, J. E. (1980) On the impossibility of informationally efficient markets. *American Economic Review* 70, 393–408.

Hayek, F. A. (1945) The use of knowledge in society. *American Economic Review* 35, 519–30.

Jordan, J. S. (1982a) Admissable market data structures: a complete characterisation. *Journal of Economic Theory* 28(1), 19–31.

Jordan, J. S. (1982b) A dynamic model of expectations equilibrium. *Journal of Economic Theory* 28(2), 235–54.

Jordan, J. S. (1983) On the efficient markets hypothesis. *Econometrica* 51, 1325–43.

Jordan, J. S. and Radner, R. (1982) Rational expectations in microeconomic models: an overview. *Journal of Economic Theory* 26, 201–23.

Kaldor, N. (1934) A classificatory note on the determinateness of equilibrium. *Review of Economic Studies* 1, 122–36.

Keynes, J. M. (1936) *The General Theory of Employment, Interest and Money.* Macmillan, London.

Knight, F. H. (1921) *Risk, Uncertainty and Profit.* Houghton Mifflin, New York.

Kreps, D. (1977) A note on fulfilled expectations equilibria *Journal of Economic Theory* 14, 32–43.

Merton, R. C. (1973) An intertemporal capital asset pricing model *Econometrica* 41, 867–88.

Meyer, P. L. (1970) *Introductory Probability and Statistical Applications.* 2nd edn Addison Wesley, Reading, Massachusetts.

Muth, J. F. (1961) Rational expectations and the theory of price movements. *Econometrica* 29, 315–35.

Plott, C. R. and Sunder, S. (1982) Efficiency of experimental security markets with insider information: an application of rational expectations models. *Journal of Political Economy* 90, 663–98.

Radner, R. (1979) Rational expectations equilibrium generic existence and the information revealed by prices. *Econometrica* 47, 655–78.

Radner, R. (1982) Equilibrium under uncertainty. In *Handbook of Mathematical Economics, vol. II*, eds K. J. Arrow and M. D. Intriligator, Amsterdam, North-Holland.

Raiffa, H. (1986) *Decision Analysis: Introductory Lectures on Choice Under Uncertainty.* Addison Wesley, Reading, Massachusetts.

Schoemaker, P. S. H. (1982) The expected utility model: its variants, purposes, evidence and limitations. *Journal of Economic Literature* 20, 529–63.

Stiglitz, J. E. (1982) Information and capital markets. In *Financial Economics: Essays in Honor of Paul Cootner.* eds W. F. Sharpe and C. M. Cootner, Prentice-Hall.

8

Information, Futures Prices, and Stabilizing Speculation

Jean-Pierre Danthine

1 INTRODUCTION

Imagine a situation in which not all relevant information is contained in the past (i.e., the properties of the underlying probability distributions) but some can be obtained through a search process focusing on the particularities of the immediate future. This paper examines the informational role of futures prices and the relationship between futures and spot prices in such a setting.

In this model, a category of agents (speculators) is endowed with advanced information as to the future economic environment. This information takes form as unbiased approximations to the unknown realization of the uncertain parameter.

The world is depicted as follows: producers purchase quantities of input today in order to deliver a desired quantity of output next period. The production process is nonrandom, but tomorrow's demand is shifting according to some exogenous stochastic process. Producers thus face an uncertain output price for their product. They also have the opportunity to trade today contracts for future delivery of the commodity at a known price p^f.

A group of speculators specializes in trading futures contracts (this is the only activity reflected in their objective function). When the market opens today, each is endowed with elements of information on the future value of the demand parameter.

The resulting market structure exhibits the following two characteristics:

Reproduced by permission from *Journal of Economic Theory* vol. 17 (1978), pp. 79–98. Copyright © 1978 by Academic Press, Inc.

This paper is based on Part III of my Doctoral Dissertation presented at Carnegie-Mellon University, April 1976. All my thanks go to R. E. Lucas, Jr. and E. C. Prescott who have inspired and directed this research. I am also indebted to J. Donaldson, T. Johnsen, L. Selden, and R. Townsend for useful comments and suggestions.

1. The role played by the futures price in the producers' decision problem turns out to be exactly analogous to the role of a certain output price. Firms act as if they were hedging the totality of their production on the futures market before speculating on the perceived futures–spot price differential. Hence production decisions are independent both of the producers' degree of risk aversion and price expectations, and they are separable from their 'portfolio' problem.
2. Speculators' information is reflected in their decision and, ultimately, in the equilibrium futures price. The latter thus acts as a signal of the information available on the market.

As a result of 1, the futures price affects[1] next period's commodity supply. Hence, the spot price distribution can only be meaningfully defined *conditional* on the value of the futures price, as a function of the uncertainty parameter's distribution.

Because of 2, the latter distribution itself, as it is perceived by market participants, is affected by the incorporation of the statistic p^f (futures price) in the information sets.

This double link between futures and spot prices is the subject of section 2, where the model is described. A competitive equilibrium is there defined as a set of decision rules and a market clearing price (function) whose ex post link with the information variables describing the state of the economy confirms the functional form expected by market agents (thus it is a price whose informational message is correctly discounted by them).

In section 3, an example of such an equilibrium price is exhibited. Being a sufficient statistic for the market information, this price formally 'summarizes all the information available on the market.' The implications of this property for the value of information is discussed in the following section, together with other results of the model. The roles and stabilizing influence of speculation in futures are taken up in section 5. A short conclusion follows.

The equilibrium concept used in the paper is an example of informative rational expectations equilibrium as developed in Lucas [13, 14], Green [4] and Grossman [6]. In [6], Grossman introduces a similar model of a futures market. His is a purely speculative model in which all speculators are either fully informed or uninformed. He discusses the ability of spot and futures prices, as statistics, to transmit information to uninformed speculators. By contrast, our speculators are differentially and never perfectly informed, and we emphasize the real (stabilizing) impact of futures speculation on commodity supply. Furthermore, our world is inhabited by speculators and producers, and risk transfer and informative roles of a futures market are both developed. The asymmetry between the initial position of a producer (hedger) and a speculator in our model turns out to constitute an important motive for speculation (in contrast with Hirshleifer [7], who claims that only information differences will stimulate speculation). It also throws new light on the value of information and the characteristics of the futures-expected spot price differential.

2 THE MODEL

2.1 Producing with futures markets: a separation result

Let us consider a world in which farmers plant a crop in period 1 and harvest it in period 2. The crop is perishable so there are no inventories. At the start of period 1, when the planting decision must be made, the period 2 market price, p, is unknown.[2] However, farmers have the opportunity, in period one, to trade futures contracts at a unit price p^f, that is, p^f is the price of a contract promising delivery of one unit of commodity in period two.

The objective of an expected utility maximizing, price taking farmer can be expressed as

$$\max_{x \geq 0, f} E[U((q - f)\tilde{p} + p^f f - x)|p^f] \tag{8.1}$$

with the notation:

f is the number of unit futures contracts supplied by the farmer. It can be positive or negative, as nothing prevents farmers from being long on the futures market.

x is the quantity of input – with price equal to one – bought by the producer.

q is the amount of output produced, related to x by the production function $q = q(x)$, $q_1 \geq 0$, $q_{11} < 0$.

U is farmers' common, strictly concave, von Neumann–Morgenstern utility function of income. It is defined on the whole real line as farmers' income can be negative. (In this two-period, partial equilibrium setup, there is no harm in assuming that farmers have other sources of income, including savings from the past and access to credit on future income, not dependent on their present decision.)

E is the expectation operator taken with respect to the conditional subjective distribution of the spot price $\tilde{p}$ given p^f. The spot price p prevailing in period 2 will result from the interaction of supply and demand forces. The latter will be summarized in a stochastic demand curve. The analysis of the former is precisely the subject of our investigation. The distribution of $\tilde{p}$ will thus be determined by consideration of the spot market equilibrium, and will depend on the same supply decisions we are now studying. To the extent that the latter are functions of the futures price, one can ascertain at this point that the spot price distribution will not be independent of p^f. It will be assumed that market agents are rational in that their subjective prior probability distributions coincide with the as yet undetermined, 'true' (equilibrium) probability distribution, and that the effect of p^f on that distribution is correctly accounted for.

As can be easily seen, the concavity of $U(\cdot)$ and $q(\cdot)$ ensures that the first-order conditions for a solution to problem (8.1) are necessary and sufficient for a maximum. They are:[3]

$$E\left[U_1(\tilde{y})\tilde{p}|p^f\right]q_1(x) \leqslant E\left[U_1(\tilde{y})|p^f\right], = \text{if} \quad x > 0, \tag{8.2}$$

$$E\left[U_1(\tilde{y})|p^f\right]p^f = E\left[U_1(\tilde{y})\tilde{p}|p^f\right]. \tag{8.3}$$

Substituting (8.3) into (8.2), we can write, for an interior solution,

$$p^f q_1(x) = 1. \tag{8.4}$$

Given the monotonicity of q_1, (8.4) defines a function between x and p^f,

$$x = x(p^f) \tag{8.5}$$

where

$$x_1(p^f) = -\frac{q_1(x)}{q_{11}(x)p^f} > 0.$$

By (8.5), $\tilde{y} = [q(x(p^f)) - f]\tilde{p} + p^f f - x(p^f)$ is a function of p, f, and p^f. Thus, the integration (8.3) over p is an implicit function in f and p^{f}[4] from which we can solve for the supply of futures, f, as

$$f = f(p^f). \tag{8.6}$$

Note that the status of p^f in the function $f(\cdot)$ is ambiguous: p^f enters not only because it affects $\tilde{y}$, the farmer's income, but also because it (potentially) modifies the probability distribution assessed to the spot price $\tilde{p}$.

The remarkable property of this solution to the farmers' problem is found in (8.4): when the possibility of trading futures contracts exists, farmers' output supply is a function of the futures price p^f (and the input price) only and, in particular, is dependent upon neither his degree of risk aversion, nor the probability distribution summarizing his expectations. In fact, the price p^f plays the same role as p in a world of certainty. Indeed, one may think of farmers as hedging all that they produce and making their production decisions based on a certain output price equal to p^f, prior to acting as speculators by readjusting their position on the futures market starting from a position $f = q$. This adjustment, in turn, depends on the level of p^f, the distribution of the spot price $\tilde{p}$, the way this distribution is affected by the knowledge of p^f, and the parameters of the utility function.

From the farmers' point of view, the existence of a futures market completes the set of markets upon which they rely. As in an Arrow–Debreu world, there is no need for them, as producers, to make probability assessments of the future as the return from their production activity is certain. Thus, provided the technology used is the same, output will be identical for all farmers, irrespective of differences in utility or in expectations. The latter differences will, in some sense, be compensated by farmers' positions in futures.

Analytically, the possibility of separating production and futures decisions in this context allows for the solving of the equilibrium spot price conditional on the outcome of the futures tradings.[5]

2.2 Conditional spot market equilibrium

Let there be a fixed number N of farmers. The aggregate supply of a commodity is

$$Q^s = Nq(x) = Nq(x(p^f)).\tag{8.7}$$

We assume the (random) market demand to be described by

$$Q^d = D(p, \eta)\tag{8.8}$$

where $D(\cdot, \cdot)$ is continuously differentiable with $D_1(p, \eta) < 0$ and $D_2(p, \eta) > 0$. $\tilde{\eta}$ is a random demand shift parameter with a continuous probability density function $g(\eta)$. For most purposes, we will assume $\tilde{\eta} \sim N(0; \sigma_\eta^2)$.

From (8.7) and (8.8), the *equilibrium* spot price is a function of the futures price p^f and the realized value of the stochastic term $\tilde{\eta}$:

$$p = p(p_t^f, \eta)\tag{8.9}$$

with

$$p_1(p^f, \eta) = \frac{Nq_1(x)x_1(p^f)}{D_1} < 0, \qquad \text{and finite,}$$

$$p_2(p^f, \eta) = -\frac{D_2}{D_1} > 0.$$

Equation (8.9) provides a first link between the future spot price and the futures price. It justifies the writing of a conditional distribution in (8.1). The first way in which p^f affects the distribution of $\tilde{p}$ is now made explicit through the relation $p(p^f, \eta)$, and the density $g(\eta)$.

2.3 Speculators

Let there also be n speculators, each of whom is identical except for his/her information set. Speculator i decides how many futures contracts, b_i to purchase on the basis of his expectation of the spot-futures price differential $(\tilde{p} - p^f)$, given his attitude toward risk.[6] Speculators are rational in the same sense as farmers are, but they have access to an additional piece of information. Before the exchange opens, speculator $i(i = 1, \ldots, n)$ observes some unbiased approximation v_i of the true value of the variable $\tilde{\eta}$, $v_i = \eta + w_i$ where the $\tilde{w}_i$'s are i.i.d $N(0; \sigma_w^2)$.

This can be interpreted as follows:[7] η is a summary measure of, e.g., the characteristics of the crop (essentially, computed as deviations from normal output), of the mood of the consumers, or of other conditions affecting demand. Speculators can obtain advanced information as to the particular value of this realization for the relevant period through, for instance, a survey of consumers' intentions, a detailed weather forecast, or a personal trip to producing countries to get a sampling of the growing conditions of the new crop, etc. These observations are not without errors, but (regarding again these two periods as a slice of a multiperiod process where learning has been taking place) speculators are assumed sufficiently skilled to avoid systematic bias in their evaluations. In this model this advance information is free to them.

The objective of a risk-averse, expected utility maximizing, price-taking speculator is to

$$\max_{b_i} \int W\left[\left(p\left(p^f, \tilde{\eta}\right) - p^f\right)b_i\right] g\left(\eta | v_i, p^f\right) d\eta \qquad (8.10)$$

with the following notation:

b_i is the contract which entitles speculator i to the delivery of b_i units of the commodity next period (alternatively $b_i < 0$, corresponds to a promise to deliver a number of units of commodity).

W is the strictly concave von-Neumann-Morgenstern utility function common to all speculators, where $W_1 > 0$, $W_{11} < 0$. It is defined on the whole real line as there is a nonnull probability of $z_i \equiv (p - p^f)b_i < 0$.

$g(\eta | v_i, p^f)$ is the conditional probability distribution of $\tilde{\eta}$ given v_i and p^f. Speculators (and farmers) make their decision *after* observing the realizations of two (one) random variables correlated with η. (That p^f satisfies their description will emerge from the following analysis). As Bayesian agents they thus solve this maximization problem using the *posterior* distribution of $\tilde{\eta}$ given the observed values of these variables. (For a theory of Bayesian statistical decision see [3, chs. 7 and 8]). $g(\eta | v_i, p^f)$ is assumed continuous in v_i and p^f. Similarly the underlying probability distribution in (8.1), $g(\eta | p^f)$ is assumed continuous in p^f. (This validates the passage from (8.3) to (8.6).)

The first-order condition for problem (8.10), necessary and sufficient for a maximum, is

$$\int W_1 \left[(p\,(p^f, \tilde{\eta}) - p^f) b_i \right] \left[p\,(p^f, \tilde{\eta}) - p^f \right] g(\eta \,|\, v_i, p^f) d\eta = 0. \qquad (8.11)$$

Under our assumptions, and using the implicit function theorem, we may solve for b_i,

$$b_i = b(p^f, v_i). \qquad (8.12)$$

Again, p^f enters both as a component of income z, and as a variable conditional on which the expectation is taken. The decision rule (8.12) is common to all our identical speculators.

2.4   The futures market equilibrium

From (8.6) and (8.12), the market clearing equation can be written as

$$Nf(p^f) - \sum_{j=1}^{n} b(p^f, v_j) = 0. \qquad (8.13)$$

Assuming monotonicity with respect of p^{f^8} of the left-hand side of (8.13), we can solve for p^f to obtain:

$$p^f = h(v_1, \ldots, v_n) \equiv h(V) \qquad (8.14)$$

where V is the row vector of speculators' observations.

This closes the model. Equation (8.14) shows the equilibrium futures price p^f as a function of speculators' individual elements of information (v_1, $\ldots, v_n$); that is, ultimately, of the current realization of the stochastic term $\tilde{\eta}$ and of speculators' observation errors ($w_1, \ldots, w_n$). These are the exogenous variables in the model. In a sense, they describe the state of the economy at the beginning of period 1. Equation (8.14) gives substance to our claim that the equilibrium futures price has an informational content which can possibly affect further the distribution of $\tilde{p}$. Indeed the functional relation between V and p^f suggests that some of the advanced information held by speculators may be 'readable' from the futures price and thus modify the agent's prior distribution on $\tilde{\eta}$.

Let us collect the preceding elements of analysis and, in this context, define an equilibrium as follows.

Definition 1   A *Competitive equilibrium* is a price $p^f \in R_+$ and a triple of real-valued functions:

$$f: R_+ \to R, \qquad b: R \times R_+ \to R, \qquad \text{and} \qquad h: R^n \to R_+$$

such that, given $V = (v_1, \ldots, v_n)$, $p = p(p^f, \eta)$, and $g(\eta)$,

(1) $p^f = h(V)$;

(2) $b(p^f, v)$ maximizes speculators' expected utility

$$\int W[(p(p^f, \tilde{\eta}) - p^f)b]g(\eta | v, p^f = h(V))d\eta, \qquad \text{over all } b \in R;$$

(3) $f(p^f)$ maximizes producers' expected utility

$$\int U[(p^f - p(p^f, \tilde{\eta}))f]g(\eta | p^f = h(V))d\eta, \qquad \text{over all } f \in R,$$

and

(4) $\displaystyle\sum_{j=1}^{n} b(p^f, v_j) = Nf(p^f).$

This definition of equilibrium incorporates the following elements:

1. All agents maximize expected utility given their information sets.
2. The market clears.
3. Expectations are in equilibrium: the distribution of $\tilde{p}$ is correctly identified as given by the function $p(\cdot, \cdot)$, the value of p^f, and the appropriate posterior distribution on $\tilde{\eta}$; traders correctly anticipate the equilibrium relationship between p^f and the vector V.

Does such an equilibrium exist? Rather than answering this question with full generality (the interested reader is referred to [1] for a complete investigation of this issue), we discuss in the following section a parametric specification of the model where an equilibrium price satisfying Definition 1 is exhibited and characterized.

3 A PARAMETRIC EXAMPLE

Let us assume the production function and the demand curve take the following forms

$$q(x) \quad = \alpha x^{1/2}, \qquad \alpha > 0,$$

$$D(p, \eta) = a - cp + \eta \quad a, c > 0, \quad \tilde{\eta} \sim N(0; \sigma_\eta^2). \tag{8.15}$$

It is then easy to solve the spot market for the equilibrium spot price (given that condition (8.6) implies the optimal $q = (\alpha^2/2)p^f$)

$$p = A - Bp^f + \frac{1}{c}\eta \quad \text{with} \quad A = \frac{a}{c} > 0, \quad B = N\frac{\alpha^2}{2c} > 0.$$

Then, the representative farmer's profit is equal to

$$\tilde{y} = \left[\frac{\alpha^2}{2}p^f - f\right]\left[A - Bp^f + \frac{1}{c}\tilde{\eta}\right] + p^f f - \frac{\alpha^2}{4}(p^f)^2,$$

while speculator i's profit equals

$$\tilde{z}_i = \left[A - (B + 1)p^f + \frac{1}{c}\tilde{\eta} \right] b_i.$$

The utility functions are assumed to be of the following form:

$$U(y) = -\exp(-\xi y), \qquad W(z) = -\exp(-\chi z)$$

where $\xi, \chi \geqslant 0$ are the Arrow-Pratt measures of absolute risk aversion.

With $\tilde{y}$ and $\tilde{z}$ normally distributed conditional on p^f, and v_i and p^f respectively,[9] these agents in fact maximize the following functions of profits (see e.g., [11]),

$$\hat{U}(\tilde{y}) = E(\tilde{y}) - \xi \operatorname{var} \tilde{y},$$
$$\hat{W}(\tilde{z}) = E(\tilde{z}) - \chi \operatorname{var} \tilde{z}.$$

Under these assumptions, the optimal choices are

$$f = -\frac{c^2}{2\xi \operatorname{var}(\tilde{\eta}|p^f)} [E(\tilde{p}|p^f) - p^f] + \frac{\alpha^2}{2}p^f$$

$$= -\frac{c^2}{2\xi \operatorname{var}(\tilde{\eta}|p^f)} \left[A - (B + 1)p^f + \frac{1}{c}E(\tilde{\eta}|p^f) \right] + \frac{\alpha^2}{2}p^f$$

$$b_i = \frac{c^2}{2\chi \operatorname{var}(\tilde{\eta}|v_i, p^f)} [E(\tilde{p}|v_i, p^f) - p^f]$$

$$= \frac{c^2}{2\chi \operatorname{var}(\tilde{\eta}|v_i, p^f)} \left[A - (B + 1)p^f + \frac{1}{c}E(\tilde{\eta}|v_i, p^f) \right]. \qquad (8.16)$$

Using the fact that $\operatorname{var}(\tilde{\eta}|v_i, p^f) = \operatorname{var}(\tilde{\eta}|v_j, p^f)\forall i,j$ for a constant σ_w^2 across speculators and solving for p^f from the market clearing equation one gets

$$p^f = \frac{1}{M} \left\{ \frac{Nc^2}{2\xi \operatorname{var}(\tilde{\eta}|p^f)} \left[A + \frac{1}{c}E(\tilde{\eta}|p^f) \right] \right.$$

$$\left. + \frac{c^2}{2\chi \operatorname{var}(\tilde{\eta}|v, p^f)} \left[nA + \frac{1}{c}\sum_j E(\tilde{\eta}|v_j, p^f) \right] \right\} \qquad (8.17)$$

where

$$M = \left(\frac{Nc^2(B + 1)}{2\xi \operatorname{var}(\tilde{\eta}|p^f)} + \frac{N\alpha^2}{2} + \frac{nc^2}{2\chi \operatorname{var}(\tilde{\eta}|v, p^f)} \right)^{-1}.$$

The informational structure of the model is as follows. Considering the market as a whole, an experiment has been performed by observing the values taken by some variable v, $v = \eta + w$ where $\tilde{w}$ is $N(0, \sigma_w^2)$, in n independent drawings. The results are summarized in the vector $V = (v_1,$ $\ldots, v_n)$; or in the sum of the v's, $\Sigma\, v_i$, which is the sufficient statistic for $V = (v_1, \ldots, v_n)$.[10]

Being a function of the observations (see (8.14)), p^f is itself a statistic used by traders in calibrating their probabilities. The question is: how good a statistic can it be? How well can the futures price summarize the information available to the market?

We are now going to construct one equilibrium price p^f, satisfying Definition 1, which is a sufficient statistic for the information available to the market; that is, which is invertible for the sufficient statistic $\Sigma\, v_j$.[11] In that case, knowledge of p^f is equivalent to the knowledge of $\Sigma\, v_j$ and farmers' and speculators' expectations coincide. They are[12]

$$E(\tilde{\eta}|p^f) = E(\tilde{\eta}|v_i, p^f) = E\left(\tilde{\eta}\Big|\sum v_j\right) = \frac{\sigma_\eta^2}{n\sigma_\eta^2 + \sigma_w^2}\sum v_j, \qquad (8.18)$$

$$\mathrm{var}(\tilde{\eta}|p^f) = \mathrm{var}(\tilde{\eta}|p^f, v_i) = \frac{\sigma_w^2\sigma_\eta^2}{n\sigma_\eta^2 + \sigma_w^2}. \qquad (8.19)$$

Using these values in (8.17), one obtains

$$p^f = F + L\sum v_j \qquad (8.20)$$

where

$$F = \frac{(N\chi + n\xi)A}{(N\chi + n\xi)\,(B + 1) + N\alpha^2\xi\chi\,\dfrac{1}{c^2}\dfrac{\sigma_w^2\sigma_\eta^2}{n\sigma_\eta^2 + \sigma_w^2}}$$

and

$$L = \frac{1}{c}\frac{\sigma_\eta^2}{n\sigma_\eta^2 + \sigma_w^2}\frac{F}{A}.$$

Equation (8.20) shows the equilibrium price p^f to be proportional to $\Sigma\, v_j$ and thus a sufficient statistic as postulated. It satisfies our definition of an equilibrium. It is a market clearing price, the result of speculators' and farmers' maximizing behavior, and it corresponds to an equilibrium state of expectations. That is, when (8.20) is the hypothesized functional relationship between p^f and v, this relationship is realized given that each agent then appropriately extracts the information $\Sigma\, v_j$ from the announcement of the equilibrium price.

No dynamic story is offered as to how such an equilibrium is reached. Nevertheless, the reader may verify that the market clearing price obtained from solving (8.15) and (8.16), with economic agents using their own information only, is itself a sufficient statistic. By modifying their posterior probability distributions, it therefore suggests revisions in their behavior (and, as such is not a full *equilibrium* price as we have defined). These ultimately lead to an equilibrium price as given by (8.20).

Sufficiency results are also discussed in Kihlstrom and Mirman [9] and Grossman [5]. In [9], the conditions for the equilibrium price to contain at least as much information as the observation v of the informed agent are explored in a context where only one agent is informed, In contrast with the present case, however, the authors use a notion of sufficiency borrowed from Blackwell and the comparison of experiments literature.[13] In that case too, sufficiency amounts to the invertibility of the price function for a sufficient statistic (in their model the entire conditional probability distribution). They show this invertibility requirement is not robust to variations in the preference structure of the informed agents. In [5], the information structure of the model and the concept of sufficiency are identical to ours. The author illustrates the nonrobustness of the sufficiency result to changes in the stochastic structure of the model (the addition of noise). Both comments apply to our model as well. In addition, it can be seen that the sufficiency result is not robust to the introduction of asymmetry among informed agents. If agents display different degrees of risk aversion, or are differently informed, their v_i's will be differently weighted in the 'market clearing' aggregation process and the sufficient statistic will not be obtainable from price information alone. Suppose, for example, that n_1 of the speculators are informed with precision (the inverse of) σ_{w1}^2, and n_2 with precision σ_{w2}^2; $\sigma_{w2}^2 > \sigma_{w1}^2$ and $n_1 + n_2 = n$. It is clearly more interesting to observe the v_i^1 than the v_i^2; and the joint sufficient statistics for the information on the market will be two separate numbers, $\Sigma^{n_1} v_i^1$, $\Sigma^{n_2} v_j^2$. Still the best information obtainable from price alone will be a weighted sum $\delta \Sigma v_i^1 + \beta \Sigma v_j^2$ from which the sufficient statistic itself cannot be disentangled.

4   SPECULATORS' PROFITS AND THE VALUE OF INFORMATION

4.1   Consequences of the model

With equilibrium prices perfectly and freely disseminating information, one would not expect information to be valued by speculators. Indeed, in a purely informative context as in [5], price sufficiency eliminates all differences among traders and thus all motives for trade (and sources of potential profit). In our model, however, speculators are compensated for sharing producers' risks and these profits vary systematically with the amount of information in the market. Specifically, speculators' average profits first increase with the quantity of information in a 'very uncertain' world, then decrease as information reduces the level of uncertainty. Thus, perhaps contrary to intuition, information is of potential value for speculators even when it is perfectly revealed to the uninformed by the price system. Before coming to this point, however, we now derive two interesting implications of the model.

1 The futures price is not an unbiased estimate of the future spot price.[14] Hence, speculators' expected profits are positive.

From (8.15) and (8.16), it is seen that at $E(\tilde{p}) = p^f$ farmers still want to trade (for hedging purposes), and speculators do not; thus the market cannot clear at that price. This implies that there is a transfer from farmers to speculators as compensation for risk reallocation. Indeed, from (8.16), we immediately obtain

$$E[(\tilde{p} - p^f)b] = \frac{c^2}{2\chi \, \text{var}(\tilde{\eta}|p^f)} E[\tilde{p} - p^f|p^f]^2$$

that is, speculators' expected profits are positive as long as there is a nonzero differential between the futures price and the expected spot price.

Of course, this result does not hold when $n \to \infty$, since uncertainty then disappears (observation errors are independent). If this was not the case, there would always be a transfer (in expected terms) from farmers to speculators, although, with the number of speculators getting larger, individual expected profits would be getting smaller.

2 Contrary to Hirshleifer's [7] contention, differences in expectations are not necessary for trading to take place.

In this model, trade occurs as long as farmers are risk averse and their initial position is riskier than the speculators'. This immediately follows from the fact that b is proportional to the expected price difference and, in equilibrium, the latter is nonzero if there is uncertainty, farmers are risk averse, and they have 'real' commitments.

Differences in risk aversion also generate trading in this context: it is easy to check from (8.15) that if there are no speculators and farmers have homogeneous expectations, trading can still take place providing rates of risk aversion differ, that is, the market clearing equation can be satisfied with not all $f_i = 0$. This implies $E(\tilde{p}|p^f) - p^f > 0$.

4.2 Ex post profits and the value of information

Defining

$$\bar{\mu} = N\alpha^2 \xi \chi,$$
$$\nu = N\chi + n\xi,$$

and refraining from being specific about the amount of information (info) available to the market, and thus shared by all agents (price sufficiency), we can rewrite (8.20) and (8.16), respectively, as

$$p^f = \frac{\bar{v}\left[A + \dfrac{1}{c}E(\tilde{\eta}|\text{info})\right]}{v(B+1) + \bar{\mu}\dfrac{1}{c^2}\text{var}(\tilde{\eta}|\text{info})}$$

and

$$b = \frac{\left[A + \dfrac{1}{c}E(\tilde{\eta}|\text{info})\right]\bar{\mu}}{2\chi\left[v(B+1) + \bar{\mu}\dfrac{1}{c^2}\text{var}(\tilde{\eta}|\text{info})\right]}.$$

Speculators' ex post profits $z = b(p - p^f)$ then equal

$$\frac{\left[\left[A + \dfrac{1}{c}E(\tilde{\eta}|\text{info})\right]\bar{\mu}\left[\left(A + \dfrac{1}{c}\eta\right)\bar{\mu}\dfrac{1}{c^2}\text{var}(\tilde{\eta}|\text{info}) + \dfrac{1}{c}v(B+1)(\eta - E(\tilde{\eta}|\text{info}))\right]\right]}{2\chi\left[v(B+1) + \bar{\mu}\dfrac{1}{c^2}\text{var}(\tilde{\eta}|\text{info})\right]^2}$$

If there is no specific information in the market, $E(\tilde{\eta}|\text{info}) = 0$, $\text{var}(\tilde{\eta}|\text{info}) = \sigma_\eta^2$, and the average (or expected *prior* to being informed) value of $z \equiv \bar{z}$ equals

$$\bar{z} = \frac{A^2\bar{\mu}^2\dfrac{1}{c^2}\sigma_\eta^2}{2\chi\left[v(B+1) + \bar{\mu}\dfrac{1}{c^2}\sigma_\eta^2\right]^2}. \tag{8.21}$$

When *n speculators observe a* $v, E(\tilde{\eta}|\text{info})$, and $\text{var}(\tilde{\eta}|\text{info})$ are given by (8.18) and (8.19), respectively, and

$$\bar{z} = \frac{\bar{\mu}^2 A^2\dfrac{1}{c^2}\dfrac{\sigma_w^2\sigma_\eta^2}{n\sigma_\eta^2 + \sigma_w^2} + \dfrac{n\sigma_\eta^4}{n\sigma_\eta^2 + \sigma_w^2}\dfrac{\bar{\mu}^2}{c^4}\dfrac{\sigma_w^2\sigma_\eta^2}{n\sigma_\eta^2 + \sigma_w^2}}{2\chi\left[v(B+1) + \bar{\mu}\dfrac{1}{c^2}\sigma_\eta^2\right]^2} \tag{8.22}$$

where we have used

$$E\left(\tilde{\eta}\sum v_j\right) = n\sigma_\eta^2$$

and

$$E\left[\left(\sum v_j\right)^2\right] = n^2\sigma_\eta^2 + n\sigma_w^2.$$

This expression is equal to zero when uncertainty disappears ($\sigma_w^2 = 0$ or $n = \infty$). It reduces to (8.19) when the variance of the observation errors, σ_w^2, tends toward infinity, that is, when the information is less and less reliable.

Denoting k our measure of uncertainty $\sigma_w^2\sigma_\eta^2/(n\sigma_\eta^2 + \sigma_w^2)$ ($= \text{var}(\tilde\eta|\Sigma v_j)$) ($k$ is monotone increasing in σ_w^2 with $k = 0$ when $\sigma_w^2 = 0$, $k = \sigma_\eta^2$ when $\sigma_w^2 = +\infty$), we can rewrite the first part of (8.22) as

$$\frac{1}{2\chi\left[\nu(B+1) + \bar\mu\dfrac{1}{c^2}k\right]^2}\left[\bar\mu^2 A^2\frac{1}{c^2}k\right].$$

This is a decreasing function of k (and thus of σ_w^2) for

$$k > \frac{(N\chi + n\xi)(B+1)}{N\alpha^2\chi\xi\dfrac{1}{c^2}}$$

and an increasing function of k when the opposite inequality is satisfied. Thus, the first part of the sum in (8.22) will be smaller than the average profits without information, equation (8.21), if σ_η^2 is small, but it will be larger if there is much uncertainty (σ_η^2 is large). Since the second part of the sum in (8.22) is positive, the latter inequality also applies for the total average profit with information, the result discussed in section 4.1. In a very uncertain world, speculators' profits, on average, are higher when a certain amount of information enables them to make more accurate 'guesses' as to the future spot price even when this accuracy is shared with other speculators and farmers. Obviously, this cannot be true all the way, since at the limit, with certainty, the market collapses and speculators can expect no profits. Thus there is an optimal level of uncertainty beyond which there is no incentive to acquire even costless information.[15]

5 STABILIZING SPECULATION

The view of futures markets emerging from this model has two facets. On the one hand, a futures market is a place where risks are reallocated between hedgers and speculators. It is easily seen that if they choose to do so, farmers can reduce the variability of their income when possibilities of trading futures exist. They are willing to compensate speculators for such activity (see the computation of speculators' expected profits) because either they are more risk averse or (and more fundamentally) because their 'real' activity requires them (inherently) to assume more risks. On the other hand, trade in futures may take place because of different expectations about the future held by different economic agents who 'speculate' on the basis of these beliefs. By providing a (not always complete) summary of the information and beliefs of the market participants, the futures price is transmitting information to all economic agents, and in particular, to the uninformed producers, who, in turn, base their supply decisions on p^f. The latter allocative role of the futures price in the spot market, i.e., on commodity supply decision, explains the positive influence of speculation in futures. Indeed, because of this property futures markets have an important stabilizing impact on spot prices. The informational message of the futures price, as summarized in the function $h(V)$, together with its role in determining the output supply, as expressed in the function $Nq(x(p^f))$, provides a link between the variations in demand and commodity output. Thus, for example, booming demand conditions, when anticipated by speculators, result in a higher futures price (assuming $(h_1(V) > 0)$ and ultimately in an above average quantity produced $(q_1(x) > 0, x_1(p^f) > 0)$. Under normal conditions, one would expect a decreased variance for the spot price.

This is illustrated in figure 8.1. Without specific information and a fortiori without a futures market, the supply curve is fixed at

$$Q^{s*} = Q(E(\tilde{p})).$$

Thus, for a realization of $\tilde{\eta} = \bar{\eta} > 0$, the equilibrium price p_1 is determined by $p_1 = p + (1/c)\bar{\eta}$. (We have drawn a linear demand curve such that $q = a - cp + \tilde{\eta}$.) If, on the other hand, speculators have some advanced idea of the particular realization $\bar{\eta}$ of $\tilde{\eta}$, p^f adjusts and induces changes in supply according to $Q^s = Nq(x(p^f))$; with increasing cost $(q_{11} < 0)$, equilibrium is likely to be at some $p_2, p_1 > p_2 > \bar{p}$, where $\bar{p}$ is the average price. This discussion has been based upon a result of section 2: $x_1(p^f) > 0$, and upon two added assumptions, $h(V)$ is an increasing function of its arguments, and V is a 'reasonable' predictor of $\bar{\eta}$. We now justify these assumptions.

The plausibility of the first assumption, $h(V)$ is increasing in V, can be appreciated by considering the opposite situation: if anticipated high demand leads to a decrease in p^f, and thus a low supply, both supply and demand elements would concur to produce a high spot price $[p = p(p^f, \eta)$, $p_1 < 0, p_2 > 0]$. Clearly, regarding p^f as an estimate (though not unbiased) of $E(\tilde{p})$, this situation (low p^f, high p) cannot correspond to an equilibrium relationship between these prices.

In fact, consistent with one's intuition, (8.20) defines (see also [1] for a formal proof) the futures price as an increasing function of speculators'

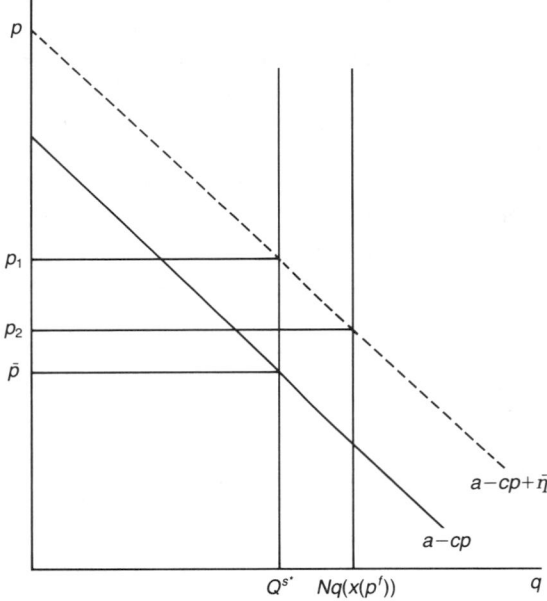

Figure 8.1

'optimism'; i.e., the expectation of a high demand produces an increase in the demand for futures which results in a higher futures price. The amplitude of this price change, in equilibrium, takes into account the opposite reaction of the spot price generated by this very price rise through an expansion of output supply. A futures price increase, however, is consistent with such an effect; indeed, even with perfect foresight, the spot price would be high in booming demand conditions because of increasing costs of production.

When does the information in V, summarized by Σv_j, lead to an improved anticipation of $\bar{\eta}$ compared with the mean of the prior $g(\eta)$?

Intuitively this will occur when $\Sigma v_i/n$ is of the same sign as $\bar{\eta}$ and, in absolute value, less than twice the absolute value of $\bar{\eta}$. Although with independent observation errors this result cannot be guaranteed, it is more likely the larger the number of speculators (i.e., of observations), the smaller their observation errors σ_w^2, and the larger the variance of $\bar{\eta}$ (i.e., the more easily $\bar{\eta}$ can be distinguished from zero).

In that perspective, it is interesting to note that for the parametric example of the previous section (and in the case of price sufficiency) the variance of the spot price with a futures market is smaller than the variance of the spot price without trading in futures, if (this is a sufficient but not necessary condition)

$$\sigma_\eta^2/\sigma_w^2 \geqslant 1/n.$$

This result, derived in the Appendix, restates the desired relationship between the three determining quantities defined above. When n increases, the precision of the collective estimation of η increases; a small σ_w^2 means that speculators' estimations are very concentrated around the mean η; a large σ_η^2 results in a more pronounced superiority of the situation with information than without as the variations in demand are more important (and with them the variability of the spot price). In this model, for any ratio σ_η^2/σ_w^2 there exists a number n of speculators for which the inequality will be satisfied.

6   CONCLUSION

This paper has supported a multirole theory of futures markets. We have emphasized the informative role of futures prices, seen as statistics used by rational traders in formulating their probability distributions. We have produced an example of an informative rational expectations equilibrium where the futures price is a sufficient statistic, i.e., a complete summary of the information in the market. And we have shown that together with the role of futures price on commodity supply decisions, this informative view of futures trading implied a stabilizing influence of speculation on spot prices.

But we have also modeled futures markets as a place where hedgers compensate speculators for sharing the risks inherent to their productive activity and have shown that this asymmetry between economic agents (some have 'real' commitments, others do not) reveals the futures price as a biased estimate of the spot price and, in its own right, can generate speculative tradings.

APPENDIX

The variance of the spot price *without* futures trading (var $\tilde{p}_{w/0}$) is larger than the variance of the spot price *with* futures trading (var $\tilde{p}_{w/}$), if $\sigma_\eta^2/\sigma_w^2 \geqslant 1/n$.

PROOF

$$\mu = N\alpha^2\chi\xi \frac{1}{c^2} \frac{\sigma_w^2\sigma_\eta^2}{n\sigma_\eta^2 + \sigma_w^2},$$

$$s = \frac{\sigma_\eta^2}{n\sigma_\eta^2 + \sigma_w^2},$$

$$\nu = N\chi + n\xi.$$

The equilibrium futures price (8.20) reads

$$p^f = \frac{\nu\left(A + (1/c)s \Sigma v_j\right)}{\nu(B + 1) + \mu},$$

and the equilibrium spot price is

$$p = \frac{A(\nu + \mu) - \nu B(1/c)s \Sigma v_j + (\nu(B + 1) + \mu)(1/c)\eta}{\nu(B + 1) + \mu}$$

$$= \frac{A(\nu + \mu) - \nu B(1/c)s \Sigma w_j + [(\nu(B + 1) + \mu)(1/c) - \nu B(1/c)sn]\eta}{\nu(B + 1) + \mu}.$$

Thus, given the stochastic independence of $\tilde\eta$ and the $\tilde w$'s,

$$\operatorname{var} \tilde p_{w/} = \left[\frac{\nu B(1/c)s}{\nu(B + 1) + \mu}\right]^2 n\sigma_w^2 + \left[\frac{1}{c} - \frac{\nu B(1/c)sn}{\nu(B + 1) + \mu}\right]^2 \sigma_\eta^2.$$

Without futures trading, $p = (1/c)(a + \eta - Q^{s*})$ and $\operatorname{var} \tilde p_{w/0} = 1/c^2$ var $\tilde\eta$. Hence,

$$\operatorname{var} \tilde p_{w/0} - \operatorname{var} \tilde p_{w/} = \frac{1}{c^2}\sigma_\eta^2 - \frac{1}{c^2}\sigma_\eta^2 + \left[\frac{2}{c}\frac{1}{c}k' - \frac{1}{c^2}k'^2\right] - \left[\frac{1}{c^2}k'^2\right]\frac{1}{n}\sigma_w^2$$

where $k' = \nu Bsn/[\nu(B + 1) + \mu]$; multiplying by c^2 and dividing by k', this difference is equal to $(2 - k')\sigma_\eta^2 - k'(1/n)\sigma_w^2$. With $0 < k' < 1$ as

$$k' = \frac{(N\chi + n\xi)B\dfrac{n\sigma_\eta^2}{n\sigma_\eta^2 + \sigma_w^2}}{(N\chi + n\xi)(B + 1) + N\alpha^2\chi\xi\dfrac{1}{c}\sigma_\eta^2},$$

$$\operatorname{var} \tilde p_{w/0} - \operatorname{var} \tilde p_{w/} > 0 \qquad \text{iff} \qquad \frac{\sigma_\eta^2}{\sigma_w^2} > \frac{k'(1/n)}{2 - k'}$$

and a fortiori if $\sigma_\eta^2/\sigma_w^2 \geqslant 1/n$.

NOTES

1. The substantive results derived in the paper depend upon the existence of a (positive) correlation between the futures price and the commodity supply. They do not seem to be contingent on as strong a property as (1), although our method to derive them is.
2. All price symbols will correspond to the period 2 value of the denoted prices. A $\sim$, e.g., $\tilde p$, will distinguish a random variable. p is a particular realization of the r.v. $\tilde p$.

3 Our notation throughout: $f_1(x, y) = \partial f(x, y)/\partial x, f_2(x, y) = \partial f(x, y)/\partial y$, etc.

4 Restrictions will be made below on the probability distribution of $\tilde{p}$ in order to validate this statement.

5 Could this result be generalized to production uncertainty? The answer is yes as long as marginal products are not affected by the uncertainty (e.g., $q = q(x) + \epsilon$, ϵ a random variable. More generally $q = q(x, \epsilon)$, $q_{12} = 0$). If this condition was not satisfied, the separation property would not hold; the demand for input (5) would then be tributary of differences in farmers' expectations (or attitudes toward risk). In our homogeneous world, however, all the following would still be valid (with a different functional form in (5)).

6 We analyze only, in its role of speculator, the behavior of an agent who may simultaneously be a consumer of the commodity, and whose final demand is, as such, included in $D(p, \eta)$.

7 In the following discussion, we allow uncertainty to originate also on the supply side. This extension to our model is warranted only under the limited conditions described in footnote 5.

8 The comparative statics analysis is made extremely complex by the necessity of distinguishing the allocative and the informative effects of price changes. See [1]. The monotonicity assumption here made is not innocuous.

9 That the priors on $\tilde{y}$ and $\tilde{z}$ are Normal follows from $\tilde{p} \sim N(0; \sigma_\eta^2)$, and the above definitions of farmers' and speculators' profits. That the posteriors also are normal will be made clear only *after* the following derivation. This again is the consequence of the equilibrium nature of our analysis.

10 For a definition of the notion of sufficient statistic and a derivation of Σv_i as the sufficient statistic for a random sample from a normal distribution with unknown mean, see [3].

11 See [15, theorem 8.4, p. 171].

12 See [3, Theorem 1, p. 167].

13 See [8] for references and discussion of these.

14 Thus, here again, as in Danthine [2], Lucas [12], and LeRoy [10] but for another reason, failure of the Martingale property to hold is *not* evidence of market inefficiency.

15 In terms of expected profits, the only incentives we have mentioned thus far. Obviously risk averse speculators have additional reason for buying variance reducing information.

REFERENCES

1 Danthine, J. P. An equilibrium analysis of speculative markets. The implications of rationality on the behavior and characteristics of equilibrium prices, Unpublished Ph. D. Dissertation, Carnegie-Mellon University, 1976.

2 Danthine, J. P. Martingale, market efficiency and commodity prices. *European Economic Review* 10 (1977), 1–17.

3 DeGroot M. H. *Optimal Statistical Decisions*, McGraw-Hill, New York, 1970.

4 Green, J. R. Information, efficiency and equilibrium, Unpublished, D. P. 284, (March 1973), Harvard University.

5 Grossman, S. On the efficiency of competitive stock markets where traders have diverse information. *Journal of Finance* 31 (1976), 573–85.

6 Grossman, S. The existence of futures markets, noisy rational expectations and informational externalities. *Review of Economic Studies* 44 (1977), 431–449.

7 Hirshleifer, J. Speculation and equilibrium: Information, risk and markets. *Quarterly Journal of Economics* 89 (1975) 519–542.

8 Kihlstrom, R. E. A Bayesian exposition of Blackwell's theorem on the comparison of experiments, Unpublished, University of Mass., Amherst & SUNY, Stony Brook, March 1974.

9 Kihlstrom, R. E. and Mirman, L. J. Information and market equilibrium. *Bell Journal of Economics* 6 (1975), 357–376.

10 LeRoy, S. P. Risk aversion and the Martingale property of stock prices. *International Economic Review* 14 (1973), 436–446.

11 Lintner, J. The aggregation of investors diverse judgment and preferences in purely competitive securities markets. *Journal of Financial and Quantitative Analysis* 4 (1969), 347–400.

12 Lucas, R. E. Jr., Asset prices in an exchange economy. *Econometrica* 46 (1978), 1426–46.

13 Lucas, R. E. Jr., An equilibrium model of the business cycle, *Journal of Political Economy* 83 (1975), 1113–44.

14 Lucas, R. E. Jr., Expectations and the neutrality of money. *Journal of Economic Theory* 4 (1972) 103–124.

15 Mood, A. M. and Graybill, F. A. *Introduction to the Theory of Statistics*, 2nd edn, McGraw-Hill, New York, 1963.

9

Futures Trading, Rational Expectations, and the Efficient Markets Hypothesis

Margaret M. Bray

1 INTRODUCTION

Prices in asset markets affect the demand for assets in two ways. Firstly and familiarly, prices determine the budget constraints which dealers face. Secondly, prices reflect dealers' information about the returns on the assets and so aggregate and transmit information between dealers.

These two aspects of price have been recognized and analyzed by a number of authors. The literature on efficient markets and the Martingale hypothesis represents one approach. (See, for example, Samuelson [18, 19] for theory; Fama [5] for a survey of empirical work.) This approach uses arbitrage arguments based on a uniform risk premium on the discount rate. More recent work has sought to model the market in more detail, approaching risk aversion through expected utility maximization. It makes explicit use of the rational expectations hypothesis that dealers form correct expectations on the basis of all the information available to them, including the asset prices.

The major issue has been, when is the strong form of the efficient markets hypothesis true; when do prices aggregate all the relevant private and public information perfectly? This has important implications for the incentives to gather information which are discussed later. The welfare implications are not pursued here, but are also important; prices are a guide to resource allocation and so the information conveyed by the price system affects welfare.

A model of a futures market is analyzed in this paper. Informational efficiency is taken to mean that the futures price is a sufficient statistic for the information available about the return on holding futures (the spot price at

I am very grateful to J. A. Mirrlees and J. E. Stiglitz who supervised the Oxford B. Phil. Thesis [3] upon which this work is based, and provided invaluable advice and encouragement. I would also like to thank the anonymous referees for many helpful comments. All responsibility for errors and ommissions of course rests with me.

the date the futures contract must be honored). The model bears many similarities to the futures market models of Grossman and Stiglitz [10, section on 'Prices as aggregators'] and Danthine [4, section titled 'A parametric example']. The stock market model of Grossman [7] is mathematically equivalent to a special case of my model. The similarities include constant absolute risk aversion utility functions and joint normality of all random variables.

The first theorem which I prove establishes a set of necessary and sufficient conditions for the futures price to be a sufficient statistic for information about the spot price. This establishes that the strong symmetry assumptions made about the information structure in the earlier models, and the identical risk aversion assumptions of Danthine [4], and Grossman and Stiglitz [10] are not necessary for their results. The essential feature of these models is that information is available about only one side of the spot market. I show that, in general, if there is information available about both spot supply and demand the two types of information 'interfere' with each other, and the futures price cannot be a sufficient statistic.

One important feature of the model presented here is that the agents who produce the commodity which is sold on the spot market are also futures traders. Their decisions on futures trades are affected by their beliefs about both the spot price and their own output. If the futures price is a sufficient statistic for information which is gathered about the spot price, there is no incentive for dealers to seek such information if it is costly. However, this observation does not generate the paradox, for the model presented here, which is described by Grossman [7] and Grossman and Stiglitz [10]. This paradox poses an existence problem; if dealers find they can learn nothing from their private information which they do not already know from the price, there is no equilibrium in which costly information is collected, because there is no incentive to collect such information. But on the other hand there is no equilibrium in which information is not collected, because then the price is uninformative and so there is an incentive to collect information. However, in the model presented here, whilst it is true that if the futures price is a sufficient statistic for information about the spot price there is no incentive to gather costly information about the spot price, there are incentives for producers to gather information about their own output, and use it in determining their futures trades. The futures price reflects this information, and as aggregate output is a major determinant of the spot price the futures price is also informative about the spot price.

Theorem 1 deals with the existence of an equilibrium in which the price is a sufficient statistic, but does not eliminate the possibility of multiple equilibria. Theorem 2 goes some way towards doing so, showing that if there is information about only one side of the spot market the unique equilibrium in which price is a linear function of the information is the sufficient statistic equilibrium. The proof of Theorem 2 makes extensive use of the 'projection characterization' of the conditional expectation of normal random variables which is set out at the beginning of the proof,[1] thereby avoiding a great deal of matrix algebra.

The model is set out in section 2, the results are stated and proved in section 3, and discussed in section 4.

2   THE MODEL

2.1   Description

This is a two-period model. A commodity is produced and traded spot at date 1. The spot price is a random variable r, which is determined by stochastic influences on spot supply and demand. At a previous date 0 there is a futures market in the commodity. Futures contracts are traded at price p and must be honored when the spot market opens at date 1. The return on holding futures is the spot price r.

The n dealers in the market are indexed by $i = 1, 2, \ldots, n$. I use the following notation for dealer i:

a_i:	private information	(realized at 0);
k_i:	risk aversion;	
R_i:	revenue	(realized at 1);
y_i:	futures sales	(realized at 0);
z_i:	production	(realized at 1);

in the two markets:

r:	spot price	(realized at 1);
p:	futures price	(realized at 0).

All these variables apart from risk aversion k_i are random. The dealers make their decisions about how much to sell forward (y_i) on the basis of their information, the realization of the random variable a_i, and the futures price p. Since y_i depends on the random variable a_i it is itself a random variable, as is the market clearing price p.

The dealers may be producers or pure speculators. Producers may be uncertain at date 0 about how much they will produce at 1 (z_i), but there is nothing they can do to influence z_i. All the production decisions have already been made so y_i is the only decision variable. For a pure speculator $z_i = 0$ in all states of the world.

Dealers sell the difference between their output z_i and their futures sales y_i on the spot market at price r. The total revenue of dealer i from spot and futures trading is[2]

$$R_i = y_i p + (z_i - y_i)r. \tag{9.1}$$

Both futures sales y_i and spot sales $z_i - y_i$ may be either positive or negative.

2.2   Assumptions

I make the following assumptions:

Assumption 1 *y_i is chosen by dealer i at date 0 to maximize the expected utility of revenue conditional upon his private information and the futures price. The utility function displays positive constant absolute risk aversion k_i. That is y_i maximizes*[3]

$$E\{ -\exp [-k_i (y_i p + (z_i - y_i)r)] | a_i, p_i\}. \tag{9.2}$$

This expression highlights the dual role of the futures price p which enters explicitly into the revenue function and also affects the conditional distribution of r and z_i.

The demand side of the spot market is described by the following *ad hoc* assumption.

Assumption 2   *Spot demand is*

$$d = -\delta r + e, \qquad \delta > 0, \tag{9.3}$$

where e is a random variable.

In addition, we make the following assumption.

Assumption 3   *The spot market clears with probability 1.*

The mathematical development of the model hinges on the following distributional assumptions:

Assumption 4   *$(a_1, \ldots, a_n, z_1, \ldots, z_n, e)$ is a multivariate normal random variable.*

The production of each dealer z_i and the stochastic disturbance to spot demand e must in the nature of things be univariate. a_i may, however, be multivariate, and a_i and $a_j (i \neq j)$ may have different dimensions.

Assumption 5   *Writing $a = (a_1, \ldots, a_n)$,*

$$\mathrm{cov} \left(e - \sum_{i=1}^{n} z_i, a \right) \neq 0. \tag{9.4}$$

That is, at least one component of the vector is nonzero.

Assumption 6

$$\text{var}\left(e - \sum_{i=1}^{n} z_i \,\big|\, a\right) > 0. \tag{9.5}$$

Assumption 7

$$E(z_i \,|\, a_i) = E(z_i \,|\, a) \qquad (i = 1, \ldots, n). \tag{9.6}$$

Assumption 8

$$(4k_i^2/\delta^2)\,\text{var}\left(e - \sum_{i=1}^{n} z_i\right)\text{var } z_i < 1 \qquad (i = 1, \ldots, n). \tag{9.7}$$

Assumptions 5–8 place restrictions on the distribution of $(a, z_1, \ldots, z_n, e)$. The role of Assumption 5 is to ensure that there is information available about the spot price – otherwise questions about the ability of the futures price to transmit such information are singularly uninteresting. Assumption 6 ensures that there is insufficient information available to eliminate all uncertainty so that the demand for futures of risk–averse dealers remains finite. Assumption 7 says that a producer's expectation of his own output, conditional on his private information, is the same as his expectation conditional on all the information. (Note that this does not imply that he can learn nothing about total production.) Assumption 8 is economically meaningless but ensures that the expected utility integrals converge. (See the Appendix.) It is always satisfied for pure speculators for whom var $z_i = 0$.

2.3 Rational expectations equilibrium

The concept of rational (or self-fulfilling) expectations equilibrium has become standard in this area. It captures the rational expectations hypothesis (Muth [16]) that agents are forming correct expectations given the model and the information available to them. In this case it is an equilibrium in the standard sense that markets clear; but more profoundly it is an equilibrium in that dealers' beliefs about the distribution of the random variables are self-fulfilling so they have no reason to change the way they form expectations.

I define a rational expectations equilibrium price for this model as a random variable p with the two following properties:

Futures market clearing[4]

$$\sum_{i=1}^{n} y_i = 0 \tag{9.8}$$

where y_i maximizes

$$E\{ -\exp\left[-k_i(y_i p + (z_i - y_i)r)\right] | a_i, p\} \qquad (i = 1, \ldots, n).$$

Price and information p is a measurable function of the information variables a.

The market clearing condition is obvious. The second condition is more subtle; it ensures that the price is unaffected by random variables which do not influence the futures market directly. The price cannot make available information which is otherwise unavailable to everyone in the market.

I shall restrict attention to prices which are linear functions of a (where $a = (a_1, \ldots, a_n)$). That is.

$$p = v_0 + \sum_{i=1}^{n} v_i a_i \tag{9.9}$$

for some $v_0 \in \mathbb{R}$, $v_i \in \mathbb{R}^{\dim a_i}$.

As a is normal, all these prices are normal. This makes explicit calculation of y_i possible. These calculations depend on the distribution of r which is determined in the spot market.

2.4   The spot market

Spot sales are the difference between production and futures sales. From (9.3) the spot market clears when

$$\sum_{i=1}^{n} (z_i - y_i) = -\delta r + e.$$

But from (9.8), $\sum_{i=1}^{n} y_i = 0$ so the spot market clearing condition is

$$\sum_{i=1}^{n} z_i = -\delta r + e. \tag{9.10}$$

Thus as $\delta > 0$,

$$r = (1/\delta) \left[e - \sum_{i=1}^{n} z_i \right]. \tag{9.11}$$

This has several useful implications. Most importantly, Assumption 4 and

(9.11) imply that $(z_1, \ldots, z_n, r, a, p)$ is a multivariate normal random variable. It can be shown that given Assumption 5, (9.4), and (9.11),[5]

$$E(r|a) \neq Er \tag{9.12}$$

and from Assumption 6 (9.5) and (9.11)

$$\text{var}(r|a_i, p) > 0 \tag{9.13}$$

for any p satisfying (9.9).

2.5   The futures market

I can now calculate explicit functional forms of the futures sales y_i which maximize expected utility

$$E\{-\exp[-k_i R_i]|a_i, p\}$$

where $R_i = y_i p + (z_i - y_i)r$. Dealer i knows the realization of p and a_i at date 0. His expected utility conditional on these realizations depends upon his choice of y_i and the conditional distribution of (z_i, r) given (a_i, p).

The calculation of the utility maximizing y_i involves some slightly tedious calculations, but no profound mathematics or economics. I have consigned these calculations to the Appendix. The methods of calculation will not be needed in the rest of this paper; the results are:

$$y_i = E(z_i|a_i, p) + \alpha_i p - \beta_i E(r|a_i, p) \tag{9.14}$$

where

$$\alpha_i = [(1 + k_i\rho_i)^2 - k_i^2\sigma_i^2\omega_i^2]/k_i\omega_i^2 > 0, \tag{9.15}$$

$$\beta_i = (1 + k_i\rho_i)/k_i\omega_i^2 > 0, \tag{9.16}$$

and

$$\begin{bmatrix} \sigma_i^2 & \rho_i \\ \rho_i & \omega_i^2 \end{bmatrix} = \text{var}(z_i, r|a_i, p). \tag{9.17}$$

Equation (9.13) ensures that $\omega_i^2 = \text{var}(r|a_i, p) > 0$, so α_i and β_i are finite. The positivity of α_i and β_i emerges from the calculations. This is economically plausible; *ceteris paribus* futures sales are an increasing function of the futures price and a decreasing function of the return on holding futures. This will be important in the arguments which follow. For a pure speculator $\sigma_i^2 = \rho_i = 0$, $\alpha_i = \beta_i = 1/k_i\omega_i^2$, and $E(z_i|a_i, p) = 0$; futures sales are proportional to the difference between the futures price and expected return.

As (z_i, r, a_i, p) is a multivariate normal random variable the conditional mean of (z_i, r) given (a_i, p) depends on both the joint distribution of (z_i, r, a_i, p) and the realization of (a_i, p), whilst the conditional variance depends only on the joint distribution. (see Anderson [2, ch. 2] for the relevant theorems on the multivariate normal distribution.) Thus α_i and β_i depend on the distribution of (z_i, r, a_i, p) but not on the realization of (a_i, p), so α_i and β_i are not random variables. This will be important in proving the theorems.

Summarizing the argument so far, the equilibrium prices in which I am interested are linear functions of the information variables, from (9.9),

$$p = \nu_0 + \sum_{i=1}^{n} \nu_i a_i \qquad (9.18)$$

for some $\nu_0 \in \mathbb{R}$ and $\nu_i \in \mathbb{R}^{\dim a_i}$, $i = 1, \ldots, n$. p satisfies the market clearing equation derived from (9.8) and (9.14):

$$\sum_{i=1}^{n} E(z_i | a_i, p) + \alpha_i p - \beta_i E(r | a_i, p) = 0, \qquad (9.19)$$

where α_i and β_i are positive functions of risk aversion and the conditional variance of (a_i, r) given (a_i, p) given by (9.15)–(9.17).

3   SUFFICIENT STATISTIC THEOREMS

3.1   Statements

These theorems are concerned with the situations in which the futures price aggregates all the information pertinent to the spot price; technically the futures price is a sufficient statistic for the information about the spot price.[6] As all the random variables are normal the conditional distribution of the spot price is completely characterized by the conditional mean and variance. The question is thus when do

$$E(r|p) = E(r|a) \qquad (9.20)$$

and

$$\text{var}(r|p) = \text{var}(r|a) \qquad (9.21)$$

where $a = (a_1, \ldots, a_n)$?

Theorem 1 gives a necessary and sufficient condition for the existence of a rational expectations equilibrium in which the price is a sufficient statistic. It is easy to show that there is at most one sufficient statistic equilibrium, which raises the question: are there other nonsufficient statistic equilibria? Theorem 2 provides a partial answer.

Theorem 1   *There is a rational expectations equilibrium in which the price is a sufficient statistic if and only if there are real numbers ϕ and β_0 such that*

$$\sum_{i=1}^{n} E(z_i|a) = \phi - \beta_0 E(r|a) \tag{9.22}$$

and

$$\beta_0 \neq -\sum_{i=1}^{n} \beta_i^* \tag{9.23}$$

where

$$\beta_i^* = \frac{(1 + k_i \operatorname{cov}(z_i, r|a))}{k_i \operatorname{var}(r|a)}. \tag{9.24}$$

No more than one sufficient statistic rational expectations equilibrium exists. If such an equilibrium does exist the equilibrium price is a linear function of a.

Theorem 2   *If (9.22) holds with*

$$\beta_0 \geqslant 0, \tag{9.25}$$

the only rational expectations equilibrium which exists with price a linear function of a is the sufficient statistic equilibrium.

The conditions of the theorems need an economic interpretation. It is helpful to distinguish three different cases:
1 (9.22) holds with $\beta_0 = \delta$. Then rewriting (9.22),

$$\sum_{i=1}^{n} E(z_i|a) = \phi - \delta E(r|a). \tag{9.26}$$

From the spot market clearing condition (9.10),

$$\sum_{i=1}^{n} E(z_i|a) = E(e|a) - \delta E(r|a). \tag{9.27}$$

(9.26) and (9.27) taken together imply that

$$E(e|a) = Ee = \phi. \tag{9.28}$$

The information a is independent of the stochastic term in spot demand e and refers only to spot supply $\sum_{i=1}^{n} z_i$.

In this case the model is almost a generalization of that of Grossman and

Stiglitz [10, section on 'Prices as aggregators']. The models differ in that I allow for the presence of pure speculators as well as producers, and do not insist on symmetrical distributions and risk aversion. Grossman and Stiglitz assume that given all the information there is no uncertainty about the spot price whilst I assume that there is always residual uncertainty. This leads to the breakdown of the market in the Grossman–Stiglitz example, as the absence of uncertainty removes any incentive to futures trading.

The model is also similar to that of Danthine [4] (a parametric example); again it differs in the greater generality of its risk aversion and distributional assumptions. Danthine analyzes the effect of futures trading on production decisions; this issue is not considered here.

2 (9.22) holds with $\beta_0 = 0$. Then

$$\sum_{i=1}^{n} E(z_i|a) = \sum_{i=1}^{n} E z_i = \phi. \tag{9.29}$$

The information a is independent of total output $\sum_{i=1}^{n} z_i$ and refers only to spot demand e.

In this case the model is mathematically equivalent to a generalization of Grossman's [7] model of a stock market, differing from Grossman's model in the greater generality of the information structure.

3 (9.26) holds with $0 \neq \beta_0 \neq \delta$. In this case from the spot market clearing condition (9.10) and (9.22),

$$\left(\sum_{i=1}^{n} E(z_i|a)\right)(1 - \beta_0/\delta) = \phi - (\beta_0/\delta)E(e|a). \tag{9.30}$$

This implies that the conditional expectations of spot supply and demand are perfectly correlated. It is difficult to imagine why this should be so; the economically interesting cases are 1 and 2 in which information is available about only one side of the spot market.

The role of the additional conditions in Theorem 1 ((9.23) and (9.24)) will become apparent in the course of the proof. Note that if these conditions fail to hold, a small change in one the parameters of the model (e.g., risk aversion) would make them hold. Thus Theorem 1 is generically true if (9.22) holds.

The condition for Theorem 2 (9.25) holds when information is available about only one side of the spot market. (Recall from Assumption 2 (9.3) that $\delta > 0$.) If (9.22) holds with information available about both sides of the spot market, (9.25) implies that the spot price is negatively correlated with supply. This seems reasonable, although it may not be true if $E(e|a)$ is positively correlated with $\sum_{i=1}^{n} E(z_i|a)$.

3.2   Proof of Theorem 1

The theorem is proved by using Grossman's [9] concept of an artificial economy. In this economy dealers pool all their information prior to trading, and trade on the basis of the conditional expectation of (z_i, r) given all the information (a), rather than (a_i, p). p^* is the Walrasian equilibrium price for this economy. The proof proceeds by showing that (9.22) is a necessary and sufficient condition for the artificial economy price to be a sufficient statistic, and then arguing in a similar fashion to Grossman that there is a rational expectations equilibrium in which the price is a sufficient statistic if and only if the artificial economy price is a sufficient statistic. The equilibrium price is the artificial economy price.

If the artificial economy price $p^* = p^*$, and $a = a$, the futures sale y_i^* is chosen to maximize

$$E\{ -\exp [-k_i (y_i^* p^* + (z_i - y_i^*)r)] | a = a\}. \tag{9.31}$$

From (9.19),

$$y_i = E(z_i | a = a) + \alpha_i^* p^* - \beta_i^* E(r | a = a). \tag{9.32}$$

p^*, the Walrasian equilibrium price for the artificial economy, satisfies

$$\sum_{i=1}^{n} E(z_i | a) + \alpha_i^* p^* - \beta_i^* E(r | a) = 0. \tag{9.33}$$

α_i^* and β_i^* are the functions of var $(z_i, r | a)$, set out in (9.15) and (9.16). Note that α_i^* and β_i^* are positive real numbers, not random variables. Also β_i^* in (9.24) and (9.32) are the same.

Equation (9.33) implies that p^* is a linear function of a. A necessary and sufficient condition for p^* to be a sufficient statistic for the information conveyed by a about r is[7]

$$E(r | p^*) = E(r | a). \tag{9.34}$$

$E(r | p^*)$ is a linear function of p^*, so (9.34) implies that $E(r | a) = \theta_0 + \theta_1 p^*$ for some (θ_0, θ_1). If $\theta_1 = 0$, $E(r | a) = \theta_0 = Er$, contradicting (9.12). Thus (9.34) implies that

$$p^* = \gamma_0 + \gamma_1 E(r | a) \tag{9.35}$$

for some real (γ_0, γ_1), $\gamma_1 \neq 0$. It is straightforward to show that (9.35) implies (9.34) by using the standard formula. Thus (9.34) and (9.35) are equivalent.

Equation (9.33) defines p^*. Given (9.33), (9.35) can hold if and only if

$$\sum_{i=1}^{n} E(z_i | a) = \phi - \beta_0 E(r | a) \tag{9.36}$$

where

$$\phi = -\gamma_0 \sum_{i=1}^{n} \alpha_i^* \tag{9.37}$$

and

$$\beta_0 = \gamma_1 \sum_{i=1}^{n} \alpha_i^* - \sum_{i=1}^{n} \beta_i^*. \tag{9.38}$$

Also

$$\gamma_1 \neq 0 \quad \text{if and only if} \quad \beta_0 \neq -\sum_{i=1}^{n} \beta_i^*. \tag{9.39}$$

Thus the postulates of the theorem hold if and only if p^*, the artificial economy price, is a sufficient statistic. The proof is completed by showing that p^* is a sufficient statistic if and only if there is a sufficient statistic equilibrium in the original model.

If the conditional distribution of (z_i, r) given (a_i, p) is the same as the conditional distribution given complete information a, dealers' trades given a realization p of p are the same as if $p^* = p$. Therefore if p is a market clearing price $p = p^*$. A rational expectations equilibrium exists in which dealers trade as if they had complete information if and only if the conditional distributions of (z_i, r) given (a_i, p^*) and a are the same $(i = 1, \ldots, n)$. (z_i, r, a) is a multivariate normal random variable and (a_i, p) is a linear function of a if and only if[8]

$$E(z_i, r | a_i, p^*) = E(z_i, r | a). \tag{9.40}$$

If p^* is sufficient statistic[9]

$$E(r | a_i, p^*) = E(r | a). \tag{9.41}$$

As p^* is a linear function of a, Assumption 7 that

$$E(z_i | a_i) = E(z_i | a) \tag{9.42}$$

implies that

$$E(z_i | a_i, p^*) = E(z_i | a). \tag{9.43}$$

Thus if p^* is a sufficient statistic for information about r, (a_i, p^*) is equivalent to complete information, and there is a rational expectations equilibrium with price p^*. Conversely every rational expectations equilibrium in which the price is a sufficient statistic must have the same price as the unique artificial economy equilibrium. Thus there is no more than one sufficient statistic equilibrium.

3.3   Proof of Theorem 2

The proof makes extensive use of the following characterization of conditional expectations of normal random variables:

Projection characterization If (x_1, x_2) is a multivariate normal random variable $E(x_1|x_2)$ is the *unique* linear function of (x_1, x_2) with the two following properties:

$$E(E(x_1|x_2)) = Ex_1 \tag{9.44}$$

and

$$\text{cov}(x_1 - E(x_1|x_2), x_2) = 0. \tag{9.45}$$

Equation (9.44) is a property of all conditional expectations. (9.45) is equivalent to the statement that if (x_1, x_2) is a zero-mean normal random variable, $E(x_1|x_2)$ is the projection of x_1 onto the subspace generated by the components of x_2 in the Hilbert space of square integrable functions.[10] This generates a series of geometrical insights; the covariance of two random variables corresponds to the dot product in Euclidean space; uncorrelated random variables correspond to orthogonal vectors. These insights yielded the intuition on which the proof is based.

The great power of this characterization is that showing that a linear function of x_2 satisfies (9.44) and (9.45) is sufficient to prove that it is the conditional expectation of x_1 given x_2. This implicit use of the projection theorem serves to eliminate a great deal of matrix algebra.

It is a matter of straightforward manipulation to show that (9.44) and (9.45) are equivalent to the standard formula when the variance matrix of x_2 is nonsingular. The result is also true when the variance matrix is singular.[11]

The proof begins by assuming that there is a rational expectations equilibrium price p which is a linear function of a. I will show that it the postulates of the theorem ((9.22)–(9.25)) hold, p must be a sufficient statistic, and so as I argued earlier $p = p^*$.

As p clears the market,

$$\sum_{i=1}^{n} E(z_i|a_i, p) + \alpha_i p - \beta_i E(r|a_i, p) = 0 \tag{9.46}$$

where α_i and β_i are positive, nonstochastic functions of $\text{var}(z_i, r|a_i, p)$. From (9.22) and (9.25),

$$\sum_{i=1}^{n} E(z_i|a) = \phi - \beta_0 E(r|a), \qquad \beta_0 \geqslant 0. \tag{9.47}$$

From Assumption 7,

$$E(z_i|a) = E(z_i|a_i, p).$$

(9.48)

Also as p is a function of a,

$$E(r|a) = E(r|a, p).$$

(9.49)

From (9.47), (9.48) and (9.49),

$$\sum_{i=1}^{n} E(z_i|a_i, p) = \phi - \beta_0 E(r|a, p).$$

(9.50)

From (9.50) and (9.46),[12]

$$p = \psi + \lambda_0 E(r|a, p) + \sum_{i=1}^{n} \lambda_i E(r|a_i, p)$$

or, letting $a_0 = a$,

$$p = \psi + \sum_{i=0}^{n} \lambda_i E(r|a_i, p)$$

(9.51)

where

$$\psi = -\phi / \sum_{i=1}^{n} \alpha_i,$$

(9.52)

$$\lambda_i = \beta_i / \sum_{i=1}^{n} \alpha_i \qquad (i = 0, 1, \ldots, n).$$

(9.53)

By assumption (9.25), $\beta_0 \geq 0$. From (9.15) and (9.16), $\alpha_i > 0$, $\beta_i > 0$, $i = 1$, $\ldots$, n. Thus

$$\lambda_0 \geq 0, \qquad \lambda_i > 0 \qquad (i = 1, \ldots, n).$$

(9.54)

(9.51) and (9.54) are the crucial equations from which the rest of the proof follows. From (9.51) as λ_i, $i = 0, \ldots, n$, and ψ are not random variables,

$$\text{cov}(r - E(r|p), p) = \sum_{i=0}^{n} \lambda_i \text{cov}(r - E(r|p), E(r|a_i, p)).$$

(9.55)

But from the 'projection characterization' (9.45)

$$\text{cov}(r - E(r|p), p) = 0.$$

(9.56)

Also

$$\text{cov}(r - E(r|p), E(r|a_i, p))$$
$$= \text{cov}(r - E(r|p), E(r|a_i, p) - E(r|p))$$

$$+ \operatorname{cov}\left(r - E\left(r|p\right), E\left(r|p\right)\right)$$

$$= \operatorname{cov}\left(r - E\left(r|p\right), E\left(r|a_i, p\right) - E\left(r|p\right)\right). \tag{9.57}$$

((9.45) and the fact that $E\left(r|p\right)$ is a linear function of p imply that $\operatorname{cov}\left(r - E\left(r|p\right), E\left(r|p\right)\right) = 0$.) But

$$\operatorname{cov}\left(r - E\left(r|p\right), E\left(r|a_i, p\right) - E\left(r|p\right)\right)$$

$$= \operatorname{var}\left(E\left(r|a_i, p\right) - E\left(r|p\right)\right)$$

$$+ \operatorname{cov}\left(r - E\left(r|a_i, p\right), E\left(r|a_i, p\right) - E\left(r|p\right)\right)$$

$$= \operatorname{var}\left(E\left(r|a_i, p\right) - E\left(r|p\right)\right) \tag{9.58}$$

(as $\operatorname{cov}\left(r - E\left(r|a_i, p\right), (a_i, p)\right) = 0$ and $E\left(r|a_i, p\right) - E\left(r|p\right)$ is a linear function of (a_i, p)). From (9.57) and (9.58),

$$\operatorname{cov}\left(r - E\left(r|p\right), E\left(r|a_i, p\right)\right) = \operatorname{var}\left(E\left(r|a_i, p\right) - E\left(r|p\right)\right) \geqslant 0$$

$$(i = 0, \ldots, n). \tag{9.59}$$

The conditional expectation, $E\left(r|a_i, p\right)$, cannot be negatively correlated with $r - E\left(r|p\right)$. From (9.55), (9.56), and (9.59),

$$0 = \sum_{i=0}^{n} \lambda_i \operatorname{var}\left(E\left(r|a_i, p\right) - E\left(r|p\right)\right). \tag{9.60}$$

As $\lambda_0 \geqslant 0$ and $\lambda_i > 0$ $(i = 1, \ldots, n)$, (9.60) implies that

$$E\left(r|a_i, p\right) = E\left(r|p\right) \qquad (i = 1, \ldots, n). \tag{9.61}$$

From (9.61) and the projection characterization,

$$\operatorname{cov}\left(r - E\left(r|p\right), a_i\right) = 0 \qquad (i = 1, \ldots, n).$$

Thus $\operatorname{cov}\left(r - E\left(r|p\right), a\right) = 0$ since $a = (a_1, \ldots, a_n)$. $E\left(r|p\right)$ is a linear function of p and thus of a, and $E\left(E\left(r|p\right)\right) = Er$. Thus $E\left(r|p\right) = E\left(r|a\right)$. p is a sufficient statistic, and thus as p is also a market clearing price $p = p^*$.

4   DISCUSSION

In this model the price does not, in general, provide information which is equivalent to complete information. This contrasts with the work of other authors (Allen [1], Grossman [7, 8, 9], Jordan [11], Kihlstrom and Mirman [12], and Radner [17].[13] The difference between this and other models, which accounts for the different results, is my assumption that some of the agents in this model are producers, who have random second period endowments (z_i) which are correlated with asset returns. The random endowments here are physical output; but there are a number of other situations in which people obtain random income from sources other than their portfolio of financial assets (for example, labor income, gifts, and bequests). The models of Grossman and Stiglitz [10] and Danthine [4] also include random endowments, but differ from this model in making the endowments the sole source of uncertainty about which dealers have any information.

Theorem 1 establishes that in this model, if there are two sources of uncertainty, one of which is endowments, the futures price is not in general a sufficient statistic. This is established by using Grossman's concept of an artificial economy in which dealers pool all their information prior to trading. There is a rational expectations equilibrium in which prices are a sufficient statistic if and only if the artificial economy prices are a sufficient statistic. If dealers' trades in the artificial economy are affected by information about both asset returns and endowments the artificial economy price reflects both types of information, and cannot in general be a sufficient statistic. This observation is similar to Grossman's [7] comment that introducing 'noise' in the form of random supply into a stock market model prevents the price from being a sufficient statistic. However, it is not clear that 'noise' is the right word for information about endowments which are correlated with asset return; in the absence of other information the 'noise' becomes the signal. A better way of describing the situation is that the artificial economy price is a function of two signals, one about asset returns, the other about random endowments which themselves affect asset returns; it is usually impossible to disentangle the effects of these signals.[14]

Another effect of the random endowments (output) is the absence of the paradox discussed by Grossman [7] and Grossman and Stiglitz [10]. The market price can only reflect the information which dealers collect. If no information is collected, the price is uninformative so dealers have an incentive to collect costly information; however, if they collect the information, it is all revealed costlessly by prices so there is no incentive to collect it. This model avoids this paradox in two ways. Firstly, price may not be a sufficient statistic. Secondly, if the price is a sufficient statistic, it aggregates information about the spot price r, so

$$E(r|a) = E(r|p). \tag{9.62}$$

(9.62) does not imply that

$$E(z_i|a) = E(z_i|p) \qquad (i = 1, \ldots, n). \tag{9.63}$$

The futures price is not a sufficient statistic for information about each dealer's output. Producers may still wish to gather information which tells them nothing about the spot price r which they cannot already infer from the futures price, because the information tells them about their own output. The futures market aggregates this information – and so the futures price is informative about the spot price. There are still incentives to gather information about output even when the futures price is a sufficient statistic for information about the spot price.

The second theorem is concerned with situations in which there is a rational expectations equilibrium in which the price is a sufficient statistic. In these circumstances (from (9.22)),

$$E\left(\sum_{i=1}^{n} z_i \,|\, a\right) = \phi - \beta_0 E\left(r \,|\, a\right). \qquad (9.64)$$

I establish that if β_0 is nonnegative there is no other rational expectations equilibrium in which the price is a linear function of a. When there is information about only one side of the spot market, (9.64) holds with $\beta_0 \geqslant 0$. If there is information about both sides of the spot market (9.64) is unlikely to hold; so the theorem covers the most economically plausible cases of a sufficient statistic equilibrium.

However, the theorem has serious limitations in dealing with the possibility of equilibria in which the price is a nonlinear function of the information variables. There can be no equilibria in which the price is a nonlinear invertible function of a linear function of information, because then the conditional distribution of (z_i, r) given (a_i, p) is normal; demand is a linear function of price and information, and so the market clearing price must be a linear function of the information. However, there might be other equilibria with nonlinear prices. The conditional distribution of (z_i, r) in these equilibria would not be normal, and the methods of this paper are not applicable.

Nevertheless the theorem does eliminate a large class of potential equilibria from consideration. It is proved by an argument which is equivalent to use of the projection theorem, which seems to be a powerful tool for the analysis of linear rational expectations models.[15]

APPENDIX

Calculation of dealers' futures sales

The objective here is to find y_i which maximizes

$$V_i = E\left(-\exp\left(-k_i R_i\right) \,|\, a_i = a_i, p = p\right)$$

where $R_i = y_i (p - r) + z_i r$. It is convenient to drop the subscript i and write

$$(\bar{z}, \bar{r}) = E\left(z, r \,|\, a = a, p = p\right)$$

and

$$\Sigma = \begin{bmatrix} \sigma^2 & \rho \\ \rho & \omega^2 \end{bmatrix} = \text{var}\ (z, r \mid a = a, p = p).$$

As (z, r, a, p) is multivariate normal, the conditional distribution of (z, r) given (a, p) is bivariate normal, Σ does not depend on the realization (a, p), and Σ is positive semi-definite. (See Anderson [2, p. 29].)

In one situation the calculation is straightforward. If $\sigma^2 = \rho = 0$, R is normal;

$$E\ (R \mid a = a, p = p) = y(p - \bar{r}) + \bar{z}\bar{r},$$

$$\text{var}\ (R \mid a = a, p = p) = (\bar{z} - y)^2 \omega^2.$$

The moment generating function of $x \sim N(\mu, \sigma^2)$ is

$$m(t) = E\ (\exp\ (tx)) = \exp\ (t\mu + \tfrac{1}{2} \sigma^2 t^2)$$

(Mood and Graybill [15, p. 126]).

Therefore, in this case

$$V = E\ (-\exp\ (-kR) \mid a, p),$$

$$V = -m(-k) = -\exp\ (-k(y(p - \bar{r}) + \bar{z}\bar{r}) + \tfrac{1}{2} k^2 (\bar{z} - y)^2 \omega^2).$$

From (9.13), $\omega^2 = \text{var}\ (r \mid a_i, p) > 0$ so V is maximized when

$$y = \bar{z} + (1/k\omega^2)\ (p - \bar{r})$$

$$= \bar{z} + \alpha p - \beta \bar{r}$$

where

$$\alpha = [(1 + k\rho)^2 - k^2 \sigma^2 \omega^2]/k\omega^2,$$

$$\beta = (1 + k\rho)/k\omega^2,$$

as

$$\sigma^2 = \rho = 0.$$

If $\sigma^2 = \text{var}\ (z_i \mid a_i, p) > 0$, R includes the nonnormal term zr so is not itself normal, and does not have a standard moment generating function. Here calculation from first principles is a tedious necessity, and conditions have to be imposed to ensure that the utility integral is finite. I give the details for the case where Σ is nonsingular: In this case,

$$V = -2\Pi |\Sigma|^{-1/2} \int_{r=-\infty}^{\infty} \int_{z=-\infty}^{\infty} \exp\ (-W) dz\, dr,$$

where

$$W = kR + \tfrac{1}{2} (z - \bar{z}, r - \bar{r}) \Sigma^{-1} (z - \bar{z}, r - \bar{r})'.$$

The first term in W arises from the utility function, the second from the normal density function. Rearranging.

$$W = \tfrac{1}{2} x' A x + b' x + c,$$

where

$$x = (z - \bar{z}, r - \bar{r})',$$

$$A = (\sigma^2 \omega^2 - \rho^2)^{-1} \begin{bmatrix} \omega^2 & \omega^2(\beta - a) \\ \omega^2(\beta - \alpha) & \sigma^2 \end{bmatrix},$$

$$\alpha = [(1 + k\rho)^2 - k^2 \sigma^2 \omega^2]/k\omega^2,$$

$$\beta = (1 + k\rho)/k\omega^2,$$

$$b = k(\bar{r}, \bar{z} - y)',$$

and

$$c = k(\bar{z}\bar{r} + y(p - \bar{r})).$$

V is finite if and only if A is positive definite. I now show that in this case α and β are positive, and that Assumption 8 is sufficient for this.

$$\det A = k\omega^2 \alpha / (\sigma^2 \omega^2 - \rho^2) > 0 \qquad \text{if and only if} \quad \alpha > 0.$$

But

$$\alpha = [1 + k(\sigma\omega + \rho)] [1 - k(\sigma\omega - \rho)]/k\omega^2.$$

As $k(\sigma\omega + \rho) > 0$, $\alpha > 0$ if and only if $1 - k(\sigma\omega - \rho) > 0$, in which case

$$\beta = \frac{1 + k\rho}{k\omega^2} > \sigma/\omega > 0,$$

so β is also positive. Now $\rho \geqslant -\sigma\omega$ so

$$1 - k(\sigma\omega - \rho) \geqslant 1 - 2k\sigma\omega;$$

so it is sufficient for $\alpha > 0$ that

$$1 > 4k^2\sigma^2\omega^2.$$

But

$$\sigma^2\omega^2 = \operatorname{var}(z|a, p) \operatorname{var}(r|a, p) \leqslant \operatorname{var} z \operatorname{var} r.$$

So a sufficient condition is

$$4k^2 \operatorname{var} r \operatorname{var} z < 1$$

or as $r = (1/\delta) (e - \Sigma_{i=1}^{n} z_i)$ (from (9.10)),

$$(4k_i^2/\delta^2) \text{ var} \left[e - \sum_{j=1}^{n} z_j \right] \text{ var } z_i < 1 \qquad (i = 1, \ldots, n).$$

This is Assumption 8.

Returning to the calculation of expected utility, on the assumption that A is positive definite,

$$A = BB'.$$

Writing $u = B'x + B^{-1}b$,

$$\int_{r=-\infty}^{\infty} \int_{z=-\infty}^{\infty} \exp\left(-W\right) \mathrm{d}z \, \mathrm{d}r = \int_{R^2} \exp\left(-\tfrac{1}{2} x'Ax - b'x - c\right) \mathrm{d}x$$

$$= |\det A|^{-1/2} \int_{R^2} \exp\left(-\tfrac{1}{2} u'u + \tfrac{1}{2} b'A^{-1}b - c\right) \mathrm{d}u$$

$$= 2\Pi |\det A|^{-1/2} \exp\left(\tfrac{1}{2} b'A^{-1}b - c\right).$$

Thus

$$V = -|\Sigma|^{-1/2}| \det A|^{-1/2} \exp\left(\tfrac{1}{2} b'A^{-1}b - c\right).$$

Σ and A do not involve y, but b and c do. Thus V is maximized when

$$\tfrac{1}{2} b'A^{-1}b - c$$

is minimized, that is, when

$$\left(\frac{\mathrm{d}b}{\mathrm{d}y}\right)' A^{-1}b - \frac{\mathrm{d}c}{\mathrm{d}y} = 0$$

or

$$y = z + \alpha p - \beta \bar{r}.$$

NOTES

1 The underlying mathematics is the projection theorem in Hilbert space, but I con-
   ·duct the argument entirely in terms of variances and covariances. Futia [6] uses
   Hilbert space theory in a more sophisticated fashion to study rational expectations equilibria in an infinite stationary sequence of speculative markets.
2 If futures payments are made at 0 and spot payments at 1 the futures price should
   be thought of as including an implicit discount factor so that R_i is revenue at
   date 1.

3 In fuller notation, given the realization p of p and a_i of a_i, y_i is chosen to maximize

$$E\{-\exp[-k_i(y_i p + (z_i - y_i)r)]|a_i = a_i, p = p\}.$$

y_i is the random variable whose realization is y_i. The function relating y_i to the realization of (a_i, p) depends on the joint distribution of (r, z_i, a_i, p). The value of the function depends on the realization (a_i, p).

4 Strictly $\Sigma_{i=1}^{n} y_i = 0$ with probability 1. Such a proviso should be included everywhere there is an equality between random variables, but it seems unnecessarily pedantic to do so.

5 The simplest way to demonstrate this uses the projections characterization (equations (9.44) and (9.45) introduced at the beginning of the proof of Theorem 2. Assumption 5 (9.4) and (9.11) imply that

$$\mathrm{cov}\,(r, a,) \neq 0.$$

If $E(r|a) = Er$,

$$\mathrm{cov}\,(r, a) = \mathrm{cov}\,(r - Er, a) = \mathrm{cov}\,(r - E(r|a), a) = 0$$

from the projection characterization. Thus $E(r|a) \neq Er$. From Assumption 6, (9.5), and (9.11), var $(r|a) > 0$, $r - E(r|a_i, p)$ is uncorrelated with (a_i, p) and therefore, since all the variables are normal, independent of (a_i, p). Thus

$$\mathrm{var}\,(r|a_i, p) = E(r - E(r|a_i, p))^2$$
$$= E(r - E(r|a) - E(r|a_i, p) + E(r|a))^2$$
$$= E(r - E(r|a))^2 + E(E(r|a_i, p) - E(r|a))^2$$
$$\geqslant E(r - E(r|a))^2 = \mathrm{var}\,(r|a) > 0$$

as $E(r|a_i, p) - E(r|a)$ is a linear function of a and so uncorrelated with $r - E(r|a)$.

6 A sufficient statistic can be defined in a variety of ways. The standard factorization criterion is that p is a sufficient statistic for the information a about r if the conditional density of a given r, $g(a|r)$, can be factored as

$$g(a|r) = g_1(p, r)g_2(a)$$

(see Mood and Graybill [15, p. 171]). Grossman [9, Appendix] shows that this condition is equivalent to

$$E[F(r)|a] = E[F(r)|p]$$

for all measurable real F. In particular this is true where F is a step function. Thus the conditional distribution function of r given a and given p are the same. When (r, a) is normal and p is a linear function of a, both conditional distributions are normal and entirely specified by the conditional mean and variance (Anderson [2, p. 29]), so (9.20) and (9.21) imply that p is a sufficient statistic.

7 If (x_1, x_2) is a multivariate normal random variable, $x_1 - E(x_1|x_2)$ is independent of x_2. (This can be readily checked from the conditional distribution for-

mula, recalling that uncorrelated normal random variables are independent.)
Thus

$$\text{var}\,(x_1\,|\,x_2) = E\,[\,(x_1 - E\,(x_1\,|\,x_2))^2\,|\,x_2] = E\,(x_1 - E\,(x_1\,|\,x_2))^2.$$

Therefore if (x_1, x_2') is also multivariate normal and

$$E\,(x_1\,|\,x_2') = E\,(x_1\,|\,x_2),$$

then

$$\text{var}\,(x_1\,|\,x_2) = \text{var}\,(x_1\,|\,x_2').$$

Thus (9.20) implies (9.21), and so (9.20) (repeated as (9.34)) is necessary and sufficient for the sufficiency of p.

8 This is another application of the argument of note 7.

9 The derivations of (9.41) and (9.43) both use the fact that if (x, a) is a multivariate normal random variable, $b(a)$ and $c(a)$ are linear functions of a, and

$$E\,(x\,|\,b(a)) = E\,(x\,|\,a),$$

then

$$E\,(x\,|\,b(a), c(a)) = E\,(x\,|\,a).$$

The simplest proof of this uses the projection characterization (equations (9.44) and (9.45)) introduced at the beginning of the proof of Theorem 2: $E\,(x\,|\,b(a))$ is a linear function of $(b(a), c(a))$, $E\,(E\,(x\,|\,b(a)) = Ex$, and as $E\,(x\,|\,b(a)) = E\,(x\,|\,a)$, $x - E\,(x\,|\,b(a))$ is uncorrelated with a and thus with $(b(a), c(a))$. Thus $E\,(x\,|\,b(a)) = E\,(x\,|\,b(a), c(a))$.

10 See Loeve [13]. Projection techniques are familiar from regression (Luenberger [14]) where realizations of random variables are considered as elements in Euclidean space. Here the random variables themselves are considered as elements of function space.

11 These formulae are: If

$$(x_1, x_2) \sim N\left[(\mu_1, \mu_2), \begin{bmatrix} \Sigma_{11} & \Sigma_{12} \\ \Sigma_{21} & \Sigma_{22} \end{bmatrix}\right]$$

the conditional distribution of x_1 given $x_2 = x_2$ is normal with mean

$$E\,(x_1\,|\,x_2 = x_2) = \mu_1 + \Sigma_{12}\Sigma_{22}^{-1}\,(x_2 - \mu_2)$$

and variance

$$\text{var}\,(x_1\,|\,x_2 = x_2) = \Sigma_{11} - \Sigma_{12}\Sigma_{22}^{-1}\Sigma_{21}.$$

(See Anderson [2, ch. 2].) If Σ_{22} is singular it can be shown that (Anderson [2, p. 24])

$$x_2 = Cx_3 + \lambda$$

where C has full column rank and var x_3 is nonsingular. As C is of full column rank cov$(x_2, y) = 0$ if and only if cov$(x_3, y) = 0$. Thus (9.44) and (9.45) imply that $E(x_1 | x_2) = E(x_1 | x_3)$.

12 The argument which follows is conducted in terms of variances. It is equivalent to more abstract argument in which equation (9.51) is projected onto the subspace of Hilbert space, generated by linear combinations of the components of a which are orthogonal to p. The left-hand side becomes zero; the right-hand side is the sum of terms, all of which are nonnegatively correlated with r, which must therefore all be zero.

13 With the exception of Jordan [11] the major thrust of these papers is to establish conditions under which prices reveal information which is equivalent to perfect information. Jordan takes the opposite approach, establishing that if the number of markets is too small relative to the dimension of the available information space the price cannot reveal all the information, except when certain conditions hold of the utility function. One of these is constant absolute risk aversion which is assumed here.

This model is not a special case of Jordan's, fundamentally because it allows for random endowments, which are correlated with returns. Jordan's model also precludes normal random variables, by assuming bounded supports.

14 In examples of this type if sufficient additional markets are opened in which trade is a function of the same information variables, the dimension of the price vector becomes high enough for it to be a sufficient statistic. Grossman [8] contains an example in which the opening of a futures market has this effect.

Allen [1] and Jordan [11] have more general results relating to the interaction of the dimension of the information space and the number of markets. Grossman [9] shows that if the information and return variables are normal, there is a riskless asset, and the market portfolio of risky assets is not a Giffen good; the dimension of the information space is effectively the number of risky assets, regardless of how many information variables there are, and prices are a sufficient statistic.

15 See also Futia [6].

REFERENCES

1 Allen, B.: Generic existence of completely revealing equilibria for economies with uncertainty when prices convey information, *Econometrica*, 49(5) (1981), 1173–99.

2 Anderson, T. W.: *An Introduction to Multivariate Statistical Analysis*. New York: John Wiley and Sons, 1958.

3 Bray, M. M.: Information in futures markets, Bachelor of Philosophy Thesis, University of Oxford, 1978.

4 Danthine, J. P.: Information, futures prices and stabilizing speculation, *Journal of Economic Theory*, 17 (1978), 79–98.

5 Fama, E. F.: Efficient capital markets: a review of theory and empirical work, *Journal of Finance*, 25 (1970), 383–416.

6 Futia, C. A.: Rational expectations in linear models, *Econometrica*, 49 (1981), 171–92.

7 Grossman, S. J.: On the efficiency of competitive stock markets where traders have diverse information, *Journal of Finance*, 31 (1976), 573–85.

8 Grossman, S. J.: The existence of futures markets, noisy rational expectations and informational externalities, *Review of Economic Studies*, 44 (1977), 431–49.

9 Grossman, S. J.: Further results on the informational efficiency of competitive stock markets, *Journal of Economic Theory*, 18 (1978), 81–101.

10 Grossman, S. J. and J. E. Stiglitz: Information and competitive price systems, *American Economic Review*, 66 (1976), 246–53.

11 Jordan, J. S.: On the efficient markets hypothesis, mimeograph, University of Minnesota, 1979.

12 Kihlstrom, R., and L. J. Mirman: Information and market equilibrium, *Bell Journal of Economics and Management Science*, 6 (1975), 357–76.

13 Loeve, M.: *Probability Theory*. Princeton: Van Nostrand, 1955.

14 Luenberger, D. G.: Optimization by vector space methods, New York: John Wiley and Sons, 1969.

15 Mood, A. M., and F. A. Graybill: *Introduction to the Theory of Statistics*. New York: McGraw-Hill, 1963.

16 Muth, J. F.: Rational expectations and the theory of price movements, *Econometrica*, 9 (1961), 315–35.

17 Radner, R.: Rational expectations equilibrium: generic existence and the information revealed by prices, *Econometrica*, 47 (1979), 655–78.

18 Samuelson, P. A.: Proof that properly anticipated prices fluctuate randomly, in *Collected Scientific Papers of P. A. Samuelson*, Vol. III. Cambridge: MIT Press, 1972, pp. 782–90.

19 Samuelson, P. A.: Proof that properly discounted present values of assets vibrate randomly, *Bell Journal of Economics and Management Science*, 4 (1973), 369–74.

Part IV

Market Liquidity

10

An Analysis of the Implications for Stock and Futures Price Volatility of Program Trading and Dynamic Hedging Strategies

S. J. Grossman

1 INTRODUCTION

The introduction of futures and options markets in stock indexes is strongly associated with the use of program trading strategies. Such strategies are used for spot/futures arbitrage, market timing, and portfolio insurance. It is this last use of program trading strategies that raises fascinating theoretical questions, the answers to which may have practical importance for understanding the impact of such strategies on the volatility of stock and futures prices.

Recent advances in financial theory have created an understanding of the environments in which a real security can be synthesized by a dynamic trading strategy in a risk-free asset and other securities.[1] The proliferation of new securities has been made possible, in part, by this theoretical work. The issuer of a new security can price the security based on the issuer's ability to synthesize the returns stream of the new security using a dynamic trading strategy in existing securities, futures, and options. This use of dynamic trading strategies has been extended even further by eliminating the 'new' security altogether and just selling the dynamic hedging strategy directly. Portfolio insurance is the best example of the latter phenomenon.

In this article I contend that there is a crucial distinction between a synthetic security and a real security. In particular, the notion that a real security is redundant when it can be synthesized by a dynamic trading

Reproduced from *Journal of Business*, vol. 61 (1988), pp. 275–98. © 1988 by the University of Chicago. All rights reserved.

An earlier version of this article was prepared for the Conference on the Impact of Stock Index Futures Trading at the Center for the Study of Futures Markets, Columbia University, June 8, 1987. Helpful comments were received from Fischer Black and Frank Edwards, but they are not responsible for any errors or opinions contained here.

strategy ignores the informational role of real securities markets.[2] The prices of real securities convey important information to market participants, and this information will not be conveyed if the real security is replaced by synthetic trading strategies. In particular, the replacement of a real security by synthetic strategies may in itself cause enough uncertainty about the price volatility of the underlying security that the real security is no longer redundant.

Portfolio insurance provides a good example of the difference between a synthetic security and a real security. One form of portfolio insurance uses a trading strategy in risk-free securities ('cash') and index futures to synthesize a European put on the underlying portfolio. If a put was traded on a securities market, then the price of the put would reveal important information about the desire of people to sell stock consequent to adverse future price moves.[3] For example, if everyone in the economy would like to get out of stocks before the price falls by more than 25 percent, then the price of such a put option would be very high. If only a few holders of stocks desired such protection, then the put option's market price would be low. The put's price thus reveals information *now* about the fraction of people with plans to get out of (or into) stocks in the *future*. The put's price reveals the extent to which the strategies of people can cohere in the future. Showing people the true cost of their plans may discourage people from attempting to purchase too much insurance in exactly those circumstances when the dynamic hedging strategy would raise stock price volatility.[4]

All of the above informational consequences of trading in a real security are absent if the real security is replaced by dynamic hedging strategies alone. How does a purchaser of a given strategy (such as a synthetic put) know the cost of insurance? Surely the cost depends on how many other people are planning to carry out similar stock selling and purchasing plans in the future. What mechanism exists to aggregate across people the information about future trading plans that will determine the cost and benefit of the current insurance strategy? Indeed, users of portfolio insurance strategies typically accept the assumption of the Black–Scholes model that the price of the underlying stock is independent of the amount of money protected by synthetic puts. This assumption is clearly false. If everyone follows the synthetic put strategy and attempts to sell stocks after a price falls, then the stock price will jump down (violating the price continuity assumption), and they will fail to achieve their desired hedge.

The marketing of *strategies* rather than *securities* has far-reaching implications for the volatility of the underlying stock and futures markets. There is no market force or price information that ensures that strategies can be implemented or informs the user of the total cost of implementation. In contrast, the purchaser of a security knows the cost of his purchase. For the economy as a whole, the price of the security reflects the cost of implementing the dynamic hedging strategy to which it may be equivalent. More important, the existence of a traded security will aggregate information (regarding future trading plans) that is currently dispersed among investors and, hence, provide valuable information about the cost of implementing the strategy.

The current price of a traded security also reveals information to people who can currently plan to take liquidity-providing positions in the future to offset the position changes implied by portfolio insurance strategies. For example, when a put option price is high, this reveals information that stock price volatility is high. Market makers, market timers, and other liquidity providers are thus informed that the future holds good opportunities for them. This leads them to make more capital available in the future to be used to take advantage of the stock price volatility. Of course, this will have the effect of reducing the actual volatility since a lot of capital will be present to invest in order to take advantage of excessive price moves.

In the absence of a real traded put option (of the appropriate striking price and maturity), there will be less information about the future price volatility associated with current dynamic hedging strategies.[5] There will thus be less information transmitted to those people who could make capital available to liquidity providers. It will therefore be more difficult for the market to absorb the trades implied by the dynamic hedging strategies. In effect, the stocks' future price volatility can rise because of a current lack of information about the extent to which dynamic hedging strategies are in place.

These points are elaborated in this paper as follows. Section 2 presents a schematic model of the impact of portfolio insurance on the stock and futures markets. Section 3 discusses the strategies used by investors who use synthetic hedging strategies and by market timers whose capital commitments can offset the effects of portfolio insurance. Section 4 develops a model of market equilibrium in a context where the number of users of dynamic hedging strategies is not known to all market participants. Section 5 discusses index arbitrage and futures trading. Section 6 discusses potential adaptations that may be useful to organized exchanges if the growth in the use of synthetic securities raises the information requirements necessary to maintain stable markets in the underlying securities.

2 THE ORGANIZATION OF THE MODEL

The purpose of this and the next two sections is to provide a schematic model of the informational consequences of trading strategies that are designed to create synthetic securities. We wish to elaborate the idea that market timers must commit capital before they know the extent of usage and the future price impact of the implementation of these strategies. This incomplete information will lessen their effectiveness in reducing the price volatility that can be caused when large portfolio insurance induced trades take place.

One purpose of the model to be developed below is to show that as the importance of portfolio insurance grows the price impact problem will also grow unless there is some mechanism by which the market can be informed in advance of the trades. The current market impact issues are minuscule relative to what would occur if 50 percent of all pension fund asset managers were to choose strategies designed to protect themselves against a loss on their stock portfolios. In order to minimize the market impact of such strategies, those who could provide substantial amounts of liquidity to the market would have to be informed substantially in advance so that they could choose not to commit their capital to other activities. In what follows, the time interval between date 1 and date 2 represents the amount of time that market timers and other liquidity providers would have to avoid committing their capital to other activities so that this capital can support the purchase or sale of securities in response to temporary price moves caused by the execution of portfolio insurance strategies.

It may help the reader to have a real example of the phenomenon under study. Such an example is the use of 'sunshine trading' strategies in stock index futures by the brokers for portfolio insurers (see Kidder, Peabody & Co., 1986). A broker using the sunshine trading technique announces to the brokerage and investment community that after a fixed period of time large orders will be brought to the trading floor and auctioned off at the best price. The purpose of preannounced trading is to give the investment community time to bring 'market-timing capital' or the orders of customers who want the other side of the trade to the exchange trading floor so that the execution of a large order will not cause an adverse price move.[6]

The simplest model that can bring out the distinction between real securities and synthetic securities has three trading dates.

At date 1. Some fraction f of security holders choose a dynamic hedging strategy. At the same time, market makers, market timers, and other liquidity providers (who I will henceforth group together under the title of market timers) decide how much capital to set aside for their attempts to profit from temporary price movements.

At date 2. News arrives about the underlying worth of the stock portfolio. This triggers trades based on the date 1 portfolio dynamic hedging strategy. The price change caused by the execution of the trades will depend on the amount of capital set aside at date 2 for market-timing activity. It may be helpful to imagine that there are two possible prices at date 2, P_{2g} and P_{2b}, depending on whether good or bad news about fundamentals arrives at date 2. The (market-clearing) prices at which trades can be executed will depend on f, as well as market-timing capital (denoted by M), available at date 2. I denote this dependence by writing $P_{2g} = P_{2g}(f, M)$ and $P_{2b} = P_{2b}(f, M)$.

At date 3. The stock price returns to its normal level, which reflects the underlying fundamental value of holding the stock portfolio. The normal level at date 3 depends on information about fundamentals, which arrives at date 3. It may be helpful to imagine that there are two possible prices at date 3, P_{3g} and P_{3b}, depending on whether good or bad news about fundamentals arrives at date 3. Of course, the news about fundamentals that arrives at date 2 will be relevant for determining the level of possible date 3 prices, and I capture this by writing $P_{3g} = P_{3g}(2g)$ if good news at date 3 was preceded by good news at date 2, or $P_{3b} = P_{3b}(2g)$ if bad news at date 3 was preceded by good news at date 2, and similarly for other combinations of date 2 and date 3 news.

Since I am focusing on the informational consequences of the substitution of synthetic securities for real securities, I assume that f is uncertain, that is, a random variable. A summary of the resolution of uncertainty follows:

Date 1. A realization f occurs that is not public information.

Date 2. News about fundamentals arrives publicly prior to trade. The dynamic hedging strategy chosen at date 1 is implemented.

Date 3. News about fundamentals arrives publicly prior to trade. Price is determined fully by fundamentals.[7]

For expositional simplicity, at this stage in the analysis I ignore transaction costs and the distinction between futures and spot transactions in the underlying stock portfolio. The purpose of the model is to show how incomplete information at date 1 about the fraction f of portfolio managers using synthetic option strategies can leave market timers unprepared at date 2 to offset the trades of portfolio hedgers and that this causes the date 2 stock price to be more volatile than it would have been had real put options been traded at date 1.[8] I begin by explaining the behavior of each of the types of traders and then analyze how the behavior determines market clearing prices.

3 TRADING STRATEGIES UTILIZED

3.1 Market makers, market timers, and other liquidity suppliers

At date 1, members of this group must decide how much capital to commit to activities that would leave their capital unavailable for market timing at date 2. That is, at date 1 capital can be committed or invested in activities for which it would be either very costly or impossible to withdraw the funds and use them to capitalize market-making transactions at date 2. For example, if a pension fund invests some of its capital in mortgages, or physical structures, then it will be very costly for it to sell them at short notice and use its capital to take advantage of a market-timing opportunity. Similarly, an investment bank may commit its capital to financing various activities other than market timing. These date 1 commitments of capital to activities for which there is a large cost of withdrawal at date 2 will lessen the funds available for date 2 market-timing activities.

How much capital will firms make available for market-timing activities? Clearly, this depends on the date 1–expected reward from taking market-timing positions at date 2. I now argue that this date 1–expected reward will be higher the larger the volatility of date 2–expected stock returns around the normal expected return. For example, if market timers at date 1 knew for certain that the expected return at date 2 for holding the stock from date 2 to date 3 would equal the normal return for holding the risk associated with the stock fundamentals, then they would have no particular incentive at date 1 to commit capital to date 2 market-timing activities.

The above point can be clarified by reference to the situation where there is either good or bad news about fundamentals. Suppose that at date 2 the two possible prices in the absence of parties using portfolio insurance would be P_{2g}^* and P_{2b}^*. These numbers have the property that portfolio owners would be willing to hold their existing stock levels, anticipating a random return of P_3/P_{2b}^*, computed from the bad news of date 2 to date 3, or P_3/P_{2g}^*, computed from the good news at date 2 to date 3.[9] Suppose that the implementation of dynamic hedging strategies will cause the date 2 price to be lower than P_{2b}^* in the bad news state and higher than P_{2g}^* in the good news state. Since, by assumption, date 3 is a point where prices are driven by fundamentals, this implies that the expected return as of the date 2 good news state (for holding the stock until date 3) will be lower than the normal expected return and the expected return in the date 2 bad news state will be higher than the normal expected return. In the date 2 bad news state, the market timers will make a net expected reward by increasing their stock holding, and in the date 2 good news state, they will make an expected reward by decreasing their holdings (possibly taking a short position).

The above argument shows that the market-timing rewards will be high the larger P_{2g} is above P_{2g}^*, and the smaller P_{2b} is below P_{2b}^*. This is precisely the statement that the larger the excess volatility is in the date 2 prices, the larger the expectation will be as of date 1 that rewards can be made from market-timing activity at date 2. Thus, given that there is a real opportunity cost of committing funds for market-timing activities, a higher date 2 excess price volatility will bring forth more market-timing capital. This supply curve for market-timing capital will be denoted by $M(V)$, where V is the excess volatility of date 2 prices as anticipated at date 1. Note that by definition M includes the possibility of leverage. That is, M gives the absolute value of the dollar size of the position that the market timer can take at date 2.

The above notion of 'volatility' is a little obscure because of the 3-period model. In the 3-period model, the stock price at date 2, P_{2b}, falls relative to its normal level, P_{2b}^*, and this causes the expected return between date 2 and date 3 to rise. It is the fact that expected returns at date 2 move inversely with P_2, which creates a supply of market-timing capital. This notion of volatility, namely that the execution of portfolio insurance orders will be associated with price reversals, is elaborated in the Appendix.

It is now possible to describe the trading activity of market timers at date 2. The fraction of $M(V)$ that is invested will depend on P_2/P_2^*. When that ratio is small (and less than one) a larger proportion of $M(V)$ will be invested but, by definition, never more than 100 percent. Similarly, when P_2/P_2^* is large (and larger than one) up to $M(V)$ dollars worth of the stocks will be sold.[10]

When market-clearing prices at date 2 are generated, it will be shown that the market timers' trading strategy serves a stabilizing function. If at date 1 the market timers know that there is going to be date 2 volatility, they will commit capital to be used at date 2 to buy stocks when the price is lower than its normal level and to sell stocks when the price is above its normal level. This argument relies crucially on the hypothesis that market timers know the date 2 volatility at date 1. We will see that if volatility is generated by the use of synthetic securities, then this volatility will be larger the larger the fraction is of portfolio managers (f) at date 1 who commit to a dynamic hedging strategy. To the extent that market timers do not know f at the time they choose M, they will find it difficult to forecast volatility.

In the absence of perfect information about volatility, market timers will choose an M that is optimal for some average level of volatility, denoted by M_a. In situations where the volatility V is high, M_a will be less than $M(V)$. In situations where V is low, M_a will be higher than $M(V)$. Therefore, the stabilizing role of market timers will be impeded by imperfect information about the determinants of price volatility.

3.2 Buy and hold portfolio managers

These parties do not follow dynamic hedging strategies. In particular, their risk preferences are such that, at prices P_{2g}^* and P_{2b}^*, they would keep their portfolio unchanged at date 2 in response to the date 2 news about fundamentals. In particular, when $f = 0$, the whole market is composed of people with these risk preferences, and P_2^* gives the price at which the expected returns from holding stock are such that a buy and hold strategy (from date 1 to date 3) is optimal.

I am making a slightly artificial distinction between market timers and those following passive investment strategies. In general, if P_2 is less than P_2^*, then investors who planned to have a passive strategy as of date 1 may find a high expected return to increasing their investment in risky assets. Thus, this group may also serve a market-timing function. However, it is my assumption that their response to temporary price moves is much smaller than that of market timers. This is because their portfolio objective specifies a particular fraction of *portfolio value* to be invested in the risky asset, and a fall in price gives them a lower portfolio value. Thus, even in the face of higher expected returns per unit risk, these investors need not increase significantly their holdings of risky assets due to the fall in their portfolio value when P_2 is less than P_2^*.

3.3   Users of synthetic securities, portfolio insurers

An investor uses a dynamic trading strategy in market contexts where the securities that would generate his desired pattern of returns across states of nature are unavailable.[11] This is a statement about the risk preferences and information of the investor, the risk preferences and information of the other market participants, and the number of explicit securities marketed. Trivially, if all investors were identical, they would all choose buy and hold strategies in the market index portfolio. However, if investors are sufficiently diverse, the only situation in which market equilibrium will involve all traders choosing buy and hold strategies at date 1 in *real* securities is when the market is explicitly complete, that is, for every state s_3 there exists a portfolio of securities that, when held to date 3, gives $1 if and only if state s_3 occurs (or equivalently, European options at all possible striking prices are marketed, where some of the striking prices may have to depend on the history that leads up to the final payoff if investors desire path-dependent final payoffs).

Our securities and futures markets allow an investor to achieve a middle ground between the above extremes. Investors may well be sufficiently diverse that a buy and hold strategy in a stock index is not optimal for everyone; however, markets are not sufficiently complete that a buy and hold strategy in a risk-free security and an option (with the investor's desired striking price) is marketed. Under the assumption of the Black–Scholes model that prices move continuously, the investor may still be able to achieve the same outcome (or close to it) by using a dynamic trading strategy to *synthesize* the desired security.[12]

Consider the following very simple example. Suppose that the stock price is $10 at date 1, and at date 2 it either rises or falls from its date 1 level by 10 percent. Suppose further that at date 3 the stock price can either rise or fall from its date 2 level by 10 percent. Thus, there are three possible date 3 prices: $8.1, $9.9, and $12.1. Let the investor start with 100 shares and assume that the risk-free interest rate is 0 percent. Suppose that the investor's preferences are such that he wants to get the highest expected date 3 wealth subject to the constraints that (1) *his date 3 wealth is no lower than $900*, and (2) *he is allowed to invest no more than his total wealth in the risky asset*.[13] If the expected return on the stock is higher than that of the risk-free asset, then it can be shown that the optimal trading strategy for the investor is to (1) invest all of his date 1 wealth in the risky asset (i.e., buy 100 shares at date 1); (2) if the price at date 2 is $9, then he sells all 100 shares and invests in the risk-free asset; (3) if the price at date 2 is $11, then he simply holds on to his 100 shares.

Notice that the above strategy makes the holdings of the risky asset very volatile. A high expected return is achieved (subject to the constraint that the portfolio have a terminal value no lower than $900) by a high initial investment in risky assets supported by a *plan* to sell off all stocks at date 2 if the price falls. This is an extreme form of portfolio insurance. A plan that did not involve the sale of all stocks at date 2 in the event of a price fall would require a smaller initial investment in the risky asset and have lower expected returns.

The strategy also has the property that the final payoff to the strategy is path dependent (i.e., the strategy has a different payoff when the price reaches $9.9 at date 3 by first reaching $9 at date 2 than would be the case if $9.9 is reached from $11 at date 2). For some reason many portfolio insurers avoid the use of such path-dependent strategies even though they yield a higher expected return for the same level of insurance.[14]

A strategy used by many portfolio insurers is a path-independent one where a dynamic trading strategy is chosen that replicates the payoff that would derive from investing an amount of $S in the stock and buying a put with a striking price of $900.[15] The value for S is found by noting that the cost of the put plus the investment in the stock S must equal the date 1 value of the portfolio, which in the above example is $1,000. This strategy has the same qualitative property as the one given above: the risky asset is sold if the date 2 price is lower than the date 1 price. However, the path of holdings in the stock is somewhat less extreme: all of the portfolio is not invested in the risky asset at date 1, and only part of the investment in risky assets is sold at date 2 if the price falls.[16]

Another form of portfolio insurance, called constant proportion portfolio insurance (CPPI), moves the investment in the risky asset linearly according to how much higher the value of the portfolio is than the insurance level. (The insurance level is $900 in the above example.)[17] This trading strategy also has the property that a fall in the stock price will lead the investor to reduce his holdings of risky assets.

In summary, the users of portfolio insurance will tend to have demands for stocks that are more price sensitive than those investors utilizing buy and hold strategies.

4 MARKET EQUILIBRIUM

In this section I tie the strategies of various investors together for the purpose of analyzing market equilibrium. I will analyze three cases. In the first case, market timers at date 1 know the extent to which dynamic hedging strategies are being used. In the second case, market timers do not know the extent to which such strategies are being used, but real put options are traded at date 1. In the third case, market timers do not know the extent to which dynamic hedging strategies are being used, and there are insufficient real index options markets to convey this information.

4.1 Extent of adoption of dynamic hedging strategies is known

For expositional simplicity, I focus on the case where there are two possible public news announcements about fundamentals at both date 2 and date 3. Hence, a model of market clearing involves finding a date 1 price, P_1, and a date 2 price for each announcement, P_{2g} or P_{2b}, such that the securities market clears at each date and state. It is clear that, if the fraction f of investors using dynamic hedging strategies is known (and the types of strategies being used are also known), then it will be possible for all parties to forecast the volatility of date 2 prices, and hence there will be prices P_1, P_{2g}, and P_{2b} such that, if all traders anticipate these prices and if the dynamic hedging strategies are indeed feasible at these prices, then the stock market will clear at those prices.

Market clearing at date 2 The above remarks may be slightly clarified by the use of the following notations.

Market timers: let $X(P_2/P_2^*, M; N)$ be the demand function of market timers at date 2, which can be thought of as a function of the price P_2 relative to its normal level, the capital that market timers can commit M, and the public news about fundamentals N. As I noted earlier, if $P_2 = P_2^*$, then they demand no shares. As P_2 falls relative to the P_2^* that is appropriate for the information N, market timers increase their holdings.

Buy and hold investors: the demand function of the buy and hold investors is also a function $Y(P_2/P_2^*; N)$ of the price relative to its normal level.

However, unlike the market timers, for the reasons given above, this demand will not be very sensitive to price changes. In the extreme case of a buy and hold investor, it will be totally insensitive. I assume that if $P_2 = P_2^*$, then $Y = 100\%$. That is, if the market was composed only of buy and hold investors, then these investors would demand 100 percent of the outstanding shares of stock.

Dynamic hedging strategy: the desired holdings of those investors who are using a dynamic hedging strategy is $Z(P_2; N)$. Their desired holdings of shares will fall as P_2 falls. There may even be a critical level beyond which they desire to hold no shares.

Given the news N, a market-clearing price P_2 will satisfy

$$X(P_2/P_2^*, M; N) + (1 - f) Y(P_2/P_2^*; N) + (f) Z(P_2; N) = 100\%$$

$$(10.1)$$

This is the statement that P_2 will adjust until 100 percent of the outstanding stock is held by those people who, at price P_2, no longer desire to trade. We write the market-clearing price as a function of f and N:

$$P_2 = P_2(f, N).$$

Note that if $f = 0$, so that no dynamic hedgers are present, then the market-clearing price will be P_2^*. This means that if goods news arrives, then $P_2 = P_{2g}^*$, and if bad news arrives, then $P_2 = P_{2b}^*$. The difference between P_{2g}^* and P_{2b}^* gives a measure of the *normal* level of volatility in the market.

Now consider the case where $f > 0$, so dynamic hedgers are present. In such a situation when bad news arrives, the market will no longer clear at P_{2b}^*. This is because the demand of the hedgers is lower than the demand of the buy and hold investors at P_{2b}^*. Market clearing will require a price lower than P_{2b}^*. How much lower depends on the impact of market timers. If market timers have a very large presence in the market, that is, M is very large, then even a very small deviation of P_2 from P_2^* will cause large trades by market timers. However, if M is small, then it will take a large deviation of P_2 from P_2^* to clear the market when f is large.

In summary, if V denotes the volatility of date 2 prices in response to news about fundamentals, then V will depend on f and M, which I write as $V(f, M)$. Volatility will rise with f and fall with M.

Market clearing at date 1

The above analysis of the market at date 2 can be used to analyze the behaviour of market participants at date 1. Under the assumption that f is known at date 1, the market timers will be able to infer the volatility of date 2 prices and, hence, their potential benefits from committing their resources, M, to market timing activities. In particular, the function $V(f, M)$ generates an aggregate demand for market-timing services (which I denote by $M^d(V;f)$) since it implies a particular return to date 1 investments in obtaining capital commitments for the purpose of date 2 market-timing activities. As we noted earlier, there are costs of obtaining market-timing capital. These costs generate a supply curve for market-timing capital, M, denoted by $M^s(V)$. The intersection of these two curves (i.e., the M such that $M = M_d(V;f) = M_s(V)$) will generate an M and a V that depend on f, denoted respectively by $M(f)$ and $V(f)$.

The less costly it is to commit capital to market-timing activities, the larger will be M for a given level of f. That is, the more it will be the case that the demands of market timers offset the demands of investors using dynamic hedging strategies. Thus, date 2 price volatility, $V = V(f) = V(f, M(f))$, will be low if it is not costly to commit capital to market-timing activities at date 1.

The feasibility of portfolio insurance

Finally, M determines the feasibility of certain types of portfolio insurance. Recall that M determines the level of the date 2 price in the presence of bad news about fundamentals, P_{2b}. An insurer would not be able to offer a dynamic strategy that assured a price higher than P_{2b}. In the event that bad news arrives at date 2, the joint execution of all the portfolio insurance strategies will force the price down to P_{2b}, so that insurers would not be able to execute stop-loss orders at a price higher than P_{2b}. Of course, if it is known at date 1 that market-timer presence will be large at date 2, then it will be possible to offer insurance at levels almost as high as P_{2b}^* since P_{2b} will be almost as high as P_{2b}^*.

4.2   Extent of adoption of dynamic hedging strategies is unknown, but real put options are traded at date 1

The previous analysis was predicated on the notion that the degree of date 2 price volatility was known at date 1. If this is not known, then it will be difficult, if not impossible, for market makers to know the benefits of their date 1 capital commitments and for date 1 insurers to know that their date 2 trading strategy can be implemented. This is exactly the type of situation where a real put options market may have a very important role.

If portfolio insurers implement their strategies via the purchase of put options at date 1, then the price of put options will reveal the fraction of investors who are using portfolio insurance strategies. Since the price of the put is a function of the anticipated volatility of the stock, the price will equivalently reveal the volatility of the stock.

To understand the ability of prices to aggregate information, imagine that a fraction f of investors decides to use portfolio insurance, and in a market where this is known, a volatility $V(f)$ would be implied. This in turn would imply a particular date 1 price for the put, say $Q(V(f)) = Q(f)$. Now suppose that traders do not know what the volatility will be because they do not know f. Suppose, for example, that this leads to a put price below $Q(f)$. Could this really represent a market equilibrium? It could not, because the users of dynamic hedging strategies would find it cheaper to use real puts to execute their trades than synthetic strategies, and this would drive up the put price. A similar argument obtains on the downside when the put price is higher than $Q(f)$. It would then be optimal for some portfolio insurers to sell puts and cover this sale with a dynamic hedging strategy.[18] In the terminology of Grossman (1976), the put price is a sufficient statistic for the one-dimensional variable V.

After all investors have learned the information about the stock's volatility from observing the option price, the option can indeed be a redundant security (in the sense that its date 2 and date 3 value can be replicated using a dynamic hedging strategy in the risk-free asset and the stock). However, since the option is not informationally redundant, the volatility of stock prices can be substantially lower in an economy where real options are traded than it would be in an economy in which market timers have no way to forecast the extent to which their capital is in demand. This is because the option price will inform market timers about the profitability of committing their capital to volatility-reducing trades at date 2. A high option price is suggestive of a high date 2 price volatility, which is suggestive of a high expected return from committing capital to market-making activity at date 2.

The above analysis assumes that the only cause of variability in volatility is the variability in (i.e., the uncertainty regarding) the intensity of portfolio insurance usage. Of course, price volatility varies for many other reasons, such as variability in the volatility of interest rates, earnings, dividends, and so forth. If I let A denote the other factors that affect volatility, then I can write $V = V(f, A)$, and the put price is $Q = Q(f, A)$. (See equation (10.2) in the Appendix, where s represents the nonportfolio insurance volatility and s is determined by the factors called A above.) In this environment, where A is important, the put price will not be a sufficient statistic for f. Recalling that intense portfolio insurance usage causes reversals in the stock price (i.e., changes in expected returns), if A represents factors in price volatility that are not associated with expected return volatility, then it is f and not A that signals market-timing opportunities. Therefore, Q is a noisy signal about f. How much information will Q reveal about f? Clearly, if portfolio insurers use synthetic puts, then the real put price Q will contain very little information about f – it will primarily reveal information about A. However, if real puts are used rather than synthetics, Q will be much more informative about f, and market-timing capital will respond appropriately.

4.3   Extent of adoption of dynamic hedging strategies is unknown, insufficient put options are traded at date 1

This is a situation where price signals about the extent of adoption of portfolio insurance strategies are absent or arrive too late.[19] At date 1, market timers must make capital commitments based on incomplete information, and investors choose dynamic hedging strategies under incomplete information. As a consequence, a put option will no longer be a redundant security, that is, it can be impossible to replicate the put option's payoff using a dynamic hedging strategy because the stock volatility is unknown.

If investors continue to use portfolio insurance strategies in the presence of uncertain volatility, then not only will volatility be uncertain but it also will be larger than it would otherwise have been. Recall that the capital commitments of market timers serve to reduce volatility. In particular, if option price or other information reveals the extent of portfolio insurance usage f, then in times of high usage market timers commit more capital. That is, capital commitments can be tailored to the anticipated volatility caused by adoption of portfolio insurance strategies. The inability to tailor capital commitments will reduce the average gain from such market timing investments. Therefore, average volatility can rise and be accompanied by a fall in market-timing capital commitments.

The above remarks can be better understood by the following example. Suppose 50 percent of the time no investors pursue portfolio insurance strategies at date 1, while the other 50 percent of the time most of the investors use portfolio insurance. (This is just a method for describing the uncertainty market timers have about the extent to which portfolio insurance strategies will cause date 2 trading.) At date 1, the market timers do not know which type of situation they are facing. If no investors are using portfolio insurance strategies, then date 2 price volatility will be very low, and the benefits from date 1 capital commitment to market timing will be low. The situation is reversed if many investors are using portfolio insurance strategies. If market timers knew which situation they were in, they would commit capital where appropriate, and actual volatility would be low. Lacking information about adoption, however, they commit an 'average' amount of capital that is correct for the 'average' situation. As a consequence, when adoption is low their capital is unnecessary, and when adoption is high their capital is inadequate to prevent excessive date two–price volatility.

It should be emphasized that in a continuous time version of this model, market participants will discover information about the intensity of portfolio insurance usage by observing *realized* stock price volatility and the extent to which expected returns are variable. If stock price volatility is variable only because insurance adoption is variable, then realized volatility will be a very good signal for adoption intensity. Further, if adoption intensity changes slowly relative to the rate at which new information about fundamentals arrives, market timers will be able to commit capital in response to observed changes in realized volatility in such a way that 'excessive' volatility is reduced.

5 INDEX ARBITRAGE, FUTURES MARKETS, AND STOCK PRICE VOLATILITY

The previous sections have not distinguished between trading activity in stock index futures and trading activity in common stocks. These issues are discussed next. Portfolio managers apply insurance strategies to cover a large basket of different stocks. In principle, they could trade individual stocks or packages of individual stocks in the stock market to implement their strategies. However, if they really want to trade in packages, they may be able to economize on transaction costs by using a futures market in a stock index.

The New York Stock Exchange (NYSE) is organized around specialists who make markets in small groups of individual stocks. There are no specialists in packages of stocks such as the Standard and Poor (S&P) 500. The S&P 500 futures market is a competitive market-maker environment where, in effect, packages of stocks can be traded. For example, if on a particular day one pension fund manager wants to decrease his holdings of the S&P 500 while another pension fund wants to increase its holdings by the same amount, then the former can take a short position and the latter can take a long position in index futures. Thus, the pension funds have transferred the price risk of the S&P 500 in a single transaction rather than in 500 separate transactions on a stock exchange. Further, if the trading times of the two institutions are slightly asynchronized, the market makers in the futures 'pit' will take a position on their own account from the first arriving order and then liquidate that position when the offsetting customer order arrives later. Thus, the existence of a futures market insulates the NYSE market makers from having to bear risk associated with slightly asynchronized order flows in baskets of stocks.

In the above example, there was no net desire to sell S&P 500 stocks at the last price. However, now suppose that at the price of the last trade, many pension fund managers want to decrease their holdings of stock, that is, there is net selling of stock index futures. If futures markets are used to reallocate packages of stock among institutional investors, then what happens when they all want to sell? Who are the 'natural' buyers? If there is a large net supply of futures because institutions want to sell stocks, then this will drive the futures price down. At that instant, index futures will be cheaper than the S&P 500 package of common stocks. Index arbitrageurs will view this differential as a profit opportunity. They will buy futures and sell common stock. They are the 'natural' buyers of futures in situations where futures are being sold because investors, in net, want to hold less common stock.

In the above scenario, the index arbitrageurs are messengers. They merely take the sell orders from the futures market (i.e., buy futures) and bring them to the stock market (i.e., sell stock). If there were no futures market (and thus no index arbitrageurs), then the institutions would have sold the common stock directly on the stock market, rather than indirectly attempting to eliminate the downside risk by selling the stock on the futures market. In the short run, this selling pressure would have to be borne totally by NYSE market makers (given the absence of an arbitrageur-linked futures market).

It is crucial to recognize that the market makers on futures markets combine with market makers on the NYSE to enhance the overall liquidity of the equity market. A given amount of institutional selling faces the buying power of market makers on both markets. Index arbitrageurs take positions that unify both markets.

The use of portfolio insurance strategies by institutional fund managers will, to some extent, raise stock price volatility irrespective of the existence of futures markets. Futures markets, by permitting low transactions cost trades in packages of stocks, allow institutions to trade more gradually than would be the case if the stock market were used directly. A larger transactions cost will cause insurers to trade less frequently, but in larger amounts per trade. In the absence of a futures market, institutions would face a larger transactions cost, and the stock market would bear the full brunt of portfolio insurance trades – without any cushion provided by the futures market.

Index arbitrageurs and futures markets are not the crucial issue in understanding large price moves. The crucial phenomenon is that, when institutions *simultaneously* attempt to use a dynamic trading strategy to synthetise a security (thereby attempting to lock in past capital gains), they will fail. The failure is caused by the fact that the dynamic trading strategy is based on the Black–Scholes model that assumes that the underlying stock price is independent of how many investors use the strategy. In the case of synthetic puts this assumption is untenable.

6   CONCLUSIONS AND RECOMMENDATIONS

The theoretical perspectives developed in this article show that a synthetic security puts quite different informational burdens on market participants than a real security. If an investor chooses a dynamic trading strategy to synthesize a European put option, then he should be very concerned with the number of other investors who have chosen similar strategies. He may very well find his own strategy infeasible if a substantial number of other traders are using the same strategy. Even if his strategy is feasible, it may cost far more than anticipated. However, if an investor could buy a real European option with the desired strike price and expiration day, then the price of the option would reveal the cost of the trading strategy. He would not have to know what other traders are doing in order to know whether his strategy is feasible.

The above informational role of prices occurs in many contexts. Hayek (1945) wrote,

> 'We must look at the price system as . . . a mechanism for communicating information if we want to understand its real function. . . . The most significant fact about this system is the economy of knowledge with which it operates, or how little the individual participants need to know in order to be able to take the right action . . . by a kind of symbol, only the most essential information is passed on.'

I have shown elsewhere how this view of prices helps illuminate the informational role of securities markets.[20] Focusing on the informational role of markets seems especially appropriate in attempting to forecast the consequences of substituting real securities for synthetic securities.

I have argued that market timers and other liquidity providers will find it difficult to engage in stabilizing trades when they have poor information about the desire for their services. In the absence of a real options market it will be difficult to forecast price volatility and, hence, difficult to forecast the effective demand for commitments of capital to market-timing activities. Equally important, portfolio insurers will not know the cost of their strategies when they do not know the intensity with which other investors are using similar strategies. If a substantial number of investors suddenly decide to use insurance strategies predicated on historical levels of stock volatility, then this will raise stock and stock index futures price volatility.

The above perspective suggests that index options play a role in providing information about the costs of insurance strategies. In investors trade in such markets, they face the true cost of their strategies. Hence, the common stock volatility problem would only be increased if the effectiveness of these markets is reduced by regulation. It should be noted that current Security and Exchange Commission regulations in the USA impose a limit on the number of (traded) stock index option contracts that can be held by a given institutional investor. These position limits effectively force large institutional managers to avoid the use of real options and instead use synthetic strategies. Excessive capital and margin requirements (erroneously imposed to limit volatility caused by 'speculation') reduce the ability of options, futures, and stock market traders from taking the opposite side from the insurance traders and, hence, increase volatility.

The above theoretical perspective should not be construed as suggesting that (1) portfolio insurance, or dynamic hedging strategies, are bad, or that (2) the increased use of such strategies has caused an increase in stock and futures price volatility. First, dynamic hedging strategies clearly play an important and useful role in increasing the feasible set of payoffs available to investors. It is costly (both privately and socially) to have liquid, real markets in every imaginable security. Dynamic hedging strategies permit us to economize on the number of active markets. Second, even if dynamic hedging strategies have contributed (or will contribute as their importance grows) to stock price volatility, it does not follow that this is, in net, socially harmful or worthy of regulation. To say that the use of a strategy imposes costs hardly implies that these costs outweigh their benefits.

How can the exchanges reduce the costs imposed if volatility increases with an increase in the adoption of dynamic hedging strategies? To answer this question, recall that the source of the problem is that market participants lack *current* information about the *future* trading plans of other participants. If many investors today adopt portfolio insurance strategies, then this implies that many will be sellers in the future when prices fall. This creates a current opportunity for market timers to commit resources, if only they were aware of the existing plans of other traders.

It hardly seems practical to solve this problem by suggesting that the exchanges require all members to publicize their plans and the plans of their customers. Aside from the obvious enforcement difficulties, it would have the effect of forcing those people who may not be 'informationless' portfolio hedgers to reveal their strategies. How could the exchanges distinguish those investors who invest resources in the collection of market-timing information from those traders who are simply pursuing 'informationless' trading for the purpose of synthesizing a put option? It surely will not help the informational efficiency of markets if the exchanges force individuals to reveal (legally obtained) information that they want to keep secret and that they have expended real resources to acquire. This would only reduce the amount of information collected in the first place and thus inhibit market-timing activities that are volatility reducing.

The maintenance of privacy for those investors who desire privacy is not a problem for our purposes if the disclosure is voluntary. An investor whose trades are for the purpose of synthesizing an option will have no need for secrecy in his trading plans. This is seen clearly in Kidder, Peabody's 'sunshine' trades for the portfolio insurance strategy firm of Leland, O'Brien, Rubinstein & Associates (Kidder, Peabody & Co., 1986). They use preannounced trading to reveal themselves to be 'informationless' and to enhance the number of investors willing to take the other side of their trades. It is interesting to note that Kidder, Peabody was unable to fully preannounce their trades because of the possible conflict with exchange rules against prearranged trading.

I think that the exchanges could avoid the problem of prearranged trading and also create a system conducive to voluntary disclosure by the following system. Each exchange could set up a system where stop-loss and other limited orders would be sent to a central computer where they are aggregated and the results made public continuously. For the NYSE a special system is feasible.[21] With many specialists already using an electronic 'book,' it is feasible to link the books across stocks and publicly display the size of the limit orders for various indexes in which there are futures or options. For example, the aggregate of buy orders could be computed under the hypothesis that each component in the S&P 500 falls in price by 1 percent. This can be done by looking at the 'book' for each component stock, finding the number of shares to be bought on the specialist's book if the price for that stock falls by 1 percent, and computing the weighted sum across the stocks in the S&P index. A similar calculation could be performed for a range of percentage up moves and percentage down moves of the stocks in the index. The final result would be a chart indicating the total buy orders in the specialist's books for the index at various relative price moves in the index. A similar chart could be constructed for sell orders. Finally, a chart could be constructed for the net buy (buy minus sell) orders for the index.

The transmittal of information about size of net buy orders at prices for the index that are away from the current price will allow investors to gauge the *depth* of the market. If net sells are very high (due to stop-loss orders of portfolio insurers) at a price just below the current price, then market timers know that there will be opportunities for advantageous trades. They will have time to raise the capital (or contact their own brokerage customers), which will lessen the impact of the execution of the stop-loss orders.

There is another adaptation for the NYSE that would interact with the above system and also enhance the execution of index trades. The exchange could set up a system by which there is a limit order (and stop-loss order) electronic book in various stock indexes. For example, members could enter such orders on the electronic book for the S&P 500 that would specify that if the index hits a particular level, then, for example, 20 units of the index should be sold. When the index hit that level the computer would cross all of the buys and sells at the current index price if the buy volume equaled the sell volume. Otherwise, it would send those orders for the components of the index to the specialists' posts for execution. The aggregate positions in the electronic book would be made public so that the public would know how many index trades can be expected to be executed at various index prices. Again, the dissemination of such information would enhance the effectiveness of market-timing activities and reduce volatility.

It is somewhat more difficult to effect similar changes on futures exchanges. However, it is crucial to realize that the index futures and options markets do not exist in a vacuum. If futures contracts are sold by a portfolio insurer as a low (transactions cost) alternative to selling the portfolio's common stock holdings, then this must have an impact on the cash (i.e., stock) market. Index arbitrage will cause the cash prices to (roughly) stay in line with the futures prices. If the cash market is illiquid, the futures market will show an increase in volatility.

The relevant adaptation for futures markets would be a system by which brokers could commit themselves to execute orders at various prices, and the exchange would aggregate these commitments and display them on a screen to various interested parties.[22] To avoid liquidity-reducing prearranged trades, the screen need not even identify the source of the orders. The exchange would have to find some method of assuring that brokers carried out their commitments. It should be noted that the physical arrangement of most trading pits and the hectic pace of activity may make it difficult for a broker to carry out his commitment. For example, a broker could always claim that he tried to carry out the commitment, but trading was too hectic. Some problems of implementation may be alleviated if a particular part of the trading pit is designated as the place where brokers with preannounced trades must stand. Of course, this may create prearrangement abuses. I do not believe that these problems are insurmountable; however, the creation of an electronic display of stop-loss and limit orders clearly creates special problems for futures markets.[23]

Finally, it should be emphasized that the suggested adaptations are for a 'problem' that may not now exist and may never exist. The implementation of any proposal contained here should await careful measurement of the market impact of synthetic hedging strategies. The purpose of this section is to illustrate the potential application of a theoretical perspective that emphasizes the informational role of markets; it should not be construed as a practical guide for regulation or for the modification of exchange rules.

APPENDIX

The 3-period model discussed in the text obscures certain ideas that I attempt to clarify below. Consider a stock price process

$$\frac{\mathrm{d}P}{P} = (u - x)\,\mathrm{d}t + s\mathrm{d}b + \mathrm{d}x, \tag{10.2}$$

where $b(t)$ is a standard Brownian motion. If x is a constant, then rates of return follow a Brownian motion with drift $u - x$ and variance s^2. However, I assume that x is a diffusion with dynamics given by

$$dx = \left(\frac{dP}{P} - u\,dt\right) l, \tag{10.3}$$

where $1 > l \geq 0$. The term dx represents the additional price move caused by portfolio insurers, and l is proportional to the intensity of portfolio insurance usage. Note that (10.3) states that an unusually large (say upward) price move will be associated with a fall in the expected return on the stock. The hypothesis in the text is that, for example, a large sell order inflow by portfolio insurers will lower stock prices and increase expected return.

The easy case to analyze is where l, u, and s are known and constant. In this case, substitution of (10.2) into (10.3) yields

$$dx = g\,(s\,db - x\,dt), \tag{10.4}$$

where $g \equiv l/(1 - l)$. Setting $x(0) = 0$, (10.4) can be solved for $x(t)$:

$$x(t) = gs\int_{o}^{t} e^{-g(t-y)}\,db\,(y). \tag{10.5}$$

Substitution of (10.4) into (10.2) yields

$$\frac{dP}{P} = \left(u - \frac{x}{1-l}\right)dt + \frac{s}{1-l}\,db, \tag{10.6}$$

and substitution of (10.5) into (10.6) yields

$$\frac{dP}{P} = u\,dt + \frac{s}{1-l}\,db\,(t) - \frac{gs}{1-l}\int_{o}^{t} e^{-g(t-y)}\,db\,(y). \tag{10.7}$$

In the text, intense portfolio insurance usage (i.e., a high f) causes increased volatility and a tendency for price reversals (e.g., expected returns at date 2 are high when the date 2 price is low). From (10.6), the instantaneous conditional variance is

$$\mathrm{var}_{t}\,\frac{dP}{P} = \frac{s^2}{(1-l)^2}, \tag{10.8}$$

and from (10.7) the conditional expected rate of return is

$$E_{t}\,\frac{dP}{P} = u\,dt - \frac{gs}{1-l}\int_{o}^{t} e^{-g(t-y)}\,db\,(y). \tag{10.9}$$

If $l = 0$ (and hence $g = 0$) we are in the standard Brownian motion case. However, as l grows (i.e., g grows), the price process becomes increasingly volatile, and expected returns move in the opposite direction from the sign of the previous price changes.

The hypothesis in the text is that l depends on the actual realization of f and on the amount of market-timing capital available, or M. With incomplete information about portfolio insurance usage, f should be modeled as a stochastic process. This causes *l* to be stochastic. The consequent stochastic volatility will make put options no longer redundant.

NOTES

1 The seminal contribution is the Black–Scholes (1973) option pricing approach, whereby it is shown how a dynamic trading strategy in a stock and risk-free asset can reproduce a European call or put option on the stock.
2 See Grossman (1977) for an elaboration of the informational role of securities and futures prices and Grossman (1988) for a summary of some of the points contained here.
3 In this article, 'stock' is often used interchangeably with 'stock index' to represent a portfolio of risky assets.
4 The cost of the strategy is the potential upside gains that are foregone to protect against downside losses. If the stock volatility is high, then this cost will be high. I will argue below that the volatility will be higher the larger the number of investors using portfolio insurance strategies. Hayne Leland, commenting on an earlier draft of this article, pointed out that the benefits of portfolio insurance can rise when volatility rises. This implies that users of synthetic put strategies face both higher costs and benefits if there is an unanticipated rise in volatility.
5 In the Black–Scholes model, the volatility is assumed constant, so that an option of any strike price and maturity can be used to infer the volatility of the stock. Clearly, the situation considered here is one where the volatility is not constant. In particular, the volatility of the stock price will be a function of the demand for put options. This is elaborated below.
6 This phenomenon shows not only that portfolio insurers are concerned about the price impact of their trades, but also that they think that the release of information *before* a trade can bring forth capital (and offset customer order flow) to enhance the liquidity of the market.
7 Date three is a theoretical device to tie down the equilibrium. The time between date 2 and date 3 is the length of time necessary for the temporary price impact of the date 2 trades to disappear. That is, the expected return from holding stocks from date 3 forward would be uncorrelated with the date 2 news event.
8 It should be emphasized that there may be incomplete information about more than just the fraction of investor capital managed with the use of portfolio insurance strategies. There may also be incomplete information about the type of strategy used, e.g., there can be incomplete information about the horizon, and/or strike price of the implicit put options being used, or both. I focus on incomplete information about *f* for expositional simplicity alone. A very appropriate alternative definition of *f* is that it represents the 'gamma' of the average synthetic put implemented by the insurance. The basic principle would be unaffected by more complex types of incomplete information.
9 Throughout this article, a price with a state subscript represents a random variable.
10 This is a crude description of the extent to which date 1 commitments enable date

2 trades. My argument requires only that the size of market timers' trades at date 2 is an increasing function of the volatility they anticipated as of date 1.

11 See Leland (1980) and Benninga and Blume (1985) for an analysis of the sources of demand for portfolio insurance.

12 See Cox and Rubinstein (1985) for an exposition of dynamic trading strategies that synthesize options and other contingent claims.

13 This form of portfolio insurance, where an objective is stated and a strategy is found that maximizes the objectives subject to constraints, is called 'optimal portfolio insurance.' See Grossman and Vila (1988).

14 The replication of such strategies in a complete market would require trading in *real securities* for which a buy and hold strategy would yield a path-dependent payoff.

15 See Rubinstein (1985) and Brennan and Schwartz (1987) for a discussion of these strategies.

16 At date 1, 68.97 shares of the stock are held, and if the price falls, then 34.48 shares are held at date 2, while if the price rises, then 97.18 shares are held at date 2.

17 See Black and Jones (1987) and Perold (1986) for a discussion of this strategy.

18 The above argument is true for situations where a given investor knows that his decision to use a portfolio insurance strategy is correlated with the decision of others, and, therefore, each investor has a little information about the overall fraction of users. One may wonder what would happen if each user of portfolio insurance did not know how many others were using it and thus would not know the volatility. This is irrelevant in a situation where the only variable that affects the put price is the volatility. In order for the put price to be below $Q(V)$, a substantial portion of the market must expect a volatility lower than V. A price below $Q(V)$, say Q_1, would be consistent with a lower volatility than V, say V_1. Each investor desiring portfolio insurance who is *certain* that the volatility is V_1 will be indifferent between the appropriate dynamic hedging strategy and holding the option at a price of Q_1. However, if the investor is even slightly uncertain about his ability to execute the appropriate dynamic hedging strategy, then he will prefer the option. The number of people who prefer the option will be proportional to the number of investors who desire portfolio insurance strategies. This will cause the price of the option to reveal the intensity of investor desire for portfolio insurance.

19 I assume that the date 1 price of the stock price index does not reveal the intensity of date 1 adoptions. Date 1 is supposed to be the date at which market timers must make capital commitments in order to attempt to profit from date 2 price volatility caused by date 1 adoptions. If the price is already varying at date 1 from its normal level because of adoptions, then dates should be relabeled and we should start the analysis at an earlier date. In general, as described in Grossman and Stiglitz (1976), there will be 'noise' in the stock price that will prevent it from completely revealing such information.

20 See Grossman (1976).

21 The New York Stock Exchange recognizes the need for providing advance information about future order flow. Its experiments with (1) disclosing 'market on close' orders prior to the close of trading and (2) disclosing order imbalances prior

to the opening of trade (on index option and futures expirations) are examples of the type of mechanism I am proposing, and its motivation is similar to mine.
22 This suggestion goes somewhat beyond current proposals to enable 'sunshine' trading. Current proposals are concerned with transmittal of information to market participants regarding a broker's commitment to execute a trade at some time in the near future. The purpose of such a proposal is to lower the market impact to a portfolio insurer for a trade that he has just decided to make. My proposal is to show the market the whole schedule of trades at prices away from the current price (aggregated over all customers who desire to participate). A floor trader could look at such a schedule and see that if the index price falls, then there will be heavy selling. This alerts the floor to the need for more liquidity before heavy selling drives the price down.
23 See Miller and Grossman (1988) for a discussion of some of the differences between futures markets and the NYSE.

REFERENCES

Benninga, S. and Blume, M. (1985) On the optimality of portfolio insurance. *Journal of Finance* 40, no. 5 (December): 1341–52.

Black, F. and Jones, R. (1987) Simplifying portfolio insurance. *Journal of Portfolio Management* 14, no. 1 (Fall): 48–51.

Black, F. and Scholes, M. (1973) The pricing of options and other corporate liabilities. *Journal of Political Economy* 81, (May–June): 637–59.

Brennan, M. and Schwartz, E. (1987) Stationary portfolio insurance strategies. Research Report no. 2–87 (January). Los Angeles: University of California, Los Angeles, Graduate School of Management.

Cox, J. and Rubinstein, M. (1985) *Options Markets*. Englewood Cliffs, NJ: Prentice-Hall.

Grossman, S. (1976) On the efficiency of competitive stock markets where traders have diverse information. *Journal of Finance* 31, no. 2 (May): 573–84.

Grossman, S. (1977) The existence of futures markets, noisy rational expectations and informational externalities. *Review of Economic Studies* 64, no. 3 (October): 431–49.

Grossman, S. (1988) Program trading and stock and futures price volatility. *Journal of Futures Markets* 8, no. 4 (August 1988).

Grossman, S. and Stiglitz, J. (1976) Information and competitive price systems. *American Economic Review* 66, no. 2 (May): 246–53.

Grossman, S. and Villa, J. I. (1988) Optimal portfolio insurance. Mimeographed. Princeton, NJ: Princeton University.

Hayek, F. (1945) The use of knowledge in society. *American Economic Review* (September).

Kidder, Peabody & Co. (1986) Stock index futures. *Weekly Commentary*. New York: Kidder, Peabody & Co. Financial Futures Department (November 4).

Leland, H. (1980) Who should buy portfolio insurance? *Journal of Finance* 35, (May): 581–94.

Miller, M. and Grossman, S. (1988) Liquidity and market structure. *Journal of Finance* 43, 617–33.

Perold, A. (1986) Constant proportion portfolio insurance. Mimeographed. Cambridge, Mass: Harvard Business School, August.

Rubinstein, M. (1985) Alternative paths to portfolio insurance. *Financial Analysts Journal* (July–August): 42–52.

11

Liquidity and Market Structure

S. J. Grossman and M. H. Miller

Keynes once observed that while most of us could surely agree that Queen Victoria was a happier woman but a less successful monarch than Queen Elizabeth I, we would be hard put to restate that notion in precise mathematical terms. Keynes' observation could apply with equal force to the notion of market liquidity. The T-bond Futures pit at the Chicago Board of Trade is surely more liquid than the local market for residential housing. But how much more? What is the decisive difference between them? Is the colorful open-outcry format of the T-bond Futures market the source of its great liquidity? Or does the causation run the other way?

Those are some of the issues we propose to consider here. Our purpose is to present a simple model of market structure that captures the essence of market liquidity. A key feature of the model is its finer partitioning of time intervals and of roles for market participants than in standard treatments of the determination of market prices. Much economic theory, in the Walrasian tradition, still proceeds as if prices were set in a gigantic town meeting in which all potential buyers and sellers participate directly. Researchers in the rapidly growing specialty, sometimes dubbed market microstructure theory, have expanded the cast to include market makers in the sense of intermediaries who can fill gaps arising from imperfect synchronization between the arrivals of the buyers and the sellers. The focus of this literature has been on the inventory-management policies of market makers (see, e.g., Stoll [11]) and on their responses to the threat of adverse information trading against them (see, e.g., Glosten and Milgrom [5]). Our intention here, however, is not to expand this important and interesting class of inventory

Reproduced by permission from *Journal of Finance*, vol. 43 (1988), pp. 617–33.

This paper was presented at the Annual Meetings of the American Finance Association, December 29, 1987, in Chicago. Helpful comments on an earlier draft were received from Kenneth Cone, Kenneth French, T. Eric Kilcollin, Andrei Shleifer, Lester Telser, and Robert Vishny.

models but to fit these intermediaries and their temporary inventory holdings into a larger framework that also encompasses the ultimate demanders and suppliers.

1   A BRIEF OVERVIEW OF THE MODEL: THE SUPPLY AND DEMAND FOR IMMEDIACY

Our model of market structure has two participant groups, and we shall refer to them, for simplicity, as *market makers*, and *outside customers*. For simplicity of exposition only, we shall take their basic tastes, including risk tolerances, as the same. Their roles are defined at this stage principally in terms of their initial endowments.

Within the group of outside customers are some who, for any of a variety of reasons, experience what we call a *liquidity event*, which leads them to perceive a gap at current prices between their desired holdings of a particular asset and their current holdings of that asset. Even if the gaps sum to zero across the whole group, as we assume, some customers might propose to remedy their portfolio imbalance immediately by undertaking a transaction in the asset; for concreteness in exposition, suppose these potential liquidity traders are net sellers. In our model the putative sellers can choose to offer the goods immediately to the market makers who happen to be in the market currently and who have no holdings of the asset, or at least no imbalance that they too are seeking to eliminate. Or, a seller can postpone the offer to sell for one stylized period until the potential buyer customers on the other side of the trade have learned of the offer and have had a chance to come to the market.

Clearly the seller faces a trade-off. By waiting until more potential buyers have been notified, the seller increases the chance of finding an eager buyer. But this delay carries risks; while the buyers are assembling, the ultimate equilibrium price may shift. The best selling price for a sale delayed to the second period may be substantially lower (or higher) than the price in a sale to a market maker in the first period. By selling immediately, that interim price risk is transferred to the market maker who then waits until the ultimate buyers have assembled. When we speak of *the demand for immediacy* by a seller, we mean the willingness to sell rather than wait. This demand depends on the volatility of the underlying price and the diversifiability of the risk of an adverse price move.

The market makers charge for bearing price risk by offering the immediate sellers a price that is not uncertain, but that is lower, on average, than the sellers could expect from delaying. The expected price rise between periods 1 and 2 is, of course, only the market maker's gross return before allowing for the costs of supplying the service. These costs include not only any direct costs of effecting and monitoring trades, but also the important, though often overlooked, cost of being available and open for business when the outside customers arrive to trade. These opportunity costs of maintaining a continuous presence in the market, which we model as fixed costs, play a key role in determining *the supply of immediacy* and market-making services.

The market makers, as emphasized earlier, must also assume the price risk that the immediacy demanders shed. That the aggregate price risk is merely shifted to the market makers does not, however, rule out efficiency gains from the arrangement. In our model, where all participants have the same risk tolerance, the gains arise essentially from diversification – the spreading of the transferred risks over the entire group of market makers. The larger that group, the lower, *ceteris paribus*, the risk and expected return per unit traded by each and hence also the lower the effective cost of immediacy to the customers. The number of market makers will adjust until, in equilibrium, the returns to each from assuming the risk of waiting to trade with the ultimate buyers just balance the costs of maintaining a continuous presence in the market. This adjustment determines the equilibrium amount of immediacy provided, i.e., the amount by which price is temporarily depressed by a typical sell order.

Our model suggests looking to differences in the cost to market makers of maintaining a market presence and to differences in the demand by customers for immediacy for the keys to market structure and market liquidity. The greater the demand for immediacy and the lower the cost to market makers of maintaining a continuous presence, the larger the proportion of the transactions between ultimate customers effected initially through market makers, and hence the more liquid the market.

2   THE LIQUIDITY SPECTRUM IN REAL-WORLD MARKET STRUCTURES

Successful futures markets are the leading examples of markets where the demand for immediacy is high. Futures markets are successful precisely for those commodities and in those time periods where price volatility, and hence the risks of delaying trading, are high. The price risks of volatility are further reinforced for potential hedger customers in those markets by the high leverage and extreme underdiversification of the underlying spot inventory positions that constitute their main line of business. Immediacy also becomes of particular concern where, as is frequently the case, the futures transaction is merely one leg of an intercontract or intermarket hedge. Little or no risk may be incurred once all the components of the hedge have been put in place, but much risk is incurred when only some of the legs have been set. When the transactor is 'naked,' to use the colorful language of the trade, the delay of even a few seconds can become critical. (See, e.g., Grossman and Miller [6].)

The demand for immediacy in successful futures markets is not only urgent, but sustained. The regular seasonal build-up and build-down of inventories, as commodities move through the production chain, creates a continual desire to *trade*, not just to *hold* futures. In financial futures markets, dealers' inventories of the underlying securities build up and down in response to periodic auctions of US Treasury issues, to the flotation of stocks or bonds by corporations, or to the restructuring of portfolios by large institutional investors.

The sustained demand for hedging and hence for trading futures quickly is often accommodated by designating a specific physical marketplace or exchange in which many competing market makers can offer their services simultaneously. Such arrangements help spread the fixed costs to market makers of maintaining a presence, as does the practice at most present-day futures exchanges of providing trading areas for many different contracts between which individual market makers can drift as trading interest changes. Many, but not all, futures exchanges also permit market makers to serve both as brokers for customers and as traders on personal account, though not, of course, on the same transaction. Most floor traders tend to specialize in one role or the other, but the freedom to switch roles can permit a quick adjustment in the number of market makers when the flow of orders changes abruptly.[1]

At the opposite extreme from the highly liquid futures markets, where intermediary market makers participate as principals in virtually all transactions, stand the highly illiquid markets, such as those for residential housing, where virtually none of the transactions pass through a dealer's temporary inventory.[2] Sellers of individual homes are typically less concerned with short-term price volatility, and hence with immediacy, than with making sure that the widest possible set of ultimate buyers can be informed of the house's availability. Potential market makers, moreover, face not only all the ordinary costs of maintaining a continuous presence in a thin market, but the additional moral hazards that arise from the owner's possibly adverse private information about the value of the property. The result is a market in which intermediaries, to the extent that they are involved at all, provide brokerage or search services, not immediacy.

3 THE STRUCTURE OF THE STOCK MARKET

Most real-world markets lie somewhere between these liquidity extremes and their structures will typically mix features from both the search markets and the liquidity markets. US stock market institutions, for example, currently involve at least four distinct forms of market organization operating simultaneously, but in different segments of the market and with somewhat different immediacy clienteles:

1 For a few of the most widely held and heavily traded securities, such as IBM or AT&T, the market at the New York Stock Exchange often approximates the open-outcry pits at the commodity exchanges. These are stocks in which the minute-to-minute order flow is highly variable relative to the arrival of news about the underlying value of the shares, and for which our model predicts a large number of market makers in equilibrium. The 'crowd' for those stocks, though substantially smaller than in the T-bond futures market, is large enough to offer a competitive discipline to the Exchange's franchised 'specialist,' who, in these particularly active markets, typically plays more the role of an auctioneer (and a commission collector) than a market maker on personal account.

2 The specialist's role as a market maker assumes greater prominence for the hundreds of smaller, less active stocks, some of which may not even trade as frequently as once a day. In such stocks, our model would not predict an equilibrium with many market makers. The designation of a specialist by the Exchange, however, does at least guarantee that someone will indeed be maintaining a physical presence in the market, ready to effect a transaction should an order happen to arrive. The potential for abuse of the specialist's monopoly position is mitigated by the same standard cross-subsidization approach long familiar in US public-utility regulation. As a condition for keeping the franchise, specialists on the New York Stock Exchange, for example, are encouraged by the Exchange to limit price changes between successive transactions to no more than one tick (normally 12½ cents per share), using personal inventory to absorb any temporary imbalances along the way. This restriction, which is in fact monitored by the Exchange, serves both to limit specialists' profit and to create the appearance of liquidity, though in practice only for very small transactions. Should a very large order arrive, however, and should it be larger than can be absorbed by the specialist or by any previously entered 'limit orders' then resting on the specialist's 'book' the market can switch to search mode. The specialist, with the permission of the Exchange, can suspend trading in the stock and institute a search for counterparties to the imbalance, either elsewhere on the floor of the Exchange or, more likely these days, off the floor at the block-trading desks of the investment bankers.

3 These desks are the third, and increasingly the dominant form of market organization for trading common stocks in the US, thanks to the concentration of so much corporate stock in a relatively small number of extremely large pension funds, mutual funds, and other institutional holders. Because relatively small portfolio adjustments by these institutional holders would be far too large to be obsorbed by any specialist firm, the large blocks of single

stocks, or sometimes whole portfolios are brought to the 'upstairs market' maintained by the investment banking firms. Until recently at least, the upstairs desks functioned primarily as a search market. The upstairs traders essentially 'shopped the block' among their customers, and when a suitable counterparty had been located and a deal struck, they reported the trade to the relevant specialists on the floor of the Exchange. In the process, they picked up on behalf of the initiating side any limit orders on the specialist's book that were transformed into market orders by the price change occasioned by the block trade.

Although search was the initial function, and still remains the major function of the upstairs market, the amount of 'positioning' and hence of market-making liquidity provided by the upstairs firms has increased substantially in recent years. The shift traces mainly to the highly liquid futures and options index markets which permit the upstairs firms to hedge their inventories while conducting the search for or waiting for the other side of the transaction.

4 Finally, at the other end of the spectrum from the upstairs, wholesale broker-dealer market lies the retail, dealer market in over-the-counter (OTC) stocks, for which, with a few well-known exceptions, the normal trading interest is typically too small to justify listing even on a regional exchange.[3] The market for such stocks is not a physical exchange floor but a set of computer terminals. When introduced originally in the 1970's, the computerized NASDAQ market system for OTC stocks offered essentially only a 'bulletin board' in which those market makers with access to the system could enter price quotes. The quotes, though deemed firm for some standard, minimum-size trade, were essentially advertisements, and the actual transactions were not executed automatically, but negotiated between the parties. The market makers in particular stocks, although they did position small inventories, assumed no obligation to maintain a continuous presence or to smooth price changes between successive transactions.[4]

All four forms of market organization for trading common stocks, along with those of the index futures and options markets, were subjected in October 1987 to what seemed to be liquidity events, in our sense, of unprecedented magnitude. We shall return briefly to those events in section 5. First, however, we turn in section 4 to set down the detailed structure of our model of market liquidity and a characterization of its equilibrium.

4 A FORMAL MODEL OF MARKET LIQUIDITY

In this section we present a formal model of the role of market makers in providing immediacy. We focus most of our attention on the consequences of a temporary order imbalance of size i in a simple world with only three dates: 1, 2, and 3. At date 1 a liquidity event occurs that creates a temporary order imbalance of size i. Market makers offset this temporary imbalance by taking trading positions that they hold until date 2. We denote the non-market makers by the term 'outside customer' although in practice, of course, individuals and firms can play either role at different times. By a temporary order imbalance we mean an asynchronization of outside-customer trading times; the net trading demand would be zero at the current price if all traders were simultaneously present in the market.

At date 2, the market makers offset their positions as other outside customers arrive to offset the imbalance. Thus, the length of time between date 1 and date 2 is the period of time needed for enough orders of outside customers to arrive at the market to offset the initial order imbalance. Date 3 is introduced only as a terminal condition for valuing the securities as of date 2.[5]

We assume two assets: a risk-free asset called cash (with zero rate of return), and a risky asset. Let $\tilde{P}_3$ be the exogenously given terminal price (or liquidation value) of the risky asset. Assume that public information about $\tilde{P}_3$ arrives before trade at period 1 and also before trade at period 2. Let $\bar{x}_t$ be the number of units of the asset owned by an outside customer after trade at time t, and let B_t be that customer's holdings of cash (in dollars). Two interpretations can be given to $\bar{x}_3$. In the first, the outside customer is a commercial hedger and the asset is a futures contract. In this case, the hedger's net holding at period 3 is $\bar{x}_3 = \bar{x}_2 + i$, where i is the number of units of the spot commodity (which may, of course, be a security) owned by the hedger. The hedger's terminal wealth is then

$$W_3 = B_2 + P_3\bar{x}_3 = B_2 + P_3\bar{x}_2 + iP_3. \tag{11.1}$$

The hedger is using the futures market to offset the spot price $\tilde{P}_3$ risk of the initial position. (Note that under this futures market interpretation, the asset is in zero supply.)

In the second interpretation, the market is a stock market, and the outside customer at time 1 has an endowment of size i in the security, which is inappropriate in the light of the customer's risk preferences and information on the risk–return pattern associated with the security. In this case, $\bar{x}_3$ is the final holding of the security at the terminal date, and $\bar{x}_3 = \bar{x}_2$. In contrast to the futures market interpretation, the asset is not in zero supply, and if i is correlated across customers, then the aggregate endowment of the asset relevant for market clearing at each date t will be affected by i.

Under either interpretation we assume that at times $t = 1, 2$ the customer chooses asset holdings $\bar{x}_t$ and a risk-free asset position B_t to maximize the expected utility of terminal (i.e., date-3) wealth

$$EU(W_3)$$

subject to

$$W_3 \quad\quad = B_2 + \bar{x}_3 \tilde{P}_3 \tag{11.2a}$$

$$\tilde{P}_2 \bar{x}_2 + B_2 = W_2 = B_1 + \tilde{P}_2 \bar{x}_1 \tag{11.2b}$$

$$P_1 \bar{x}_1 + B_1 = W_1 = P_1 i_1 + W_0, \tag{11.2c}$$

where i_1 represents the initial endowment of the asset and W_0 represents other wealth. Note that:

$i_1 = 0$ and $\bar{x}_3 = \bar{x}_2 + i$ in the futures market case;

$i_1 = i$ and $\bar{x}_3 = \bar{x}_2$ in the stock market case.

If B_1 and B_2 are eliminated from (11.2a)-((11.2c) we obtain

$$W_3 = W_0 + (\tilde{P}_2 - \tilde{P}_1)(\bar{x}_1 - i_1) + (\tilde{P}_3 - \tilde{P}_2)(\bar{x}_2 - i_1) + \tilde{P}_3 i,$$

where $\bar{x}_t - i_1$ represents the excess demand for the asset, whether it be a futures contract or a stock. Therefore, it simplifies matters to define a trader's *excess* demand to be

$$x_t = \bar{x}_t - i_1 \quad\quad t = 1, \, 2.$$

In the above notation customers choose their positions to maximize

$$EU(W_3) = EU(W_0 + (\tilde{P}_2 - P_1)x_1 + (\tilde{P}_3 - \tilde{P}_2)x_2 + \tilde{P}_3 i). \tag{11.3}$$

We will assume that $\tilde{P}$ is normally distributed at each date, and that

$$U(W) = -e^{-aW}. \tag{11.4}$$

By backward induction and (11.4), if we let x_2^{cd} denote the optimal value of x_2 (chosen at date 2), then x_2^{cd} solves

$$\max_{x_2} E_2 U(W_2 - P_2 i_1 + (\tilde{P}_3 - P_2)x_2 + \tilde{P}_3 i).$$

Using the exponential utility function, the optimal value for x_2 is

$$x_2^{cd} = \frac{E_2 \tilde{P}_3 - P_2}{a \, \mathrm{var}_2 \tilde{P}_3} - i, \tag{11.5}$$

where all means and variances are conditioned on the information at time 2. Note that the customer's excess demand is x_2^{cd} which is linear in i. Hence, if all customers are identical, except possibly with respect to i, we can take x_2^{cd} to represent the aggregate demand of customers, and i to be the aggregate potential imbalance.

We assume that there are M other traders in the market who do not hold the spot commodity and thus face no spot-price risk; these are the market makers. (Under the stock market interpretation, assume that the market makers do not hold an endowment of the security prior to their date-1 trading with outside customers.) Market makers have the same utility function, but for them $i = 0$. Hence, if the excess demand per market maker is x_2^{md}, the total excess demand by market makers in period 2 is

$$Mx_2^{md} = M \frac{E_2 \tilde{P}_3 - P_2}{a \, \text{var}_2 \tilde{P}_3}.$$

(11.6)

We now state the assumption critical to understanding the benefits of waiting from period 1 to period 2 to trade. In particular, it is that *asynchronization* of desired trades creates the demand for immediacy at time 1. Thus, the positive immediacy demand felt by the customers at time 1 is, by definition, offset by *new* customers arriving at date 2 with the opposite imbalance from those who arrived at date 1. Their aggregate excess demand is

$$\frac{E_2 \tilde{P}_3 - P_2}{a \, \text{var}_2 \tilde{P}_3} + i.$$

Market clearing at date 2 requires that the excess demand of (1) customers who arrived at date 1, plus (2) market makers, plus (3) the new customers arriving at date 2 should sum to zero:

$$\frac{E_2 \tilde{P}_3 - P_2}{a \, \text{var}_2 \tilde{P}_3} - i + M \frac{(E_2 \tilde{P}_3 - P_2)}{a \, \text{var}_2 \tilde{P}_3} + \frac{E_2 \tilde{P}_3 - P_2}{a \, \text{var}_2 \tilde{P}_3} + i = 0.$$

(11.7)

Note that in a futures interpretation, the right-hand side represents an aggregate endowment of zero, while in the stock market (11.7) means that excess demands (i.e., trades net of endowments) must sum to zero. Note also that under our convention that period 3 is merely a terminal condition, (11.7) implies:

$$E_2 \tilde{P}_3 - P_2 = 0.$$

(11.8)

The equilibrium excess demand at date 2 of the customer arriving at the market at date 1 is thus

$$x_2^{cd} = -i.$$

(11.9)

Using (11.3), (11.4), (11.8), and (11.9) we can find the date-1 demand of the customer from

$$\max_{x_1} E_1 U(W_0 + x_1 (E_2 \tilde{P}_3 - P_1) + iE_2 \tilde{P}_3).$$

(11.10)

This problem has the same form as the problem in period 2 except that the risk from the point of view of period 1 is that $P_2 = E_2 \tilde{P}_3$ is not known. As before, the customer's excess-demand function is

$$x_1^{cd} = \frac{E_1 \tilde{P}_3 - P_1}{a \operatorname{var}_1 (E_2 \tilde{P}_3)} - i, \tag{11.11}$$

where the law of iterated expectations is used to obtain $E_1 E_2 \tilde{P}_3 = E_1 \tilde{P}_3$.

4.1 Market makers and the provision of immediacy

At date 1, there are M market makers. They constantly watch the floor of the exchange either directly or through their agents on the floor. They solve the same maximization problem as the customers except that for them $i = 0$. Hence their excess-demand function is

$$x_1^m = \frac{E_1 \tilde{P}_3 - P_1}{a \operatorname{var}_1 (E_2 P_3)}. \tag{11.12}$$

Market clearing at date 1 thus requires

$$M x_1^m + x_1^{cd} = 0. \tag{11.13}$$

Using (11.11) and (11.12), it is seen that (11.13) becomes:

$$\frac{E_1 \tilde{P}_3 - P_1}{a \operatorname{var}_1 (E_2 \tilde{P}_3)} = \frac{i}{1 + M}. \tag{11.14}$$

Let $\tilde{r} = \tilde{P}_2 / P_1 - 1$ be the excess return earned by the market makers. Then

$$E_1 \tilde{r} = \frac{P_1 i}{1 + M} a \operatorname{var}_1 (\tilde{r}). \tag{11.15}$$

Thus if M is finite, a positive value of $P_1 i$ (which causes hedgers to desire to 'short') will induce a temporary fall in the market price. Note that we have defined the order imbalance to sum to zero across periods 1 and 2. In particular, no aggregate risk is associated with holding the asset across periods. Therefore, in the absence of an asynchronization of order flows, $E_1 \tilde{r} = 0$. It is the asynchronization of these flows and the finite risk-bearing capacity of market makers that leads $E_1 \tilde{r}$ to deviate from 0. Note that from (11.12) and (11.14) the value of the positions held by a typical market maker (i.e., his or her inventory) is

$$P_1 x_1^m = \frac{P_1 i}{1 + M}. $$

The larger is this inventory, the higher the expected return between period 1 and 2 to compensate the market maker for the risk that new information may arrive (causing $E_2 \tilde{P}_3 = P_2 \neq P_1$), leading to capital losses on the inventory positions.

4.2   Determination of the number of market makers

A market maker choosing always to have a presence on the trading floor is assumed to forgo opportunities elsewhere worth $c. We assume that the size and direction of the liquidity event i is not known at the time that this cost is 'sunk.' We represent i as the realization of a normally distributed random variable, uncorrelated with information about $\tilde{P}_3$. The gain from being on the floor is the ability to trade at price P_1. Then the expected utility of a market maker who pays $c out of initial wealth is

$$EU(W_0 - c + (\tilde{P}_2 - \tilde{P}_1)x_1^m),$$

where the profit between period 2 and period 3, $(\tilde{P}_3 - P_2)x_2^m$, does not appear because (11.6) and (11.8) imply that $x_2^m = 0$.

Free entry of market makers will occur until

$$EU(W_0 - c + (\tilde{P}_2 - \tilde{P}_1)x_1^m) = EU(W_0). \tag{11.16}$$

Equation (11.12) and the exponential utility assumption can be used to evaluate (11.16):

$$e^{ac} E \exp\left(-\left(\frac{a^2}{2}\right)(\mathrm{var}_1 \tilde{P}_2)\left(\frac{i}{1+M}\right)^2\right) = 1 \tag{11.17a}$$

or

$$e^{ac} E \exp\left(-\frac{t}{2}z^2\right) = 1, \tag{11.17b}$$

where

$$t = a^2 \frac{\mathrm{var}_1 \tilde{P}_2}{(1+M)^2}\,\mathrm{var}\,i, \quad \text{and} \quad z^2 = \frac{i^2}{\mathrm{var}\,i}.$$

Using the moment-generating function of the non-central chi-squared distribution, (11.17b) becomes

$$\frac{1}{\sqrt{1+t}}\exp\left(\frac{-(Ei)^2}{1+t}\left(\frac{t}{2}\right)\right) = e^{-ac}. \tag{11.8}$$

If we assume that the expectation of an order imbalance is zero, i.e., $Ei = 0$, then (11.18) becomes

$$\frac{1}{\sqrt{1+t}} = e^{-ac}. \tag{11.19}$$

Equation (11.19) implies that

$$t = a^2 \frac{(\text{var}_1 \tilde{P}_2) \text{var } i}{(1 + M)^2}$$

is determined solely by ac and is an increasing function of ac. The lower the cost of maintaining a market presence, the greater the number of market makers in equilibrium. That number would also be larger, of course, the smaller the risk-aversion parameter a for the market makers.

The quantity var i is the average size of hedging demand (since hedging demand in its average size is $E|i|$, which is proportional to var i when $\tilde{i}$ is normally distributed); $\text{var}_1 \tilde{P}_2$ is the predictability of the price change. Hence, as either of these two variances rises, the number of market makers rises.

4.3 Some empirical implications of model

The contribution of market makers shows up in the correlation between successive price changes. Since the model is only a three-period model with a single liquidity event at time 1, we define the correlation to be

$$q = \frac{\text{cov}(P_2 - P_1, P_1 - E_0 P_1)}{\sqrt{\text{var}(P_2 - P_1) \, \text{var}(P_1 - E_0 P_1)}}. \tag{11.20}$$

Using (11.14), the fact that $P_2 = E_2 \tilde{P}_3$, $E_0 \tilde{P}_1 = E_0 \tilde{P}_2$, and $E_1 \tilde{P}_2 = E_1 \tilde{P}_3$ yields

$$P_2 - P_1 = P_2 - E_1 \tilde{P}_2 + \frac{i}{1 + M} a \, \text{var}_1 (\tilde{P}_2) \tag{11.21}$$

$$P_1 - E_0 P_1 = E_1 \tilde{P}_2 - E_0 \tilde{P}_2 - \frac{i}{1 + M} a \, \text{var}_1 (\tilde{P}_2). \tag{11.22}$$

To impart a timeless quality to the uncertainty, assume that one-step-ahead variances are the same at each date, i.e.,

$$s^2 = \text{var}_1 (\tilde{P}_2 - E_1 \tilde{P}_2) = \text{var}(E_1 \tilde{P}_2 - E_0 \tilde{P}_2) = \text{var}_1 (\tilde{P}_2).$$

We can now restate q:

$$q = -\frac{t}{1 + t}. \tag{11.23}$$

Thus, from (11.19) the correlation between successive price changes is negative and is determined solely by the cost of being a market maker, c. Note that the covariance between successive price changes is

$$cov(\tilde{P}_2 - P_1, \tilde{P}_1 - E_0 \tilde{P}_1) = -\frac{a^2 \text{var } i}{(1 + M)^2} s^4 = -ts^2. \tag{11.24}$$

Hence, for a given c, since t is fixed, assets with more variability of expected price changes will have higher negative covariance.

Finally, consider the amount of immediacy provided in equilibrium. This can be measured by the amount of customer trade that is completed in period 1, x_1^{cd}, and the amount completed in period 2, $x_2^{cd} - x_1^{cd}$, which can be derived from (11.11)–(11.14):

$$x_1^{cd} = - \frac{M}{1 + M} i \tag{11.25a}$$

$$x_2^{cd} - x_1^{cd} = - \frac{i}{1 + M}. \tag{11.25b}$$

Since the total size of the trade desired is $-i$, the fraction completed in period 1 is determined by M. When M is very large the transaction is completed immediately and the market can be said to be liquid.

5   EXTENSIONS AND APPLICATIONS

Many readers will have been surprised to have come so far in a paper on market liquidity with no reference to the term 'bid–ask spread.' That term has indeed dominated academic discussions of transaction costs and market efficiency ever since the pioneering paper by Demsetz [3]; even before that, the term was the standard shorthand among practitioners for contrasting the cost of trading between markets and over time. For all its familiarity, however, and its rough common sense as a metric, we believe it does not fully capture the notion of market liquidity.

5.1 Limitations of bid–ask spread as a measure of liquidity

First (as Stoll [11] has emphasized), the bid–ask spread measures exactly the market maker's return for providing immediacy only in the special case in which the market maker simultaneously 'crosses' (i.e., executes both sides of) the trade, one at the bid and the other at the ask. But in that case, of course, the spread could not also serve as a valid measure of the cost of supplying immediacy to each of its customers; it is simply a charge by the market maker for executing their orders, rather than for providing them liquidity services.

In the more typical case that our model was designed to portray, the orders do not arrive simultaneously but are randomly separated in time. If so, the price may change between the time at which the market maker buys and sells, and the market maker may earn much more or less than the spread quoted at the time of the first leg of the transaction. And, for the same reason, the currently quoted spread cannot serve any transactor as a precise measure of the cost of trading immediately rather than delaying the order, particularly when the order is a large one. Yet that cost, as we have emphasized, is the essence of market liquidity. A customer desiring to sell is likely to be more concerned with how the bid will change over time than with the size of the current bid–ask spread.

The benefit of immediacy to a customer is the shedding of the price risk associated with waiting. In most real-world exchanges this waiting can also be achieved by means of a 'limit order' to sell, for example, at the current quoted bid price. Such a limit order will be executed if and when a buyer willing to pay this price appears and no other seller is offering to sell at a lower price. But that may never occur and the customer may have to revise the order and sell at a price lower than the bid price at the time the first limit order was sent in. Thus, if lucky, the limit-order customer gets a price higher than the bid, while if unlucky, a lower price. The customer's choice between limit orders and market orders is thus governed not by the bid–ask spread, but precisely by those considerations that our model suggests determine the supply and demand for immediacy, i.e., by the likelihood that a buyer will arrive who is willing to pay more than the current bid. (See Cohen et al. [1] for an equilibrium analysis of bid–ask spreads that emphasizes the importance of jumps in the price away from the current quotes.)

Note also that a substantial volume of transactions occurs within the prevailing quoted bid–ask spread because the traders who commit to a bid (or ask) are giving the market an option. Some traders may decide not to commit to buying or selling at particular prices and thus the quoted bid may be lower than the actual bids that appear in response to a market sell order.

The more that market orders to buy and sell are separated in time, the greater the exposure of the market maker to the risks of adverse information trading. The bid–ask spread, in addition to the pure timing-option premium, will then contain still another component, which compensates the market makers on their informationless trades for their likely losses to the informed traders. This phenomenon, as noted earlier, has been much studied in the academic literature on market microstructure. (See, e.g., Glosten and Milgrom [5].) Much less attention, however, has been directed to the inverse problem of what is likely to happen to conventional quoted bid–ask spreads in highly active markets, like futures markets, where many separate buy and sell orders are entering the trading pit virtually simultaneously. Because the adverse-selection problem arises only when a market maker cannot hope to offset a position immediately, and because the costs of maintaining a market presence are mainly (and, in our model, entirely) fixed costs, it might seem that quoted bid–ask spreads and market makers' profits from what amounts to crossing trades would be driven towards zero by the competitive entry of new market makers.[6] Where the fixed costs are large relative to the entry-inhibiting trading risks, a competitive market may not be viable because the market makers would have no way of recovering their fixed costs of maintaining a presence on the floor.[7] To keep markets viable, therefore, exchanges may limit the number of 'seats' available to market makers (or designate a regulated specialist).

Exchanges also typically define a minimum price-change unit (called a 'tick'), which, in highly active markets, serves also to set a minimum on both the quoted bid–ask spread and the profits a 'scalper' makes from a quick turnaround. This somewhat subtle and frequently overlooked role of the minimum tick helps explain, among other things, the seeming paradox of finding many traders in an obviously highly competitive pit fighting (sometimes literally) to execute an order. This behavior suggests that the quoted bid–ask spread of one tick, and hence the profit from a quick turn on a standard-size trade, are actually higher in an active market than they would be in the absence of the minimum-tick rule. Part of the art of managing a futures exchange is finding a minimum tick size for its contracts, high enough to sustain a viably competitive supply of floor traders, but not so high as to give rise to the problems of rationing and queue discipline so often encountered under price controls.[8]

5.2   Limitations of the 'liquidity ratio' as a measure of market liquidity

Another widely used empirical measure in intermarket comparisons of market liquidity is the 'liquidity ratio,' defined as the ratio of average dollar volume of trading to the average price change during some interval. (See, e.g., Dubofsky and Groth [4], Cooper, Groth, and Avers [2], and Martin [8].) A high value for the ratio is taken to indicate that many shares were traded with little price change, and a low value is taken to suggest that a trader bringing a large block to market will induce a large adverse price change.

These measures, of course, tell us at best only about past average associations between price changes and volume. They do not answer the critical question of how the sudden arrival of a larger-than-average order would affect price. Nor do they distinguish adequately among the sources of price volatility. A particular market may display high price variability not because it is illiquid but because new fundamental information arrives frequently. High price volatility can occur without high volumes of trading; in fact, when the import of the news is unambiguous, there may be no trading at all.

The liquidity ratio, in sum, fails to capture what we have called the immediacy that the market's structure offers. At best, and with all due regard for the pitfalls of estimating simultaneous equations, it might hope to measure the average elasticity of the market's demand curve for transactions. What we need, however, is a measure of how well the market makers are providing customers with an effective substitute for the delays in a search for a more inclusive set of counterparties. Whether so complex a notion can ever be distilled down to a single scalar is still far from clear. Our equations (11.24) and (11.25) (a) and (b) with their focus on reversals offer some promising new leads (similar in spirit to those opened earlier by Roll [10]), which we hope to follow up in future empirical research.

The need for new ways of measuring and comparing the liquidity of different market structures takes on added urgency in the light of the dramatic stock market events of October 1987 and especially of the many policy proposals for market reform that surfaced in the wake of the crash and were actively debated in the press and in Congress. But even in the absence of numerical calibrations of liquidity we believe that the model of market liquidity presented in the previous section can offer a helpful perspective on the main events of those hectic days.

5.3 Market liquidity and the crash of October 1987

We hasten to add that our interpretation of the recent crash in terms of our model of market liquidity must not be taken as signifying our belief that the event was entirely, or even primarily, a matter of liquidity rather than of fundamentals. (See Miller et al. [9] for a discussion of the events preceding and surrounding the crash.) Whatever the precipitating cause, a massive liquidity event, in our earlier sense of an imbalance in the demand for immediacy, clearly occurred at the opening of the markets on October 19. Both the futures market and the cash spot market were hit simultaneously with a flood of sell orders of unprecedented size.

Each of the two markets responded immediately to the imbalances, but in ways appropriate to their characteristic and, as we had noted earlier, quite different structures. The rules of the NYSE permit – indeed, encourage– specialists to delay the opening of trading when the overnight accumulation of orders for a particular stock is too far out of balance to allow market clearing at a price near the previous close. The delayed opening gives the specialist time to search the floor and the upstairs block-trading desks for balancing orders on the other side. Under ordinary conditions, when most other stocks have opened and are trading normally, that search is completed successfully, and trading is resumed (though, typically, with a somewhat larger than usual price gap) in a matter of a few minutes. At the opening of the 19th, however, the order imbalances were so widespread and so large that no immediate help from on or off the floor was available to the beleaguered specialists of many of the most heavily traded shares. An hour after the opening bell, more than a third of the stocks in the Dow-Jones Index (including such widely followed international companies as IBM, Sears, and Exxon) had yet to start trading.

By contrast, the S&P 500 futures market at the Chicago Mercantile

Exchange, like other futures markets, seeks to provide a setting in which prices can most speedily reflect the best current information. If the outcry at the opening call on a futures exchange shows the overnight accumulation of orders to be heavily unbalanced, then the price will jump directly to a level at which trading can immediately take place.[9] The previous closing price plays no explicit role in setting the level or the path to reach it. This contrast in opening procedures between the futures and the stock markets is fully understandable in the light of our model. The high demand for immediacy by firms that use futures markets to hedge inventory risk causes those markets to be organized precisely to provide maximal immediacy of order execution. The costs of delayed execution being normally less for stock trading, the market makers there seek to provide more search service relative to immediacy than in the futures markets.

On Monday, October 19, opening prices in New York had to fall some 10 percent below the Friday close – an enormous gap by past standards – before trading in all stocks could begin.[10] By 11:00 a.m. or so, New York time, however, all the major delayed-opening stocks had resumed trading, and the two markets were now virtually back in step. Although the price fall had been large, the two markets, from all outward appearances, appeared to have handled successfully the enormous imbalance of sell orders that had accumulated at the opening. But the capital resources of their regular market makers on or around the floor had by then been heavily committed. In Chicago, many of the smaller market makers had left the floor, either voluntarily or under pressure from their clearing firms. Those that remained were unwilling to take on large positions in such a volatile market except at price concessions far larger than normal. When a further wave of sell orders hit both markets somewhat after noon, New York time, there was less resistance from the market makers and the fabled 'meltdown' was soon under way. Or, to use the less colorful language of our model, both markets had by then become highly illiquid and virtually incapable of supplying immediacy at the low cost their users in the past had come to expect.

That illiquidity was evidenced in the spot market by (1) the virtual impossibility of executing market sell orders at the bid quoted at the time of order entry, and (2) the delays in executing and confirming trades on Monday afternoon and again, after the opening on Tuesday.[11] On the futures exchange, order flows that might have moved the market by at most a tick or two in the week before, were moving the market by 10 or 20 times that amount or more in the early afternoon of Tuesday, October 20. Despite the evident rise in the cost of immediacy to sellers, the inflow of sell orders continued, and perhaps even accelerated in what took on all the appearances of a classic, self-reinforcing panic. By early afternoon on Tuesday, trading had been suspended in many NYSE stocks and in the main options and futures markets. With virtually no market-making capacity remaining, the burden of equilibration had to be assumed by the search for buyers off the market, culminating in the cavalry-like ride to the rescue on Tuesday afternoon by large US corporations instituting buy-back programs of their own shares. At the same time, the Federal Reserve System was directly and indirectly encouraging banks to support dealer inventory positions. By the end of the day, these infusions of buying power had pushed prices nearly back to their levels before the Monday noon collapse and substantial market-making capacity was back in place.

Effective market-making capacity in the period immediately after the crash, however, as well as at several critical junctures during the crash, was reduced by restrictions imposed on 'program trading', which cut the normal arbitrage linkage between the market makers in the spot and futures markets. Arbitragers, by taking offsetting positions in both markets close to simultaneously, can transmit some of the pressure of order imbalances from the market first impacted to the market makers in the other. Market makers' resources in both markets can thus be brought to bear on the initiating imbalance more effectively, much as they would be if the number of active market makers had been increased. Price concessions and hence the cost of transacting can be kept smaller in both markets, thanks to arbitrage program trading, than might otherwise be the case.[12] How ironic then to find arbitrage program trading still so often blamed for undermining investor confidence in the market.

NOTES

1 For a discussion of the benefits and the supposed abuses of dual trading on futures exchanges, see Grossman and Miller [6].

2 Although the fraction of potential trades executed immediately by market makers rather than delayed for search is higher for futures exchanges than in virtually any other market setting, search plays a role even there. A case in point is so-called 'sunshine trading' in which pending large and presumably informationless orders by portfolio insurers are publicized in advance throughout the investment community with a view to attracting a large inflow of counterparties prepared to take the other side. Whether such sunshine trading violates long-standing regulatory prohibitions against 'prearranged trading' is a policy issue currently much in dispute.

3 Some corporations of substantial size, however, may nevertheless choose to list in this market because there are fewer restrictions on size and capital structure (such as a one-share, one-vote rule) than on the NYSE or AMEX.

4 In addition to the four markets so far listed, there may now be as many as six distinct stock markets if one counts the 'after-hours' market (which now includes the trading of big-name US stocks on foreign exchanges) and the so-called 'fourth market' in which large pension funds, especially those following 'passive' or

indexing strategies, transfer baskets of stocks directly to and from each other in essentially informationless trades. The futures and options markets in stocks, of course, constitute still another form of stock market at least for the trading if not the holding of stocks.

Many European stock markets, where the volumes of trading are still quite small by US standards, use 'batch' or 'periodic call' systems rather than any of the continuous-trading systems we find here. For a comprehensive survey of trading practices overseas, see Whitcomb [12].

5   The reader is referred to Ho [7] for a model of equilibrium market making in a continuous-time, Poisson-arrival-of-orders setting.

6   Remember that, in our model, market makers take risky positions as well as match orders. Entry occurs to the point where the market makers earn a return on their risky positions plus any profits from simultaneous matching that just balances the trading risks and the fixed costs of maintaining a continuous presence.

7   In terms of the notation in our model, the nonviability of a competitive equilibrium would occur when c becomes large relative to a.

8   A closely related but somewhat different problem is faced by the designers of computerized, automatic execution systems like the much-publicized (but little used) INTEX exchange in Bermuda. Because the users can hit directly any bids or offers showing on the screen, no intermediary can hope to earn a living by 'scalping' the bid–ask spread on quick trades. This keeps market makers, who might otherwise provide immediacy when orders do not match, from being able to recover their opportunity costs of maintaining a continuous presence in the market.

9   The Chicago Board of Options Exchange opens with an auctioneer establishing provisional opening prices for each traded option. But with so many separate maturities and striking prices involved, the process of finding simultaneous, viable trading ranges is far from easy when prices are moving rapidly. On the morning of the 19th, and again on the 20th, by the time the 'rotation,' as the opening process is called, had worked its way around to the last series, the earlier, tentatively established trading ranges had become hopelessly wide of the mark. The process had to be repeated, and on Tuesday, October 20, trading did not in fact begin until far after the regular opening time.

10 This difference in opening procedures in the two markets undoubtedly contributed to the widespread (but misleading) impression at the time that the futures market in Chicago, if not actually dragging down stock prices in New York, was at least signaling to an already panicky public that heavy new selling pressure was on its way to the market in New York.

11 In the case of the NASDAQ bulletin board, market prices were sometimes changing at a faster rate than the quotes were being updated. When the best offer to sell is entered below the best bid to buy, a market is deemed crossed, and under the then-standing NASDAQ rules only the bid showed on the screen. No further transactions could be made until the obsolete bid was updated, which often involved substantial delay.

12 For a futher discussion of arbitrage program trading and especially its interaction with portfolio insurance, see chapter 10 of this volume.

REFERENCES

1 K. Cohen, S. Mair, R. Schwartz, and D. Whitcomb. Transaction costs, order placement strategy and the existence of the bid-ask spread. *Journal of Political Economy* 89 (April 1981).

2 K. Cooper, J. C. Groth, and W. E. Avers. Liquidity, exchange listing, and common stock performance. Working paper, Texas A&M University, August 1983.

3 H. Demsetz. The cost of transacting. *Quarterly Journal of Economics* 82 (February 1968).

4 F. Dubofsky and J. Groth. Exchange listing and liquidity. Department of Finance, Texas A&M University, mimeo, February 1984.

5 Lawrence R. Glosten and Paul R. Milgrom. Bid, ask and transaction prices in a specialist market with heterogeneously informed traders. *Journal of Financial Economics* 14 (March 1985), 71–100.

6 Sanford J. Grossman and Merton H. Miller. Economic costs and benefits of the proposed one-minute time bracketing regulation. *Journal of Futures Markets 6 (Spring 1986), 141–66.*

7 T. Ho. Dealer market structure: a dynamic competitive model. New York University working paper, March 1984.

8 P. Martin. Analysis of the impact of competitive rates on the liquidity of NYSE stocks. *Economic Staff Paper* 75-3, Securities and Exchange Commission (July 1975).

9 Merton H. Miller, John D. Hawke Jr., Burton Malkiel, and Myron Scholes. *Preliminary Report of the Committee of Inquiry Appointed by the Chicago Mercantile Exchange to Examine the Events Surrounding October 19, 1987* (December 22, 1987), mimeo.

10 Richard Roll. A simple implicit measure of the effective bid-ask spread in an efficient market. *Journal of Finance* 39 (March 1984), 1127–39.

11 Hans R. Stoll. Alternative views of market making. In Y. Amihud, T. Ho, and R. Schwartz (eds), *Market Making and the Changing Structure of the Securities Industry.* Lexington Books, 1985, 67–92.

12 David Whitcomb. An international comparison of stock exchange trading structures. In Y. Amihud, T. Ho, and R. Schwartz (eds), *Market Making and the Changing Structure of the Securities Industry.* Lexington Books, 1985, 237–56.

12

A Theory of Futures Market Manipulations

Albert S. Kyle

The great liquidity of futures markets and the anonymity that goes along with futures trading make it feasible for one large trader to acquire a substantial long position without having a large effect on prices and without being noticed by the other traders in the market. If a large trader in this position subsequently pushes prices higher by either threatening to take delivery or actually doing so, then we have a market manipulation, which is usually called a corner or a squeeze.

This chapter develops a simple model of futures trading in which market manipulations, which take the form of squeezes, discourage the use of futures markets by increasing the cost of hedging. The model contains three kinds of traders: hedgers, speculators, and a squeezer. In a well-functioning market where market manipulations do not occur, speculators who are risk-neutral have the risks faced by hedgers transferred to them at unbiased prices. When squeezes become a possibility, speculators bid up futures prices to levels that accurately reflect the probability of a squeeze. In this situation, futures prices, which are unbiased from the point of view of speculators, become biased against hedgers from the point of view of hedgers.

How is it that futures prices which appear unbiased or fair from the point of view of speculators nevertheless are compatible with the squeezer's making profits and hedgers' losing money consistently? The squeezer trades in such a way that speculators cannot tell from observing the trading process how much the squeezer is buying and how much the hedgers are selling. In

This chapter originally appeared as chapter 5 in *The Industrial Organization of Futures Markets*, edited by Ronald W. Anderson (Lexington, Mass.: Lexington Books, D. C. Heath and Company. Copyright 1984, D. C. Heath and Company), pp. 141–75. Reprinted by permission of the publisher.

Financial support from the Center for The Study of Futures Markets is gratefully acknowledged. The views expressed in this paper are those of the author and do not necessarily express those of The Center for The Study of Futures Markets.

early trading, the squeezer acquires a large long position when short hedging is active and acquires a large short position when hedging is inactive. To speculators, the amount of trade appears constant; it is thus impossible for speculators to learn whether a squeeze is in the works or not. It becomes apparent whether or not a squeeze is on when hedgers try to liquidate their positions. When hedging is active, the squeezer hangs on to his long positions, the squeeze is on, and hedgers must bid up prices to high levels to get out of their short positions. When hedging is inactive, the squeezer and hedgers both liquidate their positions at lower no-squeeze prices. Because initial prices discount the probability of a squeeze, the squeezer makes money both ways. He makes money on the long side as prices rise when there is a squeeze, and he makes money on the short side as prices fall when there is no squeeze. Hedgers, on the other hand, lose money consistently. When hedging is active, hedgers lose money on large short positions; when hedging is inactive, hedgers make money on small short positions. It is the asymmetric size of the positions when gains and losses occur – losses on large positions and gains on small positions – that is responsible for hedgers consistently losing money.

In equilibrium, hedgers adjust the amount of futures trading they do in light of the costs imposed on them by squeezers. The probability of squeezes, on the other hand, depends endogenously on the amount of hedging that takes place in the futures market. The equilibrium level of hedging and the equilibrium probability of squeezes are thus determined simultaneously in much the same way that equilibrium quantities and prices are determined by the intersection of supply and demand curves in the standard theory of supply and demand.

This chapter is organized into several sections. First, I justify using the concepts of liquidity and anonymity to explain squeezes as a futures market phenomenon. I then define corners and squeezes as two different kinds of market manipulations (squeezes are the kind of manipulation discussed here). Then the relationship between squeezes and the cheapest-to-deliver concept of delivery is discussed, followed by a simple model of squeezes, in which hedgers are assumed to behave exogenously. Despite the apparent simplicity of the basic model, the equilibrium is rather tricky to discuss mathematically. It is shown that the probability of a squeeze depends on the amount of hedging and the size of deliverable stocks.

I then show that when delivery is costly, threats to take or make delivery become important but that the model can be applied to the situation in which the squeezer uses threats to obtain the best outcome from his point of view. Next, the equilibrium behavior of hedgers is modeled to allow us to determine simultaneously the amount of hedging and the probability of squeezes in the market. Finally, I examine the effectiveness of various policies to control squeezes, including different delivery differentials, additional deliverable supply, cash settlement, and position limits.

1 THE ROLE OF LIQUIDITY AND ANONYMITY IN SQUEEZES

To explain corners and squeezes as futures market phenomena, it is useful to examine first the features of futures trading that distinguish it from other forms of market organization. Two basic approaches have been used to explain futures trading: the insurance approach and the liquidity approach.

According to the insurance approach, futures markets provide a step toward complete markets – a set of markets in which it is possible to exchange every conceivable kind of risk – by making it possible to exchange risks that would not be possible to exchange using combinations of other kinds of assets. However, the insurance approach, as emphasized by Telser (1981), does not distinguish futures markets from ordinary insurance markets. Insurance markets and futures markets are clearly different forms of market organization, the former distinguished by large numbers of con-tracts uniquely tailored for specific risks borne by specific firms or individuals in specific situations, the latter distinguished by a small number of contracts, each of which is traded actively by a large number of traders for a variety of reasons. The insurance approach does not help explain why we see one form of market organization in some situations and another form of market organization in another situation.

A better explanation of futures trading is the liquidity approach, advanced recently by Telser (1981) but reminiscent of Working (1953). According to this approach, futures markets are a form of market organization designed, as Telser puts it, to 'facilitate trade among strangers,' or, as Working puts it, to reduce transactions costs. The advantage of the liquidity approach to futures trading is that it helps explain those institutional features of futures trading which distinguish it from other forms of market organization. These institutional features – small numbers of perfectly fungible contracts with well-defined terms, trading by open outcry on an organized exchange floor under well-defined rules, book-entry accounting of open positions, clearing of trades by a central clearing house, margins and mark-to-market settle-ment of accounts on a daily basis by a clearing organization, centralized monitoring of the financial positions of member firms – all reduce the costs of trading by centralizing the search, bookkeeping, and credit activities that are part of trading.

A feature of futures trading closely connected with liquidity is anonymity, a fact reflected in Telser's statement that futures markets 'facilitate trade among strangers.' The organizational structure of futures trading makes it unnecessary for traders to know individually the principals on the other side of their transaction, because the brokers on the trading floor bring traders off the floor together behind a wall of anonymity and because the clearing house of the exchange guarantees the integrity of positions on both sides of the market. In fact, the anonymity of futures trading is closely related to its low transactions costs, in that the high costs of trading in other markets are in large part the result of the costs of keeping detailed records of positions with a large number of trading partners and the cost of assessing the financial integrity of each of them.

The anonymity of futures markets tends to change the nature of the market dramatically, because knowledge of who is trading what is in many cases a valuable commodity itself. Traders sometimes go to great lengths to conceal their identities while simultaneously going to equally great lengths to figure out what other traders in the market are doing. It is clear that both liquidity and anonymity make futures markets an attractive form of market organization.

In our model, we assume that hedgers, who are basically buyers of insurance, use futures contracts because of their liquidity. Implicitly, we assume that cash markets are too costly to be used as a hedging device but that futures markets are, at a transactional level, essentially costless. Thus, hedgers use futures markets even though the risk and delivery characteristics of the contracts do not mesh perfectly with the hedgers' inventories. As we shall see, this imperfect fit between inventories and futures positions is important when thinking about squeezes because a hedger who is persuaded by the liquidity of the market to short a futures contract against a cash market position that is not most deliverable leaves himself in a vulnerable position when the longs in the market decide to take delivery.

Although hedgers are attracted to the futures market mainly because of its liquidity, the squeezer is attracted mainly because of its anonymity. It seems clear that if the rest of the market knew what the squeezer was up to, prices would adjust quickly to levels such that the squeezer could not engineer a squeeze in which he expected to make a profit.

2 DISTINGUISHING BETWEEN CORNERS AND SQUEEZES

In a market manipulation, prices are manipulated not because supply is prevented from being equal to demand but because the manipulator holds positions that, at the margin, could be liquidated at current prices and reacquired later at more favorable prices (even after adjusting for storage and interest costs). A perfect competitor would not be willing to hold a position in this situation because it would be unprofitable, but an imperfect competitor may be willing to do so if it enables him to liquidate his inframarginal positions at better prices.

The terms corner and squeeze are often used interchangeably to describe the market manipulations in futures markets. However, it is useful to distinguish between these two different kinds of market manipulations. In a corner, the manipulator acquires control over large enough stocks to set up a temporary monopoly in the commodity. He then supplies stocks to the market gradually, keeping prices high by exploiting intertemporal elasticities in demand and supply. In a squeeze, the manipulator exploits the delivery mechanism of the futures contract by taking advantage of the fact that not all stocks of the commodity are easily available for delivery on favorable terms. The squeezer makes his profits either by threatening to take delivery and thereby forcing shorts to bail out at high prices to avoid the high costs of bringing supplies into deliverable position or by taking delivery of so much of the commodity that the shorts must deliver goods that would not ordinarily be cheapest to deliver.

The difference between a corner and a squeeze is that a squeeze, which exploits the delivery mechanism, is essentially over once delivery is made. In contrast, a corner, which exploits intertemporal elasticities of supply and demand, is in some sense just getting started when delivery is made. In a squeeze, the prices that have been bid up for specific qualities and locations (the ones treated most favorably by the futures contract) fall quickly back to normal levels once delivery is made. In a corner, a generalized rise in the price of all qualities and locations occurs, and prices fall back more slowly once delivery is made, as the cornerer works off his stocks slowly at high prices.

The distinction between a corner and a squeeze is not sharp. Individual market manipulations may have characteristics of both corners and squeezes. In this chapter, market manipulations are modeled as squeezes because we are concerned with the transactions technology of futures markets and the delivery mechanism of the futures contract rather than with the underlying fundamentals of demand and supply. However, the mathematics of a model of a corner would be similar to the mathematics of a model of a squeeze.

3   SQUEEZES AND THE DELIVERY MECHANISM

In most futures contracts the cash prices and futures prices are tied together at delivery by the cheapest to deliver concept. To explain how the cheapest to deliver concept works, suppose that there are two qualities of the asset, quality one and quality two. Let p_1^M and p_2^M denote the market prices of these qualities at the time of delivery in a market where no squeeze takes place. We call these no-squeeze prices. Let p^F denote the futures price at the time of delivery. Let p_1^D and p_2^D denote the prices at which the different qualities can be delivered against the futures contract. The prices p_1^D and p_2^D are determined in the specifications of the contract as functions of the futures prices p^F. We will assume that the delivery prices are determined by adjusting the futures price p^F by adding constants Δ_1 and Δ_2, so that

$$p_1^D = p^F + \Delta_1$$
$$p_2^D = p^F + \Delta_2$$

defines the delivery prices. The quantities Δ_1 and Δ_2 are part of the specifications of the futures contract. Positive values of Δ_1 and Δ_2 denote premiums and negative values denote discounts.

In most futures contracts, the seller has the option to decide what qualities are delivered. This option is given to the seller because the flexibility made possible by this option makes it more difficult for the buyer to squeeze the seller by insisting on the delivery of particular qualities. If sellers have the option to choose the quality delivered, and if there is at least one competitive trader in the market, the relationship between cash prices and futures prices will be determined according to the cheapest-to-deliver concept, which states that the seller breaks even by delivering at least one quality and does not make a profit delivering any quality. Mathematically, this relationship can be written

$$\max(p^F + \Delta_1 - p_1^M, p^F + \Delta_2 - p_2^M) = 0$$

If good 1 is the cheapest to deliver, then $p_1^M = p^F + \Delta_1 = p_1^D$ and $p_2^M \geqslant p^F + \Delta_2 = p_2^D$. The cheapest-to-deliver constraint makes it possible to calculate the equilibrium futures price p^F given equilibrium cash prices p_1^M, p_2^M and contract specifications Δ_1, Δ_2. The equilibrium futures price p^F is by definition the price at which no arbitrage is possible.

The delivery mechanism creates an opportunity for squeezes in the following way. Suppose for simplicity that it is known that good 1 will be cheapest to deliver and let d denote the cost advantage of delivering good 1 instead of good 2 when cash prices are determined under the assumption that there will be no squeeze. Then it is straightforward to show that

$$d = (\Delta_2 - \Delta_1) - (p_2^M - p_1^M)$$

that is, d is the difference between the arbitrary contract relationships used for delivery purposes and the basis relationships prevailing in the open market. It is also clear that the equilibrium futures price is given by

$$p^F = p_1^M - \Delta_1$$

that is, the futures price is perfectly correlated with the cash price for good 1 and differs from the cash price by the delivery adjustment Δ_1. Let x_1 and x_2 denote the supplies of good 1 and good 2 available for delivery against the futures contract.

The possibility for a squeeze exists if a trader can purchase such large quantities of futures contracts at prices close to p^F that the shorts are forced to deliver underlying qualities which would not otherwise be cheapest to deliver. If a position whose size is in excess of x_1 (the total available supply of cheapest-to-deliver quality) can be acquired, then the trader, by taking delivery of his contracts, can force the shorts to deliver expensive to deliver good 2 on some of the contracts. If the trader purchases the futures contracts at price $p_1^M - \Delta_1$, and sells the qualities he has delivered at prices p_1^M and p_2^M, then the trader breaks even on deliveries of good 1 and makes a profit of d on deliveries of good 2. (If the trader purchases positions in excess of the total available supply $x_1 + x_2$, the shorts must either cover at prices dictated by the squeezer or default on some contracts.) Thus, if the squeezer acquires at no-squeeze price a position of size x, where $x_1 \leqslant x \leqslant x_1 + x_2$, then squeezer's profits are $(x - x_1)d$.

When a squeeze is on, the no-squeeze prices p_1^M, p_2^M will not be the ones prevailing in the market. Because during a squeeze there is not enough of the cheapest-to-deliver quality available to make all of the deliveries necessary, the shorts will bid up the cash market price of the cheapest-to-deliver qualities to a point where both qualities are equally deliverable. This bidding up of cash market prices on cheapest-to-deliver qualities, which occurs in line with the bidding up of futures prices, will only occur on cash market forward contracts that settle on or before delivery of the futures contract. For cash market transactions with delivery after this point, there will be no bidding up of prices. Implicitly, the market is expecting the spot prices of the cheapest-to-deliver quality, which have been run up sharply before delivery, to collapse immediately after delivery back to the no-squeeze levels (assuming another squeeze is not expected at maturity of the next futures contract.)

If traders expect spot prices for the cheapest-to-deliver quality to collapse immediately after delivery is made, why will any competitive trader be willing to hold inventories of the cheapest-to-deliver quality during the delivery period? In fact, only the squeezer himself will be willing to do so, because he is the only trader who is not a perfect competitor. He is willing to hold inventories of the cheapest-to-deliver commodity and take a loss on them, because doing so allows him to acquire the expensive-to-deliver quality at favorable terms – which is essentially what the squeeze is all about.

The squeezer is in effect able to internalize an externality that crops up in the delivery mechanism. To explain this externality, we compare the price a competitive short is willing to pay to buy back his position with the price a competitive long is willing to accept to liquidate his short. The marginal cost of making delivery is the price at which the short breaks even delivering the expensive commodity, because the cheapest-to-deliver commodity is also bid up before delivery to this level. As a result, a competitive short is willing to pay anything up to this price to liquidate his short position.

A competitive long, on the other hand, looks at the value of the delivered qualities after delivery. Because the cheapest-to-deliver quality will have fallen back to its no-squeeze value at this point, he is looking at lower prices than a short. Let us suppose that the delivery mechanism works as follows. During delivery the qualities that the shorts tender for delivery are allocated randomly to the longs, and no bargaining is allowed between shorts or longs over the question of who gets delivered what. Then the value to the long of taking delivery is the weighted average value of the qualities delivered, where the cheapest-to-deliver quality has its lower, post-delivery value. A competitive long is willing to sell at any price greater than this weighted average value.

Because the marginal cost of taking delivery for the competitive long is less than the marginal cost of making delivery for a competitive short, the longs are better off liquidating at prices close to the marginal cost of making delivery for the shorts than by taking delivery. As a result, the only trader left on the long side of the market will be the squeezer.

The nature of the externality present during a squeeze is now clear. When an extra long position and an extra short position are created during a squeeze, the marginal quality delivered by the short is the expensive quality but the marginal quality delivered to the long is the average of the qualities delivered. The extra delivery of the expensive quality at the margin tends to raise average quality, but almost all these benefits of improved quality are captured by the inframarginal longs already present in the market and not by the long with whom the trade occurs. This externality discourages accumulation of open interest and in fact causes open interest to liquidate. The only trader with no incentive to liquidate is the squeezer. He has no incentive to liquidate because he internalizes the externality by also holding all of the inframarginal long positions and takes this into account in making his trading decisions.

4 A SIMPLE MODEL

In this section we examine a simple model of squeezes that has many of the properties discussed intuitively in the preceding sections. Assume that futures trading takes place in two trading periods, at equilibrium prices p_1^F, p_2^F. Before trading in the first period, there is no open interest, and the open interest remaining after trading in the second period is liquidated through delivery. The exogenous deliverable supply consists of z_1 units of quality 1 and z_2 units of quality 2. Immediately after delivery, quality 1 will have a value of $\tilde{v}$ and quality 2 will have a value of $\tilde{v} + d$, where d is a positive constant known by all traders and $\tilde{v}$ is a random variable. During the first period of trade, traders know the distribution of $\tilde{v}$ but not its outcome. During the second period of trade, the outcome $\tilde{v}$ is known with certainty by all traders. Both qualities of the commodity can be delivered against the futures contract (with no differentials). Thus, good 1 is cheapest to deliver and good 2 is d dollars more expensive.

There are three types of traders: hedgers, speculators, and a squeezer. The model is a game played by speculators and the squeezer. In this game, hedgers' trade is exogenous – that is, hedgers do not trade strategically.

Hedgers trade exogenously by selling a random quantity of contracts, denoted $\tilde{H}$, in period 1 and purchasing back the $\tilde{H}$ contracts in period 2. The random variable $\tilde{H}$, which is distributed independently of $\tilde{v}$, assumes two outcomes, H_0 and H_1, where

$$\tilde{H} = \begin{cases} H_0 & \text{with probability } 1 - \lambda \\ H_1 & \text{with probability } \lambda \end{cases}$$

We assume $0 < H_0 < H_1$, so an outcome of H_0 corresponds to inactive hedging and an outcome of H_1 corresponds to active hedging. (The assumption that the quantities H_0 and H_1 are positive is not actually necessary.

The strategy choice of the squeezer consists of two measurable functions, denoted $\tilde{X}_1(\cdot)$ and $\tilde{X}_2(\cdot, \cdot, \cdot)$, where $\tilde{X}_1(\cdot)$ maps the space of real numbers into the space of random variables distributed independently from $\tilde{v}$, and $X_2(\cdot, \cdot, \cdot)$ maps R^3 into the space of random variables distributed independently from $\tilde{v}$. The quantities traded by the squeezer in periods 1 and 2, denoted $\tilde{x}_1$ and $\tilde{x}_2$ respectively, are given by

$$\tilde{x}_1 = \tilde{X}_1(\tilde{H}_1)$$

and

$$\tilde{x}_2 = \tilde{X}_2(\tilde{H}_1, \tilde{x}_1, \tilde{v})$$

where positive quantities denote purchases and negative quantities denote sales. This method of defining the trading strategy of the squeezer captures the idea that the squeezer observes the quantity $\tilde{H}$ traded by the hedgers before choosing the quantity he wishes to trade himself. Furthermore, the squeezer is allowed to randomize the quantities he trades in ways that do not anticipate the future spot price $\tilde{v}$. The fact that $\tilde{x}_2$ can depend on $\tilde{x}_1$ and $\tilde{v}$ allows the squeezer to adjust the quantity traded in period 2 in light of the quantity traded in period 1 and in light of the value $\tilde{v}$ revealed in period 2 (but this is not an important feature of the equilibrium).

The behavior of the speculators is specified by two measurable functions

$P_1(\cdot)$ and $P_2(\cdot, \cdot, \cdot)$, which map R^1 and R^3, respectively, into R^1. The futures prices in periods 1 and 2 are given by

$$\tilde{p}_1^F = p_1(\tilde{x}_1 - \tilde{H})$$

and

$$\tilde{p}_2^F = p_2(\tilde{x}_1 - \tilde{H}, \tilde{x}_2 + H, \tilde{v})$$

In setting $\tilde{p}_1^F$, the speculators observe the aggregate quantity traded in period 1, denoted by $\tilde{y}_1 = X_1(\tilde{H}) - \tilde{H}$, but they do not observe the individual quantities $\tilde{X}_1(\tilde{H})$ and $\tilde{H}$ traded by the squeezer and the hedgers respectively. In setting the price in period 2, the speculators observe trade in period 1, trade in period 2, and the realized value $\tilde{v}$. Although the insider randomizes the quantity he trades, the pricing functions $P_1(\cdot)$ and $P_2(\cdot, \cdot, \cdot)$ are nonstochastic.

Let the notation $\tilde{X}_1, \tilde{X}_2, P_1, P_2$ denote in more abbreviated form the strategy choices $\tilde{X}_1(\cdot)$ and $\tilde{X}_2(\cdot, \cdot, \cdot)$ of the squeezer and the choices $P_1(\cdot)$ and $P_2(\cdot, \cdot, \cdot)$ of the speculators. Let $\tilde{\pi}(\tilde{X}_1, \tilde{X}_2, P_1, P_2)$ denote the profits of the insider as a function of these strategy choices. It is clear that $\tilde{\pi}(\tilde{X}_1, \tilde{X}_2, P_1, P_2)$ is a random variable given by

$$\tilde{\pi}(\tilde{X}_1, \tilde{X}_2, P_1, P_2) = \tilde{X}_1(\tilde{v} - \tilde{p}_1) + \tilde{X}_2(\tilde{v} - \tilde{p}_2) +$$
$$\max\{\tilde{x}_1 + \tilde{x}_2 - z_1, 0\}d,$$

or, expressed explicitly in terms of $\tilde{X}_1, \tilde{X}_2, P_1, P_2$, by

$$\tilde{\pi}(\tilde{X}_1, \tilde{X}_2, P_1, P_2) = X_1(\tilde{H}) \cdot [\tilde{v} - p_1(\tilde{X}_1(\tilde{H}) - \tilde{H})]$$
$$+ \tilde{X}_2(\tilde{H}, \tilde{X}_1(\tilde{H}), \tilde{v}) \cdot [\tilde{v} - P_2(\tilde{X}_1(\tilde{H}) - \tilde{H}, \tilde{X}_2(\tilde{H}, \tilde{X}_1(\tilde{H}), \tilde{v})$$
$$+ \tilde{H}, \tilde{v})] + \max\{\tilde{X}_1(\tilde{H}) + \tilde{X}_2(\tilde{H}, \tilde{X}_1(\tilde{H}), \tilde{v}) - z_1, 0\}d.$$

In this expression, the first term gives no-squeeze profits on trade made in period 1, the second term gives no-squeeze profits on trade made in period 2, and the third term gives additional profits captured when there is a squeeze.

An equilibrium is defined as a set of strategy choices $\tilde{X}_1, \tilde{X}_2, P_1, P_2$ such that three conditions hold. For all alternate strategies $\tilde{X}_1', \tilde{X}_2'$

$$E\{\tilde{\pi}(\tilde{X}_1, \tilde{X}_2, P_1, P_2)\} \geq E\{\tilde{\pi}(\tilde{X}_1', \tilde{X}_2', P_1, P_2)\} \tag{12.1}$$

The function P_1 satisfies $P_1(y) = E\{\tilde{p}_2 | \tilde{x}_1 - \tilde{H} = y\}$, or explicitly

$$P_1(y) = E\{P_2[\tilde{X}_1(\tilde{H}) - \tilde{H}, \tilde{X}_2(\tilde{H}, \tilde{X}_1(\tilde{H}), \tilde{v}) + \tilde{H}, \tilde{v}] \,|$$
$$\tilde{X}_1(\tilde{H}) - \tilde{H} = y\} \tag{12.2}$$

The function P_2 is given by

$$P_2(y_1, y_2, v) = \begin{cases} v & \text{if } y_1 + y_2 \leqslant z_1 \\ v + d & \text{if } y_1 + y_2 > z_1 \end{cases} \qquad (12.3)$$

According to this equilibrium concept, the squeezer maximizes his expected profits, taking into account the effect that a change in his trading has on future prices. Speculators are assumed to trade in such a way that the expected profits of acquiring a futures position at market-clearing prices, then liquidating it later through trade or through delivery, are zero. In effect, we assume that speculators are risk-neutral, perfect competitors who compete with one another so fiercely that their extra profits are driven to zero, but we do not model explicitly the auction process that generates this outcome. To both the speculators and the insider, the equilibrium reflects fulfilled expectations in the sense that traders utilize models which are not contradicted in equilibrium by observations of variables in their respective information sets.

In order to understand this equilibrium concept, it is important to keep in mind two points. First, the squeezer's strategy choices $\tilde{X}_1$ and $\tilde{X}_2$ are not arguments of the speculators' pricing functions p_1 and p_2. That is, we are in effect using a Nash concept of equilibrium rather than a Stackelberg concept in which the squeezer moves first. If the squeezer contemplates changing his strategy $\tilde{X}_1$, $\tilde{X}_2$, he assumes that speculators do not change theirs in response. Instead, the speculators merely react to the actual quantities traded. Because of the Nash equilibrium concept, the squeezer will not follow a random strategy unless the various random outcomes all generate the same expected profits conditional on the squeezer's information. Furthermore, there will be no sense in which the squeezer, say, sacrifices expected profits when hedging is inactive to increase profits when hedging is active because such behavior implicitly assumes that the squeezer gets the speculators to change their strategies in response to changes in his own. Finally, the Nash concept automatically makes the equilibrium dynamically consistent by ruling out credibility issues involving whether the squeezer will still want to follow the second-period strategy $\tilde{X}_2$ after first-period trade has already occurred.

Second, remember the nature of the conditional expectation defining $P_1(y_1)$ in condition (12.2) of equilibrium. The function $P_1(\cdot)$ must be defined for all values of $\tilde{y}_1$, where $\tilde{y}_1$, the equilibrium quantity traded in period 1, is given by $\tilde{y}_1 = \tilde{X}_1(\tilde{H}) - \tilde{H}$. Because $\tilde{H}$ assumes only two outcomes, the equilibrium distribution of $\tilde{y}_1$ may well be massed at only one or two points, so almost all of the admissible outcomes of $\tilde{y}_1$ will never be realized. For those sets of outcomes y_1 with probability zero of occurring, the value of $P_1(y_1)$ can be changed without affecting the fact that $P_1(y_1)$ is the conditional expectation because conditional expectations are only defined up to sets of probability zero. Thus, condition (12.2) does not define $P_1(y_1)$ uniquely (except for those values of y_1 which have positive probability of occurring). In equilibrium, however, the prices $P_1(y_1)$ corresponding to values of y_1 that never occur play an important role. The prices corresponding to these y_1 values must be such that for all outcomes $\tilde{H}$, the squeezer is never induced to trade in such a way that the corresponding y_1 values are realized. In other words, although almost all values of y_1 will never be realized, the function $P_1(\cdot)$, which is not uniquely defined by condition (12.2), must be chosen in such a way that it sustains the equilibrium in which they are not realized, by making it unattractive for the squeezer to trade in such a way that they are.

In the rest of this section, we show how to characterize the equilibria in this model. We show that an equilibrium exists and also show that except for trivial changes in $\tilde{X}_1$, $\tilde{X}_2$, P_1, P_2, the equilibrium is unique. In particular, there exists a unique probability that a squeeze occurs and a unique equilibrium pricing process. However, the quantities traded by the insider and the prices that occur with probability zero are not necessarily uniquely defined.

Because of the way in which equilibrium is defined, it is possible to calculate the equilibria for the model by working backward from period 2. As a first step, we show that in any equilibrium, no second-period trading strategy for the squeezer dominates the strategy of not trading.

Lemma 1 For all $\tilde{X}_1$, $\tilde{X}_2'$, P_1, P_2, the trading strategy $\tilde{X}_2 = 0$, defined by $\tilde{X}_2(\tilde{H}, \tilde{x}_1, \tilde{v}) = 0$ with probability 1, has the property that

$$\tilde{\pi}(\tilde{X}_1, 0, P_1, P_2) \geqslant \tilde{\pi}(\tilde{X}_1, \tilde{X}_2', P_1, P_2)$$

PROOF From the definition of $\tilde{\pi}(\tilde{X}_1, \tilde{X}_2, P_1, P_2)$, we have

$$\tilde{\pi}(\tilde{X}_1, 0, P_1, P_2) - \tilde{\pi}(\tilde{X}_1, \tilde{X}_2', P_1, P_2)$$

$$= \max\{\tilde{X}_1(\tilde{H}_1) - z_1, 0\} - \max\{\tilde{X}_1(\tilde{H}) + \tilde{X}_2'(\tilde{H}, \tilde{X}_1(\tilde{H}), z_1), 0\}d$$

$$- \tilde{X}_2'(\tilde{H}, X_1(\tilde{H}), \tilde{v})[\tilde{v} - P_2(\tilde{X}_1(\tilde{H}) - \tilde{H}, \tilde{X}_2(\tilde{H}, \tilde{X}_1(\tilde{H}), \tilde{v})$$

$$+ \tilde{H}, \tilde{v})]$$

We wish to show that the preceding expression is always nonnegative. Letting $x_1 = \tilde{X}_1(\tilde{H})$, $x_2 = \tilde{X}_2'(\tilde{H}, \tilde{X}_1(\tilde{H}), \tilde{v})$, $\tilde{H} = h$, $\tilde{v} = v$, the right side of the preceding expression can be expressed as $J(x_1, x_2, h, p)$, where J is defined by

$$J(x_1, x_2, h, p) = \max\{x_1 - z_1, 0\} \cdot d - \max\{x_1 + x_2 - z_1, 0\} \cdot d$$

$$- x_2(v - P_2(x_1 + h, x_2 - h, v))$$

From the definition of P_2 (property (12.3) of the definition of equilibrium), it is a straightforward exercise to show the whenever $x_1 - z_1$ has the same sign as $x_1 + x_2 - z_1$, then $J = 0$, and whenever $x_1 - z_1$ is opposite in sign to $x_1 + x_2 - z_1$, then $J = |x_1 - z_1| \cdot d$. Thus, J is always nonnegative, and the result is proved.

The intuition behind this result is quite simple. Because speculators observe whether or not there will be a squeeze before p_2^F is determined, the squeezer cannot trick the speculators into trading at unfavorable prices in period 2. This being the case, he has no incentive to trade in period 2 at all. The squeezer is actually indifferent between trading $x_2 = 0$ and any other x_2 that leaves the sign of $x_1 - z_1$ the same as the sign of $x_1 + x_2 - z_1$. Because there will be a squeeze if and only if $x_1 + x_2 - z_1$ is positive, the squeezer determines whether or not there will be a squeeze by his trading in period 1. In period 2, he does anything that does not alter this determination. Without loss of generality, we can therefore assume $\tilde{X}_2 = 0$, that is, the squeezer does not trade in period 2.

Because P_2 is defined in part (12.3) of the definition of equilibrium and because $\tilde{X}_2$ is (without loss of generality) zero, the problem of characterizing equilibrium collapses back to determining period 1 strategies $\tilde{X}_1$ and $\tilde{P}_1$.

Letting $\tilde{\pi}_1(\tilde{X}_1, P_1)$ denote the profits of the insider with $\tilde{X}_2$ and P_2 substituted out, we obtain

$$\tilde{\pi}_1(\tilde{X}_1, P_1) = \tilde{X}_1(\tilde{H}) \cdot [\tilde{v} - P_1(\tilde{X}_1(\tilde{H}) - \tilde{H})] + \max(\tilde{X}_1(\tilde{H})$$
$$- z_1, 0) \cdot d$$

$\tilde{X}_1$ and P_1 generate an equilibrium provided

$$E\tilde{\pi}_1(\tilde{X}_1, P_1) \geqslant E\tilde{\pi}_1(\tilde{X}_1', P_1) \text{ for all } \tilde{X}_1',$$

$$P_1(y_1) = E\tilde{v} + \text{Prob}\{\tilde{X}_1(\tilde{H}) - z_1 > 0 | \tilde{X}_1(\tilde{H}) - \tilde{H} = y_1\} \cdot d$$

The conditional expectation in the preceding equation is defined uniquely only up to sets of probability zero.

Now, given the function P, define the functions $\Pi_p(\cdot, \cdot)$, measuring expected squeezer profits when the squeezer trades x and hedgers trade h, and $\Pi_p^*(\cdot)$, measuring maximized profits, by

$$\Pi_p(x, h) = (E\tilde{v} - P(x - h))x + \max(x - z_1, 0) \cdot d,$$

$$\Pi_p^*(h) = \max_x \Pi_p(x, h)$$

For the conditions $E\pi_1(\tilde{X}_1, P) > E\pi_1(\tilde{X}_1', P)$ to hold for all $\tilde{X}_1'$, it is necessary that

$$\text{Prob}\{\Pi_p(\tilde{X}_1(H_i), H_i) = \Pi_p^*(H_i)\} = 1 \qquad i = 0, 1.$$

As a first step toward characterizing equilibrium, we show that if squeezes occur with positive probability in equilibrium, the squeezer is always short when hedging is inactive.

Lemma 2 *If* $\text{Prob}\{\tilde{X}_1(\tilde{H}) - z_1 > 0\} > 0$ *in equilibrium, then* $\tilde{X}_1(H_0) < 0$ *with probability* 1, $P(\tilde{X}_1(H_0) - H_0) > E\tilde{v}$ *with probability* 1, *and* $\Pi_p^*(H_0) > 0$.

PROOF Consider an equilibrium where $\text{Prob}\{\tilde{X}_1(\tilde{H}) - z_1 > 0\} > 0$. Because squeezes occur with positive probability, it must be the case that $\text{Prob}\{\tilde{H} = H_0$ and $P(\tilde{X}(\tilde{H}) - \tilde{H} > E\tilde{v}\} > 0$ since otherwise speculators could infer from $P(\tilde{X}_1(\tilde{H}) - \tilde{H}) > E\tilde{v}$ that $\tilde{H} = H_1$, and, knowing that a squeeze was going to occur, would set $P(\tilde{X}(\tilde{H}) - \tilde{H}) = E\tilde{v} + d$; but this would make the squeeze unprofitable for the squeezer and hence cannot be an equilibrium.

Clearly, for the squeezer not to lose money when $P(\tilde{X}_1(H_0) - H_0) > E\tilde{v}$, it must be the case that either $\Pi_p^*(H_0) = 0$ (and $\tilde{X}_1(H_0) = 0 - H_0$) when $P(\tilde{X}_1(H_0) - H_0) > E\tilde{v}$ or $\Pi_p^*(H_0) > 0$ and $\tilde{X}_1(H_0) < 0$ when $P(\tilde{X}_1(H_0) - H_0) > E\tilde{v}$.

Suppose (to be contradicted) that $\tilde{X}_1(H_0) = 0$ when $P(\tilde{X}_1(H_0) - H_0) > E\tilde{v}$. For $\tilde{X}_1(H_0) = 0$ to be maximizing, it must be the case that $P(y) \leqslant E\tilde{v}$ for $y < -H_0$; otherwise the squeezer could sell short and make positive profits. Clearly, for $\tilde{X}_1(H_0) = 0$ to hold when $P(\tilde{X}_1(H_0) - H_0) > E\tilde{v}$, we must have $P(-H_0) > E\tilde{v}$. Since $\tilde{X}_1(H_0) = 0$ with positive probability, we must have $\tilde{X}_1(H_1) = H_1 - H_0$ with positive probability since otherwise speculators could infer from $\tilde{X}_1(\tilde{H}) - \tilde{H} = -H_0$ that $\tilde{H} = H_0$ and $\tilde{X}_1(\tilde{H}) = 0$, and would thus set $P(-H_0) = E\tilde{v}$. Because of the left discontinuity in $P(y)$ at $y = -H_0$, the squeezer makes greater profits setting $\tilde{X}_1(H_1) = H_1 - H_0 - \varepsilon$ for small $\varepsilon > 0$ than from $\tilde{X}_1(H_1) = H_1 - H_0$. This contradicts the fact that $\tilde{X}_1(H_1) = H_1 - H_0$ maximizes profits when $\tilde{H} = H_1$; thus the original supposition that $\tilde{X}_1(H_0) = 0$ when $P(\tilde{X}_1(H_0) - H_0) > E\tilde{v}$ must be false.

From this contraction, we conclude that $\Pi_p^*(H_0) > 0$ and $\tilde{X}_1(H_0) < 0$ when $P(\tilde{X}_1(H_0) - H_0) > E\tilde{v}$. When futures prices are not greater than $E\tilde{v}$, it is clear that futures prices equal $E\tilde{v}$ since lower prices (with positive probability) are inconsistent with equilibrium. When $P(\tilde{X}_1(H_0) - H_0) = E\tilde{v}$, it must be the case that the squeezer engineers a squeeze to achieve strictly positive profits $\Pi_p^*(H_0)$. But this is inconsistent with prices being equal to $E\tilde{v}$. It follows that conditional on $\tilde{H} = H_0$, futures prices are greater than $E\tilde{v}$ with probability 1 and $\tilde{X}_1(H_0)$ is negative with probability 1 - the desired result.

The next lemma amplifies the previous result by showing that in equilibria where squeezes occur, the short position taken by the squeezer when hedging is inactive is unique (nonrandom). Futhermore, whenever the squeezer attempts a squeeze, he purchases a unique (nonrandom) quantity.

Lemma 3   *Suppose* Prob $\{\tilde{X}_1(\tilde{H}) - z_1 > 0\} > 0$ *in equilibrium. Then there exists a constant $y*$ satisfying $y* + H_0 < 0 < z_1 < y* + H_1$ such that*

1.   Prob $\{\tilde{X}_1(H_0) = y* + H_0\} = 1$,

2.   Prob $\{\tilde{X}_1(H_1) > z_1\} = $ Prob$\{\tilde{X}_1(H_1) = y* + H_1\}$

PROOF   Define the function $\pi(\cdot, \cdot)$ by

$$\pi(x, p) = (E\tilde{v} - p)x + \max\{x - z_1, 0\}d$$

For equilibrium profit levels $\Pi_p^*(H_0)$ and $\Pi_p^*(H_1)$, define the sets $B(H_i)$, $I(H_i), i = 0, 1$, by

$$B(H_i) = \{ (y, p): z_1 - H_1 < y < -H_0, \Pi(y + H_i, p) = \Pi_p^*(H_i)\},$$

$$I(H_i) = \{ (y, p): z_1 - H_1 < y < -H_0, \Pi(y + H_i, p) > \Pi_p^*(H_i)\},$$

We claim that in equilibrium $I(H_0) \cap I(H_1) = \phi$. To prove this claim observe that over x values such that $x = y + H_0$, $z - H_1 < y < -H_0$ implies that $z_1 - (H_1 - H_0) < x < 0$. Since x is negative, $\pi(x, p)$ is strictly quasiconcave in x and p and increasing in p. Thus, $I(H_0)$ is convex if it contains (y, p); it also contains (y, p') for all $p' \geqslant p$. Similarly, observe that over x values such that $x = y + H_1$, $z_1 - H_1 < y < -H_0$ implies that $z_1 < x < H_1 - H_0$. Since x is greater than z_1, $\Pi(x, p)$ is strictly quasi-concave and decreasing in p. Thus, $I(H_1)$ is convex, and if it contains (y, p) it also contains (y, p') for all $p' \leqslant p$ (see figure 12.1).

Now suppose (to be contradicted) that $I(H_0) \cap I(H_1)$ is nonempty and let $(y, p) \in I(H_0) \cap I(H_1)$. There clearly exists no p' such that $(y, p') \notin I(H_0)$ and $(y, p') \notin I(H_1)$ because $I(H_0)$ contains all (y, p') with $p' \geqslant p$ and $I(H_1)$ contains all p' with $p' < p$. Thus, no matter how $P(y)$ is defined, the squeezer can do better than his equilibrium strategy by choosing $x = y + H_i$ when either $\tilde{H} = H_0$ or $\tilde{H} = H_1$. This is clearly a contradiction, from which we conclude that $I(H_0) \cap I(H_1) = \phi$.

Now it follows from the properties of convex sets that since $I(H_0)$ and $I(H_1)$ do not intersect, their boundaries $B(H_0)$ and $B(H_1)$ intersect in at most one point. Call this point, if it exists, $\langle y*, p* \rangle$. (See figure 12.1.)

We now claim that

$$\text{Prob}\{ (\tilde{X}_1(\tilde{H}) - \tilde{H}, P(\tilde{X}_1(\tilde{H}) - \tilde{H})) \in B(H_0) \cap B(H_1) |$$

$$P(\tilde{X}(\tilde{H}) - \tilde{H}) > E\tilde{v}\} = 1$$

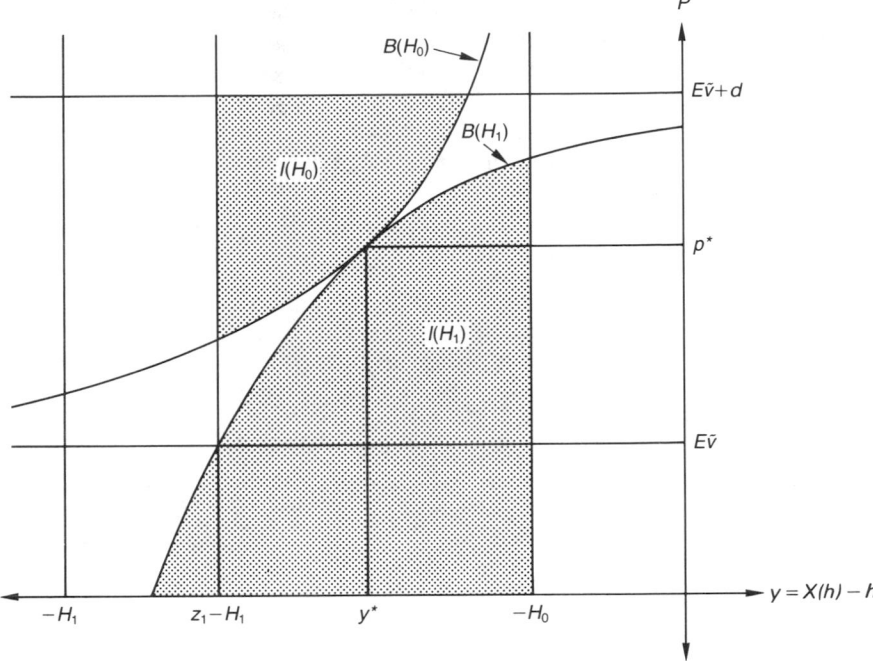

Figure 12.1 Equilibrium with squeezes

From this claim, it follows that whenever $\tilde{p}_1^F > E\tilde{v}$, the observed quantity-price outcome is $\langle y^*, p^* \rangle$, from which the desired results stated in Lemma 3 follow immediately from Lemma 2. To prove the claim, observe that a quantity-price outcome consistent with prices greater than $E\tilde{v}$ must be such that it is impossible to infer whether or not there will be a squeeze, since if it is possible to infer that there will be no squeeze (with probability 1), the price would be $E\tilde{v}$; and since if it is possible to infer that there will be a squeeze (with probability 1), the price would be $E\tilde{v} + d$ and the squeezer would be losing money. Clearly, $z_1 - H_1 < y$ and $\Pi(y + H_1, p) = \Pi_p^*(H_1)$ because otherwise it can be inferred that there will not be a squeeze, and $y < H_0$ and $\Pi(y + H_0, p) = \Pi_p^*(H_0)$ because otherwise it can be inferred (from Lemma 2) that there will be a squeeze. This is enough to put the price-quantity outcome in the set $B(H_0) \cap B(H_1)$ (with probability 1), which proves the desired claim. This completes the proof of the lemma.

Define the quantity μ^* by

$$\mu^* = \text{Prob}\{\tilde{X}_1(H_1) > z_1\}$$

The quantity μ^* is the conditional probability of a squeeze given $\tilde{H} = H_1$. From Lemma 3 we can conclude that it is necessary for all equilibria to fall under one of the following three cases, classified according to whether $\mu^* = 0, 0 < \mu^* < 1$, or $\mu^* = 1$.

Type 1. $\mu^* = 0$: Squeezes occur with probability 0. The equilibrium price is $E\tilde{v}$ with probability 1.

Type 2 $0 < \mu^* < 1$: Squeezes occur with probability $\lambda\mu^*$. There exists a pair (y^*, p^*) such that $z_1 - H_1 < y^* < -H_0$ and

$$X(H_0) = y^* + H_0 \quad \text{with probability 1}$$

$$X(H_1) \begin{cases} = y^* + H_1 & \text{with probability } \mu^* \\ < z_1 & \text{with probability } 1 - \mu^* \end{cases}$$

$$\tilde{p}_1^F = P(\tilde{X}_1(\tilde{H}) - \tilde{H}) = \begin{cases} p^* = E\tilde{v} + \dfrac{\mu^*\lambda}{1 - \lambda + \mu^*\lambda} d & \begin{array}{l}\text{when } X_1(\tilde{H}) - \tilde{H} = \\ y^*, \text{ which occurs} \\ \text{with probability} \\ 1 - \lambda + \mu^*\lambda\end{array} \\ \\ E\tilde{v}, & \text{otherwise} \end{cases}$$

These conditions do not define the distribution of $\tilde{X}_1(H_1)$ uniquely for $\tilde{X}_1(H_1) < z_1$ and do not define the values of the function $P(y)$ uniquely for $y \neq y^*$. In this case, $\Pi_p^*(H_1) = 0$, that is, the squeezer makes zero profits when there is a squeeze. The squeezer makes positive profits by shorting the market when there will be no squeeze.

Type 3 $\mu^* = 1$: Squeezes occur with probability λ. There exists a pair (y^*, p^*) such that $z_1 - H_1 < y^* < -H_0$ and

$$\tilde{X}_1(H_0) = y^* + H_0 \quad \text{with probability 1}$$

$$\tilde{X}_1(H_1) = y^* + H_1 \quad \text{with probability 1}$$

$$\tilde{P}_1^F = P(\tilde{X}_1(\tilde{H}) - \tilde{H}) = P^* = E\tilde{v} + \lambda d \quad \text{with probability 1}$$

These conditions do not define the values of the function $P(y)$ for $y \neq y^*$. Also, the squeezer always expects positive profits – he makes positive profits on the long side when there is a squeeze and positive profits on the short side when there is no squeeze.

We now show that an equilibrium for the model always exists, and that each of the three cases can be an equilibrium, depending on the size of $H_1 - H_0$. As $H_1 - H_0$ increases exogenously, the equilibrium changes from type 1 to type 2 to type 3.

Theorem *There exists an equilibrium. Depending on the size of $H_1 - H_0$, the equilibrium is one of the following three types.*

Type 1. $0 < H_1 - H_0 \leqslant z_1$: Squeezes occur with probability

0 and $\tilde{p}_1^F = E\tilde{v}$ with probability 1

Type 2. $z_1 \leqslant H_1 - H_0 < \dfrac{z_1}{(1-\lambda)^2}$: then $\mu^* = \left[\left(\dfrac{H_1 - H_0}{z_1} \right)^{1/2} - 1 \right] \dfrac{1-\lambda}{\lambda}$

$\tilde{X}_1(H_0) = (H_1 - H_0)^{1/2} z_1^{1/2} - (H_1 - H_0)$ with probability 1

$$\tilde{X}_1(H_1) \begin{cases} = (H_1 - H_0)^{1/2} z_1^{1/2} & \text{with probability } \mu^* \\ < z_1 & \text{otherwise} \end{cases}$$

$$p_1^F = \begin{cases} E\tilde{v} + \left[1 - \left(\dfrac{z_1}{H_1 - H_0} \right)^{1/2} \right] d & \begin{array}{l} \text{when } X_1(H) - H = \\ (H_1 - H_2)^{1/2} z_1^{1/2} - H_1 \\ \text{which occurs with probability} \\ 1 - \lambda + \mu^* \lambda \end{array} \\ E\tilde{v}, & \text{otherwise} \end{cases}$$

Type 3. $\left(\dfrac{z_1}{(1-\lambda)^2} \right) \leqslant H_1 - H_0$: Then, with probability 1, we have

$X_1(H_0) = \lambda(H_0 - H_1),$

$X_1(H_1) = (1 - \lambda)(H_0 - H_1),$

$p_1^F = E\tilde{v} + \lambda d.$

Proof Suppose first that $H_1 - H_0 \leqslant z_1$. Since there exists no y^* such that $y^* + H_0 < 0$ and $z_1 < y^* + H_1$, the conclusion of lemma 3 cannot hold, so any equilibrium must have zero probability of squeezes. To show that such an equilibrium does exist, we must specify functions P and $\tilde{X}$ that generate an equilibrium. One such example is given by

$$P(y) = \begin{cases} E\tilde{v} & \text{if } y \leqslant -H_0 \\ E\tilde{v} + d & \text{if } y > -H_0 \end{cases}$$

$\tilde{X}(\tilde{H}) = 0$ with probability 1

To prove that this is an equilibrium, observe that when $\tilde{H} = H_1$, the squeezer must pay $E\tilde{v} + d$ to buy enough to squeeze, which is unprofitable, and if he does not squeeze, can at best break even by trading at price $E\tilde{v}$.

When $\tilde{H} = H_0$, the squeezer cannot take a short position at any price except $E\tilde{v}$ and hence cannot make positive expected profits in this case either. Because the squeezer makes zero profits when $\tilde{H} = H_0$ and zero profits when $\tilde{H} = H_1$, no strategy dominates the no-trade strategy. Note that the equilibrium P and $\tilde{X}$ are not unique. No other equilibrium, however, generates a positive probability of squeezes – that is, all such equilibria are type 1.

Now suppose $H_1 - H_0 > z_1$. We claim that squeezes must have a positive probability of occurring. To prove this claim, observe that for y satisfying $z_1 - H_1 < y < H_0$, we must have $\Pi_p^*(H_0) > 0$ unless $P(y) = E\tilde{v}$ and we must have $\Pi_p^*(H_1) > 0$ if $P(y) = E\tilde{v}$. It is thus impossible to have $\Pi_p^*(H_0) = \Pi_p^*(H_1) = 0$, which is necessary if squeezes never occur.

Because squeezes occur with positive probability, there exists a y^* satisfying Lemma 3 and an associated p^* as discussed in the proof of that lemma. Recall that in the proof of Lemma 3, it was shown that to satisfy the condition $E\tilde{\pi}_1(\tilde{X}_1, P) \geqslant E\tilde{\pi}_1(\tilde{X}_1', P)$ for all $\tilde{X}_1'$, it is necessary that there exist profit levels $\Pi_p^*(H_0) > 0$ and $\Pi_p^*(H_1) \geqslant 0$ such that $\{(y^*, p^*)\}$ is the intersection of the boundaries $B(H_0)$ and $B(H_1)$, and the interiors $I(H_0)$ and $I(H_1)$ do not intersect. For this necessary condition to be sufficient to satisfy the condition $E\tilde{\pi}_1(\tilde{X}_1, P) \geqslant E\tilde{\pi}_1(\tilde{X}_1', P)$ for all $\tilde{X}_1'$, we must be able to define the function P such that the following two conditions hold:

1. For the restricted domain $z_1 - H_1 < y < H_0$, the graph of P separates the interiors $I(H_0)$ and $I(H_1)$.
2. For y outside this domain, P must be defined so that the profit levels $\Pi_p^*(H_0)$ and $\Pi_p^*(H_1)$ cannot be dominated either.

To prove that condition 1 then can be satisfied, we know from the properties of convex sets (the indifference curves $B(H_0)$ and $B(H_1)$ are both nowhere vertical) that a linear function P exists, but the actual P chosen need not be linear. To satisfy condition 2, we can choose $P(y) = E\tilde{v}$ for $y \leqslant z_1 - H_1$ and $P(y) = E\tilde{v} + d$ for $y \geqslant H_0$, but again, many other definitions of P work just as well (see figure 12.2).

The (y^*, p^*) combinations consistent with equilibrium lie along a contract curve defined as a set of points (y^*, p^*) satisfying $z_1 - H_1 \leqslant y^* < -H_0$ and such that there exists a nonnegative profit level $\Pi_p^*(H_1)$ with

$$(y^*, p^*) = \operatorname*{argmax}_{y, p} \{ (E\tilde{v} - p)(y + H_0) :$$

$$(E\tilde{v} - p + d)(y + H_1) - z_1 d \geqslant \Pi_p^*(H_1) \}$$

To calculate the locus of points defining this contract curve, we obtain from the Lagrangian

$$L = (E\tilde{v} - p)(y + H_0) - \alpha[(E\tilde{v} - p + d)(y + H_1) - z_1 d - \Pi_p^*(H_1)]$$

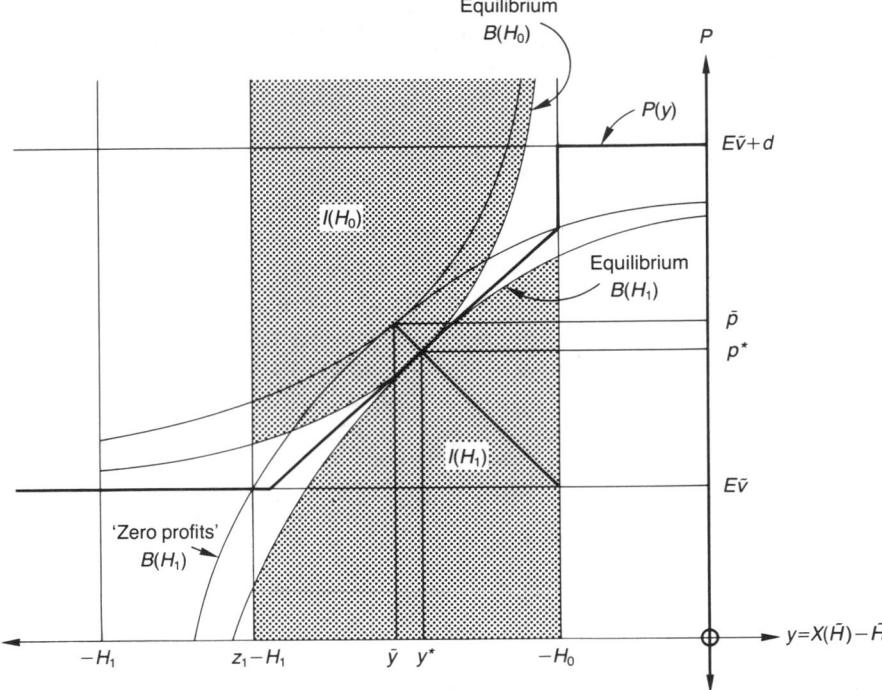

Figure 12.2 Equilibrium futures price function

(with Lagrange multiplier α) the first-order conditions

$$y^* + H_0 = \alpha(y^* + H_1),$$

$$E\tilde{p} + p^* = \alpha(E\tilde{v} - p^* + d)$$

It is not hard to show that these conditions imply

$$(H_1 - H_0)(E\tilde{v} - p^* + d) = (y^* + H_1)d,$$

from which it is apparent that the contract curve is a straight line segment. The left endpoint of the contract curve, denoted $(\bar{y}, \bar{p})$, corresponds to the solution of the maximization problem when $\Pi_p^*(H_1) = 0$, and is given by

$$\bar{y} = (H_1 - H_0)^{1/2} z_1^{1/2} - H_1$$

$$\bar{p} = E\tilde{v} + \left[1 - \left(\frac{z_1}{H_1 - H_0} \right)^{1/2} \right] d$$

Note that the condition $z_1 - H_1 \leqslant \bar{y} < H_0$ is satisfied. The right endpoint of the contract curve is defined by $y^* = -H_0$, $p^* = E\tilde{v}$. Because we have already shown that the equilibrium condition $E\pi_1(\tilde{X}, P_1,) \geqslant E\tilde{\pi}_1(\tilde{X}_1', P_1)$ for all $\tilde{X}_1'$ is satisfied, the points along the contract curve will generate equilibria provided the market-efficiency condition

$$P(y) = E\tilde{v} + \text{Prob}\{\tilde{X}_1(\tilde{H}) - z_1 > 0 \,|\, \tilde{X}_1(\tilde{H}) - \tilde{H} = y\} \cdot d$$

is also satisfied. There are two cases to consider:

Case 1: $\Pi_p^*(H_1) = 0$. Then we have a type 2 equilibrium with $(y^*, p^*) = (\bar{y}, \bar{p})$. The parameter μ^* gives the probability of a squeeze conditional on $\tilde{H} = H_1$. The market-efficiency condition holds provided first, $p_1^F = E\tilde{v}$ with probability 1 conditional on $\tilde{X}_1(\tilde{H}) - \tilde{H} \neq \bar{y}$ and second

$$\bar{p} = E\tilde{v} + \frac{\mu^*\lambda}{1 - \lambda + \mu^*\lambda} d$$

Condition 1 holds because P was defined so that $P(y) = E\tilde{v}$ for all $y < z_1 - H_1$ (other definitions of P would work just as well). From the definition of $\bar{p}$, condition 2 holds provided

$$\mu^* = \frac{1 - \lambda}{\lambda} \left[\left(\frac{H_1 - H_0}{z_1} \right)^{1/2} - 1 \right]$$

Because μ^* is a probability, we must have $\mu^* \in [0, 1]$, which occurs provided

$$z_1 < H_1 - H_0 < \frac{z_1}{(1 - \lambda)^2}$$

Case 2 $\Pi_p^*(H_1) > 0$. Then we have a type 3 equilibrium. The market-efficiency condition holds if and only if $p^* = E\tilde{v} + \lambda d$, from which we obtain $y^* = -\lambda H_1 - (1 - \lambda)H_0$. The point (y^*, p^*) is on the contract curve provided

$$H_1 - H_0 \geqslant \frac{z_1}{(1 - \lambda)^2}$$

We have now characterized equilibrium when $H_1 - H_0 > z_1$ in a manner consistent with the statement of the theorem. This completes the proof of the theorem.

It is interesting to observe what happens as the size of the market, as measured by $H_1 - H_0$, increases from some small initial value. For $H_1 - H_0 < z_1$, there are no squeezes. When $H_1 - H_0$ gets slightly larger than z_1, squeezes begin to occur occasionally but are never expected to be profitable for the squeezer; however, the bidding up of prices in anticipation of squeezes allows the squeezer to earn positive profits by shorting the market when no squeeze is going to occur. Finally, when $H_1 - H_0 > z_1 / (1 - \lambda)^2$, squeezes occur with probability λ.

Now define λ^* by

$$\lambda^* = \min \left[\lambda, \max \left(1 - \left(\frac{z_1}{H_1 - H_0} \right)^{1/2}, 0 \right) \right]$$

The quantity λ^* measures the conditional probability of a squeeze given that $\tilde{X}_1(\tilde{H}) - \tilde{H} = y^*$. The expected losses of hedgers, denoted L, are given by

$$L = \lambda^* (1 - \lambda)(H_1 - H_0)$$

and the expected profits of the squeezer are given by

$$E\tilde{\pi}_1(X_1, P) = \lambda^* [(1 - \lambda)(H_1 - H_0) - \mu\lambda z_1]$$

The difference between L and $E\tilde{\pi}_1(\tilde{X}_1, P)$ is the transfer of resources to the holders of the cheap quality because its price is bid up in anticipation of squeezes.

5 WHAT HAPPENS WHEN DELIVERY IS COSTLY?

A typical squeeze situation is often thought to involve a great deal of threatening and bluffing. The squeezer acquires a large long position but does not really want to take delivery. Instead, the squeezer wants to set the futures price at a high level and persuade the shorts to liquidate at the high price that he dictates. If the shorts can be persuaded, the squeeze can be successful, even though few actual deliveries are made.

This threatening and bluffing is missing from the model described in the previous section. It is missing because the marginal qualities involved in the delivery process, which are the expensive qualities, are worth to the squeezer exactly what they cost the shorts to deliver. The squeezer has nothing to lose by taking delivery so he does not need to threaten to do so. In fact, we showed in the previous section that the squeezer is indifferent between taking delivery of all the positions he acquires in period 1 and taking delivery of only slightly more than is necessary to soak up all of the cheap quality. He is indifferent because the difference, which represents the high-quality deliveries, can be liquidated in period 2 at the high squeeze price.

Threats and bluffs enter the picture when it costs the shorts more to make delivery than it is worth to the squeezer to take delivery. It is easy to see how this situation can arise in practice. Contract specifications call for deliverable stocks to be stored at particular delivery points. When stocks at these delivery points are low, shorts are forced to transport the stocks from non-deliverable points to deliverable points, even though at postdelivery prices the value premium for stocks stored at the deliverable points over non-deliverable points may not be enough to cover transportation and other delivery costs. In fact, it is possible that stocks are worth more at non-deliverable than at deliverable points, when valued at no-squeeze prices, and moving them not only involves a transportation cost but destroys some of their value as well. In this situation, delivery of the commodity is economically inefficient and involves a deadweight cost that must be borne by the squeezer or the shorts. With costly delivery, an incentive is created for both sides to liquidate their contracts before delivery. The problem of course, involves setting the price at which liquidation will occur.

The squeezer would like to set a price slightly below what it costs the shorts to make delivery. To do so, he must threaten to take delivery of contracts that will be worth much less to him. The shorts, on the other hand, would like to set a price only slightly above what the contracts would be worth to the squeezer. In doing so, they implicitly threaten to make delivery at a cost that is much higher than this price. The equilibrium price that emerges and the number of deliveries, if any, that are made will be determined in part by the game theoretic structure of the delivery process.

Because the shorts are fragmented competitors, it may seem appropriate to model the delivery process as a game in which the squeezer forces liquidation on his terms. However, if the leader tries to force liquidation on his terms, the shorts may not remain fragmented competitors. Instead, one short may allow the others to buy out of their positions at prices slightly lower than the squeezer is offering. It costs him little to do this because he always preserves the option of caving in to the squeezer and taking a small loss. He has a great deal to gain, however, if – having bought out the other shorts – he can use a stronger bargaining position with the squeezer to achieve a better price. This reasoning suggests that open interest on both sides of the market will become concentrated near delivery and that the delivery process should be modeled as a game with a small number of players on both sides of the market. The actual outcome may be indeterminate, in the sense that there is either no equilibrium or are multiple equilibria, but we do not pursue this idea in detail here.

The question remains whether the model discussed in the previous section is relevant at all when there is costly delivery. In fact, that model can be interpreted as modeling a situation in which the shorts cave in to the squeezer and liquidate before delivery on his terms. To make this interpretation, a few trivial changes are needed. First, the underlying value of the expensive qualities $\bar{v} + d$ is interpreted not as its value to the squeezer but rather as its delivered cost to the shorts. For example, we can assume that there is really only one quality and that it is worth $\bar{v}$ regardless of whether it is stored at deliverable or nondeliverable points. Let z_1 denote stocks at the deliverable storage point, let z_2 denote stocks at the nondeliverable point, and let d

denote the cost of transporting stocks from one point to another. Then stocks at the nondeliverable point are worth $\tilde{v}$ to the squeezer when delivered but cost the shorts $\tilde{v} + d$ to deliver.

The second change concerns the second period of trading. In the second period, the squeezer, rather than being indifferent about delivery, prefers not to take delivery and liquidates almost all of his position in excess of z_1 at the squeeze price $\tilde{v} + d$, thus cashing in almost all of his profits through liquidation. Taking delivery of slightly more than z_1 units forces the shorts to deliver some expensive stocks and keeps the period 2 price high.

With these minor changes, the period 1 game remains unchanged and prices and profits are exactly the same as discussed in the previous section. Thus, that model remains applicable when there is costly delivery. The model gives the squeezer the power to make a credible threat by forcing him to move first in period 2 and not letting him trade more later.

6 ENDOGENOUS HEDGING

The model discussed in the preceding section takes as given the amount of hedging H_0 and H_1. In this section we make the amount of hedging endogenous by constructing a simple model of endogenous hedging.

Supoose that there are N potential hedgers. We suppose that there are two states, where state zero corresponds to inactive hedging and state one corresponds to active hedging. In state i, $i = 0, 1$, a fraction η_i of the hedgers have an inventory of one unit of the commodity and the remaining fraction $1 - \eta_i$ of hedgers have no inventory. We assume $0 < \eta_0 < \eta_1 < 1$, so the states differ only with respect to the percentage of the population of hedgers who have inventories to hedge. The problem for a hedger is to decide how large a futures position to take, given the size of the hedger's inventory. The hedger does not know whether there will be active hedging or inactive hedging, but he can use Baye's theorem to calculate the probabilities conditional on his inventory as follows:

$$\text{Prob (inactive hedging} | \text{one unit)} = \frac{(1 - \lambda)\eta_0}{(1 - \lambda)\eta_0 + \lambda\eta_1}$$

$$\text{Prob (active hedging} | \text{one unit)} = \frac{\lambda\eta_1}{(1 - \lambda)\eta_0 + \lambda\eta_1}$$

$$\text{Prob (inactive hedging} | \text{zero units)} = \frac{(1 - \lambda)(1 - \eta_1)}{(1 - \lambda)(1 - \eta_0) + \lambda(1 - \eta_1)}$$

$$\text{Prob (active hedging} | \text{zero units)} = \frac{\lambda(1 - \eta_0)}{(1 - \lambda)(1 - \eta_0) + \lambda(1 - \eta_1)}$$

From the previous section, expected returns on a futures position between period 1 and period 2 are given by

$$E(p_2^F - p_1^F | \text{inactive hedging}) = -\lambda^* d$$

$$E(p_2^F - p_1^F | \text{active hedging}) = \frac{\lambda^*}{\lambda}(1 - \lambda)d$$

Using these conditional expecatations and the conditional probabilities listed previously, the hedger can calculate the expected return on futures contracts conditional on the information revealed to him by the size of his endowment. These are given by

$$E(p_2^F - p_1^F | \text{one unit}) = \frac{(1 - \lambda)\lambda^* d(\eta_1 - \eta_0)}{(1 - \lambda)\eta_0 + \lambda\eta_1}$$

$$E(p_2^F - p_1^F | \text{zero units}) = \frac{-(1 - \lambda)\lambda^* d(\eta_1 - \eta_0)}{(1 - \lambda)(1 - \eta_0) + \lambda(1 - \eta_1)}$$

Suppose that each hedger is a risk-averse expected utility maximizer and that each hedger's inventory is a mixture of qualities 1 and 2 held in the same proportions as the other hedgers. Let $S_1(\lambda^*)$ denote the net unhedged position taken (after futures trading) by a hedger with one unit of the commodity and let $S_0(\lambda^*)$ be the position taken by a hedger with no inventory. It can be shown, under reasonable conditions, that $S_1(\lambda^*)$ is positive and increasing in λ^*.

The aggregate futures position taken by the hedgers in the two states H_0 and H_1 is given by

$$H_i = [\eta_i(1 - S_1(\lambda^*)) + (1 - \eta_i)S_0(\lambda^*)]N \qquad i = 0, 1$$

and the difference in hedging between the two states $H_1 - H_0$ is given by

$$H_1 - H_0 = (\eta_1 - \eta_0)(1 - (S_1(\lambda^*) + S_0(\lambda^*)))N$$

An equilibrium with endogenous hedging is generated by values of λ^* and $H_1 - H_0$ such that the preceding equation holds and such that

$$\lambda^* = \min\left(\lambda, \max\left[1 - \left(\frac{z_1}{H_1 - H_0}\right)^{1/2}, 0\right]\right)$$

(See figure 12.3.) The downward-sloping demand for hedging curve plots the equation for $H_1 - H_0$ above, and the upward-sloping supply of squeezes curve plots the equation for λ^*. The intersection of the two curves, represented by point E in figure 12.3, determines simultaneously the probability of a squeeze λ^* and the difference between active and inactive hedging $H_1 - H_0$.

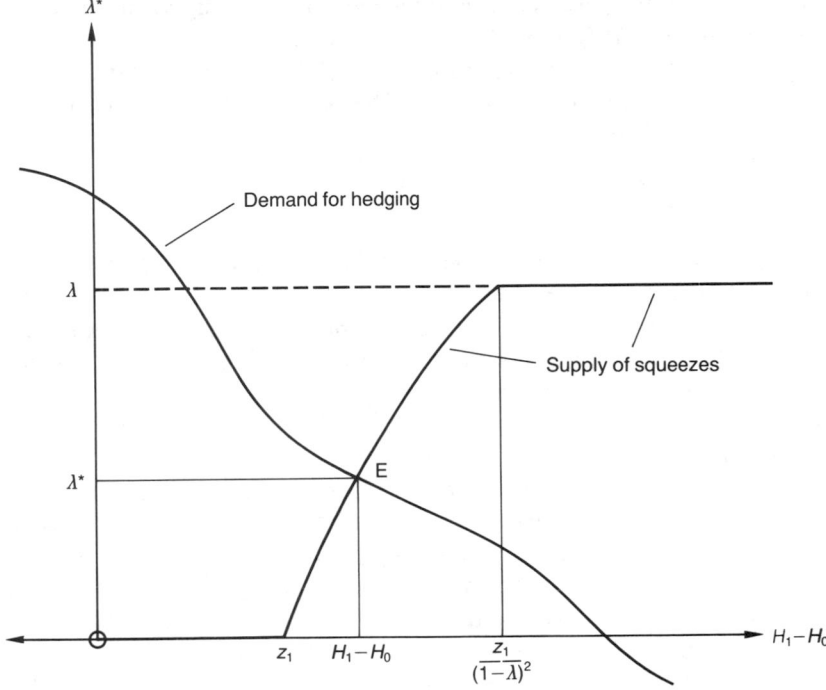

Figure 12.3 Equilibrium with endogenous hedging

From this equilibrium model of hedging, it is clear that one of the welfare costs of squeezes is that hedging is discouraged. As a result, risk-averse hedgers bear risk, even though there are other traders in the economy who are risk-neutral. Implicitly, we are assuming that other markets in the economy are not used for hedging. These markets are not used because, for example, the transactions costs of finding trading partners is too high.

7   POLICY APPLICATIONS

Our model of corners and squeezes shows that when corners and squeezes are possible, the profits of the squeezer come at the expense of hedgers; furthermore, squeezes also create benefits for the holders of the cheaply delivered quality, and these benefits also come at the expense of hedgers. The costs that fall upon hedgers induce them to hedge only part of the risks that would be fully hedged in a futures market without squeezes. The resulting misallocation of risk-bearing represents the social cost of squeezes.

In this section, we examine briefly several policies designed to reduce the effect of squeezes: different delivery differentials, additional deliverable supply, cash settlement, and position limits. These policies might be either the result of government regulation or the result of self-regulation by the exchanges themselves.

7.1   Delivery differentials

A reduction in the delivery differential d between quality 1 and quality 2, holding hedging behavior constant, leaves the probability of squeezes unchanged but decreases their profitability proportionately with the reduction in d. To hedgers, the decreased profitability of squeezes represents a lowered cost of hedging. With endogenous hedging, hedgers expand their hedging activities, and squeezes tend to become more frequent, even though the allocation of risk is made more efficient.

Reduction of d to zero eliminates squeezes entirely. Why, then, are differentials not always set equal to actual market differentials? The reason is that, in practice, market differentials change but their value in any particular case cannot be objectively verified by a government or commodity exchange bureaucracy, even if market participants know what they are. Suppose that the difference in market values $\tilde{d}$ is a random variable whose distribution can be objectively verified but whose outcome in any particular case cannot be objectively verified. Our model then represents a market outcome conditional on a particular outcome of $\tilde{d}$ and a delivery differential of zero. This leads us to pose the following question: What delivery differential d, chosen as a function of deliverable supplies z_1, and z_2 and the distribution of $\tilde{d}$ (but not its outcome), results in the most efficient use of the market as a hedging device? Although this question is well posed, answering it takes us beyond the scope of this paper. Suffice it to observe that the optimal value of d is not the mean or median of the distribution of $\tilde{d}$. It is easy to convince oneself that the optimal differential d depends on the relative supplies of qualities 1 and 2 and that optimal differentials will in many cases be chosen such that the quality in greatest supply is the cheapest to deliver.

7.2   Additional deliverable supply

If the supply of the cheapest-to-deliver quality z_1 is increased, squeezes become less profitable and tend to become less likely. Figure 12.4 illustrates the effect of an increase in deliverable supply on λ^*, using the same format as figure 12.3. The increase in z_1 shifts outward the supply curve, which tends to improve the allocation of risk-bearing by increasing the amount of hedging .

One way to increase deliverable supply in this way is to add delivery

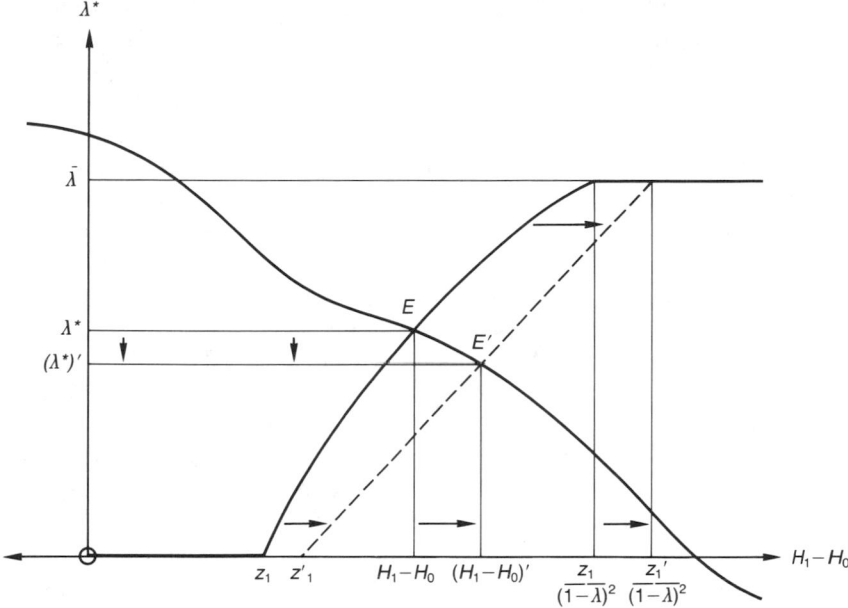

Figure 12.4 Increases of deliverable supply

points that have the property that quantities delivered to these points have no-squeeze market values which are perfectly correlated with no-squeeze market values of the cheapest-to-deliver quality. When the new delivery points have values that are perfectly correlated with neither quality 1 nor quality 2, the result is a multiquality model, which again takes us beyond the scope of this paper. Within the context of such a multiquality model, however, choosing the optimal combination of delivery points and delivery differentials for these points is clearly a well-posed problem. Given the joint probability distribution of the vector of market differentials, one suspects that the optimal delivery differentials – chosen as a function of this distribution but not actual outcomes – will in many cases have the property that one cluster of qualities (delivery points) whose values are closely correlated will tend to be cheapest to deliver.

7.3 Cash settlement

Cash settlement has been proposed as a device that eliminates squeezes as an exploitation of the delivery mechanism by eliminating delivery itself. In the context of our model, cash settlement can be modeled in the following way.

Instead of liquidating through delivery the open interest remaining in period 2, positions are liquidated at a price that is some function of the cash market prices of qualities 1 and 2, evaluated at the end of period 2. Although various functions can be used (a weighted average is typical), the function consistent with our delivery mechanism is the minimum of the cash market prices of the two qualities. In the model with delivery, the cash prices at the end of period 2 of qualities 1 and 2 are $\bar{v}$ and $\bar{v} + d$ when there is no squeeze and $\bar{v} + d$ for both qualities when there is a squeeze. The price of quality 1 is higher when there is a squeeze because traders with short positions are willing to buy it to deliver it immediately to the squeezer, who immediately suffers a loss d as the price falls back to the no-squeeze price $\bar{v}$.

With cash settlement, traders with short positions would not be willing to pay a premium of size d for quality 1. Does this mean that the cash price of quality 1 would be $\bar{v}$ instead of $\bar{v} + d$ even in the squeeze situation where the squeezer has a futures position in excess of z_1? It is easy to see that, in this situation, the squeezer himself has an incentive to bid up the price of quality 1, even if this means that he must purchase the entire available supply, z_1. If the squeezer bids the price to $\bar{v} + d$ and purchases the entire deliverable supply z_1, his profits are exactly the same as they would be with delivery. We conclude that cash settlement has no effect on the incentive to engage in squeezes. It only transfers some of the manipulative activity into the cash market.

Cash settlement is also proposed as a method for reducing the costs associated with use of the delivery mechanism. To the extent that transactions costs for utilizing the futures market delivery mechanism play into the hands of the squeezer, cash settlement might be thought to be a way to avoid these costs and reduce the power of the squeezer. In fact, cash settlement merely replaces the cost of using the futures market delivery mechanism with the costs of utilizing the cash market delivery mechanism. If these costs are the same, then cash settlement again has no effect on the incentive to engage in squeezes.

7.4   Position limits

Position limits are often ineffective because it is difficult in practice to tell whether positions owned by different traders are in fact being managed cooperatively. If, however, effective position limits can be devised, our model suggests that they have beneficial effects.

Suppose that a position limit of size x_L is imposed on long positions. If the position limit is less than the available supply of the cheapest-to-deliver quality, squeezes are eliminated entirely. It can be shown that if the position limit is greater than the supply of the cheapest-to-deliver commodity, but less than the quantity the squeezer buys when he squeezes, squeezes may – but need not – be, mitigated to some extent (figure 12.5). Without position limits, the equilibrium can be represented as some point along the contract curve $O\bar{E}$, the particular point depending upon the exogenous value of λ. At the equilibrium corresponding to point E, for example, the squeezer buys x_E when $\tilde{H} = H_1$, sells $H_1 - H_0 - x_E$ when $\tilde{H} = H_0$, and the price in period 1 is $p_E = E\tilde{v} + \lambda d$. Now suppose that a position limit of size x_L with $z_1 < x_L < x_E$, is imposed on long positions. Let $\bar{E}_L$ denote the intersection of the vertical line $y = x_L - H_1$ and the concave indifference curve $B(H_1)$ passing through $\bar{E} = (\bar{y}, \bar{p})$. It can be shown (but we do not prove it here) that all equilibria affected by the position limit are in effect replaced by equilibria along the new contract curve $O_L \bar{E}_L$; furthermore, there are two cases to consider, depending on whether the old equilibrium is northwest or southeast of the point M, defined as the point on the old contract curve lying on the horizontal line through $\bar{E}_L$.

Case 1: For old equilibria lying on the line segment OM (that is, southeast

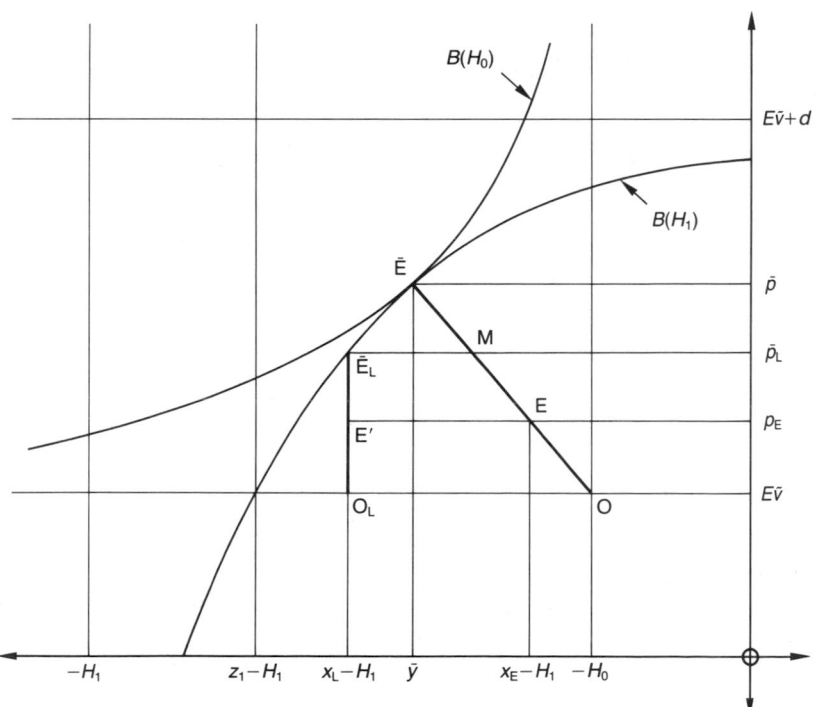

Figure 12.5 Imposition of position limits

of M), such as point E in figure 12.5, the new equilibrium is the point on the new contract curve lying along the same horizontal line as the old equilibrium (point E' in figure 12.5). The new equilibrium has virtually the same economic properties as the old. In particular, the equilibrium price is the same, the occurrence of squeezes is the same, and the expected profits of the squeezer are the same. The only difference is that the squeezer takes a smaller long position when squeezing, thus earning smaller profits, while taking a larger short position when not squeezing, thus earning greater profits.

Case 2:   For old equilibria lying on the line segment M$\bar{\text{E}}$ (that is, northwest of M), the new equilibrium corresponds to point $\bar{\text{E}}_L$. The new equilibrium point $\bar{\text{E}}_L$ has quite different economic properties from the old: lower equilibrium prices, less frequent squeezes, and lower expected profits for the squeezer, who now makes all of his profits on the short side when he does not squeeze.

It is clear that in case 2, position limits will have an expansionary effect on hedging because the downward shift in the supply curve in figure 12.6

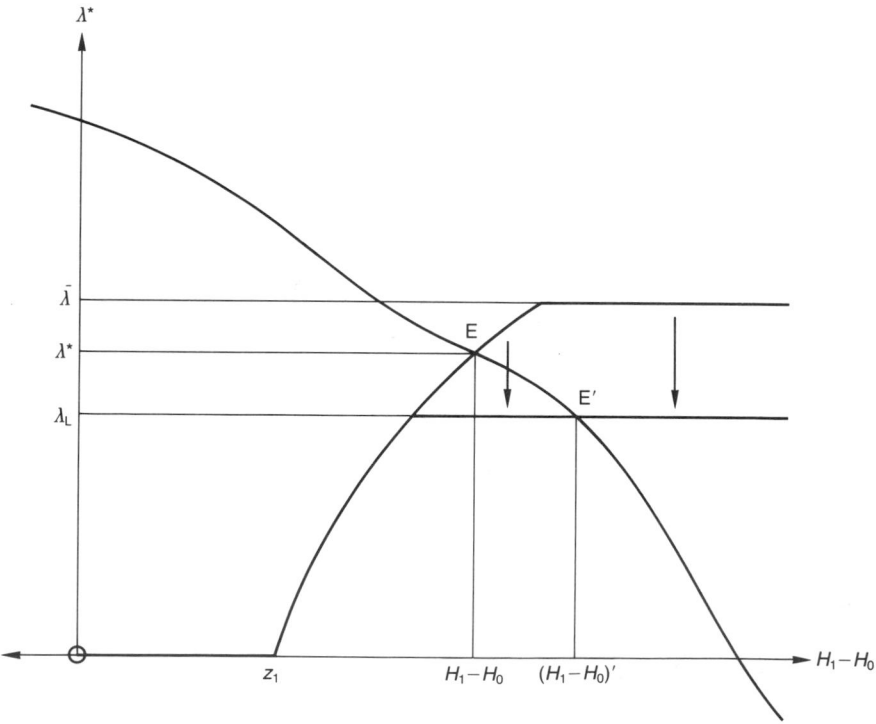

Figure 12.6   Effects of position limits on hedging

induces a beneficial downward movement along the demand curve, corresponding to more hedging. In case 1, the downward shift in the supply curve only occurs for points on the supply curve above the equilibrium, and therefore has no welfare consequences.

8   CONCLUSION

Our model is based upon some very special informational and game-theoretic assumptions that might be relaxed in future research. The squeezer, who has private information about what hedgers are doing, for example, faces no threat from potential entrants who also have such private information. He earns a rent based on his unchallenged large market power and information about the order flow from hedgers. Other kinds of information, such as inside information (in period one) about the outcome of $\tilde{v}$ might be added to the model. In the hands of a large trader, such information might become more valuable if squeezes are possible. Clearly, the model can be extended by using a more complicated process generating hedge trade, more deliverable qualities, and more trading periods.

The principal advantage of this simple model is that it illustrates clearly how a large trader with information about the order flow of hedgers can use the anonymity of the trading process to accumulate a large enough position to engineer a successful squeeze. Price fluctuations, which are perceived to be fair game from the point of view of speculators, are simultaneously perceived to be an unfair game from the point of view of hedgers. As a result, even though prices have the random features of an efficient market from the point of view of speculators, the increased cost of hedging resulting from squeezes reduces the amount of hedging, leads to a misallocation of risks in the economy, and calls for some policies designed to make squeezes more difficult.

REFERENCES

Telser, Lester G. (1981). Why there are organized futures markets, *Journal of Law and Economics*, vol. 24, pp. 1–22.
Working, Holbrook (1953). Futures trading and hedging, *American Economic Review*, vol. 43, pp. 314–43.

Index